PAYROLL ACCOUNTING:
A COMPLETE GUIDE
TO PAYROLL

NOV

NOV 2

PAYROLL ACCOUNTING: A COMPLETE GUIDE TO PAYROLL

2001 Edition

FRANK C. GIOVE

Niagara University

HOUGHTON MIFFLIN COMPANY   BOSTON   NEW YORK

Publisher: Charles Hartford
Senior Sponsoring Editor: Bonnie Binkert
Associate Sponsoring Editor: Joanne M. Dauksewicz
Associate Editor: Damaris R. Curran
Project Editor: Patricia English
Production/Design Coordinator: Jodi O'Rourke
Manufacturing Manager: Florence Cadran
Marketing Manager: Steve Mikels

Printed in the U.S.A.

Library of Congress Catalog Card Number: 00-133846

ISBN: 0-395-95997-7

1 2 3 4 5 6 7 8 9-B-04 03 02 01 00

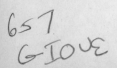
657
GIOVE

CONTENTS

PREFACE
2001 EDITION

Perhaps no topic in the field of business is as pervasive as payroll. Usually, it is the largest single expense of most businesses and a continuing management challenge in terms of cost control. This book provides comprehensive coverage of the payroll accounting process, including a rarely glimpsed perspective on the internal control procedures and cost-saving techniques used by management.

The text introduces the subject of payroll by first presenting the federal rules and regulations governing employment, compensation, and payroll taxes. It then takes the reader step-by-step through the entire payroll process—from timekeeping, computation of gross earnings, determining federal income tax and other payroll tax withholdings; to preparing and distributing the payroll; to the final, vital step of recording or accounting for wages, tax liabilities, and payments or deposits. The last two chapters focus on the various policies and measures companies establish to keep payroll costs under control.

The field of payroll management is certainly growing. Payroll managers, as this book shows, can have a profound effect on the successful operation of a business. Even with outside payroll services and direct deposit, the payroll manager must still control the timekeeping systems used by the company, provide the necessary input to any outside service, and establish and oversee the direct deposit system. Therefore, it is of vital importance for the payroll manager—as well as the payroll clerk—to be well versed in all aspects of payroll operations.

Readers interested in learning payroll accounting and payroll management will find this book to be a valuable training tool. Those readers who are currently employed as payroll assistants, clerks, or managers can use the book as a resource and reference manual. Other readers who will benefit from the text are those already familiar with general accounting or business management. The in-depth coverage and organizational focus will help these readers to become more knowledgeable about payroll and gain practical information about internal control and cost-saving techniques.

Features

My goal has been to provide a comprehensive and practical book that presents payroll procedures and issues in an accessible and interesting way. The text is published as an annual edition, incorporating yearly tax revisions to keep the coverage as up-to-date and useful as possible. In addition, the entire book is structured to clarify and explain the payroll process.

An *ongoing case* begins each part and chapter, highlighting the various steps in the payroll process at Nioga Gear, Inc., a fictitious but true-to-life company.

Learning objectives open each chapter and provide readers with an overview of new concepts.

Highlighted inserts, entitled "In the News" and "Payroll in Action," illuminate current payroll issues and stimulate reader interest.

Review questions are straightforward, cover basic material in the book, and are designed to elicit answers that reinforce learning.

Discussion questions are thought-provoking, deal with current issues in payroll, and will encourage lively discussion with widely contrasting points of view.

Exercises are relatively short computational questions that illustrate a single procedure or principle.

Problems are longer computational questions involving several employees or a combination of computations.

A *continuing case problem* at the end of each chapter focuses on a service company, Frontier Landscaping, and relates directly to the chapter material it follows.

Payroll Practice Sets

Two complete payroll practice sets are available for use with *Payroll Accounting. Lawson's Supply Center, Inc.* can be worked either manually or by computer (using Houghton Mifflin's General Ledger program and the data disk supplied with the practice set). Students take on the role of payroll clerk at Lawson's, a merchandising business that sells building materials and supplies; they must follow the entire payroll process for a quarterly period.

The second practice set, *Oak Creek Canyon Jewelers,* is a computerized payroll practice set designed to be used with Peachtree Accounting for Windows (Release 3.5 or Release 5.0). In this simulation, students take on the role of payroll clerk for Oak Creek Canyon Jewelers, a sole proprietorship retail operation. Students record all payroll transactions for the fourth quarter and prepare end-of-quarter and end-of-year reports.

Instructor's Resource Manual with Solutions

For instructors using this book in an academic setting, the *Instructor's Resource Manual* is an all-inclusive aid. It contains three separate sections to enhance teaching of the material:

Teaching Notes. Each chapter contains a review of learning objectives and key terms. Also, a complete lecture outline provides a comprehensive review of the chapter material.

Solutions. Solutions are provided for all end-of-chapter reinforcement material: answers to review and discussion questions, solutions to exercises, problems, and the continuing case problem. Each solution is carefully and logically presented so that procedures and the concepts behind them can be fully understood.

Transparency Masters. Key figures, tables, and exhibits have been reproduced as transparency masters for classroom use.

Practice Set Instructor Manuals

For each practice set, *Lawson's Supply Center, Inc.* and *Oak Creek Canyon Jewelers,* an instructor manual with solutions is available to help instructors guide students in completing the simulations.

Achievement Test Masters

Payroll Accounting is also accompanied by a set of Achievement Tests. These ready-to-reproduce test masters cover each chapter of the text and are available to adopters upon request. The tests reflect the updated payroll requirements, forms, and tables in the 2001 Edition and have been thoroughly accuracy-tested. Solutions are also provided.

Acknowledgments

Although this text was a labor of love, it would not have been possible without the conscientious and generous contributions of the fine staff at Houghton Mifflin. I owe a sincere thanks to Ray Deveaux and Don Golini for encouraging me and giving me the opportunity to write this text and its annual updates. I am also indebted to an excellent group of editors at Houghton Mifflin who assisted in each of the annual updates. I am especially grateful to Ann West, Margaret Kearney, Penny Stratton, and Linda Burkell who helped me develop the first edition of the text. I would also like to thank Damaris Curran, Patricia English, and Jodi O'Rourke, who worked on this edition. In particular, I would like to thank Joanne Dauksewicz, who helped put together each edition we've published.

I would also like to thank my word processor at Niagara University, Diane Rowe. Without her dedication, this book would have been most difficult to complete. I am also grateful to the following reviewers who provided valuable comments and suggestions:

David J. Andrews
Robert Morris College

Nancy Atwater
Brown Institute

Courtney Baillie
Southeast Community College

Thomas M. Bock
Berkeley College

Michael Choma
New Kensington Commercial School

Karen A. DeJulio
Bradford School

Freda Dibble
Patricia Stevens College

Chris Finley
Missouri Vocational Center

Barbara Kramer
Lewis-Clark State College

Cathy Xanthaley Larson
Middlesex Community College

Linda C. Lott
Illinois Central College

Shirl Mallory
Coosa Valley Technical Institute

Martha McDonald
Metro Business College

Jon Nitschke
*Montana State University College
of Technology—Great Falls*

Sandro O'Meara
Santa Barbara City College

Frank A. Paliotta
Berkeley College

Gail Reed
National College

Debbie K. Reeder

R. Becki L. Saylor
Sanford Brown College

Michael Scully
Catherine College

Warren W. Smock
Ivy Tech State College

Ginger Dudley Tuton
Coastal Carolina Community College

Carolyn Woodbury
*The University of Montana
College of Technology—Missoula*

My deepest appreciation goes to my daughter, Kathryn Blackman, also a CPA, who tested and worked on the solutions to the exercises and problems and provided inspirational support in my efforts. She stood in the shoes of my late dear wife, who always encouraged me to put my thoughts and knowledge on paper.

F. C. G.

PART I

PAYROLL LAWS AND RECORDKEEPING REQUIREMENTS

Julia Jones works as a telephone sales representative for Nioga Gear, Inc., an athletic shoe manufacturer. Operating out of her home, Julia makes telephone sales calls to small exercise equipment outlets and clothing stores that carry athletic clothes to ask them to consider becoming local distributors of Nioga's walking shoe. She spends ten hours a week making cold calls, for which she is paid $2.00 per call, and the rest of her time following up on leads and servicing accounts, for which she receives an hourly wage. Her work hours range from 30 to 50 hours a week, depending on the time she spends on follow-up. She is paid once a week.

Julia, a home-based employee working alone and outside the Nioga office, is considered an employee rather than an independent contractor because her employer, Nioga, controls the details of all her work and the results to be accomplished. As an employee, Julia is protected by a variety of federal and state laws pertaining to employment and compensation. Such laws guarantee her, among other things, a minimum hourly wage; an overtime wage that is 1½ times her regular hourly rate of pay; a piece rate that equals or surpasses the minimum wage rate; and pay that is equal to the earnings of others doing the same job.

As Julia's employer, Nioga Gear is bound by some other laws; for example, it must verify that Julia is a U.S. citizen or is authorized to work in the United States. In addition, Nioga must follow the rules and regulations put forth in a variety of federal and state payroll tax laws. For instance, it must withhold a certain amount from Julia's gross pay for the payment of federal and state income and Social Security and Medicare taxes. Nioga must also set aside from its own funds an amount equal to a certain percentage

1

of Julia's gross pay to cover the company's contribution to Social Security, Medicare, and unemployment taxes. All of these requirements involve a substantial amount of recordkeeping and government reporting.

In the meantime, Julia has a job to do, one she does quite well. She reports to a supervisor at Nioga Gear and attends monthly sales meetings and annual sales conferences. She hopes to be promoted to a sales manager position in the spring, at which time she would move "in-house," be switched to a monthly salary and a sales commission, and receive a substantial raise.

Nioga provides Julia with a weekly paycheck and some implied assurances about the accuracy of the calculations done to prepare that check—that is, that everything from time- and recordkeeping to calculating gross earnings to figuring withholding amounts and employer contributions has been done in conformity with current employment and tax laws. Abiding by these laws requires a well-organized payroll department and efficient, orderly, and effective procedures for each of the payroll functions. We'll begin our study of payroll accounting by taking a close look at the payroll laws and their effect on the payroll process.

CHAPTER 1

EMPLOYMENT AND PAYROLL LAWS

LEARNING OBJECTIVES

On completing this chapter, you will be able to:

1. Distinguish between employees and independent contractors, statutory employees and statutory nonemployees, and exempt and nonexempt employees.
2. Explain the main provisions of the Fair Labor Standards Act and their effect on the computation of gross earnings.
3. Review the various laws that provide equal rights in employment and prohibit discrimination based on race, color, religion, sex, national origin, age, or disability.
4. Differentiate the employer's liability for taxes and the meaning of employer under the various tax laws.
5. Discuss the state laws on employment, those that parallel federal laws and others specifically reserved for state action.
6. Describe other laws regarding payroll recordkeeping related to retirement plans and immigration reform.

At first glance, payroll accounting appears to be a relatively simple process. An employer pays an employee wages for work completed and withholds portions of the employee's earnings for payroll taxes, which are then handed over to the taxing authorities. However, to carry out this operation successfully, a payroll manager needs to have a good understanding of employment and payroll laws, personnel management, recordkeeping techniques, and accounting. That is our task in this text—to make the novice familiar enough with these areas to be an effective payroll manager.

This chapter will discuss the employment and payroll laws that pertain to payroll accounting. But before we address these laws, we need to examine the rules that dictate whether a worker is considered an employee and thus covered by these laws or an independent contractor who is not covered by them.

EMPLOYEE VERSUS INDEPENDENT CONTRACTOR

Common-law test *A test that, for FICA purposes, defines an employee as one subject to the will and control of the employer in the performance of services.*

Independent contractor *An individual or company hired by the public, often by contract, with discretion on when, where, and how to accomplish a specific job and generally with an investment in equipment, tools, and facilities.*

Statutory employee *An individual who does not qualify as an employee under the common-law test but who, nevertheless, is an employee by law which designates certain full-time workers performing services with no substantial investment in the business—is subject to withholding of FICA taxes but exempt from withholding of federal income taxes.*

Statutory nonemployee *An individual who does not qualify as an employee under the common-law test but, unlike the statutory employee, has been designated as a statutory nonemployee or independent contractor—is exempt from withholding of FICA and federal income taxes.*

The distinction between an employee and an independent contractor is an important one because employers must withhold federal income tax and withhold and match Social Security and Medicare taxes from employees' paychecks. Employers need not withhold taxes from payments to independent contractors, although they must furnish the Internal Revenue Service (IRS) with a record of payments made to the independent contractors.

The employer makes the decision as to whether a worker is an employee or an independent contractor, based on whether or not a common-law relationship exists between them. Under the **common-law test**, if the employer has the right to control both what will be done and how it will be done, then the relationship is an employer-employee one. If not, then the worker is an independent contractor.

In general, an **independent contractor** is one who controls a business, i.e., one who

- determines when, where, and how to work, often works under a contract, and may offer services to the general public;
- receives compensation in a lump sum or from commissions (not on an hourly, weekly, or monthly basis) and incurs expenses that may lead to a profit or loss for the business;
- has an investment in equipment, tools, and/or facilities.

Often, however, the distinction between employee and independent contractor is not clear-cut; the particular facts of each case must govern the determination. The employer who is not sure can use Form SS-8 (Exhibit 1-1) to establish worker status for purposes of income and employment taxes. Upon review of the completed form, the Internal Revenue Service (IRS) makes a determination as to whether the individual is an employee or an independent contractor.

In general, the common-law test determines whether an individual is an employee or not. The IRS, however, has taken the initiative to define certain groups of employees without strict adherence to the test, as long as the individuals work full-time, perform services, and have no investment in the business. Two such groups, called **statutory employees**, are life insurance agents and outside salespeople. In contrast, the IRS has decided that real estate agents and direct sellers of consumer products are independent contractors or **statutory nonemployees**.

Form **SS-8**
(Rev. June 1997)
Department of the Treasury
Internal Revenue Service

Determination of Employee Work Status for Purposes of Federal Employment Taxes and Income Tax Withholding

OMB No. 1545-0004

Paperwork Reduction Act Notice

We ask for the information on this form to carry out the Internal Revenue laws of the United States. You are required to give us the information. We need it to ensure that you are complying with these laws and to allow us to figure and collect the right amount of tax.

You are not required to provide the information requested on a form that is subject to the Paperwork Reduction Act unless the form displays a valid OMB control number. Books or records relating to a form or its instructions must be retained as long as their contents may become material in the administration of any Internal Revenue law. Generally, tax returns and return information are confidential, as required by Code section 6103.

The time needed to complete and file this form will vary depending on individual circumstances. The estimated average time is: **Recordkeeping,** 34 hr., 55 min.; **Learning about the law or the form,** 12 min.; and **Preparing and sending the form to the IRS,** 46 min. If you have comments concerning the accuracy of these time estimates or suggestions for making this form simpler, we would be happy to hear from you. You can write to the Tax Forms Committee, Western Area Distribution Center, Rancho Cordova, CA 95743-0001. **DO NOT** send the tax form to this address. Instead, see **General Information** for where to file.

Purpose

Employers and workers file Form SS-8 to get a determination as to whether a worker is an employee for purposes of Federal employment taxes and income tax withholding.

General Information

Complete this form carefully. If the firm is completing the form, complete it for **ONE** individual who is representative of the class of workers whose status is in question. If you want a written determination for more than one class of workers, complete a separate Form SS-8 for one worker

from each class whose status is typical of that class. A written determination for any worker will apply to other workers of the same class if the facts are not materially different from those of the worker whose status was ruled upon.

Caution: Form SS-8 is **not** a claim for refund of social security and Medicare taxes or Federal income tax withholding. Also, a determination that an individual is an employee does not necessarily reduce any current or prior tax liability. A worker must file his or her income tax return even if a determination has not been made by the due date of the return.

Where to file.—In the list below, find the state where your legal residence, principal place of business, office, or agency is located. Send Form SS-8 to the address listed for your location.

Location:	Send to:
Alaska, Arizona, Arkansas, California, Colorado, Hawaii, Idaho, Illinois, Iowa, Kansas, Minnesota, Missouri, Montana, Nebraska, Nevada, New Mexico, North Dakota, Oklahoma, Oregon, South Dakota, Texas, Utah, Washington, Wisconsin, Wyoming	Internal Revenue Service SS-8 Determinations P.O. Box 1231, Stop 4106 AUSC Austin, TX 78767
Alabama, Connecticut, Delaware, District of Columbia, Florida, Georgia, Indiana, Kentucky, Louisiana, Maine, Maryland, Massachusetts, Michigan, Mississippi, New Hampshire, New Jersey, New York, North Carolina, Ohio, Pennsylvania, Rhode Island, South Carolina, Tennessee, Vermont, Virginia, West Virginia, All other locations not listed	Internal Revenue Service SS-8 Determinations Two Lakemont Road Newport, VT 05855-1555
American Samoa, Guam, Puerto Rico, U.S. Virgin Islands	Internal Revenue Service Mercantile Plaza 2 Avenue Ponce de Leon San Juan, Puerto Rico 00918

Name of firm (or person) for whom the worker performed services

Name of worker

Address of firm (include street address, apt. or suite no., city, state, and ZIP code)

Address of worker (include street address, apt. or suite no., city, state, and ZIP code)

Trade name

Telephone number (include area code) ( )

Worker's social security number

Telephone number (include area code) ( )

Firm's employer identification number

Check type of firm for which the work relationship is in question:
☐ Individual ☐ Partnership ☐ Corporation ☐ Other (specify) ▶

Important Information Needed To Process Your Request

This form is being completed by: ☐ Firm ☐ Worker

If this form is being completed by the worker, the IRS **must** have your permission to disclose your name to the firm.

Do you object to disclosing your name and the information on this form to the firm? . . . . ☐ Yes ☐ No

If you answer "Yes," the IRS cannot act on your request. **Do not complete the rest of this form unless the IRS asks for it.**

Under section 6110 of the Internal Revenue Code, the information on this form and related file documents will be open to the public if any ruling or determination is made. However, names, addresses, and taxpayer identification numbers will be removed before the information is made public.

Is there any other information you want removed? . . . . ☐ Yes ☐ No

If you check "Yes," we cannot process your request unless you submit a copy of this form and copies of all supporting documents showing, in brackets, the information you want removed. Attach a separate statement showing which specific exemption of section 6110(c) applies to each bracketed part.

Cat. No. 16106T

Form **SS-8** (Rev. 6-97)

EXHIBIT 1-1 Form SS-8 Determination of Employee Work Status

(Exhibit continues.)

Form SS-8 (Rev. 6-97)   Page **2**

This form is designed to cover many work activities, so some of the questions may not apply to you. **You must answer ALL items or mark them "Unknown" or "Does not apply."** *If you need more space, attach another sheet.*

Total number of workers in this class. (Attach names and addresses. If more than 10 workers, list only 10.) ▶ _____

This information is about services performed by the worker from _____ to _____
                                                                           (month, day, year)   (month, day, year)

Is the worker still performing services for the firm? . . . . ☐ **Yes** ☐ **No**

● If "No," what was the date of termination? ▶ _____
                                                    (month, day, year)

1a Describe the firm's business ....

 b Describe the work done by the worker ....

2a If the work is done under a written agreement between the firm and the worker, attach a copy.

 b If the agreement is not in writing, describe the terms and conditions of the work arrangement ....
....

 c If the actual working arrangement differs in any way from the agreement, explain the differences and why they occur ....
....

3a Is the worker given training by the firm? . . . . ☐ **Yes** ☐ **No**
  ● If "Yes," what kind? ....
  ● How often? ....

 b Is the worker given instructions in the way the work is to be done (exclusive of actual training in 3a)? . ☐ **Yes** ☐ **No**
  ● If "Yes," give specific examples ....

 c Attach samples of any written instructions or procedures.

 d Does the firm have the right to change the methods used by the worker or direct that person on how to
   do the work? . . . . ☐ **Yes** ☐ **No**
  ● Explain your answer ....
....

 e Does the operation of the firm's business require that the worker be supervised or controlled in the
   performance of the service? . . . . ☐ **Yes** ☐ **No**
  ● Explain your answer ....
....

4a The firm engages the worker:
   ☐ To perform and complete a particular job only
   ☐ To work at a job for an indefinite period of time
   ☐ Other (explain) ....

 b Is the worker required to follow a routine or a schedule established by the firm? . . . . ☐ **Yes** ☐ **No**
  ● If "Yes," what is the routine or schedule? ....
....

 c Does the worker report to the firm or its representative?. . . . . ☐ **Yes** ☐ **No**
  ● If "Yes," how often? ....
  ● For what purpose? ....
  ● In what manner (in person, in writing, by telephone, etc.)? ....
  ● Attach copies of any report forms used in reporting to the firm.

 d Does the worker furnish a time record to the firm? . . . . ☐ **Yes** ☐ **No**
  ● If "Yes," attach copies of time records.

5a State the kind and value of tools, equipment, supplies, and materials furnished by:
  ● The firm ....
....

  ● The worker ....
....

 b What expenses are incurred by the worker in the performance of services for the firm? ....
....

 c Does the firm reimburse the worker for any expenses? . . . . ☐ **Yes** ☐ **No**
  ● If "Yes," specify the reimbursed expenses ....

EXHIBIT 1-1   Form SS-8 Determination of Employee Work Status *(cont.)*

6a Will the worker perform the services personally? . . . . ☐ **Yes** ☐ **No**

b Does the worker have helpers? . . . . ☐ **Yes** ☐ **No**
  - If "Yes," who hires the helpers? ☐ Firm ☐ Worker
  - If the helpers are hired by the worker, is the firm's approval necessary? . . . . ☐ **Yes** ☐ **No**
  - Who pays the helpers?   ☐ Firm ☐ Worker
  - If the worker pays the helpers, does the firm repay the worker? . . . . ☐ **Yes** ☐ **No**
  - Are social security and Medicare taxes and Federal income tax withheld from the helpers' pay? . . ☐ **Yes** ☐ **No**
  - If "Yes," who reports and pays these taxes?   ☐ Firm   ☐ Worker
  - Who reports the helpers' earnings to the Internal Revenue Service? ☐ Firm ☐ Worker
  - What services do the helpers perform? ....

7 At what location are the services performed? ☐ Firm's ☐ Worker's ☐ Other (specify) ....

8a Type of pay worker receives:
  ☐ Salary   ☐ Commission ☐ Hourly wage   ☐ Piecework ☐ Lump sum   ☐ Other (specify) ....

b Does the firm guarantee a minimum amount of pay to the worker? . . . . ☐ **Yes** ☐ **No**

c Does the firm allow the worker a drawing account or advances against pay? . . . . ☐ **Yes** ☐ **No**
  - If "Yes," is the worker paid such advances on a regular basis? . . . . ☐ **Yes** ☐ **No**

d How does the worker repay such advances? ....

9a Is the worker eligible for a pension, bonus, paid vacations, sick pay, etc.? . . . . ☐ **Yes** ☐ **No**
  - If "Yes," specify ....

b Does the firm carry worker's compensation insurance on the worker? . . . . ☐ **Yes** ☐ **No**

c Does the firm withhold social security and Medicare taxes from amounts paid the worker? . . . ☐ **Yes** ☐ **No**

d Does the firm withhold Federal income tax from amounts paid the worker? . . . . ☐ **Yes** ☐ **No**

e How does the firm report the worker's earnings to the Internal Revenue Service?
  ☐ Form W-2 ☐ Form 1099-MISC   ☐ Does not report ☐ Other (specify) ....
  - Attach a copy.

f Does the firm bond the worker? . . . . ☐ **Yes** ☐ **No**

10a Approximately how many hours a day does the worker perform services for the firm? ....

b Does the firm set hours of work for the worker? . . . . ☐ **Yes** ☐ **No**
  - If "Yes," what are the worker's set hours? _____ a.m./p.m. to _____ a.m./p.m. (Circle whether a.m. or p.m.)

c Does the worker perform similar services for others? . . . . ☐ **Yes** ☐ **No** ☐ **Unknown**
  - If "Yes," are these services performed on a daily basis for other firms? . . . . . ☐ **Yes** ☐ **No** ☐ **Unknown**
  - Percentage of time spent in performing these services for:
    This firm .... % Other firms .... %   ☐ **Unknown**
  - Does the firm have priority on the worker's time? . . . . ☐ **Yes** ☐ **No**
  - If "No," explain ....

d Is the worker prohibited from competing with the firm either while performing services or during any later period? . . . . ☐ **Yes** ☐ **No**

11a Can the firm discharge the worker at any time without incurring a liability? . . . . ☐ **Yes** ☐ **No**
  - If "No," explain ....

b Can the worker terminate the services at any time without incurring a liability? . . . . ☐ **Yes** ☐ **No**
  - If "No," explain ....

12a Does the worker perform services for the firm under:
  ☐ The firm's business name   ☐ The worker's own business name   ☐ Other (specify) ....

b Does the worker advertise or maintain a business listing in the telephone directory, a trade journal, etc.? . . . . ☐ **Yes** ☐ **No** ☐ **Unknown**
  - If "Yes," specify ....

c Does the worker represent himself or herself to the public as being in business to perform the same or similar services? . . . . ☐ **Yes** ☐ **No** ☐ **Unknown**
  - If "Yes," how? ....

d Does the worker have his or her own shop or office? . . . . ☐ **Yes** ☐ **No** ☐ **Unknown**
  - If "Yes," where? ....

e Does the firm represent the worker as an employee of the firm to its customers? . . . . ☐ **Yes** ☐ **No**
  - If "No," how is the worker represented? ....

f How did the firm learn of the worker's services? ....

13 Is a license necessary for the work? . . . . ☐ **Yes** ☐ **No** ☐ **Unknown**
  - If "Yes," what kind of license is required? ....
  - Who issues the license? ....
  - Who pays the license fee?

(Exhibit continues.)

14 Does the worker have a financial investment in a business related to the services
performed? . . . . ☐ **Yes**   ☐ **No**   ☐ **Unknown**
  ● If "Yes," specify and give amount of the investment . . . .

15 Can the worker incur a loss in the performance of the service for the firm? . . . . ☐ **Yes**   ☐ **No**
  ● If "Yes," how? . . . .

16a Has any other government agency ruled on the status of the firm's workers? . . . . ☐ **Yes**   ☐ **No**
  ● If "Yes," attach a copy of the ruling.

  b Is the same issue being considered by any IRS office in connection with the audit of the worker's tax
return or the firm's tax return, or has it been considered recently? . . . . ☐ **Yes**   ☐ **No**
  ● If "Yes," for which year(s)? . . . .

17 Does the worker assemble or process a product at home or away from the firm's place of business? ☐ **Yes**   ☐ **No**
  ● If "Yes," who furnishes materials or goods used by the worker? ☐ **Firm**   ☐ **Worker**   ☐ **Other**
  ● Is the worker furnished a pattern or given instructions to follow in making the product? . . . . . ☐ **Yes**   ☐ **No**
  ● Is the worker required to return the finished product to the firm or to someone designated by the firm? ☐ **Yes**   ☐ **No**
18 Attach a detailed explanation of any other reason why you believe the worker is an employee or an independent contractor.

Answer items 19a through o only if the worker is a salesperson or provides a service directly to customers.

19a Are leads to prospective customers furnished by the firm? . . . . ☐ **Yes** ☐ **No**   ☐ **Does not apply**
  b Is the worker required to pursue or report on leads? . . . . ☐ **Yes** ☐ **No**   ☐ **Does not apply**
  c Is the worker required to adhere to prices, terms, and conditions of sale established by the firm? . . ☐ **Yes**   ☐ **No**
  d Are orders submitted to and subject to approval by the firm? . . . . ☐ **Yes**   ☐ **No**
  e Is the worker expected to attend sales meetings? . . . . ☐ **Yes**   ☐ **No**
  ● If "Yes," is the worker subject to any kind of penalty for failing to attend? . . . . ☐ **Yes**   ☐ **No**
  f Does the firm assign a specific territory to the worker? . . . . ☐ **Yes**   ☐ **No**
  g Whom does the customer pay?   ☐ **Firm**   ☐ **Worker**
  ● If worker, does the worker remit the total amount to the firm? . . . . ☐ **Yes**   ☐ **No**
  h Does the worker sell a consumer product in a home or establishment other than a permanent retail
establishment? . . . . ☐ **Yes**   ☐ **No**
  i List the products and/or services distributed by the worker, such as meat, vegetables, fruit, bakery products, beverages (other
than milk), or laundry or dry cleaning services. If more than one type of product and/or service is distributed, specify the
principal one . . . .
  j Did the firm or another person assign the route or territory and a list of customers to the worker? . . ☐ **Yes**   ☐ **No**
  ● If "Yes," enter the name and job title of the person who made the assignment . . . .
  k Did the worker pay the firm or person for the privilege of serving customers on the route or in the territory? ☐ **Yes**   ☐ **No**
  ● If "Yes," how much did the worker pay (not including any amount paid for a truck or racks, etc.)? $ . . . .
  ● What factors were considered in determining the value of the route or territory? . . . .
  l How are new customers obtained by the worker? Explain fully, showing whether the new customers called the firm for service,
were solicited by the worker, or both . . . .
  m Does the worker sell life insurance? . . . . ☐ **Yes**   ☐ **No**
  ● If "Yes," is the selling of life insurance or annuity contracts for the firm the worker's entire business
activity? . . . . ☐ **Yes**   ☐ **No**
  ● If "No," list the other business activities and the amount of time spent on them . . . .
  n Does the worker sell other types of insurance for the firm? . . . . ☐ **Yes**   ☐ **No**
  ● If "Yes," state the percentage of the worker's total working time spent in selling other types of insurance . . . . %
  ● At the time the contract was entered into between the firm and the worker, was it their intention that the worker sell life
insurance for the firm: ☐ on a full-time basis   ☐ on a part-time basis
  ● State the manner in which the intention was expressed . . . .
  o Is the worker a traveling or city salesperson? . . . . ☐ **Yes**   ☐ **No**
  ● If "Yes," from whom does the worker principally solicit orders for the firm? . . . .
  ● If the worker solicits orders from wholesalers, retailers, contractors, or operators of hotels, restaurants, or other similar
establishments, specify the percentage of the worker's time spent in the solicitation . . . . %
  ● Is the merchandise purchased by the customers for resale or for use in their business operations? If used by the customers
in their business operations, describe the merchandise and state whether it is equipment installed on their premises or a
consumable supply

Under penalties of perjury, I declare that I have examined this request, including accompanying documents, and to the best of my knowledge and belief, the facts
presented are true, correct, and complete.

Signature ▶   **Title ▶**   **Date ▶**

If the firm is completing this form, an officer or member of the firm must sign it. If the worker is completing this form, the worker must sign it. If the worker wants a
written determination about services performed for two or more firms, a separate form must be completed and signed for each firm. Additional copies of this form may
be obtained by calling 1-800-TAX-FORM (1-800-829-3676).

✪ *Printed on recycled paper*   *U.S. Government Printing Office: 1997 - 417-677/60200

EXHIBIT 1-1   Form SS-8 Determination of Employee Work Status *(cont.)*

EXAMPLE   Ralph Ryan cleans a doctor's office once a week. Because he has 15 other clients in different locations whose offices he cleans and who each pay him directly, he is considered an independent contractor.   ▲

EXAMPLE   Janine Cruz cleans offices in three executive office suites. She is paid by the building manager and is dispatched to offices as needed. Because the building owner pays her wages and directs her work, Janine is considered an employee.   ▲

We've seen how workers qualify as employees under the IRS guidelines. Determining employee status is important because employees, unlike independent contractors, are protected by a number of laws that address compensation and employment. These include the Fair Labor Standards Act, federal laws protecting equal rights in employment, and both federal and state laws having to do with employment, compensation, disability, unemployment, and the withholding of taxes (Table 1-1). Our study of these laws begins with the Fair Labor Standards Act.

FAIR LABOR STANDARDS ACT

Fair Labor Standards Act (FLSA)   A 1938 federal law that regulates wages and hours of work, sets standards for minimum wage and overtime rates, prohibits discrimination in compensation, restricts child labor, and sets out recordkeeping requirements.

The **Fair Labor Standards Act** of 1938 (FLSA), also known as the Federal Wage and Hour Law, is considered the most important law in payroll operations. Amended several times since its original enactment, this law has a pervasive effect not only on payroll but on the economy as well. It provides the basis for requirements relating to:

1. Minimum wage rates.
2. Overtime (maximum hour) pay.
3. Nondiscrimination in compensation.
4. Child labor restrictions.

TABLE 1-1		
Summary of Federal Laws on Compensation and Employment		
Year	Law	Major Effects
1938	Fair Labor Standards Act	Set standards for wages and hours
1963	Equal Pay Act	Outlawed pay differentials based on sex
1964	Civil Rights Act	Prohibited discrimination based on sex, race, religion, national origin
1967	Age Discrimination in Employment Act	Barred age discrimination of those over 40 years of age
1972	Equal Employment Opportunities Act	Authorized legal action in cases of discrimination
1974	Employment Retirement Income Security Act	Imposed funding and disclosure standards for pension plans
1986	Immigration Reform and Control Act	Required verification of employment eligibility
1990	Americans with Disabilities Act	Banned discrimination based on physical or mental disability
1993	Family and Medical Leave Act	Permitted eligible employees up to 12 weeks leave for family or medical reasons

Employment Coverage

Interstate commerce Business, economic activity, or trade involving sales, production, and distribution not confined within any one state, but crossing one or more state lines.

An employer must abide by the provisions of the FLSA if two or more employees engage in interstate commerce or in the production of goods and services for interstate commerce. **Interstate commerce** refers to any trade (buying and/or selling), communication, or transportation across state lines. If the business is not engaged in interstate commerce, employees are still covered if the business has annual gross sales of at least $500,000. In addition, employees of certain types of enterprises are covered regardless of sales volume. These include workers employed in the construction trades, those employed by hospitals or schools (profit and nonprofit), those engaged in repairing clothes or fabric and in laundry services, and those employed by a public agency.

Enterprise coverage Provisions that define coverage of the employees of an organization under the Fair Labor Standards Act based on certain characteristics of the organization itself.

All of these instances are part of **enterprise coverage**, coverage that includes all employees of the enterprise. Another form of coverage, called **individual employee coverage**, extends to an individual employee who meets the interstate commerce requirement regardless of what the business itself or other employees do. For example, the law may cover an ice cream shop employee who makes regular trips out of state to pick up ice cream, even if the business itself does not meet the requirements for enterprise coverage. Also, individual employee coverage under the FLSA guidelines applies to domestic workers such as full-time baby sitters or housekeepers who receive wages in cash from one employer of at least $1,000 a calendar year or who work at least eight hours a week for one or more employers.

Individual employee coverage Coverage applicable to the Fair Labor Standards Act if any employee sells, produces, distributes, or is engaged in any other economic activity in interstate commerce.

Wage-Hour Provisions

Major provisions of the Fair Labor Standards Act deal with wages and hours, such as minimum wage rates, overtime pay, and nondiscrimination in compensation.

Minimum Wage Rate. While the FLSA established the structure for the minimum wage, Congress has since enacted several laws and amendments that have increased the minimum wage to keep up with inflation and/or changed specific regulations. The minimum wage established by the 1938 Act was 25 cents an hour. The federal hourly wage rate in effect as of April 1, 1991, was $4.25 per hour. Legislation passed in 1996 changed the minimum wage to $4.75 per hour, effective October 1, 1996, and $5.15 per hour beginning September 1, 1997. A state's minimum wage applies if it exceeds the federal minimum. Instead of the hourly rate, the employer may use a piece-rate method to calculate wages (see Chapter 2) as long as the **gross earnings** of each piece-work employee exceed the minimum wage rate for the hours worked.

Gross earnings Total regular earnings plus total overtime earnings.

An employee covered by the FLSA must receive at least the federal minimum hourly wage for each hour worked during the workweek. Averaging wages between workweeks so that overages in later weeks make up for shortages in earlier weeks is not permissible. But employers can deduct the value of certain items from the employee's pay regardless of whether deductions or allowances reduce the employee's pay to less than the required minimum wage.

PAYROLL IN ACTION

THE HOME AS A WORKPLACE

In colonial days, the principal workplace was the home. With the advent of the Industrial Revolution, factories sprang up and workers left their homes to pool their abilities in the production of goods. As service businesses grew, workers gathered in offices to serve the needs of their clients or customers.

We are now witnessing a dramatic return to the old methods of producing goods or rendering services. More and more people are working at home—aided by personal computers, modems, telephone answering systems, fax machines, and other communication devices. Recent figures reveal that more than 20 million persons work at home with about half of those people doing all their work at home. There are two types of home workers: home-based employees, who receive the same benefits as regular office or factory workers, and cottage workers, who are really independent contractors responsible for paying their own payroll taxes and providing their own benefits.

The securities industry is a good example of an industry that has fragmented into several groups of workers: regular office staff, home-based employees, and cottage workers. Both stockbrokers and investment managers are leaving the confines of their noisy ticker-tape environments in the city to set up shop in the suburbs or country—or anywhere they choose. These financial analysts generally have a following of loyal customers and can conduct business as usual at a distance, either continuing as home-based employees or setting up their own businesses as cottage workers. All this becomes possible through sophisticated stock quotation microcomputers and direct electronic communication systems hooked up to those at the main office and/or financial institutions. With the greater availability and affordability of equipment once found only in the office, we can expect the number of workers-at-home to continue increasing.

The permitted deductions are, in effect, part of gross wages and include:

1. Meals and lodging furnished by the employer. An employer can deduct the reasonable cost of meals and lodging if furnished for the employer's convenience and accepted voluntarily by employees, even though this may reduce cash wages below the minimum wage. The deduction for meals and lodging cannot, however, affect the computation of an employee's overtime rate.

2. Other supplies such as tools and uniforms furnished by the employer. These deductions follow the same rule as for meals and lodging except that they cannot reduce wages below the minimum level when the items are furnished for the employer's convenience.

3. Voluntary deductions authorized by the employee for savings plans, union dues, charitable donations, or insurance premiums. These deductions may reduce pay below the minimum wage, but cannot affect the computation for overtime.

4. Loan repayments. Loan repayments may reduce pay to less than the minimum wage, but interest or fees on loans cannot take the pay below the minimum wage or affect the overtime rate.

5. Customer tips. An employer can apply a credit for customer tips of up to 50% of the minimum wage of an employee who receives $20 a month or more in tips.

An employer can make a number of other deductions, such as deductions for work-rule infractions or cash shortages, as long as they do not bring the employee's wages below the minimum level. Deductions not allowed against the minimum wage usually cannot be applied to computation of the overtime rate. For example, an employer can dock an employee an hour for reporting to work late. However, that deduction cannot reduce the employee's pay to less than the minimum wage nor result in a reduction of the overtime rate. If the employee has worked overtime, the deduction for the penalty hour cannot be at the overtime rate but must be at employee's regular hourly rate. Deductions for cash shortages or lost checks cannot reduce wages below the minimum level, unless the employee has misappropriated funds.

Overtime *Hours worked over 40 in a workweek.*

Flextime *A plan that permits nonexempt employees to schedule their own flexible hours. A workday consists of certain required hours (or core time) and optimal hours (or flextime). Employees can schedule the flextime at their own convenience and are paid time-and-a-half if they elect to work more than 40 hours in a workweek.*

Irregular or fluctuating workweek *A work arrangement agreed to in writing, whereby an employee receives a fixed salary per week, regardless of the hours worked, but also receives an extra half-time premium of the average hourly rate for hours over 40 unless an exempt employee.*

White-collar exemption test *Criteria relating to duties, responsibilities, level of discretionary authority, and salary requirements for certain categories of employees (executive, administrative, professional, and outside salespersons) to determine whether such employees are exempt from the minimum wage, overtime, and certain recordkeeping requirements of the FLSA.*

Overtime Pay. The FLSA requires **overtime** pay at 1½ times the regular hourly rate for hours worked in excess of 40 per week. The averaging of weeks is not permissible and each workweek must stand on its own; employees cannot waive their statutory right to overtime.

Employers with nontraditional workweeks—due to **flextime**, workweeks of more or less than five days, or other **irregular** or **fluctuating workweeks**—must carefully calculate overtime allowances to stay within the law. A schedule of flexible hours for employees eligible for overtime must include no more than 40 hours in the regular workweek; hours beyond 40 must be paid at the overtime rate. The FLSA *does* permit different groups of workers to be on different workweeks, provided the workweeks are permanent or scheduled in advance.

The 40-hour test includes only those hours the employee actually works. In other words, the employer does not have to count time during which the employee did not perform services, even if paid for this time. Examples of paid hours that do not count for overtime are sick time, time spent on unauthorized work, travel time to and from different work stations, and preliminary or follow-up activities unless part of the job.

Exemptions from Minimum and Overtime Wage Rates. Certain types of employees meeting specific criteria (the so-called **white-collar exemption test**) are exempt from minimum wage or overtime regulations. The **exempt employees** are of four basic types: executives, administrators, professionals, and outside salespersons. These exemptions, in all cases, require that no more than 20% (40% if retail) of the workweek be spent in nonexempt work and that the minimum salary be $155 per week for executives and administrators and $170 per week for professionals.

Except for outside salespersons, all of the exempt positions describe workers who have management functions and/or who exercise discretion in their jobs. If the employee's salary is between $155 and $250 weekly, the following criteria must be met:

1. Executives must manage an enterprise or department, direct at least two workers, and have hiring and firing authority and discretionary powers.

2. Administrators must perform office management work or administer a school system, including staff employees with special assignments (such as purchasing agents or auditors), and must use independent judgment and discretion.

3. Professionals must apply originality, creativity, or specialized knowledge obtained from advanced study and must use independent judgment and discretion.

If the employee's salary is at least $250 weekly, the white-collar exemption test is less severe; the assumption is that a salary of this level implies that executives, administrators, and professionals exercise discretionary powers and their work requires a high degree of independent judgment. Consequently, proof of these characteristics is unnecessary.

The only other employees exempt from the minimum wage and overtime provisions are employees who are classified as learners, apprentices, or students and handicapped persons. Enterprises that are exempt from these provisions include retail and service establishments that meet certain statutory qualifications; amusement and recreational businesses having seasonal peaks; forestry, fishing, and offshore seafood processing businesses; railroads, express companies and water, motor and air carriers; and agriculture.

Nondiscrimination in Compensation. The FLSA prohibits unjustified wage differentials and prescribes that wage differentials be eliminated by raising the pay of those at the lower rates rather than by reducing the pay of those at the higher rates. This provision also applies to labor union scales. The employer may differentiate in wages based on seniority and merit but must maintain records that support these differences, such as job descriptions and evaluations, documentation of merit and **seniority systems**, and union or employment contracts.

Seniority system *A company policy to promote employees, pay them higher wages, or provide extra benefits based on length of service.*

Child Labor Restrictions

The child labor provisions of the FLSA prohibit oppressive child labor. Oppressive child labor is employment of a child under 16, subject to exceptions determined by the Secretary of Labor, or the employment of minors between 16 and 18 years of age in occupations determined by the Secretary to be hazardous to their health and well-being. The child labor laws apply to all businesses that engage in or produce goods for interstate or foreign commerce. It prohibits employment of:

• *Minors under age 14,* unless working in certain jobs (actor, news carrier) or employed by a parent in a nonhazardous industry.

The law limits employment of:

• *Minors age 14 and 15* to working not more than 3 hours per day and 18 hours per week during school months or not more than 8 hours per day and 40 hours per week during school vacation periods. The hours worked must fall between 7 A.M. and 7 P.M. or from June 1 to Labor

Day between 7 A.M. and 9 P.M. Under this law, a 14-year-old might work as a grocery store bagger weekends during the school year for a total of 18 hours a week and weekdays during the summer for a total of 40 hours a week.

- *Minors age 16 and 17* to working in nonhazardous jobs. Some jobs considered hazardous are work in manufacturing or processing plants; excavation and wrecking work; work in coal mines; and any work requiring use of power-operated machines, with the exception of office work.

Recordkeeping Requirements

An important provision of the Fair Labor Standards Act concerns recordkeeping. For each employee, the employer must have on file certain permanent information—home address, sex, date of birth, Social Security number, and occupation—as well as certain changing employment information—day and time of day the workweek begins, regular hourly rate of pay, basis of wage payments, hours worked per day and per week, daily or weekly straight-time pay, amount and nature of exempt pay, weekly overtime pay, total additions to or deductions from wages, total remuneration for a payroll period, and date of payment.

Every employer subject to any provision of the Fair Labor Standards Act must maintain records of employees and of the wages, hours, and other conditions and practices of employment for such periods of time prescribed by the Secretary of Labor, as necessary or appropriate for enforcement of the act. Furthermore, the act may regulate, restrict, or prohibit industrial home-based work as appropriate to prevent the circumvention of the minimum wage rate.

The Secretary of Labor has the authority to call witnesses and subpoena books, papers, and documents in an investigation regarding the keeping of employment records. Violators are subject to criminal proceedings, lawsuits by employees for unpaid wages, and wage collections by the government.

The Wage and Hour Division of the U.S. Department of Labor enforces most of the FLSA provisions. Exceptions are provisions of the Equal Pay Act of 1963. The Equal Employment Opportunity Commission (EEOC) enforces these provisions.

FEDERAL LAWS PROTECTING EQUAL RIGHTS IN EMPLOYMENT

Several major federal laws affect payroll operations in the area of equal rights. The *Civil Rights Act of 1964, Title VII,* as amended by the *Equal Employment Opportunities Act of 1972,* forbids employer and union discrimination based on race, color, religion, sex, or national origin. The *Equal Pay Act of 1963* requires equal pay for men and women doing equal work. The *Age Discrimination in Employment Act of 1967,* as amended in 1978, forbids discriminatory hiring practices against job applicants between the ages of 40 and 70. The *Rehabilitation Act of 1973* protects the handicapped from discrimination by employers performing federal contract work. In addition, *Executive Order 11246*, which has the force and effect of a statute enacted by Congress, specifically regulates contractors and subcontractors doing business with the federal government. Not only does this order prohibit discrimination against minorities, but in certain situations it also mandates that employers take affirmative action to improve employment opportunities for minorities.

The *Americans with Disabilities Act of 1990* prohibits discrimination in employment of individuals with disabilities. Employers must examine all steps of the employment process to eliminate and avoid any discriminatory practices from recruitment to retirement. The effective date of the law for employers of 25 or more employees was July 1, 1992, while July 1, 1994 was the effective date for employers of 15 to 24 employees.

Let's examine these laws in more detail.

Civil Rights Act of 1964, Title VII (amended 1991)

Title VII of the Civil Rights Act of 1964 outlawed discrimination in employment based on race, religion, national origin, or gender. The act covers any employer of at least 15 workers in each of 20 or more weeks in the current or preceding calendar year and whose business affects interstate commerce. Such employers cannot base hiring or firing decisions on an individual's race, color, religion, sex, or national origin, nor otherwise discriminate with respect to compensation, terms, conditions, or privileges of employment.

Equal Employment Opportunity Commission (EEOC) *A government agency that investigates violations of the Civil Rights Act of 1967 prohibiting discrimination in employment based on race, religion, national origin, or sex.*

The act established the **Equal Employment Opportunity Commission** (EEOC) to investigate violations of the law. A victim of discrimination must first try to work out any complaint through the EEOC before filing a lawsuit against the employer. The EEOC itself may initiate proceedings against any employer or group of persons that is in violation of the provisions of the law. After investigating any violations, the EEOC takes steps to remedy the situation through conciliation, conferences, and persuasion and can bring suit in federal district courts if necessary.

Bona fide occupational qualification (BFOQ) *A qualification for employment based on religion, national origin, or sex.*

Certain employers are exempt from the provisions of this law: the federal government, U.S.-government-owned corporations, Indian tribes, private tax-exempt membership clubs, and certain religious societies. The act also permits exceptions in cases where religion, national origin, or gender is a **bona fide occupational qualification** (usually referred to as a **BFOQ**). For example, a religious organization may legally employ only those of its faith in certain positions, just as a men's health club may hire only men to work in its locker room.

The Civil Rights Act of 1991 amends several sections of Title VII. The amendment strengthens and improves the Federal civil rights laws, provides for damages in case of intentional employment discrimination, and clarifies provisions. Title II sets up a commission to focus attention on, and complete a study relating to, the existence of artificial barriers to the advancement of women and minorities in the workplace and to make recommendations for overcoming such barriers.

Equal Employment Opportunities Act of 1972

The Equal Employment Opportunities Act of 1972 amended Title VII in several important respects. The class of persons covered under Title VII was expanded to include state and local governments and their political subdivisions. The act also eliminated the exemption for educational institutions with respect to teachers and professional and nonprofessional staff members engaged in educational activities.

The act also authorized the EEOC to institute court actions on behalf of the charging party if conciliation failed. Under the act, the EEOC received authority to bring class action lawsuits and to initiate lawsuits in response to allegations of a pattern of discrimination.

Equal Pay Act of 1963

The Equal Pay Act of 1963 prohibits pay differentials between men and women if they are doing equal work on jobs requiring equal skill, effort, and responsibility. This act has led to the theory of comparable worth; that is, a person should be paid as much as someone of the opposite sex who is performing work that is comparable, even if the job is not the same.

The act outlaws any variation in wage rates paid men and women that are based solely on gender. Whereas the FLSA provides exceptions based on seniority and merit, the Equal Pay Act permits variations that result from quantity or quality of production or any other differential based on a factor other than gender. For instance, a male and a female hairdresser may receive different compensation based on number of customers served or types of services rendered.

EXAMPLE Raoul, a stylist, earns more than Rachel, who does shampoos, because he performs a more costly service. His higher wage is acceptable under the Equal Pay Act because of the difference in the type of work performed. ▲

Age Discrimination in Employment Act of 1967

The Age Discrimination in Employment Act of 1967 (ADEA) as amended in 1978 forbids discrimination against men and women over 40 years of age by employers, unions, and employment agencies. The ADEA also forbids a mandatory retirement age. The act expands "employer" to include state and local governments; Executive Order 11141 prohibits age discrimination by government contractors and federal agencies.

The EEOC is responsible for enforcing the ADEA. Like the BFOQ exception of the Civil Rights Act, employers may establish reasonable age limitations on certain high-stress jobs requiring excellent physical condition.

Americans with Disabilities Act of 1990

The Americans with Disabilities Act of 1990 banned discrimination based on physical or mental disability. This law makes it illegal for employers with more than 15 employees to refuse employment to job candidates who might require difficult or costly accommodations. In other words, the goal of the law is to have employers focus on an individual's strengths or abilities, not weaknesses or disabilities.

Whether an individual will get the job should depend solely on whether the candidate can perform the work or "essential functions" of the job with or without reasonable accommodation. This condition means that the employer must establish whether certain functions are essential and, if not, restructure the job or have other employees carry out these functions. In essence, the law requires employers to make reasonable accommodations for qualified individuals with disabilities.

OTHER FEDERAL LAWS AFFECTING EMPLOYMENT

Several other federal laws affect employment and payroll management. The Employment Retirement Income Security Act of 1974 (ERISA), the Immigration Reform and Control Act of 1986 (IRCA), and the Family and Medical Leave Act of 1993 are three of the most important of these laws.

Employment Retirement Income Security Act of 1974

Vesting *The interest or rights to receive benefits from a pension plan as a result of years of service to the plan sponsor and not contingent on future service or employment.*

Pension plans became an important part of employee compensation in the late 1940s and early 1950s. With little federal regulation at the time, numerous instances of pension fund mismanagement and abuse took place. Inadequate funding and overly complex eligibility and **vesting** rights (the granting of rights to the benefits of a pension plan should an employee leave before retirement age) created confusion, with many employees receiving much less or none of the pension they expected. In response to the public demand for better retirement protection, Congress enacted the Employment Retirement Income Security Act, known as ERISA.

ERISA does not require any employer to provide a pension plan, but it does impose standards on both private and public employers to make sure that employees receive pension benefits they are due, commensurate with their years of employment. It also requires pension plan administrators to disclose to employees and the government financial information about plans offered. The provisions of ERISA also apply to other employee benefit plans established by employers, commonly termed *welfare plans*. Welfare plans usually provide medical coverage, disability benefits, death benefits, vacation pay, and unemployment benefits. They may also cover other programs such as day-care centers and scholarship awards.

Fiduciary *A person entrusted with property or power for the benefit of others.*

Prudent man rule *A legal guideline stating that a fiduciary must act as a so-called prudent man would in the same capacity under similar circumstances.*

Although the welfare or pension plan fund is a separate entity, the employer usually serves as trustee or administrator. As a **fiduciary**, the employer is responsible for keeping records on the contributions and other income of the fund, its expenses, and the interest of each participant. A fiduciary must follow the **prudent man rule** and thus must diversify the investments of the fund to minimize risk.

Welfare and pension plans require extensive disclosure. The employer as a fiduciary must file informational returns with the Department of

Labor, the IRS, and, in the case of pension plans, the Pension Guarantee Benefit Corporation. These reports present details of the plans—eligibility, participation, termination, funding—and include audited financial statements with the current value of plan assets and liabilities as well as receipts and disbursements. Participants also receive summary reports.

Immigration Reform and Control Act of 1986

The Immigration Reform and Control Act of 1986 (IRCA) forbids employers from knowingly hiring illegal aliens and provides criminal and civil penalties for violations. The act requires the employer to verify that each new employee hired after November 6, 1986, has authorization to work in the United States. The Immigration and Naturalization Service (INS) has designated Form I-9 as the official verification form to comply with the IRCA (Exhibit 1-2).

.The prospective employee must attest to being a U.S. citizen or to having INS authorization to work in the United States and must present documents that support the person's right to work in the United States. These documents may include a U.S. passport, a certificate of naturalization, an unexpired foreign passport with attached visa authorizing U.S. employment, or an Alien Registration Card with photograph. The employer must complete a Form I-9 within three days of the date the employee begins work and must retain completed forms for three years after the date of hire or one year after the date of termination, whichever is later. The INS can assess fines of between $100 and $1,000 for failure to comply.

Family and Medical Leave Act of 1993

The Family and Medical Leave Act of 1993 (FMLA) permitted eligible employees as much as 12 weeks leave for family or medical reasons without fear of job layoff or dismissal. The law applied to employers with 50 or more employees within a 75 mile radius during at least 20 weeks in the current or preceding calendar year, including part-time, temporary, and seasonal employees. To be eligible for a leave, an employee must have worked for the employer for at least 1,250 hours during the previous 12 months.

Employees are eligible for a total of 12 weeks paid or unpaid leave during any 12 month period for events such as the birth of a child; adoption; foster care; caring for a spouse, child, or parent with a serious health condition; or a personal health condition serious enough to impede job performance. An employer must continue to provide health insurance benefits to employees during the leave, but can recover the premiums paid for an employee not returning to work, unless such failure is due to a valid reason. At the discretion of the employees or employer, the employees may substitute accrued (earned but not used) paid vacation, personal leave or sick leave for family leave taken for birth, adoption, or foster care.

U.S. Department of Justice
Immigration and Naturalization Service

OMB No. 1115-0136
Employment Eligibility Verification

Please read instructions carefully before completing this form. The instructions must be available during completion of this form. **ANTI-DISCRIMINATION NOTICE.** It is illegal to discriminate against work eligible individuals. Employers CANNOT specify which document(s) they will accept from an employee. The refusal to hire an individual because of a future expiration date may also constitute illegal discrimination.

Section 1. Employee Information and Verification. To be completed and signed by employee at the time employment begins

Print Name: Last	First	Middle Initial	Maiden Name

Address (Street Name and Number)	Apt. #	Date of Birth (month/day/year)

City	State	Zip Code	Social Security #

I am aware that federal law provides for imprisonment and/or fines for false statements or use of false documents in connection with the completion of this form.

I attest, under penalty of perjury, that I am (check one of the following):
☐ A citizen or national of the United States
☐ A Lawful Permanent Resident (Alien # A_____)
☐ An alien authorized to work until ___/___/___
(Alien # or Admission # _____)

Employee's Signature   Date (month/day/year)

Preparer and/or Translator Certification. (To be completed and signed if Section 1 is prepared by a person other than the employee.) I attest, under penalty of perjury, that I have assisted in the completion of this form and that to the best of my knowledge the information is true and correct.

Preparer's/Translator's Signature   Print Name

Address (Street Name and Number, City, State, Zip Code)   Date (month/day/year)

Section 2. Employer Review and Verification. To be completed and signed by employer. Examine one document from List A OR examine one document from List B **and** one from List C as listed on the reverse of this form and record the title, number and expiration date, if any, of the document(s)

List A	OR	**List B**	AND	**List C**
Document title: _____		_____		_____
Issuing authority: _____		_____		_____
Document #: _____		_____		_____
Expiration Date (if any): ___/___/___		___/___/___		___/___/___
Document #: _____				
Expiration Date (if any): ___/___/___				

CERTIFICATION - I attest, under penalty of perjury, that I have examined the document(s) presented by the above-named employee, that the above-listed document(s) appear to be genuine and to relate to the employee named, that the employee began employment on (month/day/year) ___/___/___ and that to the best of my knowledge the employee is eligible to work in the United States. (State employment agencies may omit the date the employee began employment).

Signature of Employer or Authorized Representative	Print Name	Title

Business or Organization Name	Address (Street Name and Number, City, State, Zip Code)	Date (month/day/year)

Section 3. Updating and Reverification. To be completed and signed by employer

A. New Name (if applicable)	B. Date of rehire (month/day/year) (if applicable)

C. If employee's previous grant of work authorization has expired, provide the information below for the document that establishes current employment eligibility.

Document Title:_____ Document #:_____ Expiration Date (if any): ___/___/___

I attest, under penalty of perjury, that to the best of my knowledge, this employee is eligible to work in the United States, and if the employee presented document(s), the document(s) I have examined appear to be genuine and to relate to the individual.

Signature of Employer or Authorized Representative	Date (month/day/year)

Form I-9 (Rev. 11-21-91) N

EXHIBIT 1-2 Employment Eligibility Verification (Form I-9)

STATE EMPLOYMENT LAWS

The states have their own laws regarding employment regulations. State regulations affect minimum/maximum wage rates; pay periods; pay for call-in and waiting time; and work conditions such as rest and meal periods, absences, meals and lodging, tips, uniforms, and other items. In addition, the states have their own recordkeeping and payroll tax requirements. Although most states provide for the same types of employee protection, the specifics of each program vary widely from state to state. Those responsible for setting up or operating a payroll program must be as knowledgeable about their own state regulations as they are about federal regulations.

Minimum Wage and Maximum Hours Laws

All states have regulations regarding minimum wage and maximum hour (overtime) standards. In the case of minimum wage and overtime rates, if an employee is covered under both the federal and the state standards, the higher of the two wage rates prevails.

Workers' Compensation Laws

Most states require employers to provide employees with workers' compensation insurance, which protects against job-related accidents, disability, or death. An employer obtains such insurance through the state's compensation fund or a private insurance company. The premiums are a percentage of the total payroll. To process a claim, the employer must provide information to the insurer about the employee's earnings.

Disability Benefit Laws

Disability insurance *Insurance that provides protection for employees and their families against loss of income due to non-job-related accidents or disability.*

A number of states have laws that require employers to provide **disability insurance** to employees who cannot work due to illnesses or accidents that are not job-related. The financing of this insurance may be joint (by both the employer and the employee) or may be the sole responsibility of the employer.

PAYROLL TAX LAWS

Tax laws are among the most complex of all federal regulations. And, because of their withholding, deposit, and reporting requirements, they play a major role in payroll recordkeeping and operations. The tax laws that require regular payroll deductions and/or employer contributions include:

1. The Current Tax Payment Act of 1943, otherwise known as the Federal Income Tax Withholding Law (FITW)
2. The Federal Insurance Contributions Act of 1935 (FICA)
3. The Self-Employment Contributions Act (SECA)
4. The Federal Unemployment Tax Act (FUTA)

Employers liable for payroll taxes must keep accurate records that support the tax liability for at least the past four years. The retention period begins after the due date of the tax for the return period to which the records relate or the date of the tax payment, whichever is later. The required documentation should be kept in safe and accessible locations and must be available for IRS inspection at all times.

Let's examine these laws in more detail.

Federal Income Tax Withholding Law (FITW)

A federal income tax went into effect in 1913 with the passage of a constitutional amendment allowing Congress to levy a tax on the income of individuals and corporations. Since then, Congress has passed a variety of federal income tax laws, including the complex federal income tax regulations that make up the Internal Revenue Code (or federal tax law).

Current Tax Payment Act A 1943 federal law that requires employers to withhold federal income taxes from the wages of employees.

The **Current Tax Payment Act** of 1943, often referred to as the Federal Income Tax Withholding Law (FITW), is the most important law affecting payroll tax withholding. This law provides for the collection of federal income taxes at the source of wages and is enforced by the Internal Revenue Service of the Department of the Treasury. In a sense, this law turned over the responsibility for tax collection to employers, at the same time providing a steady flow of tax income to the federal government. Before the enactment of the Current Tax Payment Act, individuals paid their taxes once a year when they filed their tax returns. The liability for payroll taxes arises at the same time as gross wages are earned. The employer withholds from each employee's check an amount based on the current tax formula and makes regular payments of these withholdings to the IRS or to a bank authorized by the IRS. The employer must also make quarterly reports (Form 941) to the IRS detailing amounts withheld and deposited. The 1943 act included some recordkeeping requirements as well. Employers must have on file the names and addresses of employees, period of employment, amounts subject to withholding, and dates of payment.

Another law passed more recently affects payroll tax computations. The *Tax Reform Act of 1986* drastically changed tax rates, exemptions, and allowable deductions, requiring commensurate changes for payroll managers in terms of withholding calculations. Other tax law changes in subsequent years have also changed these calculations. The deposit requirements and other regulations are topics covered in later chapters.

Federal Insurance Contributions Act (FICA)

Federal Insurance Contributions Act (FICA) A 1935 federal law that provides old-age and survivors' benefits and disability insurance, financed by contributions from both employees and employers.

The **Federal Insurance Contributions Act** (FICA) implements the Social Security Act of 1935, which provides funding for financial security of workers and their families. FICA requires an equal employee/employer contribution toward the cost of old-age and survivors' benefits and disability (Social Security) and hospital insurance (Medicare). Employers withhold a certain percentage of each employee's earnings each payroll period and match these withholdings. The employers deposit the total amounts withheld and matched for all employees in an authorized bank or with the IRS and file periodic reports. The act also requires detailed records on earnings, tax liabilities, and deposits.

Self-Employment Contributions Act (SECA)

Self-Employment Contri-
butions Act (SECA) A
1951 federal law that re-
quires self-employed persons
to pay taxes comparable to
FICA taxes; the act provides
equivalent Social Security
and Medicare benefits.

The **Self-Employment Contributions** Act (SECA) complements FICA by providing the same benefits for self-employed persons. This act covers anyone independently operating an unincorporated trade or business. A trade or business is generally an activity carried on for a livelihood or in good faith to make a profit. The business need not actually make a profit as long as pursuing a profit is the primary motivating factor. Ongoing efforts to further the interest of the business, regularity of activities and transactions, and the production of income are important elements of the definition.

Self-employment income is subject to self-employment tax. The self-employed person can use any of three methods to compute the tax: the regular method and two optional methods. The optional methods, described in more detail in Chapter 4, are useful if an individual wants to continue Social Security and hospital benefits coverage and has self-employment income of $1,600 or even a loss.

Federal Unemployment Tax Act (FUTA)

Federal Unemployment
Tax Act (FUTA) *A law*
providing unemployment
benefits to eligible employees
without jobs, financed by con-
tributions from the employer.

The **Federal Unemployment Tax Act** represents the other fund-raising arm of the Social Security Act. FUTA, together with the state unemployment systems, provides for payment of unemployment compensation to eligible employees who have lost their jobs.

Only the employer must make contributions—the employee is not subject to any withholding to fund the program. The act makes no provisions for direct federal benefit payments, but only for payments under unemployment compensation laws of the various states and territories.

Employer Liability under the Tax Laws

An employer can be an individual, corporation, partnership, trust, estate, joint-stock company, association, unincorporated business, tax-exempt organization, or an entity making supplemental unemployment benefit payments equivalent to wages. Employers also include governments of the United States, U.S. territories, Puerto Rico, the District of Columbia, and the 50 states.

Employer *An entity or or-*
ganization that has control
over the payment of wages to
employees or employees' per-
formance of services.

Definition of Employer for Tax Purposes. An employer may or may not be subject to the federal payroll tax laws. An employer can also be subject to some payroll tax laws and not to others, simply because the rules that establish an employer's liability are sometimes different for FITW than for FICA and FUTA. For FITW purposes, an **employer** is an entity or organization for whom an individual performs any service as an employee. However, if the entity or organization receives services but does not have control of the payment of wages, the employer is the entity or organization that controls the payment of wages. This distinction often arises in the case of parent-subsidiary corporations or brother-sister relationships (common stockholders of two or more businesses). The entity that controls the payment of wages is the employer for FITW purposes, while the entity that controls the workers is the employer for FICA and FUTA purposes.

The common-law test, described earlier in this chapter, determines the employer for FICA purposes. Under this test, every worker who performs services subject to the will and control of the employer both as to the method and results of the work is an employee. Thus, an employer is the entity or organization that has the final authority to control the worker in performing services (in contrast to the FITW test where the employer is the entity paying the wages).

For the FUTA tax, the liability results from meeting the *1-in-20* test or the *wage* test. Under the 1-in-20 test, employers must pay FUTA tax if they employ at least one individual for some portion of the day in each of 20 days during the current or preceding calendar year, each day being in a different calendar week. The calendar weeks don't have to be consecutive, and the one required employee doesn't have to be the same worker on each of the 20 days.

Under the wage test, FUTA applies to employers who pay wages of $1,500 ($1,000 for household employees) during any quarter in the current or preceding calendar year. The purpose of this test is to cover seasonal employers—those that periodically employ workers, but not for 20 weeks in any one calendar year.

Period of Liability for Employer.   For both FITW and Medicare, the liability extends from the first to the last day of nonexempt employment. However, in the case of Social Security and FUTA, the liability for an employee ends when that employee reaches a designated taxable wage limit.

If employment meets either the 1-in-20 or the wage test, the liability under FUTA continues for at least two years. If the employer fails to meet the coverage tests during two consecutive years, liability ends as of January 1 of the second year.

State Income Tax Withholding Laws

Many states and some cities and towns impose income taxes on individuals, and their laws require withholdings, the filing of reports, and the prepayment of taxes. In those cases where the states or localities have income tax laws, the employers must follow the applicable government's regulations.

State Unemployment Tax Acts (SUTA)

All the states have enacted unemployment insurance laws that dovetail with the Federal Unemployment Tax Act (FUTA). An employer receives a credit against the FUTA tax for contributions to the state's unemployment insurance fund.

Good recordkeeping is essential to carrying out the unemployment insurance program, and employers may be subject to penalties for failure to maintain the proper records and file the required reports.

REVIEW QUESTIONS

1–1. Who decides if a person is an employee or independent contractor and on what basis? Does or can the IRS have a voice in this process?

1–2. Define *independent contractor* with respect to control of work, form of compensation, and investment in equipment.

1–3. Name three groups exempt from the overtime pay provisions of the FLSA under the so-called white-collar exemption test.

1–4. What is the effect of different salary levels on the exemption from the overtime pay provisions of the Fair Labor Standards Act?

1–5. Define *statutory employee*. Explain the taxability of compensation for such an employee, giving examples.

1–6. What is a *statutory nonemployee*? Give examples.

1–7. How can an employer justify differences in wage rates under the FLSA? under the Equal Pay Act of 1963?

1–8. Define *oppressive child labor*. How does the FLSA prohibit and limit the employment of minors?

1–9. What information does the FLSA require in respect to employment data?

1–10. What size of enterprise is subject to the Civil Rights Act of 1964, Title VII?

1–11. Name five classes of employers exempt from the Civil Rights Act of 1964.

1–12. What is meant by a bona fide occupational qualification (BFOQ)? Give two examples.

1–13. Describe the purpose of the Equal Pay Act of 1963 and the theory of comparable worth.

1–14. To what age group does the Age Discrimination in Employment Act of 1967 apply? What agency is responsible for the enforcement of the act?

1–15. Name the four laws that govern the imposition and payment of payroll taxes.

1–16. Define a trade or business according to the Self-Employment Contributions Act (SECA).

1–17. What circumstances determine the employer responsible for payment of FITW taxes? FICA taxes? FUTA taxes?

1–18. Define *employer* in terms of services received, wages paid, and workers controlled.

1–19. What are the 1-in-20 test and the wage test used with the Federal Unemployment Tax Act?

1–20. Differentiate the liability under FITW as compared to FICA and FUTA.

1–21. What is the period of liability under FITW, FICA, and FUTA?

1–22. What is the difference between workers' compensation and disability benefit insurance?

1–23. From what two sources may an employer obtain workers' compensation insurance? What are two methods of financing disability benefit insurance?

Review Questions (cont.)

1–24. What types of plans are covered by the Employment Retirement Income Security Act of 1974 (ERISA)? What is the responsibility of the trustee or administrator as fiduciary in these plans? What are the filing requirements for pension plans?

1–25. What is the purpose of the Immigration Reform and Control Act of 1986? What form must a prospective employee complete? What documents provide evidence in support of the application?

DISCUSSION QUESTIONS

1–1. The Crestview Nursing Home paid its nurses' aides the minimum wage. The nurses' aides wore uniforms, which they paid for at their own expense. In what way(s) has the Crestview Nursing Home violated the FLSA? How can Crestview comply with the law?

1–2. Occasionally, line operators at the Crunched Cereal Company were asked to do work during their break time (rest periods) for which they were not paid. Following their supervisor's instructions, the line operators signed their timecards indicating that they had taken their scheduled break times. Did the Crunched Cereal Company violate any provisions of the FLSA?

1–3. Prior to this year, the Thomas Cafeteria paid its hourly food service employees at least the minimum wage and permitted them to purchase meals at a discount. Starting this year, Thomas instituted a new policy. Employees were required to buy their meals from a limited menu and no longer paid for their meals directly. Instead, Thomas deducted $.45 per hour from their wages as the reasonable cost of the meals. This deduction resulted in some employees receiving less than minimum wage. Did the Thomas Cafeteria violate the minimum wage provision of the FLSA?

1–4. The Professional Ambulance Service employed ambulance drivers and attendants on a work shift that extended from 8 A.M. until 8 A.M. the following day. The employees understood that they would receive an hourly rate in excess of the minimum wage rate for all time worked plus time-and-a-half for all hours over 40 hours per week. They would be paid for 10 hours per 24-hour shift, even in the absence of any ambulance calls.

The company furnished living quarters for its employees in the area of its operations and gave its employees the option of using these quarters or other premises of their choice. During their work shift, the employees were free to leave the facilities on personal business as long as they advised the telephone answering service where they could be reached. Did the Professional Ambulance Service violate the overtime provision of the FLSA?

1–5. The Burger Boutique regards its assistant managers, who are paid $250 a week, as exempt employees and, therefore, not entitled to time-and-a-half for overtime hours. The assistant managers schedule employees, assign work, oversee product quality, and converse with customers. They also train employees, set the schedule for producing food, and perform various recordkeeping, inventory, and cash reconciliation duties, according to standard operating procedures of the company. A number of the other tasks performed by the assistant managers are the same as those of hourly employees. They spend approximately 40% of their time taking and expediting orders, preparing food, and performing general housekeeping tasks. Do you believe the assistant managers should be exempt or nonexempt? Present arguments for both sides.

1–6. On May 10, 2000, Martha Travis completed an application for employment at the Ridge Road Machine Shop, listing her date of birth as April 3, 1982, when in fact she was born April 3, 1984. On passing a physical examination and having her application approved, Martha began work on June 1, 2000, as a punch press operator. A week later, Martha broke her arm in an accident on the job. In the course of her application for medical benefits, the company discovered that Martha had lied about her birth date on the employment application and at the time of hiring was 16 years of age. Is Ridge Road responsible for the violation of the child labor provisions of the FLSA? What action might the company have taken prior to hiring Martha?

1–7. Rainbow Airlines has a policy of hiring only females for the job of flight attendant. In Rainbow's opinion, being a female is a bona fide occupational qualification (BFOQ) reasonably necessary to the normal operation of the airline. According to Rainbow, most passengers prefer female flight attendants and females were able to carry out the mechanical functions of the job in a more effective manner than most men. Do you agree with Rainbow's position? Explain.

1–8. Brady Knudsen was an employee of Trans America Bus Lines. After several years with Trans America, Brady joined the World Church of Christ, a religion that observed the Sabbath by not performing any work from sunset on Friday until sunset on Saturday or on religious holidays.

The company was willing to transfer Knudsen to another job, but the union would not permit the transfer because it violated the seniority provisions of the collective bargaining agreement. Knudsen was then transferred to another job that required Saturday work. When he refused to report for work on Saturdays, Trans America fired him. Is the company in violation of the antidiscrimination provisions of the Civil Rights Act of 1974, Title VII?

1–9. Northeast Commuter Lines requires its flight engineers to retire at age 60. The Age Discrimination in Employment Act of 1967 (ADEA) generally prohibits mandatory retirement before age 70, but provides an exception where age is a bona fide occupational qualification (BFOQ) reasonably necessary to the normal operation of the particular business. Do you agree with the position of Northeast? How might the company prove its case?

1–10. Attorney Kathryn Stephens was hired as an associate in a large law firm. The firm indicated that she would become a partner after six years, provided she received satisfactory evaluation reviews. Stephens received excellent reviews during the six years but was denied a partnership. Stephens alleged sex discrimination but the firm replied that Title VII did not apply because partnership selection involves a change in status from employee to employer. Do you agree with the position of the firm? Comment.

RUNNING A PAYROLL

In Chapter 1, we saw the impact of federal and state laws on employee compensation and recordkeeping. In the next several chapters, we'll examine the effects of these laws on each step of the payroll process. As we go along, we'll use examples from Nioga Gear, Inc., the hypothetical company described in Part I, and from other hypothetical businesses to illustrate how these laws and a payroll accounting system interact.

Let's start by describing Nioga's operations in more detail. Nioga Gear started in business three years ago with the production of a special type of walking shoe. Using a regional distribution system, the company was able to steadily increase sales. Last year, the company sold 25,000 units in the Nioga Walker Line, and gross income from the sales of shoes and accessories exceeded $2 million. Nioga has just added a new line—a general-purpose sport shoe that will be suitable for tennis, racquetball, and handball. The company's success to date has resulted from a limited but effective advertising campaign based on a sincere approach featuring homespun axioms. For example, one magazine advertisement uses the phrase "comfortable as an old shoe" and radio spots use the phrase "if the shoe fits, wear it." In addition, Nioga has opened up new distributorships for its walking shoe by aggressively pursuing small retail outlets and offering excellent discounts. The ads and distribution plan have earned the company a place on the *Inc.* magazine list of most promising small companies in the United States.

Nioga has 94 employees. These include the president Harry Weimer, vice president Rachel Mollone, and treasurer Bruce Jackson. The company has 65 production workers, including several

supervisors; 16 salespersons, including 4 telephone sales representatives and 4 sales managers; and 10 office workers, including
a personnel manager, payroll manager Clark Barr, and his assistant Lois Arruda.

The Nioga payroll manager, Clark Barr, has been training his
assistant Lois Arruda on what it takes to run a payroll department.
He believes you must satisfy your employer, the government, and
your employees—not necessarily in that order. Clark would like to
move up with the company and he has been teaching Lois all that
she needs to know to take over his job. However, Clark has done
such a good job that his boss, Bruce Jackson, is reluctant to replace
him. Bruce has heard the stories of payroll errors and fraud that
have cost companies money, embarrassment, or both.

CHAPTER 2

TIMEKEEPING AND COMPUTING GROSS EARNINGS

LEARNING OBJECTIVES

On completing this chapter, you will be able to:

1. Describe the various methods of timekeeping: time records, timecards, time sheets, work records, and production and sales records.

2. Compute gross earnings on the hourly rate plan, salary plan, overtime pay, piece-rate plan, commission plan, and combination plan.

3. Explain worktime eligibility for compensation, the nature of taxable compensation, and other compensation methods—bonuses, profit-sharing payments, and tips—and also supplemental wages.

As described in the part introduction, Nioga's payroll manager, Clark Barr, is preparing Lois Arruda, currently his assistant, to take over the payroll duties. She is learning fast, and Clark now believes she is ready to get into the real substance of working up a payroll. He plans to cover three major components in determining employee compensation: timekeeping, the methods to divide time worked into payroll periods and to track employee time; methods of computing pay, which can vary among employees depending on the type of work done; and the forms of compensation offered.

29

TIMEKEEPING

A timekeeping system is necessary for compliance with the Fair Labor Standards Act. However, what the law mandates is also essential for ordinary business operations.

Payroll Periods

Payroll period *The number of days, weeks, or parts of a month or year—that is, the frequency of employee compensation: weekly, biweekly, semimonthly, and monthly.*

Biweekly *Every two weeks, resulting in 26 pay periods.*

Semimonthly *Twice a month, resulting in 24 pay periods.*

A **payroll period** may cover one week, two weeks, half a month, or one month—periods referred to as weekly, **biweekly**, **semimonthly**, and monthly, respectively. The employer selects a payroll period that best serves the needs of the organization. Often the employer may pay one category of employee (such as production workers) on a weekly basis and another category of employee (such as managerial employees) on a monthly basis.

The date for paying employees follows the end of the payroll period and allows for a period of time to prepare and distribute the payroll. For example, suppose a weekly payroll period ends on Friday; payday may be on the following Tuesday. Or, for a monthly payroll period, the payroll distribution may take place four business days after the end of the month (Figure 2-1).

At Nioga Gear, the production employees are paid weekly, on the Wednesday following the workweek ending Saturday. Managerial employees are paid either biweekly (every two weeks), on the Wednesday

OCTOBER
20XX

SUN	MON	TUES	WED	THURS	FRI	SAT
					1	2
3	4	5 Payday Week Ended Friday 10/1	6 Payday Month of September	7	8	9
10	11	12 Payday Week Ended Friday 10/8	13 Payday Biweekly Period Ended Friday 10/8	14	15	16
17	18	19 Payday Week Ended Friday 10/15	20	21	22	23
24 / 31	25	26 Payday Week Ended Friday 10/22	27 Payday Biweekly Period Ended Friday 10/22	28	29	30

FIGURE 2-1 Typical Paydays for Various Payroll Periods

following their second workweek, or monthly, on the first Wednesday after the end of the month. Some companies have no time lag and pay their salaried employees on the last day of the month.

Timekeeping Records

Accurate timekeeping is an essential part of an efficient payroll system. Every business must have an orderly method of recording the hours employees worked during the payroll period. The Fair Labor Standards Act requires that time records show the date and the time the workweek starts, the number of hours worked each day, and the total hours worked during the week. The only exception to this rule is for employees who are exempt from the overtime pay requirement. (See the white-collar exemption test described in Chapter 1.) After preparing the payroll, the payroll clerk files the timecards for safekeeping for up to three years, according to FLSA requirements. Well-maintained records prove invaluable should questions arise later regarding hours worked and wages paid to employees.

The most common methods of timekeeping use a time clock with timecards or a time sheet.

Timecard *A form used to record the exact hours worked by an employee.*

Timecards. A mechanical or electronic clock with **timecards** is the time-keeping method used most often for production or shift workers (those who work in a big factory or a large service establishment, such as a hotel with more than 100 rooms). Each employee receives a timecard; all the cards are arranged in numbered slots in a rack next to the time clock. The employees punch in and out as they arrive and depart for the day and at meal times (see Figure 2-2). A supervisor collects the timecards at the end of the week. Either the supervisor or the payroll clerk adds up the hours each employee worked during the period.

By law, employees must be paid for all the time they work, including fractional parts of an hour. As a result, most time clocks record time in and time out to the minute. Employers may round the starting and stopping times to the nearest 5 minutes, tenth of an hour, or quarter of an hour as long as they can demonstrate that their system averages out to the full amount of time worked. The system selected out of many that are available is usually a part of the collective bargaining agreement.

Nioga uses a quarter-hour system to compute the time worked by production employees. Arrival and departure times are rounded to the nearest quarter-hour. Any time seven minutes before or seven minutes after the quarter-hour is recorded as of that quarter-hour (Table 2-1). For example, if an employee arrives for work at 8:05, it would be counted as 8:00. If, however, the employee arrived at 8:08, it would be counted as 8:15.

Badge Readers. A computerized system using *badge readers* is beginning to replace the time clock at some companies. Employees pass their badges or identification cards through an electronic eye device. This badge reader is connected to a computer system and enters the arrival and departure times directly into the computer. The computer can then calculate the hours worked, providing the data for the computation of gross wages.

NIOGA GEAR, INC.

Week Ending: *October 16*   20*XX*

No. **38**

Name: *William Johnson*

DAY	MORN. IN	NOON OUT	NOON IN	NIGHT OUT	EXTRA IN	EXTRA OUT	TOTAL
M	7^{55}	12^{00}	1^{00}	5^{02}			8
Tu	7^{57}	12^{02}	12^{58}	5^{04}			8
W	7^{59}	12^{00}	12^{55}	5^{01}	5^{30}	7^{35}	10
Th	7^{58}	12^{01}	12^{59}	5^{00}			8
F	8^{01}	12^{03}	1^{01}	5^{02}			8
S	7^{56}	12^{02}					4

Total Time: *46*   hours

Rate: *$8.00 per hour*

Total wages for week: *$392.00*

FIGURE 2-2   Timecard

Time sheet   *A time record on which the employee or supervisor enters arrival and departure times.*

Time Sheets.   Many smaller businesses or those with a staff working the same hours (such as office workers) use **time sheets** rather than timecards to record hours worked. The use and format of time sheets can vary a great deal depending on the size of the company and the type of work per-

TABLE 2-1				
Recording Fractional Parts of an Hour				
Fractional Part of Hour	No. of Minutes	Range (Minutes Before and After)	Actual Times	Equal to
1/12	5	2 before–2 after	7:58–8:02	8:00
			8:03–8:07	8:05
1/4	15	7 before–7 after	7:53–8:07	8:00
			8:08–8:22	8:15

Nioga Gear, Inc.
Weekly Time Sheet

EMPLOYEE NAME: _Helen Yee_

DEPARTMENT: _Personnel_

REPORT FOR WEEK ENDING: _October 16, 20XX_

DAY	TIME IN	TIME OUT	HOURS WORKED	EXCEPTIONS
Sunday	—	—	—	—
Monday	8:03	10:05	2	S-6
Tuesday	7:56	4:45	7.75	
Wednesday	7:55	4:30	7.50	
Thursday	7:35	5:15	8.75	
Friday	8:03	4:45	7.75	
Saturday	—	—	—	—
		WEEKLY TOTAL:	33.75	6

Exception Code
S - Sickness   H - Holiday   Employee's Signature: _Helen Yee_

V - Vacation   E - Other   Approved by: _Lois Arruda_

FIGURE 2-3   Weekly Time Sheet

formed. Generally, however, the sheet covers a weekly period and has spaces for an employee or a supervisor to enter the times for arrival, break for and return from lunch, and departure for the day. At some companies, employees record their own arrival and departure times, signing the sheet each day. At other companies, a timekeeper is assigned to track the employees in a department; employees sign their sheets at the end of the week. Time may be recorded on the quarter-hour, tenth-hour, or five-minute system.

At Nioga, the office staff uses time sheets; work hours are calculated to the nearest quarter hour (Figure 2-3). At the end of the week, the payroll clerk (in this case, Lois Arruda) determines the total number of hours each employee worked during that period.

Job Time Tickets.   The job time ticket, illustrated in Figure 2-4, is a specialized version of the timecard. Instead of showing hours worked per person per day, it show hours worked per job per day. The record provided by the

EMPLOYEE	JOB NO.	CLOCK TIME IN	OUT	TIME minutes		
Barney Gates	463	1040	1055	15		
Jane Storm	463	950	1000	10		
Larry Ottman	463	1010	1035	25		
Leigh Ward	463	1120	1150	30		

FIGURE 2-4   Job Time Ticket

job time ticket facilitates a sophisticated cost accounting system whereby a company has control over costs and production.

Work Records

In some businesses, employee wages depend on units of output produced during the payroll period (with a minimum wage guaranteed by provisions of the FLSA). The employer must keep both time and work records on these employees in order to compute their wages and fulfill the requirements of the Fair Labor Standards Act. At Nioga, the production workers are on a piecework system; the number of units they produce in combination with the number of hours they work determines their wages.

Nioga uses production records that include space for both the time worked, recorded by a time clock, and the number of items produced, usually entered by hand (Figure 2-5). Likewise, the Nioga salespeople are on commission, and their wages relate to the value of the units they sell. As with many other businesses, Nioga does not keep time records for salespeople whose wages consist of commissions on sales. A sales and commission report, illustrated in Figure 2-6, provides data for computing commissions for Nioga's salespeople.

METHODS OF PAYROLL COMPUTATION

Incentive payment plan
A compensation plan whereby the employee receives additional amounts based on higher than normal or regular performance, i.e., earnings related to units produced (piecework) or dollars sold (commissions).

Lois is now ready to learn the methods used for computing wages and salaries. Each of the more common methods has its place at Nioga since the management and administrative staff receive salaries and the production workers and salespeople are on **incentive payment plans**—a piecework plan for production workers and a commission plan for salespeople.

Compensation for time worked may be calculated according to a time rate (hourly, weekly, biweekly, semimonthly, or monthly), at a piece rate, on a commission basis, or a combination of these. Although the term *wages*

Nioga Gear, Inc.

Production Record for Week Ending October 16, 20XX

EMPLOYEE	DAY	HOURS WORKED	NO. OF SHOES POLISHED	(a) EARNINGS PER SHOES POLISHED	(b) DAILY EARNINGS
Barney Gates	M	8	100	$ .50	$ 50.00
	T	10	170	.50	85.00
	W	—	absent	—	—
	T	8	116	.50	58.00
	F	8	109	.50	54.50
				TOTAL:	$ 247.50
Jane Storm	M	8	100	$ .50	$ 50.00
	T	10	150	.50	75.00
	W	8	105	.50	52.50
	T	8	107	.50	53.50
	F	8	103	.50	51.50
				TOTAL:	$ 282.50
Larry Ottman	M	12	180	$ .50	$ 90.00
	T	10	150	.50	75.00
	W	8	110	.50	55.00
	T	8	100	.50	50.00
	F	8	107	.50	53.50
				TOTAL:	$ 323.50
Leigh Ward	M	12	217	$ .50	$ 108.50
	T	10	130	.50	65.00
	W	8	120	.50	60.00
	T	10	160	.50	80.00
	F	8	110	.50	55.00
				TOTAL:	$ 368.50

FIGURE 2-5 Production Record

Nioga Gear, Inc.
Commission Report

No. 84
Maria Lopez

Week Ending 10/16/XX

SALES

Monday	$2,000
Tuesday	1,000
Wednesday	1,600
Thursday	2,000
Friday	1,400
Saturday	—
Total Sales	$8,000
Commission Rate - 6%	.06
Total Wages	$ 480

FIGURE 2-6   Sales and Commission Report

Wages *Compensation based on an hourly, weekly, or piecework basis.*

Hourly rate plan *A compensation method whereby employees receive a fixed amount for each hour worked.*

Regular earnings *Earnings for the first 40 hours worked in a week.*

usually refers to all taxable compensation for services, it can have different meanings depending on its use. For our purposes here, **wages** refers to compensation paid on an hourly, weekly, or piecework basis, whereas salaries cover compensation paid on a weekly, biweekly, semimonthly, or monthly basis.

Hourly Rate Plan

Employees paid on an **hourly rate plan** receive a fixed amount for each hour they work. An employee's **regular earnings** are equal to the employee's hourly rate multiplied by the number of hours worked (usually to the nearest quarter of an hour) during the payroll period.

EXAMPLE Joanne Klein, the receptionist at Nioga, earns a regular hourly rate of $7 an hour. During one week, she worked 40 hours. Her regular earnings were $280 (40 hours × $7 per hour). ▲

Salary Plan

Salaried employees receive a fixed amount for each payroll period, whether weekly, biweekly, semimonthly, or monthly. For example, Nioga's personnel manager Sallie Foster receives a salary of $480 per week. The sales manager Michael Carson receives a salary of $2,080 per month. Computations to find regular earnings for employees on salary are not necessary, provided they work the required number of hours during the payroll period. If an employee on the **salary plan** works less than the **regular hours** during a payroll period, the employer may deduct for the time lost, although in most cases the employer does not make such a deduction. If the employer did deduct for time lost, however, the employee's hourly rate would first have to be calculated. Regular earnings would be determined by multiplying that hourly rate by the actual number of hours the employee worked during the payroll period.

EXAMPLE   Sallie Foster, the personnel manager at Nioga, receives a salary of $480 a week for a 40-hour week. If she took off 5 hours one week for personal reasons, she would receive $420 for the week, computed as follows:

1. Regular Hourly Rate

   Weekly Salary ÷ Regular Weekly Hours = Regular Hourly Rate

   $480 per week ÷   40 Hours per Week   = $12 per Hour

2. Regular Earnings

   Regular Hourly Rate × Actual Hours = Regular Earnings

   $12 per Hour   ×   35 Hours   = $420   ▲

Overtime Pay

At one time, each individual business established its own rate of overtime pay. In some cases, the rate was well below the regular hourly rate. Today, all businesses must comply with the overtime regulations of the Fair Labor Standards Act. The regulations require employers to pay all but exempt employees a special overtime rate 1½ times the regular rate for time worked beyond the regular 40 hours per week.

Special rules define the meaning of overtime. Generally, these rules count toward overtime any hours over 40 per week that are physically worked; compensated time does not count. In other words, no overtime is due on sick pay, holiday pay, or vacation pay. Overtime results from working extra hours per week, not extra hours per day.

Overtime rules apply only to hours when the employee is physically present on the job site. Time spent waiting or preparing to work count for overtime purposes. Company-sanctioned seminars and travel to seminars also count since the company has approved these activities to be done on company time. However, the physical presence rule does not allow overtime for call-back and show-up time. (Call-back and show-up time refers to the time an employee stands by waiting for a work assignment, after the shift is complete or before workers are selected for the shift.) This rule also means that time spent "on call" is not considered part of overtime hours, just as travel time to and from work is not considered as overtime. In some cases, hours may qualify toward the calculation of regular wages, but not toward overtime hours. For instance, hours worked and paid for on a guaranteed wage plan, if treated as a discretionary bonus, do not count for overtime.

Overtime earnings *Earnings for time worked beyond 40 hours in a week.*

A computation for **overtime earnings** is separate from the calculation for regular earnings. Gross earnings then become regular plus overtime earnings.

EXAMPLE   Will Johnson, the janitor at Nioga, worked 46 hours one week. With a regular hourly rate of $8 an hour, his gross earnings were $392, calculated as follows:

1. Regular Wages
    Regular Hourly Rate × Regular Weekly Hours = Regular Weekly Earnings
        $8 per Hour   ×   40   = $320
2. Overtime Rate
    Regular Hourly Rate × Overtime Multiple = Overtime Rate
        $8 per Hour   ×   1½   = $12 per Hour
3. Overtime Pay
    Overtime Rate × Overtime Hours = Overtime Pay
     $12 per Hour ×   6 Hours   = $72
4. Gross Earnings
    Regular Wages + Overtime Pay = Gross Earnings
         $320   + $72   = $392   ▲

Salaried employees, such as managers and supervisors, who are not exempt from the overtime pay requirement, must also receive at least 1½ times their regular hourly rate for all work beyond 40 hours in any week.

EXAMPLE   Helen Yee, a personnel interviewer at Nioga, receives $360 a week for a 40-hour week. If Helen worked 44 hours during one week, she would have earned $414, computed as follows:

1. Regular Hourly Rate
    Weekly Salarly ÷ Regular Weekly Hours = Regular Hourly Rate
    $360 per Week ÷   40 Hours per Week   = $9 per Hour
2. Overtime Rate
    Regular Hourly Rate × Overtime Multiple = Overtime Rate
        $9 per Hour   ×   1½   = $13.50 per Hour
3. Overtime Pay
    Overtime Hours × Overtime Rate = Overtime Pay
        4 Hours   × $13.50 per Hour = $54
4. Gross Earnings
     Weekly Salary + Overtime Pay = Gross Earnings
    $360 per Week + $54   = $414   ▲

An additional step is necessary to find the regular hourly rate of a salaried employee paid on a semimonthly or monthly basis. In these cases, the annual salary is computed first, and then the hourly rate, using the conversion factor of 2,080 hours, as shown in Table 2-2.

EXAMPLE   Michael Carson, a sales manager at Nioga, receives a monthly salary of $2,080 for a regular workweek of 40 hours. Although Michael earns over $250 a week and regularly supervises more than two full-time employees,

TABLE 2-2			
Work Days and Hours by Payroll Period			
	Period	Work Days per Period	Hours per Period
Weekly	52	5	40
Biweekly	26	10	80
Semimonthly	24	10.83	86.67
Monthly	12	21.67	173.33
Yearly	1	260	2,080

he spends more than 20% of his time in nonexempt work; thus, he is not exempt from overtime pay. One month, he worked 12 hours overtime. His gross earnings were computed as follows:

1. Yearly Salary
    Monthly Salary × Months per Year = Yearly Salary
    $2,080 per Month ×   12 Months   = $24,960 per Year
2. Regular Hourly Rate
    Yearly Salary   ÷   Hours per Year   = Regular Hourly Rate
    $24,960 per Year ÷ 2,080 Hours per Year = $12 per Hour
3. Overtime Rate
    Regular Hourly Rate × Overtime Multiple = Overtime Rate
        $12 per Hour   ×   1½   = $18 per Hour
4. Overtime Pay
    Overtime Hours × Overtime Rate = Overtime Pay
        12 Hours   × $18 per Hour = $216
5. Gross Earnings
    Monthly Salary   + Overtime Pay = Gross Earnings
    $2,080 per Month + $216   = $2,296

The multiplier used to determine annual salary is 24 for a semimonthly pay period and 12 for a monthly pay period. Dividing the yearly salary by 2,080 hours per year yields the regular hourly rate. ▲

The conversion factors to determine the hourly rate for a weekly or biweekly salary are 40 and 80 hours, respectively, as shown in Table 2-2.

EXAMPLE Joe Grady, a sales analyst at Nioga, receives a biweekly salary of $580. During one biweekly period, he worked 10 hours overtime for gross earnings of $688.80, calculated as follows:

1. Regular Hourly Rate
    Biweekly Salary ÷ Conversion Factor = Regular Hourly Rate
    $580 per Period ÷ 80 Hours per Period = $7.25 per Hour
2. Overtime Rate
    Regular Hourly Rate × Overtime Multiple = Overtime Rate
        $7.25 per Hour   ×   1½   = $10.88 per Hour

3. Overtime Pay
   Overtime Hours × Overtime Rate = Overtime Pay
      10 Hours   × $10.88 per Hour = $108.80
4. Gross Earnings
   Biweekly Salary + Overtime Pay = Gross Earnings
   $580 per Period + $108.80   = $688.80   ▲

Overtime for Irregular Workweek. As described in Chapter 1, a specific set of rules apply when paying for overtime with an irregular or fluctuating workweek. Under certain conditions, the employer may arrange to pay some hourly employees straight time for *all* the hours they work in a week (sometimes called a **guaranteed wage**) instead of just the first 40 hours. The employer and the employee agree in writing that the employer has hired the individual not to work a certain number of hours, but to do a job and that job involves irregular hours per day or per week. An overtime premium must be paid for all hours worked over 40 in a week. The hourly rate is determined by dividing the guaranteed wage by the actual number of hours worked during the week. The employer must then add an extra half-time premium for all hours over 40.

Guaranteed wage *A written agreement to pay an employee a guaranteed minimum amount, regardless of hours worked, with an extra half-time premium for hours over 40.*

EXAMPLE An employee who earns $360 at straight time for a regular 40-hour workweek worked 48 hours during one week. Under the irregular workweek arrangement, the employee earns $390 calculated as follows:

1. Irregular Hourly Rate
   Guaranteed Wage ÷ Actual Hours = Actual Hourly Rate
      $360   ÷   48 Hours   = $7.50 per Hour
2. Overtime Rate
   Actual Hourly Rate × Overtime Multiple = Overtime Rate
      $7.50 per Hour   ×   ½   = $3.75 per Hour
3. Overtime Pay
   Overtime Hours × Overtime Rate = Overtime Pay
      8 Hours   × $3.75 per Hour = $30
4. Gross Earnings
   Guaranteed Wage + Overtime Pay = Gross Earnings
      $360   + $30   = $390

On a regular workweek arrangement, the employee would earn $468, calculated as follows:

1. Regular Hourly Rate
   Regular Wages ÷ Regular Weekly Hours = Regular Hourly Rate
   $360 per Week ÷ 40 Hours per Week = $9.00 per Hour
2. Overtime Rate
   Regular Hourly Rate × Overtime Multiple = Overtime Rate
      $9.00 per Hour   ×   1½   = $13.50 per Hour
3. Overtime Pay
   Overtime Hours × Overtime Rate = Overtime Pay
      8 Hours   × $13.50 per Hour = $108

4. Gross Earnings
   Regular Wages + Overtime Pay = Gross Earnings
   $360 per Week + $108   = $468   ▲

The irregular or fluctuating workweek arrangement may seem one-sided but the advantage to the employee is a guaranteed weekly wage, regardless of the hours worked during that week.

Piece-Rate Plan

Piece-rate plan A compensation plan whereby employee earnings depend on the units produced.

Production workers paid on a **piece-rate plan** or for piecework receive a certain amount for each item produced. Gross earnings are the result of multiplying the rate per item times the number of items produced during the payroll period. (See Figure 2-5.)

EXAMPLE Perry Worth is a Nioga production worker sewing shoes. Perry is paid a piece rate of $2 a shoe. He completed 150 shoes during one week and, thus, had gross earnings of $300.   ▲

Sometimes the employee earns a different piece rate for different levels or types of production.

EXAMPLE Perry Worth receives $2.00 per shoe for sewing up to 200 shoes in one week and $2.20 per shoe for anything above 200 shoes. During one week, Perry completed 210 shoes. His gross earnings were $422, computed as follows:

1. Earnings on Base Level Production
   Units Produced ×   Piece Rate   = Base Level Earnings
      200 Units   × $2.00 per Unit = $400
2. Additional Earnings on Extra Production
   Units over Base Level ×   Piece Rate   = Additional Earnings
      10 Units   × $2.20 per Unit = $22
3. Gross Earnings
   Base Level Earnings + Additional Earnings = Gross Earnings
         $400   + $22   = $422   ▲

According to the minimum wage requirement of the Fair Labor Standards Act, employers must ensure that the weekly earnings of piece-rate employees are at least equal to the minimum wage. This requirement does not apply to occupations normally exempt from the minimum wage regulation such as work in agriculture, in amusement or recreational businesses with seasonal peaks, casual babysitting, most professional occupations including teaching and school administration, work in limited circulation newspapers (under 4,000 copies), and outside sales positions.

Nioga is not exempt from the minimum wage requirement. To ensure compliance, Lois computes the regular hourly rate of each piece-rate employee for the week and compares this rate to the current minimum wage ($5.15 per hour since September 1, 1997).

EXAMPLE   Ann Grable produced 200 shoe soles in a week in which she worked 40 hours. Her piecework earnings for the week are less than she could make at the minimum wage rate so she received $206, computed as follows:

1. Gross Earnings
   Units Produced × Piece Rate = Gross Earnings
      200 Units   × $.75 per Unit = $150
2. Hourly Rate
   Gross Earnings ÷ Actual Hours = Hourly Rate
       $150   ÷   40 Hours   = $3.75 per Hour
3. Gross Earnings as Adjusted
   Actual Hours × Minimum Wage Rate = Gross Earnings
      40 Hours   × $5.15 per Hour = $206   ▲

When the piece-rate employee works more than 40 hours a week, the employer uses one of two methods to compute overtime earnings. The method used is the result of an agreement between the employee and employer before performance of the work. With the first method, the employee receives one-half of the regular hourly rate for each overtime hour.

EXAMPLE   Sue Foster is a quality control inspector at Nioga. She worked 44 hours during one week when she had piece-rate earnings of $396. Her overtime earnings were $18 and her gross earnings were $414, computed as follows:

1. Hourly Rate
   Piece-rate Earnings ÷ Actual Hours = Hourly Rate
       $396   ÷   44 Hours   = $9 per Hour
2. Premium Rate or Overtime Piecework Rate
   Hourly Rate × Premium Multiple = Premium Rate
   $9 per Hour ×   ½   = $4.50 per Hour
3. Overtime Pay
   Overtime Hours × Premium Rate = Overtime Pay
      4 Hours   × $4.50 per Hour = $18
4. Gross Earnings
   Piece-rate Earnings + Overtime Pay = Gross Earnings
       $396   + $18   = $414   ▲

The second method of computing overtime pay for piece-rate employees is determined by company policy and is based on the regular piece rate of pay. The employee receives at least 1½ times the regular piecework rate for any items produced after 40 hours during the week.

EXAMPLE   One week, Perry Worth sewed 200 shoes in 40 hours and 16 shoes in 4 overtime hours. His regular piece rate is $2 a shoe and the overtime rate is

$3 a shoe. His regular earnings were $400 and overtime earnings were $48 for gross earnings of $448, computed as follows:

1. Regular Piece-rate Earnings
    Units Produced × Piece Rate = Piece-rate Earnings
       200 Units   × $2 per Unit = $400
2. Overtime Pay
    Units Produced × Overtime Piece Rate = Overtime Pay
       16 Units   × $3 per Unit   = $48
3. Gross Earnings
    Regular Piece-rate Earnings + Overtime Pay = Gross Earnings
             $400   + $48   = $448

If Perry Worth had been paid on the basis of hours, his gross earnings would have been computed as follows:

1. Regular Piece-rate Earnings
    Units Produced × Piece Rate = Regular Piece-rate Earnings
       216 Units   × $2 per Unit = $432
2. Regular Hourly Rate
    Regular Piece-rate Earnings ÷ Actual Hours = Regular Hourly Rate
             $432   ÷   44 Hours = $9.82 per Hour
3. Premium Rate or Overtime Piece Rate
    Regular Hourly Rate × Premium Multiple = Premium Rate
          $9.82   ×   ½   = $4.91 per Hour
4. Overtime Pay
    Overtime Hours × Premium Rate = Overtime Pay
       4 Hours   × $4.91 per Hour = $19.64
5. Gross Earnings
    Regular Piece-rate Earnings + Overtime Pay = Gross Earnings
             $432   +   19.64   = $451.64   ▲

Do you remember Julia Jones, Nioga's telephone salesperson from the introduction to Part I? She receives both piecework and hourly wages. During the week of January 15, she made 40 calls to independent retailers in her 10-hour cold calling time and spent another 35 hours making follow-up calls to current clients. Julia gets $2 per cold call and $7 per hour for follow-up time. As was the case for Perry Worth, Julia's gross earnings can be computed by using either of two methods. The method that is used is the result of an agreement between Nioga and Julia. Initial calls are the basis for overtime computations.

Method 1 — Overtime Pay Based on Hours Worked

1. Regular Piece-rate Earnings
    Units produced × Piece Rate = Regular Piece-rate Earnings
       40 Units   × 2.00 per Unit = $80
2. Non-piecework Earnings
       40 Hours less
    Piecework Hours × Regular Hourly Rate = Non-piecework Earnings
       (40 − 10) Hours × $7 per Hour   = $210

3. Overtime Rate

Regular Hourly Rate × Overtime Multiple = Overtime Rate

$7 per Hour   ×   1½   = $10.50

4. Overtime Pay

Overtime Hours × Overtime Rate = Overtime Pay

5 Hours   × $10.50 per Hour = $52.50

5. Gross Earnings

Regular   Non-piece-rate

Piece-rate Earnings +   Earnings   + Overtime Pay = Gross Earnings

$80   + $210   + $52.50   = $342.50

Method 2 — Overtime Pay Based on Piecework Rate

1. Hourly Production Rate

Units Produced ÷ Piece-rate Hours = Hourly Production Rate

40 Units   ÷   10 Hours   =   4 Units per Hour

2. Regular Production

                                                                Regular

Regular Piece-rate Hours × Hourly Production Rate = Production

5 Hours   ×   4 Units per Hour   =   20 Units

3. Regular Piece-rate Earnings

Regular Production ×   Piece Rate   = Regular Piece-rate Earnings

20 Units   × $2.00 per Unit = $40

4. Overtime Production

                                                                Overtime

Overtime Piece-rate Hours × Hourly Production Rate = Production

5 Hours   ×   4 Units per Hour   =   20 Units

5. Overtime Piece-rate Earnings

Units Produced × Overtime Piece Rate = Overtime Piece-rate Earnings

20 Units   × $3 per Unit   = $60

6. Non-piecework Earnings

Actual Hours × Regular Hourly Rate = Non-piecework Earnings

35 Hours   × $7 per Hour   = $245

7. Gross Earnings

Non-piecework Earnings + Piecework Earnings = Gross Earnings

$245   + $40 + $60   = $345

Commission Plan

Commission plan *A compensation method whereby employees receive a percentage of sales.*

Sales **commission plans** vary greatly from company to company but are generally based on the sales made during a payroll period. At Nioga, each salesperson receives a certain percentage or commission rate on sales for the period. This type of plan requires detailed sales records in order to accurately compute the commissions due the salespeople.

EXAMPLE   Maria Lopez sells shoes for Nioga at a 6% commission rate. During one week, her sales totaled $8,000 and her gross earnings were $480, computed as follows:

Gross Earnings

Sales for Week × Commission Rate = Gross Earnings

$8,000   ×   .06   = $480   ▲

As is the case for piecework, some employees on the commission plan may not be exempt from the minimum wage requirement of the Fair Labor Standards Act. The employer must determine the regular hourly rate for each nonexempt salesperson during the week and make sure this rate is at least equal to the minimum wage rate.

Combination Plan

Combination plan *A compensation method whereby employees receive a fixed amount of salary for each payroll period plus an extra amount for production (piecework) or sales (commission).*

Many businesses pay their salespeople both a salary and a commission. Such a **combination plan** provides some security but still offers an incentive for superior sales.

EXAMPLE

Martin Galley is a sales manager at Nioga with both selling and administrative duties. Martin receives a salary of $360 a week and a 6% commission on sales over a quota of $2,000 per week. During one week he sold $6,000 worth of shoes. His gross earnings for the week were $600, computed as follows:

1. Commission Earnings
   Sales over Quota × Commission Rate = Commission Earnings
   ($6,000 − $2,000) ×   .06   = $240
2. Gross Earnings
   Weekly Salary + Commission Earnings = Gross Earnings
        $360   + $240   = $600   ▲

Julia Jones, Nioga's telephone sales representative, did eventually receive her promotion. She began to receive a commission on the efforts of the three telephone representatives reporting to her. She continued to receive $2.00 per cold call and $7.00 per hour for follow-up work, but she also received $.50 per call made by the other three reps. As the previous example shows, Julia earned $342.50 (by Method 1) on her production and time. If the three other reps made 120 calls between them during the week, her gross earnings would be $342.50 plus $60.00 ($.50 × 120), or $402.50.

Worktime Eligibility for Compensation

Employees receive compensation for all hours worked. Hours worked means all hours under the employer's control, including nonproductive time. Whether hours on the job will warrant compensation, i.e., are compensable time, depends on the circumstances, for example:

Meal and Rest Periods. Meal periods are not working time if the employee has no responsibilities, performs no work and the time allotted is 30 minutes or longer (sometimes shorter by agreement). The employee should be free to pursue any activity or personal interests during the meal period.

Travel Time. Commuting time or home-to-work time is generally not working time, although by union contract or custom, the employee may receive separate payment for this time. This rule also applies where an employee uses a company vehicle for commuting. Situations where travel time counts as compensable worktime include emergency calls requiring substantial distance or special one-day assignments, involving travel after regular workday hours. Travel time that is an integral part of the job is compensable worktime, including travel during regular working hours, even if on a nonworking day.

On-Call and Waiting Time. On-call time or time where the employee must be ready to work on the employers' premises or in the vicinity is compensable worktime. In this case, the test is whether the employee needs to limit personal activities in order to be available.

　　Where the employee is on the premises and "engaged to be waiting," the time is compensable since the time usually is insufficient for personal pursuits. On the other hand, time spent "waiting to be engaged" is not compensable because the time usually allows for personal matters.

Meetings and Seminars. Required attendance at meetings, seminars and lectures outside of working hours or for a purpose unrelated to the job and without performance of productive work is compensable worktime.

Preparing to Work. Unless a union contract or custom provides otherwise, activities preliminary or postliminary to the principal work activity are not compensable worktime. Thus, time spent getting ready to begin or leave work is not compensable unless necessary for the principal work activity. However, changing clothes or cleaning-up or receiving medical treatment where required by law is compensable worktime. Also, receiving medical attention during regular work hours is compensable.

De Minimis Time. Time so insignificant it is not measurable and does not count for compensation. Early or late punch-in times, i.e., time before and after regular hours is not compensable because the employee is not working.

TAXABILITY OF COMPENSATION

Nature of Taxable Compensation

For purposes of employment taxes, an employer must differentiate payments made to employees between taxable and nontaxable compensation or wages. Unless specifically excluded, compensation for services, whether called wages, salaries, commissions, bonuses, profit sharing or tips, is taxable for federal income tax withholding (FITW) and usually for other employment taxes. In the next chapter, we also consider other payments sometimes equivalent to wages—noncash fringe benefits, employee business expense reimbursements, and sick pay.

Even the method of payment has no bearing on the definition of taxable wages or compensation. Payment can be in noncash form: goods, lodging, meals, stocks, bonds, or other forms of property—all measured at fair market value.

In later chapters, we will consider various payments that are exempt from these taxes. Examples of these exempt items include sickness and injury payments under a worker's compensation plan, excludable moving expense reimbursements, and employer contributions to a qualified retirement plan.

Other Incentive Compensation Methods

So far, we have reviewed various compensation methods based either on a time or incentive basis. The incentive methods include paying employees by piecework or commission as well as variations of these approaches and other incentive compensation methods. Let's look at three other incentive methods of compensation: bonuses, profit-sharing payments, and tips.

Bonus *Extra compensation paid to an employee for services over and above those normally performed.*

Bonuses. A **bonus** plan can take a number of different forms. Some bonuses are based on profitable operations of the business and are paid at year-end. A common type of bonus paid to salespeople may be offered for selling certain kinds of goods, such as slow-moving items. A third type of bonus plan, one that may be part of an employment agreement, pays managers if the yearly sales or profits are over a certain level.

EXAMPLE

In addition to her yearly salary of $40,000, Penny Seaver, an institutional salesperson with Nioga, receives 1% of her annual salary for each whole increment of $20,000 of the company's net income over a base level of $100,000. Last year, Nioga had earnings of $185,000. Penny's gross earnings in the year were $41,600, computed as follows:

1. Percentage Bonus
   Total Net Income − Base-level Net Income ÷ $20,000
      ($185,000   − $100,000)   ÷ $20,000 = 4.25
      4.25 ÷ 100 = 4.25% ≅ 4% (or .04)
2. Bonus Earnings
   Yearly Salary × Percentage Bonus
      $40,000   ×   .04   = $1,600
3. Gross Earnings
   Yearly Salary + Bonus Earnings
      $40,000   + $1,600   = $41,600   ▲

Profit-sharing plan *An employee benefit plan whereby the employer rewards employees, based on profitability of the company, with additional compensation in the form of cash, company stock, or a pension plan interest.*

Profit-Sharing Payments. A **profit-sharing plan**, like a bonus plan, can take a number of different forms. An employer may elect to pay cash to employees, give them stock in the business, or set up a deferred compensation fund for retirement.

EXECUTIVE SALARIES

The last several years have witnessed a public outcry over the large salaries paid to corporate officers, particularly chief executive officers (CEOs). Corporate layoffs and cutbacks taking place at the same time CEOs receive pay hikes and stock bonanzas has infuriated the general public as well as the stockholders of companies.

The issue has received major media attention. *Business Week, Fortune,* and *USA Today* have run cover stories on CEO pay and even Congress has considered holding inquiries and passing legislation to somehow restrict executive compensation. Polls suggest that the public believes CEO salaries of $1 million or more may be excessive, even when the company achieves an earnings increase. When the company performs poorly, paying these salaries raises the ire of not only investors but also the general public.

Most CEOs who receive high compensation are sensitive to the issue. Their companies have attempted to conceal the facts while complying with Securities and Exchange Commission (SEC) disclosure rules. Proxy statements sent to stockholders present a piecemeal picture of the various forms of compensation—salary, bonus, stock options, and other arrangements. Only a CPA or a labor compensation expert could add the pieces together to arrive at a total figure. In many cases, the total package is huge by any standard.

Tip *A gift or an additional amount of money received from a customer as recognition of services rendered by the employee.*

Tips.   In certain businesses, employees receive compensation in the form of gratuities or tips. A **tip** is an additional amount from a customer for services rendered. Bartenders and restaurant servers usually receive tips in addition to wages. Hair stylists and taxi drivers also depend on tips as a major source of income. Any employee receiving tips in excess of $30 a month (FLSA) is called a *tipped* employee ($20 under FITW and FICA). As discussed in Chapter 1, employers can pay such employees wages below the minimum rate because tips enter into the computation of the regular hourly rate. The "tip credit" has risen to 50% in the last few years, which means employers may credit up to $3.02 per hour ($5.15 current minimum wage less 50% of $4.25 former minimum wage).

The employers must take into account the actual tips received by an employee before determining how much of the maximum 50% credit toward the minimum wage is allowable. The tipped employee uses Form 4070, Employee's Report of Tips to Employer, to report the receipt of tips by the 10th day of the month following the month in which the tips were received (Exhibit 2-1). With this information, the employer can determine how much more than 50% toward minimum wage must be paid in order to meet the minimum wage requirement of the FLSA. Employees may use Form 4070-A, Employee's Daily Record of Tips, to help keep track of tips they receive each month. Form 4070-A does not have to be sent to the employer or filed with the IRS, but would be beneficial for tax compliance and for personal tax recording.

EXAMPLE   Alice Piero is earning college tuition by working at a resort over the summer. It is not unusual for her to earn as much as $100 a night in tips and at least $350 in tips for a 35-hour workweek. Her employer takes advantage

Form **4070** (Rev. July 1996) Department of the Treasury Internal Revenue Service	**Employee's Report** **of Tips to Employer** ▶ For Paperwork Reduction Act Notice, see back of form.	OMB No. 1545-0065
Employee's name and address		Social security number
Employer's name and address (include establishment name, if different)		1 Cash tips received
		2 Credit card tips received
		3 Tips paid out
Month or shorter period in which tips were received from , 19 , to , 19		4 Net tips (lines **1 + 2 - 3**)
Signature		Date

Paperwork Reduction Act Notice.—We ask for the information on these forms to carry out the Internal Revenue laws of the United States. You are required to give us the information. We need it to ensure that you are complying with these laws and to allow us to figure and collect the right amount of tax.

You are not required to provide the information requested on a form that is subject to the Paperwork Reduction Act unless the form displays a valid OMB control number. Books or records relating to a form or its instructions must be retained as long as their contents may become material in the administration of any Internal Revenue law. Generally, tax returns and return information are confidential, as required by Code section 6103.

The time needed to complete Forms 4070 and 4070A will vary depending on individual circumstances. The estimated average times are: **Recordkeeping**—Form 4070, 7 min.; Form 4070A, 3 hr. and 23 min.; **Learning about the law**—each form, 2 min.; **Preparing** Form 4070, 13 min.; Form 4070A, 55 min.; and **Copying and providing** Form 4070, 10 min.; Form 4070A, 14 min.

If you have comments concerning the accuracy of these time estimates or suggestions for making these forms simpler, we would be happy to hear from you. You can write to the Tax Forms Committee, Western Area Distribution Center, Rancho Cordova, CA 95743-0001.

Purpose.—Use this form to report tips you receive to your employer. This includes cash tips, tips you receive from other employees, and credit card tips. You must report tips every month regardless of your total wages and tips for the year. However, you do not have to report tips to your employer for any month you received less than $20 in tips while working for that employer.

Report tips by the 10th day of the month following the month that you receive them. If the 10th day is a Saturday, Sunday, or legal holiday, report tips by the next day that is not a Saturday, Sunday, or legal holiday.

See **Pub. 531**, Reporting Tip Income, for more information.

You can get additional copies of **Pub. 1244**, Employee's Daily Record of Tips and Report to Employer, which contains both Forms 4070A and 4070, by calling 1-800-TAX-FORM (1-800-829-3676).

EXHIBIT 2-1   Form 4070, Employee's Report of Tips

of the full 50% tip credit toward the minimum wage ($3.02 × 35 = $105.70). While her weekly tips average $350, her weekly wage is $74.55 ($5.15 × 35 − $105.70 = $180.25 − 105.70). ▲

EXAMPLE   Sandy Becker, who works in a coffee shop frequented by Nioga employees, works 40 hours a week and receives a $124 salary plus tips. Her employer is currently using a 50% (or $103) credit toward the minimum wage. She must make at least $206, including tips, in order to make a minimum wage ($5.15 × 40 hours). However, her tips average only $50, so she is still not making minimum wage ($124 salary + $50 tips = $174). She informs her boss about this discrepancy when filing her Form 4070.

He raises her salary to $156 and is no longer in violation of the Fair Labor Standards Act.   ▲

Supplemental Wages

Supplemental wages
Forms of compensation that differ from regular wages because they are computed on a different compensation plan or rate, based on a different payroll period, or paid at a different time.

All the forms of compensation that qualify as regular wages, except for vacation pay and vacation advances, which are specifically excluded from supplemental wages, may also qualify as supplemental wages. **Supplemental wages** differ from regular wages only in that they may be based on a different payroll period, computed on a different compensation plan or rate, or paid at a different time than regular wages. In addition, certain payments are, by their nature or timing, supplemental wages. Such payments include retroactive pay increases, severance pay, and vacation pay on termination. Thus, most forms of compensation can be either regular wages or supplemental wages.

The distinction between regular and supplemental wages is important because special rules apply to withholdings on supplemental wages. If the employer does not specifically indicate the amount of supplemental versus regular wages given in a single payment, FITW applies to the total of the supplemental and regular wages (aggregate method). On the other hand, if the employer pays an employee regular and supplemental wages in a single payment and specifically identifies each, federal income tax may be withheld on the portion of the payment representing supplemental wages at a flat 28% (flat rate method), e.g. if an employee receives a bonus of $2,000, the total tax is a tax on wages before the bonus plus a flat 28% of $2,000, or $560.

REVIEW QUESTIONS

2–1. Name four payroll periods.

2–2. Distinguish between wages and salaries.

2–3. Name five types of compensation other than salaries and wages.

2–4. What are the three bases for determining wages?

2–5. What is the hourly rate plan? What is the basis for overtime pay under this plan?

2–6. How is the regular hourly rate used to compute overtime for an employee on
   a. salary?
   b. a piece-rate plan?

2–7. How may a quota system be part of a commission plan?

2–8. How does the minimum wage affect piecework and commission compensation?

2–9. For purposes of employment taxes, what are taxable wages?

2–10. Give two examples of wages exempt from tax withholding.

2–11. Explain a typical bonus plan arrangement.

2–12. What effect might tips have on the minimum wage?

2–13. When are bonuses and commissions considered regular wages and when are they considered supplemental wages? What difference does it make to the employee?

2–14. Explain the method of compensation for an irregular workweek.

Review Questions
(cont.)

2–15. What is the difference between regular and supplemental wages?

2–16. Name two forms of compensation always considered supplemental wages and two forms of compensation that are not considered supplemental wages.

2–17. Describe two general methods of withholding taxes on supplemental wages.

DISCUSSION QUESTIONS

2–1. From time to time various labor and other organizations advocate a fewer number of days per workweek—a 4-day, 10-hour-per-day week for a 40-hour workweek.

    a. How do you feel about this proposal?

    b. What favorable effects might it have?

    c. What might be some of its disadvantages?

2–2. Only the state of Alaska pays overtime based on time worked over 8 hours per day. In other states an employee can work a double shift, and if the hours for the week do not exceed 40 hours, the employee will not receive overtime pay for any hours over the regular 8 hours per day.

    a. Do you think it is fair to pay regular time for more than 8 hours work in a day?

    b. Should employers follow the practice of paying employees overtime rates for daily hours in excess of 8 hours per day? Why or why not?

2–3. Many companies pay their salespeople a straight salary plus a commission based on sales or a bonus based on profits. If you had a choice and were in sales,

    a. Would you want to be paid a straight salary with no commission or bonus, a straight salary with a commission based on sales, or a straight salary with a bonus based on profits?

    b. Would your answer be different for a company with increasing sales and earnings or fluctuating sales and earnings?

    c. What type of person would be inclined to choose each of the methods of compensation?

2–4. Employees who are paid on a piece-rate or commission basis receive compensation related to the benefits they provide the employer. The compensation of other employees is based on an hourly, weekly, monthly, or other time basis. As an employer,

    a. How would you determine whether time-basis employees are doing an effective job?

    b. Can the process of evaluating employees' work be as objective as for the piece-rate or commission worker?

    c. What methods would you use for making the process less subjective and more objective?

2–5. Tipped employees, if their tips total $103 per week for a 40-hour week, may receive in wages only 50% of the minimum wage.

    a. Do you think the tip credit available to employers of tipped employees is fair to the employees?

    b. Would some other method of compensation be preferable?

    c. Should businesses where tipping is traditional forbid tips and pay employees the minimum wage and more?

EXERCISES

Note: For the exercises and problems in this and all subsequent chapters, use $5.15 as the minimum hourly wage unless otherwise stated.

2–1. Patti Trotta, the receptionist at Trotta's Portraits, receives a regular hourly rate of $7 an hour, with overtime pay over 40 hours at time-and-a-half. One week she worked 46 hours. What were Patti's regular and overtime earnings for the week?

regular $ _____

overtime $ _____

2–2. Sue Blaker, the personnel manager at Diet Workouts, receives a salary of $480 a week for a 40-hour week. One week she worked 32 hours; the following week, she worked 46 hours.

     a. If the company deducts for time lost, what were Sue's gross earnings for the first week?

$ _____

     b. If the company pays for overtime, what were Sue's gross earnings for the second week?

$ _____

2–3. Jerry James, a sales manager at Best Cars Agency, is on a monthly salary of $2,080 for a regular workweek of 40 hours. One month he worked 16 hours overtime. What were Jerry's gross earnings for the month if he is an exempt employee?

$ _____

2–4. Terry Gross is a production worker at Neocraft Designs making widgets. He earns a piece rate of $2.00 per widget for production up to 200 widgets and $2.20 per widget above that level. One week he completed 225 widgets. What were Terry's gross earnings for the week?

$ _____

2–5. Amy Lord is a production worker at Modern Fashions. She sews hemlines on dresses at a piece rate of $.75 per dress. One week she worked 40 hours and sewed 210 hemlines. What were Amy's gross earnings for the week?

$ _____

2–6. Morton Graves, a sales manager at Modern Fashions, receives a weekly salary of $450 for administrative duties and a 6% commission on sales above $2,000. One week he sold $7,000 worth of dresses. What were Morton's gross earnings for the week?

$ _____

2–7. Hortense Smith, a Best Cars salesperson, earns a 1.5% sales commission. During one week she sold two cars, for total sales of $37,500. What were Hortense's gross earnings for the week?

$ _____

Exercises (cont.)

2–8. Arlie Bragg is a Neocraft quality control inspector. He receives $1.50 for each widget inspected. During one week he inspected 190 widgets in the first 40 hours and 20 widgets in an additional 2 hours. What were Arlie's gross earnings for the week assuming

    a. an overtime piecework rate at ½ the regular hourly rate for overtime hours.

$ _____

    b. an overtime piecework rate at 1½ times the regular piece rate for additional production.

$ _____

2–9. Pamela Stewart, an institutional salesperson with Trotta's Portraits, is a member of the executive bonus plan. At the end of the year, she receives an extra 1% of her yearly salary of $40,000 for each full $20,000 of net income over a base level of $100,000 (maximum 10 percent). In the latest year, Trotta's had audited net income of $225,000. What was Pamela's bonus at year-end?

$ _____

2–10. Sandy Becker works in the Have-a-Snack Coffee Shop near the Nioga Gear plant. She works a 40-hour week and receives $120 plus tips. If she receives $45 in tips in a week, what were her gross earnings for the week?

$ _____

PROBLEMS

2–1. Roger Hart works for the Grace Plumbing and Heating Company. One week Roger worked the hours shown on the timecard with an hour off for lunch. Roger's regular wage rate is $7 per hour for a regular workweek of 40 hours and time-and-a-half for overtime. Grace records time on the quarter-hour system. Using the timecard data, compute regular, overtime, and gross earnings for Roger Hart.

No. 83
Name: *Roger Hart*

Day	In	Out	In	Out	Hours Worked
M	7:54	5:00	5:30	8:30	_____
T	8:12	5:02			_____
W	7:57	5:00	5:30	9:30	_____
T	8:09	4:58			_____
F	8:00	5:00			_____

Total Hours _____

Regular Earnings $ _____

Overtime Earnings _____

Gross Earnings $ _____

Problems (cont.)

2–2. The Simpson Games Company pays its production workers according to the piece-rate plan. The report for one week shows the following:

	Chess Pieces	Chess Piece Earnings	Checkers	Checker Earnings	Markers	Marker Earnings	Total Earnings
Robert Lunt	360	$_____	440	$_____	500	$_____	$_____
Quinn O'Brien	420	_____	420	_____	400	_____	_____
Art Scholl	440	_____	360	_____	600	_____	_____
Sylvia Dunn	360	_____	440	_____	520	_____	_____
Dora Capelli	380	_____	460	_____	540	_____	_____

The piece rates are $.25 for each chess piece, $.15 for each checker, and $.10 for each marker. Compute total earnings for the five employees.

2–3. Roger Stimm sells cheese to supermarkets for the Cheese Factory. He earns $150 per week and receives a 7% commission on daily sales over $4,000. One week Roger's commission report showed the following sales:

	Sales	Commission Earned
M	$5,400	$_____
T	3,800	_____
W	6,000	_____
T	5,000	_____
F	4,200	_____

Total Wages $_____

Compute Roger's daily commission and total wages for the week.

2–4. The Unique Jig-Saw Puzzle Company pays its employees according to the following piece-rate schedule:

Output	Rate
1–100 puzzles	$.75
101–200 puzzles	.80
201–300 puzzles	.85

The piece rate is the same for all units produced except that the company also pays 1½ times the regular piece rate for all pieces produced during overtime hours. During one week the production report showed the following:

	Total Hours	Units Produced Regular	Units Produced Overtime	Piecework Earnings	Overtime Earnings	Gross Earnings
Lois O'Toole	44	140	40	$_____	$_____	$_____
Marty Fortunna	42	220	20	_____	_____	_____
Estelle Barrie	44	130	20	_____	_____	_____
Betty Wynne	42	150	30	_____	_____	_____
Bruce Gardener	42	210	10	_____	_____	_____

Problems (cont.)

Compute piecework, overtime, and gross earnings for the five employees. (Hint: Compare gross earnings computed with minimum wage.)

2–5. Harrison Motors pays its employees on a commission basis. During one week the output report showed the following sales and commission rates:

	No. of Escorts Sold	No. of Tempos Sold	No. of Tauruses Sold	No. of Lincolns Sold	Total Earnings
Gary Brooks	2	3	3	1	$_____
Betty Good	4	4	1	—	_____
Robert Chen	2	2	4	—	_____
Eve Grant	1	1	3	2	_____
David Parks	1	1	4	2	_____

The salespeople are paid $100 for each Escort or Tempo sold and .5% for each Taurus or Lincoln sold, using a base price of $14,000 for Taurus and $28,000 for Lincoln.

Compute the total earnings of these five employees.

2–6. Esther Barone works an irregular workweek by agreement with her employer, Pauline's Interiors. Esther receives $510 a week regular wages plus overtime pay if she works over 40 hours. One week she worked 45 hours. Compute her gross earnings for the week. (Round to two decimal places in computations.)

$ _____

2–7. George Chadwick cleans carpets for Hogan's Carpet Cleaning Service. George has a regular workweek of 40 hours and receives $7.00 per hour. He also earns $.25 for each square foot of carpet cleaned in excess of 12,000 square feet per week. During one week, George worked overtime and cleaned 12,400 square feet of carpeting. Compute George's gross earnings for the week assuming that the piecework rate method applies to the overtime pay.

Overtime Piecework Earnings $ _____

Regular Weekly Earnings _____

Gross Earnings $ _____

2–8. Judy Blake and Charles Lane work as hairdressers for Quik Cut and Curl Shoppe. Judy averages $65 a week and Charles $30 a week in tips during a 35-hour week. What salaries should Quik Cut pay Judy and Charles so that it is not in violation of the FLSA? What dollar amount of tip credit can it take for them?

Judy's Tip Credit $ _____   *Salary* $ _____

Charles's Tip Credit $ _____   *Salary* $ _____

2–9. At the Monaco Dress Shop, Susan Garrett worked 36 hours at $10 an hour in her job as a hostess for fashion shows and 10 hours at $12 an hour as a buyer. If she is paid overtime for her work as a hostess and also receives a

56 Part II Running a Payroll

Problems (cont.)

bonus of $10 per week, what are her gross earnings? (Use the lower paying job as the basis for overtime pay.)

Regular Earnings	$ _____
Overtime Earnings	_____
Bonus	_____
Gross Earnings	$ _____

2–10. Henry Riggins is an institutional salesperson for Computer Applications, Inc. Henry also writes original software programs for the company and gets a commission on the sales of a program for the first 18 months it is on the market. Henry receives a monthly salary of $5,000 per month and 10% of the sales of his new Ogre Orgy video game. During May, Computer Applications sold $4,000 worth of the O-O video game. What are Henry's total earnings for the month of May?

Monthly Salary	$ _____
Commission Earnings	_____
Gross Earnings	$ _____

2–11. Employees on the assembly line of Jupiter Toys, Inc., work 40 hours a week and receive time-and-a-half for overtime. Using the following data, compute the overtime hourly rate, regular wages, overtime wages, and gross wages for each employee.

Employee	Hours Worked	Regular Hourly Rate	Overtime Hourly Rate	Regular Wages	Overtime Wages	Gross Wages
Lola Prince	46	$7.50	$_____	$_____	$_____	$_____
Howie Rooker	48	6.50	_____	_____	_____	_____
Bea Quinn	44	8.80	_____	_____	_____	_____
Clay Pease	42	7.80	_____	_____	_____	_____

2–12. Jupiter Toys, Inc., pays its production workers on a piece-rate plan. These workers receive $2.00 per 50 units for the first 250 units, $2.50 per 50 units for the next 250 units and $2.25 per 50 units for all units over 500. Assuming an 8-hour workday, compute the piece-rate earnings and the hourly rate to two decimal places for each employee.

Employee	Units Produced/Day	Daily Piece-rate Earnings	Hourly Rate
Tamara Rome	1,600	$_____	$_____
Christine Craven	2,600	_____	_____
Teddy Bunker	3,400	_____	_____
Mel Dopson	2,000	_____	_____

2–13. Middle managers at Jupiter Toys, Inc., receive weekly salaries. Based on a 40-hour week and assuming downward as well as upward adjustment in the salaries for actual hours worked, compute the gross earnings for each employee.

Problems (cont.)

Employee	Hours Worked	Salary	Gross Earnings
Douglas Finn	44	$420	$_____
Aggie Martin	38	460	_____
Bill Rhodes	36	440	_____
Meg A. Young	46	480	_____

2-14. Jupiter Toys, Inc., pays its outside salespeople a commission on sales. They receive a 5% commission on the first $5,000 of sales and a 6% commission on any sales over $5,000. Assuming a 40-hour week, compute the commission and hourly rate for each employee.

Employee	Sales	Commission Earned	Hourly Rate
Ford Lane	$7,600	$_____	$_____
Terri Klink	8,000	_____	_____
Win Orton	5,800	_____	_____
Ann Yount	6,800	_____	_____

2-15. Sales managers at Jupiter Toys, Inc., receive a salary plus a commission on sales. Assuming a 2% commission on sales, compute the total earnings for each employee.

Employee	Weekly Salary	Sales	Commission	Total Earnings
Carol Lund	$400	$4,000	$_____	$_____
Al Legett	400	5,000	_____	_____
Virginia Dann	360	6,000	_____	_____
Parker Davis	380	5,000	_____	_____
Elaine Frame	360	4,000	_____	_____

2-16. Aaron Henry works as a waiter in the Bugle Restaurant near the Jupiter Toys plant. He receives a weekly wage and averages tips of $130 for a 40-hour week. If Aaron's employer claims a tip credit of $50, what is the weekly wage and the hourly rate that the Bugle must pay Aaron?

Weekly Wage $ _____

Hourly Rate _____

2-17. Dwayne Morse and Terri Grant are full-time students and work part-time at Central State University near Jupiter Toys, Inc. Dwayne earns $3.80 an hour while Terri makes $4.00 an hour. During one week in July, Dwayne worked 30 hours and Terri, 24 hours. Are the hourly rates being paid Dwayne and Terri in violation of the FLSA? Depending on your answer to this question, what should the university pay Dwayne and Terri? $ _____

2-18. Compute the hourly wage rate for the following employees of Jupiter Toys, Inc.

    a. Helga Stein, sales supervisor, earns $1,800 each month for a 40-hour week.

$ _____

b. Ron Black, advertising copywriter, receives an annual salary of $22,400 for a 52-week year and 40 hours per week.

$ _____

c. Debra Payne, a financial analyst, earns $475 per week for a 37½-hour week.

$ _____

2–19. Jupiter Toys, Inc., pays its toy assemblers piecework rates based on an incentive schedule of $.15 each for the first 1,200 units produced and $.16 for any units over this amount. Compute the piecework earnings for each of the following employees. Assume a 35 hour week.

Employee	Units Produced/Week	Piecework Earnings
Stuart Wright	1,320	$_____
Stella Dempsey	1,180	_____
Hortense Slade	1,410	_____
Roger Munn	1,280	_____

2–20. Inside sales personnel at Jupiter Toys, Inc., receive a base salary plus an 8% commission on sales above assigned quotas. Compute the gross earnings for the following employees.

	Base Salary	Annual Sales	Sales Quotas	Gross Earnings
Joe Cermack	$20,000	$100,000	$ 80,000	$_____
Audrey Shaw	18,000	120,000	80,000	_____
Beryl Caine	24,000	140,000	100,000	_____
Bill Green	19,000	100,000	70,000	_____

CONTINUING CASE PROBLEM

Starting in this chapter, we will look at a continuing case problem involving a new corporation: Frontier Landscaping, Inc. We will visit this company at various points throughout the text to illustrate the successive steps in a payroll operation, from paying employees and depositing payroll taxes to recording the payroll.

Frontier Landscaping, although a small company by the usual criteria, is one of the larger companies in its specialized field and in its area of operations—the suburbs around Boston. The company does landscaping for large, private estates, the residences of some of the most prominent executives in the Boston metropolitan area. The homes of its customers range in value from $400,000 to $5,000,000; the average price is over $1,000,000.

The company takes pride in its ability to use landscaping to complement the homes and reflect the personality of the owners as well as the homes.

During the busy season (late spring to early fall), Frontier has eight hourly and two salaried employees. The hourly employees are paid for hours actually worked with time worked recorded in quarter-hour intervals. The standard workweek consists of 40 hours, with all but exempt employees being paid time-and-a-half for hours worked over 40.

Continuing Case
Problem (cont.)

Payday is the Tuesday following the end of the workweek, which is Saturday. The payday for the week ending May 15 is May 18. The data applicable to each employee are as follows:

Employee Name	Hourly Wage or Salary	Hours Worked	Reg. Hours	Reg. Earnings	Overtime Hours	Overtime Earnings	Gross Earnings
Carrie Barnes	$5.40 per hr.	40	_____	$_____	_____	$_____	$_____
Melissa Trane	5.60 per hr.	48	_____	_____	_____	_____	_____
Horace Glenn	5.40 per hr.	38	_____	_____	_____	_____	_____
Brenda Toomey	5.40 per hr.	40	_____	_____	_____	_____	_____
Frank Granto	5.80 per hr.	44	_____	_____	_____	_____	_____
Harry Fein	6.00 per hr.	40	_____	_____	_____	_____	_____
Jose Lopez	6.00 per hr.	48	_____	_____	_____	_____	_____
Julie Brown	5.60 per hr.	44	_____	_____	_____	_____	_____
Kathy Wood	$1,500 salary per wk.	44	_____	_____	_____	_____	_____
David Wood	$1,250 salary per wk.	46	_____	_____	_____	_____	_____

COMPUTE:

a. Regular hours and overtime hours worked for each employee.
b. Regular earnings, overtime earnings, and gross earnings for each employee. Salaried employees are exempt employees.

CHAPTER 3

WITHHOLDING INCOME TAXES

LEARNING OBJECTIVES

On completing this chapter, you will be able to:

1. Explain the use of Form W-4, the method by which an employee establishes exemption allowances.
2. Compute the amount of federal income tax withholding using the wage-bracket and percentage methods, as well as the annualized wages, cumulative wages, and part-year employment methods.
3. Enumerate nontaxable fringe benefits and the taxability of other benefits.
4. Describe the requirements and procedures for the advance payment of the earned income credit.
5. Discuss state and local income tax withholding, using New York state as an example.

Now that Lois Arruda, with Nioga Gear, understands how to compute gross wages, Clark Barr believes Lois is ready to learn about the payroll tax deductions made for each employee.

Fifty years ago, individuals were responsible for paying their own taxes on income earned during the year. The enactment of the Current Tax Payment Act of 1943 radically changed that system by mandating that taxes be paid at the source, that is, taken out of each paycheck. Today, federal income taxes are only one of the many government and employee-authorized deductions from the average paycheck. The payroll process may involve other deductions required by law or requested by the employee.

Clark begins to describe the federal income tax deductions required by law.

61

WITHHOLDING FEDERAL INCOME TAXES

Withholding allowance
An allowance that reduces taxable income by a fixed amount, adjusted for inflation.

The Current Tax Payment Act of 1943 requires employers to deduct federal income taxes from employees' earnings at the end of each payroll period. The amount of money withheld depends on an employee's estimated taxable annual income and the number of **withholding allowances** claimed by the employee. Lois has learned about the concept of taxable wages. Clark now shows Lois the method for determining the number of withholding allowances and the effect of this information on the income taxes withheld.

Withholding Allowances

Employee's Withholding Allowance Certificate (Form W-4) *A form used to claim allowances, to request the withholding of an additional amount, or to claim an exempt status.*

When hired, each employee fills out a **Form W-4, Employee's Withholding Allowance Certificate** (Exhibit 3-1). The purpose of Form W-4 is to help employees determine the number of allowances they receive so that the total amount withheld from their paychecks closely approximates their annual tax liability. Employees determine the number of allowances they should receive, based on the number of their dependents. Basically, the number of allowances depends on marital or tax-filing status and the number of dependents; other factors, however, such as a working spouse, a second job, income not subject to withholding, dependent care expenses, and itemized deductions, may affect the allowances claimed. The Form W-4 takes into account these variables.

For a new employee, the allowance figure is effective as of the first wage payment. If a new employee does not complete a Form W-4, the payroll clerk must withhold tax as if that person is single and claims no withholding allowances. This results in the largest amount of federal income tax withheld. Such withholding acts as a penalty for failure to file a Form W-4 and as an incentive for filing.

A Form W-4 remains in effect until the employee completes a new one. When an employee submits a new Form W-4, the employer *may* make the change effective with the first wage payment after filing of the form. In any event, the change must be in effect no later than the first payroll period ending on or after the 30th day after the new Form W-4 is filed.

Change in Allowances.   Certain changes in an employee's life may require a change in withholding allowances. Marriage, birth of a child, or new responsibilities related to caring for an elderly or dependent relative are examples of some changes that might necessitate revising Form W-4. These changes translate into increases in withholding allowances. The filing of a new Form W-4 is optional, but the employee should file a new form to reflect the higher allowances. By law, the employee *must* provide a new Form W-4 within ten days after certain decreases in allowances, such as:

1. Divorce, if claiming married status or if the ex-spouse now claims an allowance on a separate Form W-4.
2. Decrease in the number of dependents or in expected deductions that form the basis for claiming an allowance.

Form W-4
Department of the Treasury
Internal Revenue Service

Employee's Withholding Allowance Certificate

▶ **For Privacy Act and Paperwork Reduction Act Notice, see page 2.**

OMB No. 1545-0010

20

1 Type or print your first name and middle initial	Last name	2 Your social security number

Home address (number and street or rural route)	3 ☐ Single ☐ Married ☐ Married, but withhold at higher Single rate.
	Note: If married, but legally separated, or spouse is a nonresident alien, check the Single box.

City or town, state, and ZIP code	4 If your last name differs from that on your social security card, check here. **You must call 1-800-772-1213 for a new card** . . . ▶ ☐

5 Total number of allowances you are claiming (from line **H** above **OR** from the applicable worksheet on page 2)   **5** ____

6 Additional amount, if any, you want withheld from each paycheck . . . .   **6** $ ____

7 I claim exemption from withholding for 2000, and I certify that I meet **BOTH** of the following conditions for exemption:
 • Last year I had a right to a refund of **ALL** Federal income tax withheld because I had **NO** tax liability **AND**
 • This year I expect a refund of **ALL** Federal income tax withheld because I expect to have **NO** tax liability.
 If you meet both conditions, write "EXEMPT" here . . . . ▶ **7** ____

Under penalties of perjury, I certify that I am entitled to the number of withholding allowances claimed on this certificate, or I am entitled to claim exempt status.

Employee's signature
(Form is not valid
unless you sign it) ▶   Date ▶

8 Employer's name and address (Employer: Complete lines 8 and 10 only if sending to the IRS.)	9 Office code (optional)	10 Employer identification number

Cat. No. 10220Q

EXHIBIT 3-1   Form W-4, Employee's Withholding Allowance Certificate

An employee whose spouse has died during the year can still claim married status for the year on Form W-4. If the spouse died in either of the two preceding tax years, the employee can claim married status if the employee claims an exemption for a child or stepchild and the employee could have filed a joint return in the year of the spouse's death.

If an employee returns to work after a layoff or authorized leave, the payroll clerk should request a new Form W-4 to avoid overwithholding or to change the basis of withholding to a part-year method. Publications 505 and 919 from the Internal Revenue Service contain worksheets and examples of how to determine the optimum number of withholding allowances.

Let's see how one of Nioga's employees filled out his Form W-4 (Exhibit 3-2). Tom Wilson expects to earn $37,000 in wages for the year at Nioga. His wife Trudy expects to make $26,000 at Jupiter Toys. They estimate their interest and dividend income for the year to be $300. The Wilsons have two dependent children and expect to have itemized deductions of about $9,250 on their Form 1040 for 2000. In addition, Tom pays $4,000 in alimony to his former wife. Tom completed the Personal Allowance Worksheets on page 1 of Form W-4 as follows:

Line A: 1, Tom's personal allowance

Line B: 0, since Trudy earns more than $1,000

Line C: 0, since Trudy is a working spouse

Line D: 2, the number of dependent children

Line E: 0, since Tom is not filing as head of household

Line F: 0, since child care expenses are under $1,500

Line G: 1, the Child Tax Credit for Tom and Trudy

Line H: 4, the sum of lines A through G

In most cases, employees need go no further. Since the Wilsons plan to itemize deductions and their combined income exceeds $55,000, Tom completed the second page of Form W-4.

Form W-4 (20)

Purpose. Complete Form W-4 so your employer can withhold the correct Federal income tax from your pay. Because your tax situation may change, you may want to refigure your withholding each year.

Exemption from withholding. If you are exempt, complete only lines 1, 2, 3, 4, and 7, and sign the form to validate it. Your exemption for 2000 expires February 16, 2001.

Note: *You cannot claim exemption from withholding if (1) your income exceeds $700 and includes more than $250 of unearned income (e.g., interest and dividends) and (2) another person can claim you as a dependent on their tax return.*

Basic instructions. If you are not exempt, complete the **Personal Allowances Worksheet** below. The worksheets on page 2 adjust your withholding allowances based on itemized

deductions, adjustments to income, or two-earner/two-job situations. Complete all worksheets that apply. They will help you figure the number of withholding allowances you are entitled to claim. **However, you may claim fewer (or zero) allowances.**

Child tax and higher education credits. For details on adjusting withholding for these and other credits, see **Pub. 919,** How Do I Adjust My Tax Withholding?

Head of household. Generally, you may claim head of household filing status on your tax return only if you are unmarried and pay more than 50% of the costs of keeping up a home for yourself and your dependent(s) or other qualifying individuals. See line E below.

Nonwage income. If you have a large amount of nonwage income, such as interest or dividends, you should consider making estimated tax payments using **Form 1040-ES,** Estimated Tax for Individuals. Otherwise, you may owe additional tax.

Two earners/two jobs. If you have a working spouse or more than one job, figure the total number of allowances you are entitled to claim on all jobs using worksheets from only one Form W-4. Your withholding usually will be most accurate when all allowances are claimed on the Form W-4 prepared for the highest paying job and zero allowances are claimed for the others.

Check your withholding. After your Form W-4 takes effect, use Pub. 919 to see how the dollar amount you are having withheld compares to your projected total tax for 2000. Get Pub. 919 especially if you used the **Two-Earner/Two-Job Worksheet** on page 2 and your earnings exceed $150,000 (Single) or $200,000 (Married).

Recent name change? If your name on line 1 differs from that shown on your social security card, call 1-800-772-1213 for a new social security card.

Personal Allowances Worksheet (Keep for your records.)

A   Enter "1" for **yourself** if no one else can claim you as a dependent . . . . **A**   _1_

B   Enter "1" if: {   • You are single and have only one job; or
           • You are married, have only one job, and your spouse does not work; or . .   **B**   _0_
           • Your wages from a second job or your spouse's wages (or the total of both) are $1,000 or less.

C   Enter "1" for your **spouse.** But, you may choose to enter -0- if you are married and have either a working spouse or more than one job. (Entering -0- may help you avoid having too little tax withheld.) . . . . **C**   _0_

D   Enter number of **dependents** (other than your spouse or yourself) you will claim on your tax return . . . . **D**   _2_

E   Enter "1" if you will file as **head of household** on your tax return (see conditions under **Head of household** above) .   **E**   _0_

F   Enter "1" if you have at least $1,500 of **child or dependent care expenses** for which you plan to claim a credit . .   **F**   _0_

G   **Child Tax Credit:**
     • If your total income will be between $18,000 and $50,000 ($23,000 and $63,000 if married), enter "1" for each eligible child.
     • If your total income will be between $50,000 and $80,000 ($63,000 and $115,000 if married), enter "1" if you have two
       eligible children, enter "2" if you have three or four eligible children, or enter "3" if you have five or more eligible children   **G**   _1_

H   Add lines A through G and enter total here. **Note:** *This may be different from the number of exemptions you claim on your tax return.* ▶   **H**   _4_

For accuracy, complete all worksheets that apply.   {
     • If you plan to **itemize or claim adjustments to income** and want to reduce your withholding, see the **Deductions and Adjustments Worksheet** on page 2.
     • If you are **single,** have **more than one job** and your combined earnings from all jobs exceed $34,000, OR if you are **married** and have a **working spouse or more than one job** and the combined earnings from all jobs exceed $60,000, see the **Two-Earner/Two-Job Worksheet** on page 2 to avoid having too little tax withheld.
     • If **neither** of the above situations applies, **stop here** and enter the number from line H on line 5 of Form W-4 below.

----- Cut here and give Form W-4 to your employer. Keep the top part for your records. -----

Form **W-4**
Department of the Treasury
Internal Revenue Service

Employee's Withholding Allowance Certificate

▶ **For Privacy Act and Paperwork Reduction Act Notice, see page 2.**

OMB No. 1545-0010

20

1 Type or print your first name and middle initial Last name	2 Your social security number
Thomas , *Wilson*	843 26 1899

Home address (number and street or rural route)
2247 Pine Street

3   ☐ Single   ☑ Married   ☐ Married, but withhold at higher Single rate.
Note: *If married, but legally separated, or spouse is a nonresident alien, check the Single box.*

City or town, state, and ZIP code
Niagara, NY 14307

4   If your last name differs from that on your social security card, check here. **You must call 1-800-772-1213 for a new card** . . . ▶ ☐

5   Total number of allowances you are claiming (from line **H** above **OR** from the applicable worksheet on page 2)   **5**   _1_

6   Additional amount, if any, you want withheld from each paycheck . . . .   **6** $

7   I claim exemption from withholding for 2000, and I certify that I meet **BOTH** of the following conditions for exemption:
     • Last year I had a right to a refund of **ALL** Federal income tax withheld because I had **NO** tax liability **AND**
     • This year I expect a refund of **ALL** Federal income tax withheld because I expect to have **NO** tax liability.
     If you meet both conditions, write "EXEMPT" here . . . . ▶   **7**

Under penalties of perjury, I certify that I am entitled to the number of withholding allowances claimed on this certificate, or I am entitled to claim exempt status.

Employee's signature
(Form is not valid
unless you sign it) ▶ *Thomas Wilson*   Date ▶ *1/5*   *00*

8 Employer's name and address (Employer: Complete lines 8 and 10 only if sending to the IRS.)	9 Office code (optional)	10 Employer identification number

Cat. No. 10220Q

EXHIBIT 3-2   Determining Withholding Allowances

Form W-4 (2000)   Page **2**

Deductions and Adjustments Worksheet

Note: *Use this worksheet only if you plan to itemize deductions or claim adjustments to income on your 2000 tax return.*

1 Enter an estimate of your 2000 itemized deductions. These include qualifying home mortgage interest, charitable contributions, state and local taxes, medical expenses in excess of 7.5% of your income, and miscellaneous deductions. (For 2000, you may have to reduce your itemized deductions if your income is over $128,950 ($64,475 if married filing separately). See **Worksheet 3** in Pub. 919 for details.) . . . 1 $ *9,250*

2 Enter:
- $7,350 if married filing jointly or qualifying widow(er)
- $6,450 if head of household
- $4,400 if single
- $3,675 if married filing separately

    2 $ *7,350*

3 **Subtract** line 2 from line 1. If line 2 is greater than line 1, enter -0- . . . . 3 $ *1,900*

4 Enter an estimate of your 2000 adjustments to income, including alimony, deductible IRA contributions, and student loan interest 4 $ *4,000*

5 **Add** lines 3 and 4 and enter the total (Include any amount for credits from **Worksheet 7** in Pub. 919.) . 5 $ *5,900*

6 Enter an estimate of your 2000 nonwage income (such as dividends or interest) . . . . 6 $ *300*

7 **Subtract** line 6 from line 5. Enter the result, but not less than -0- . . . . 7 $ *5,600*

8 **Divide** the amount on line 7 by $3,000 and enter the result here. Drop any fraction 8 *1*

9 Enter the number from the **Personal Allowances Worksheet**, line H, page 1 . . . . 9 *4*

10 **Add** lines 8 and 9 and enter the total here. If you plan to use the **Two-Earner/Two-Job Worksheet,** also enter this total on line 1 below. Otherwise, **stop here** and enter this total on Form W-4, line 5, page 1 . 10 *5*

Two-Earner/Two-Job Worksheet

Note: *Use this worksheet only if the instructions under line H on page 1 direct you here.*

1 Enter the number from line H, page 1 (or from line 10 above if you used the **Deductions and Adjustments Worksheet**) 1 *5*

2 Find the number in **Table 1** below that applies to the **LOWEST** paying job and enter it here 2 *4*

3 If line 1 is **MORE THAN OR EQUAL TO** line 2, subtract line 2 from line 1. Enter the result here (if zero, enter -0-) and on Form W-4, line 5, page 1. **Do not** use the rest of this worksheet 3 *1*

Note: *If line 1 is **LESS THAN** line 2, enter -0- on Form W-4, line 5, page 1. Complete lines 4–9 below to calculate the additional withholding amount necessary to avoid a year end tax bill.*

4 Enter the number from line 2 of this worksheet . . . . 4 _____

5 Enter the number from line 1 of this worksheet . . . . 5 _____

6 **Subtract** line 5 from line 4 . . . . 6 _____

7 Find the amount in **Table 2** below that applies to the **HIGHEST** paying job and enter it here . . . . 7 $ _____

8 **Multiply** line 7 by line 6 and enter the result here. This is the additional annual withholding needed . . 8 $ _____

9 **Divide** line 8 by the number of pay periods remaining in 2000. For example, divide by 26 if you are paid every other week and you complete this form in December 1999. Enter the result here and on Form W-4, line 6, page 1. This is the additional amount to be withheld from each paycheck . . . . 9 $ _____

Table 1: Two-Earner/Two-Job Worksheet

Married Filing Jointly				All Others			
If wages from **LOWEST** paying job are—	Enter on line 2 above	If wages from **LOWEST** paying job are—	Enter on line 2 above	If wages from **LOWEST** paying job are—	Enter on line 2 above	If wages from **LOWEST** paying job are—	Enter on line 2 above
$0 - $4,000	0	41,001 - 45,000	8	$0 - $5,000	0	65,001 - 80,000	8
4,001 - 7,000	1	45,001 - 55,000	9	5,001 - 11,000	1	80,001 - 100,000	9
7,001 - 13,000	2	55,001 - 63,000	10	11,001 - 17,000	2	100,001 and over	10
13,001 - 19,000	3	63,001 - 70,000	11	17,001 - 22,000	3		
19,001 - 25,000	4	70,001 - 85,000	12	22,001 - 27,000	4		
25,001 - 31,000	5	85,001 - 100,000	13	27,001 - 40,000	5		
31,001 - 37,000	6	100,001 - 110,000	14	40,001 - 50,000	6		
37,001 - 41,000	7	110,001 and over	15	50,001 - 65,000	7		

Table 2: Two-Earner/Two-Job Worksheet

Married Filing Jointly		All Others	
If wages from **HIGHEST** paying job are—	Enter on line 7 above	If wages from **HIGHEST** paying job are—	Enter on line 7 above
$0 - $50,000	$420	$0 - $30,000	$420
50,001 - 100,000	780	30,001 - 60,000	780
100,001 - 130,000	870	60,001 - 120,000	870
130,001 - 250,000	1,000	120,001 - 270,000	1,000
250,001 and over	1,100	270,001 and over	1,100

Privacy Act and Paperwork Reduction Act Notice. We ask for the information on this form to carry out the Internal Revenue laws of the United States. The Internal Revenue Code requires this information under sections 3402(f)(2)(A) and 6109 and their regulations. Failure to provide a **properly** completed form will result in your being treated as a single person who claims no withholding allowances; **providing fraudulent information may also subject you to penalties.** Routine uses of this information include giving it to the Department of Justice for civil and criminal litigation, to cities, states, and the District of Columbia for use in administering their tax laws, and for use in the National Directory of New Hires.

You are not required to provide the information requested on a form that is subject to the Paperwork Reduction Act unless the form displays a valid OMB control number. Books or records relating to a form or its instructions must be retained as long as their contents may become material in the administration of any Internal Revenue law. Generally, tax returns and return information are confidential, as required by Code section 6103.

The time needed to complete this form will vary depending on individual circumstances. The estimated average time is: **Recordkeeping 46 min., Learning about the law or the form** 13 min., **Preparing the form** 59 min. If you have comments concerning the accuracy of these time estimates or suggestions for making this form simpler, we would be happy to hear from you. You can write to the Tax Forms Committee, Western Area Distribution Center, Rancho Cordova, CA 95743-0001. **DO NOT** send the tax form to this address. Instead, give it to your employer.

 Printed on recycled paper   *U.S. Government Printing Office: 1999 — 456-119

Line 1: $9,250, the amount of itemized deductions the Wilsons expect

Line 2: $7,350, the Wilsons expect to file a joint return

Line 3: $1,900, the difference between lines 2 and 1

Line 4: $4,000, since Tom pays this amount in alimony to his ex-wife

Line 5: $5,900, the sum of lines 3 and 4

Line 6: $300, the Wilsons' expected interest and dividend income for the year

Line 7: $5,600, the difference between lines 5 and 6

Line 8: 1, the result of dividing $5,600 by $3,000 and dropping the fraction

Line 9: 4, from line H on page 1

Line 10: 5, the sum of lines 8 and 9

Tom also completed the Two-Earner/Two-Job Worksheet on Form W-4 because both he and Trudy have jobs and their combined earnings are over $55,000.

Line 1: 5, from line 10 of the Deductions and Adjustments Worksheet

Line 2: 4, the number for Trudy's $26,000 salary (the lower-paying job) from Table 1

Line 3: 1, the difference between lines 1 and 2. Tom also enters this number on line 5 of page 1.

Thus, the Wilsons can claim one allowance on Form W-4. Tom claims this one allowance so that the taxes withheld will approximate the Wilsons' actual tax liability. On her Form W-4, Trudy claims no allowances.

Exemption from Withholding.   An employee may claim an exemption from withholding taxes. The exemption applies only to income taxes, not to FICA taxes. To be eligible for an exemption, the employee must have had no tax liability for the prior year and no expectation of any for the current year. Although no one is automatically exempt, students who work part-time or during the summer and individuals age 65 or older and blind often qualify for such an exemption.

Verification of Withholding Allowances.   The payroll department retains the Form W-4 in the employee's file. A copy of the Form W-4 is sent to the IRS for verification when the employee claims

1. more than ten withholding allowances or
2. exemption from withholding when wages are expected to be more than $200 a week.

Methods of Withholding

Several different methods are available for determining the deduction for federal income tax once the employee has completed Form W-4. All these methods attempt to approximate the tax liability the employee will be subject to on the year-end tax return (Form 1040). However, since the Form W-4 worksheets and the withholding methods do not account for all possible situations, the amount withheld may be off the mark. This situation most often happens when both spouses work, when the employee has more than one job, or when the employee has substantial nonwage income such as interest, dividends, alimony, or self-employment income. Nevertheless, the different withholding methods are flexible enough to cover most situations.

Wage-Bracket Method. The simplest and most widely used method of determining withholding among smaller businesses is the **wage-bracket method**. This method relies on a set of withholding tables furnished by the Internal Revenue Service in *Circular E*, **Employer's Tax Guide**. The tables indicate the amount of federal income tax to be deducted for wage brackets or ranges, with separate tables for single and married persons and for daily, weekly, biweekly, semimonthly, monthly, and miscellaneous payroll periods. Exhibit 3-3 shows a partial tax table for single employees and a weekly payroll period. The tax tables for all variations are contained in Appendix A at the back of this book.

Wage-bracket method *A federal income tax withholding method that takes into account gross earnings, the payroll period, marital status, and the number of withholding allowances.*

Circular E, **Employer's Tax Guide** *An IRS publication describing withholding methods and the advance earned income credit; includes withholding tables and other charts.*

Let's use the wage-bracket tables to find the federal income tax withholding for Wilma Holden, a sales analyst at Nioga Gear. Wilma is single and, since she supports her mother, has two withholding allowances. During the last week, she earned $366. Follow these steps to determine the correct amount of federal income tax withholding.

1. Use the table for single persons, weekly payroll period (see Exhibit 3-3).

2. Using the first two columns, locate the line that reads "At least $360 but less than $370."

3. Follow that line across the table to the column for the number of withholding allowances the employee claims. For Wilma, that number is 2. The amount where the row and column intersect is the amount to be withheld. In the case of Wilma Holden, the correct amount of income tax withholding is $31.

As the example shows, four separate pieces of information are essential to determine the federal income tax withholding by this method: marital status, length of payroll period, number of withholding allowances claimed by the employee, and gross wages.

Percentage Method. The **percentage method** can be used any time but may be most appropriate when the number of allowances claimed is greater than 10 or the wages are greater than the last figures cited in the wage-bracket tables. Under the percentage method, the withholding is determined by applying a formula that contains both fixed and variable components (Exhibit 3-4). This method is based on the same four pieces of information as the wage-bracket method—marital status, length of payroll period, number of withholding allowances, and gross wages.

Percentage method *A federal income tax withholding tax method that applies a formula with both fixed and variable components to the wages amount.*

The first step is to determine the withholding allowance amount using the allowance values listed in Table 3-1. The next step is to subtract the withholding allowance amount from gross wages. The resulting balance, with the correct line from the table in Exhibit 3-4, yields the appropriate formula to calculate the amount to withhold.

SINGLE Persons—WEEKLY Payroll Period

(For Wages Paid in 2000)

If the wages are—		And the number of withholding allowances claimed is—										
At least	But less than	0	1	2	3	4	5	6	7	8	9	10
		The amount of income tax to be withheld is—										
$0	$55	0	0	0	0	0	0	0	0	0	0	0
55	60	1	0	0	0	0	0	0	0	0	0	0
60	65	2	0	0	0	0	0	0	0	0	0	0
65	70	2	0	0	0	0	0	0	0	0	0	0
70	75	3	0	0	0	0	0	0	0	0	0	0
75	80	4	0	0	0	0	0	0	0	0	0	0
80	85	5	0	0	0	0	0	0	0	0	0	0
85	90	5	0	0	0	0	0	0	0	0	0	0
90	95	6	0	0	0	0	0	0	0	0	0	0
95	100	7	0	0	0	0	0	0	0	0	0	0
100	105	8	0	0	0	0	0	0	0	0	0	0
105	110	8	0	0	0	0	0	0	0	0	0	0
110	115	9	1	0	0	0	0	0	0	0	0	0
115	120	10	2	0	0	0	0	0	0	0	0	0
120	125	11	3	0	0	0	0	0	0	0	0	0
125	130	11	3	0	0	0	0	0	0	0	0	0
130	135	12	4	0	0	0	0	0	0	0	0	0
135	140	13	5	0	0	0	0	0	0	0	0	0
140	145	14	6	0	0	0	0	0	0	0	0	0
145	150	14	6	0	0	0	0	0	0	0	0	0
150	155	15	7	0	0	0	0	0	0	0	0	0
155	160	16	8	0	0	0	0	0	0	0	0	0
160	165	17	9	1	0	0	0	0	0	0	0	0
165	170	17	9	1	0	0	0	0	0	0	0	0
170	175	18	10	2	0	0	0	0	0	0	0	0
175	180	19	11	3	0	0	0	0	0	0	0	0
180	185	20	12	4	0	0	0	0	0	0	0	0
185	190	20	12	4	0	0	0	0	0	0	0	0
190	195	21	13	5	0	0	0	0	0	0	0	0
195	200	22	14	6	0	0	0	0	0	0	0	0
200	210	23	15	7	0	0	0	0	0	0	0	0
210	220	25	17	8	0	0	0	0	0	0	0	0
220	230	26	18	10	2	0	0	0	0	0	0	0
230	240	28	20	11	3	0	0	0	0	0	0	0
240	250	29	21	13	5	0	0	0	0	0	0	0
250	260	31	23	14	6	0	0	0	0	0	0	0
260	270	32	24	16	8	0	0	0	0	0	0	0
270	280	34	26	17	9	1	0	0	0	0	0	0
280	290	35	27	19	11	3	0	0	0	0	0	0
290	300	37	29	20	12	4	0	0	0	0	0	0
300	310	38	30	22	14	6	0	0	0	0	0	0
310	320	40	32	23	15	7	0	0	0	0	0	0
320	330	41	33	25	17	9	1	0	0	0	0	0
330	340	43	35	26	18	10	2	0	0	0	0	0
340	350	44	36	28	20	12	4	0	0	0	0	0
350	360	46	38	29	21	13	5	0	0	0	0	0
360	370	47	39	31	23	15	7	0	0	0	0	0
370	380	49	41	32	24	16	8	0	0	0	0	0
380	390	50	42	34	26	18	10	2	0	0	0	0
390	400	52	44	35	27	19	11	3	0	0	0	0
400	410	53	45	37	29	21	13	5	0	0	0	0
410	420	55	47	38	30	22	14	6	0	0	0	0
420	430	56	48	40	32	24	16	8	0	0	0	0
430	440	58	50	41	33	25	17	9	1	0	0	0
440	450	59	51	43	35	27	19	11	3	0	0	0
450	460	61	53	44	36	28	20	12	4	0	0	0
460	470	62	54	46	38	30	22	14	6	0	0	0
470	480	64	56	47	39	31	23	15	7	0	0	0
480	490	65	57	49	41	33	25	17	9	0	0	0
490	500	67	59	50	42	34	26	18	10	2	0	0
500	510	68	60	52	44	36	28	20	12	3	0	0
510	520	70	62	53	45	37	29	21	13	5	0	0
520	530	71	63	55	47	39	31	23	15	6	0	0
530	540	73	65	56	48	40	32	24	16	8	0	0
540	550	75	66	58	50	42	34	26	18	9	1	0
550	560	78	68	59	51	43	35	27	19	11	3	0
560	570	81	69	61	53	45	37	29	21	12	4	0
570	580	84	71	62	54	46	38	30	22	14	6	0
580	590	87	72	64	56	48	40	32	24	15	7	0
590	600	89	74	65	57	49	41	33	25	17	9	1

EXHIBIT 3-3   Wage-Bracket Table

TABLE 3-1
Allowance Table

Allowance Table	And wages are paid-							
	Weekly	Biweekly	Semi-monthly	Monthly	Quarterly	Semi-annually	Annually	Daily or Misc.
If the number of withholding allowances is:	The total amount of withholding allowances for the payroll period is:							
0	$ 0	$ 0	$ 0	$ 0	$ 0	$ 0	$ 0	$ 0
1	53.85	107.69	116.67	233.33	700.00	1,400.00	2,800.00	10.77
2	107.70	215.38	233.34	466.66	1,400.00	2,800.00	5,600.00	21.54
3	161.55	323.07	350.01	699.99	2,100.00	4,200.00	8,400.00	32.31
4	215.40	430.76	466.68	933.32	2,800.00	5,600.00	11,200.00	43.08
5	269.25	538.45	583.35	1,166.65	3,500.00	7,000.00	14,000.00	53.85
6	323.10	646.14	700.02	1,399.98	4,200.00	8,400.00	16,800.00	64.62
7	376.95	753.83	816.69	1,633.31	4,900.00	9,800.00	19,600.00	75.39
8	430.80	861.52	933.36	1,866.64	5,600.00	11,200.00	22,400.00	86.16
9	484.65	969.21	1,050.03	2,099.97	6,300.00	12,600.00	25,200.00	96.93
10	538.50	1,076.90	1,166.70	2,333.30	7,000.00	14,000.00	28,000.00	107.70

The percentage method is easier to do than to describe, so let's use this method for Wilma Holden from our previous example. Remember, Wilma is single, has two withholding allowances, and earned $366 last week. Follow these steps to determine the correct amount of federal income tax withholding under the percentage method. Use the rules for rounding that appear in the Payroll in Action box on page 72.

1. Locate in Table 3-1 the allowance value for the payroll period and the number of withholding allowances the employee claims. For Wilma, the withholding allowance amount is $107.70.

2. Subtract that amount from the employee's wages to determine the taxable wages.

$$\$366.00 - \$107.70 = \$258.30 = \$258$$

3. Using the table for a weekly payroll, single person (Table 1 of Exhibit 3-4), locate the correct percentage formula and determine the amount the employee's taxable wages exceed the base amount. Wilma's taxable wages are over $51 but not over $536. Therefore, subtract the $51 base amount from Wilma's earnings.

$$\$258 - \$51 = \$207$$

4. Multiply the excess amount by the percentage indicated to determine the amount to be withheld. For Wilma, the income tax to be withheld under the percentage method is $31.

$$\$207 \times .15 = \$31.05 = \$31$$

The payroll clerk can use the wage-bracket or percentage tables to determine withholding. Either method is suitable, and the payroll clerk can

Tables for Percentage Method of Withholding
(For Wages Paid in 2000)

TABLE 1—WEEKLY Payroll Period

(a) SINGLE person (including head of household)—

If the amount of wages (after subtracting withholding allowances) is:

The amount of income tax to withhold is:

Not over $51 . . . . . $0

Over—	But not over—		of excess over—
$51	—$536	. . 15%	—$51
$536	—$1,152	. . $72.75 plus 28%	—$536
$1,152	—$2,581	. . $245.23 plus 31%	—$1,152
$2,581	—$5,576	. . $688.22 plus 36%	—$2,581
$5,576	. . . . .	. $1,766.42 plus 39.6%	—$5,576

(b) MARRIED person—

If the amount of wages (after subtracting withholding allowances) is:

The amount of income tax to withhold is:

Not over $124 . . . . . $0

Over—	But not over—		of excess over—
$124	—$931	. . 15%	—$124
$931	—$1,942	. . $121.05 plus 28%	—$931
$1,942	—$3,192	. . $404.13 plus 31%	—$1,942
$3,192	—$5,633	. . $791.63 plus 36%	—$3,192
$5,633	. . . . .	. $1,670.39 plus 39.6%	—$5,633

TABLE 2—BIWEEKLY Payroll Period

(a) SINGLE person (including head of household)—

If the amount of wages (after subtracting withholding allowances) is:

The amount of income tax to withhold is:

Not over $102 . . . . . $0

Over—	But not over—		of excess over—
$102	—$1,071	. . 15%	—$102
$1,071	—$2,304	. . $145.35 plus 28%	—$1,071
$2,304	—$5,162	. . $490.59 plus 31%	—$2,304
$5,162	—$11,152	. . $1,376.57 plus 36%	—$5,162
$11,152	. . . . .	. $3,532.97 plus 39.6%	—$11,152

(b) MARRIED person—

If the amount of wages (after subtracting withholding allowances) is:

The amount of income tax to withhold is:

Not over $248 . . . . . $0

Over—	But not over—		of excess over—
$248	—$1,862	. . 15%	—$248
$1,862	—$3,885	. . $242.10 plus 28%	—$1,862
$3,885	—$6,385	. . $808.54 plus 31%	—$3,885
$6,385	—$11,265	. . $1,583.54 plus 36%	—$6,385
$11,265	. . . . .	. $3,340.34 plus 39.6%	—$11,265

TABLE 3—SEMIMONTHLY Payroll Period

(a) SINGLE person (including head of household)—

If the amount of wages (after subtracting withholding allowances) is:

The amount of income tax to withhold is:

Not over $110 . . . . . $0

Over—	But not over—		of excess over—
$110	—1,160	. . 15%	—$110
$1,160	—$2,496	. . $157.50 plus 28%	—$1,160
$2,496	—$5,592	. . $531.58 plus 31%	—$2,496
$5,592	—$12,081	. . $1,491.34 plus 36%	—$5,592
$12,081	. . . . .	. $3,827.38 plus 39.6%	—$12,081

(b) MARRIED person—

If the amount of wages (after subtracting withholding allowances) is:

The amount of income tax to withhold is:

Not over $269 . . . . . $0

Over—	But not over—		of excess over—
$269	—$2,017	. . 15%	—$269
$2,017	—$4,208	. . $262.20 plus 28%	—$2,017
$4,208	—$6,917	. . $875.68 plus 31%	—$4,208
$6,917	—$12,204	. . $1,715.47 plus 36%	—$6,917
$12,204	. . . . .	. $3,618.79 plus 39.6%	—$12,204

TABLE 4—MONTHLY Payroll Period

(a) SINGLE person (including head of household)—

If the amount of wages (after subtracting withholding allowances) is:

The amount of income tax to withhold is:

Not over $221 . . . . . $0

Over—	But not over—		of excess over—
$221	—$2,321	. . 15%	—$221
$2,321	—$4,992	. . $315.00 plus 28%	—$2,321
$4,992	—$11,183	. . $1,062.88 plus 31%	—$4,992
$11,183	—$24,163	. . $2,982.09 plus 36%	—$11,183
$24,163	. . . . .	. $7,654.89 plus 39.6%	—$24,163

(b) MARRIED person—

If the amount of wages (after subtracting withholding allowances) is:

The amount of income tax to withhold is:

Not over $538 . . . . . $0

Over—	But not over—		of excess over—
$538	—$4,033	. . 15%	—$538
$4,033	—$8,417	. . $524.25 plus 28%	—$4,033
$8,417	—$13,833	. . $1,751.77 plus 31%	—$8,417
$13,833	—$24,408	. . $3,430.73 plus 36%	—$13,833
$24,408	. . . . .	. $7,237.73 plus 39.6%	—$24,408

EXHIBIT 3-4   Percentage Method Withholding Tables

Tables for Percentage Method of Withholding (Continued)
(For Wages Paid in 2000)

TABLE 5—QUARTERLY Payroll Period

(a) SINGLE person (including head of household)—

If the amount of wages (after subtracting withholding allowances) is:		The amount of income tax to withhold is:
Not over $663		$0

Over—	But not over—		of excess over—
$663	—$6,963	. 15%	—$663
$6,963	—$14,975	. $945.00 plus 28%	—$6,963
$14,975	—$33,550	. $3,188.36 plus 31%	—$14,975
$33,550	—$72,488	. $8,946.61 plus 36%	—$33,550
$72,488	. . . . .	. $22,964.29 plus 39.6%	—$72,488

(b) MARRIED person—

If the amount of wages (after subtracting withholding allowances) is:		The amount of income tax to withhold is:
Not over $1,613		$0

Over—	But not over—		of excess over—
$1,613	—$12,100	. 15%	—$1,613
$12,100	—$25,250	. $1,573.05 plus 28%	—$12,100
$25,250	—$41,500	. $5,255.05 plus 31%	—$25,250
$41,500	—$73,225	. $10,292.55 plus 36%	—$41,500
$73,225	. . . . .	. $21,713.55 plus 39.6%	—$73,225

TABLE 6—SEMIANNUAL Payroll Period

(a) SINGLE person (including head of household)—

If the amount of wages (after subtracting withholding allowances) is:		The amount of income tax to withhold is:
Not over $1,325		$0

Over—	But not over—		of excess over—
$1,325	—$13,925	. 15%	—$1,325
$13,925	—$29,950	. $1,890.00 plus 28%	—$13,925
$29,950	—$67,100	. $6,377.00 plus 31%	—$29,950
$67,100	—$144,975	. $17,893.50 plus 36%	—$67,100
$144,975	. . . . .	. $45,928.50 plus 39.6%	—$144,975

(b) MARRIED person—

If the amount of wages (after subtracting withholding allowances) is:		The amount of income tax to withhold is:
Not over $3,225		$0

Over—	But not over—		of excess over—
$3,225	—$24,200	. 15%	—$3,225
$24,200	—$50,500	. $3,146.25 plus 28%	—$24,200
$50,500	—$83,000	. $10,510.25 plus 31%	—$50,500
$83,000	—$146,450	. $20,585.25 plus 36%	—$83,000
$146,450	. . . . .	. $43,427.25 plus 39.6%	—$146,450

TABLE 7—ANNUAL Payroll Period

(a) SINGLE person (including head of household)—

If the amount of wages (after subtracting withholding allowances) is:		The amount of income tax to withhold is:
Not over $2,650		$0

Over—	But not over—		of excess over—
$2,650	—$27,850	. 15%	—$2,650
$27,850	—$59,900	. $3,780.00 plus 28%	—$27,850
$59,900	—$134,200	. $12,754.00 plus 31%	—$59,900
$134,200	—$289,950	. $35,787.00 plus 36%	—$134,200
$289,950	. . . . .	. $91,857.00 plus 39.6%	—$289,950

(b) MARRIED person—

If the amount of wages (after subtracting withholding allowances) is:		The amount of income tax to withhold is:
Not over $6,450		$0

Over—	But not over—		of excess over—
$6,450	—$48,400	. 15%	—$6,450
$48,400	—$101,000	. $6,292.50 plus 28%	—$48,400
$101,000	—$166,000	. $21,020.50 plus 31%	—$101,000
$166,000	—$292,900	. $41,170.50 plus 36%	—$166,000
$292,900	. . . . .	. $86,854.50 plus 39.6%	—$292,900

TABLE 8—DAILY or MISCELLANEOUS Payroll Period

(a) SINGLE person (including head of household)—

If the amount of wages (after subtracting withholding allowances) divided by the number of days in the payroll period is:		The amount of income tax to withhold per day is:
Not over $10.20		$0

Over—	But not over—		of excess over—
$10.20	—$107.10	. 15%	—$10.20
$107.10	—$230.40	. $14.54 plus 28%	—$107.10
$230.40	—$516.20	. $49.06 plus 31%	—$230.40
$516.20	—$1,115.20	. $137.66 plus 36%	—$516.20
$1,115.20	. . . . .	. $353.30 plus 39.6%	—$1,115.20

(b) MARRIED person—

If the amount of wages (after subtracting withholding allowances) divided by the number of days in the payroll period is:		The amount of income tax to withhold per day is:
Not over $24.80		$0

Over—	But not over—		of excess over—
$24.80	—$186.20	. 15%	—$24.80
$186.20	—$388.50	. $24.21 plus 28%	—$186.20
$388.50	—$638.50	. $80.85 plus 31%	—$388.50
$638.50	—$1,126.50	. $158.35 plus 36%	—$638.50
$1,126.50	. . . . .	. $334.03 plus 39.6%	—$1,126.50

PAYROLL IN ACTION

RULES FOR ROUNDING

Although it has provided no specific guidelines and confusion reigns on the methods for implementation, the U.S. Treasury Department encourages rounding to whole-dollar amounts. The income tax withholding amounts in the wage-bracket tables are already rounded. The percentage method allowance table lists the withholding allowances in dollars and cents, which should not be rounded. However, the wage amount after deducting the allowances should be rounded, as well as the tax computed from the percentage method tables.

The wage-bracket tables for advance EIC (earned income credit) payments are already rounded to whole-dollar amounts. Advance EIC payments calculated by the percentage method should likewise be rounded to the nearest dollar.

Consistent use of rounding is important. The rules are to round *up* any amounts of $.50 or more and round *down* any amounts less than $.50. For example, $4.50 is rounded to $5.00 and $4.49 is rounded to $4.00.

use one method for one group of employees and another method for a different group. However, for employees paid on a quarterly, semiannual, or annual basis, the percentage method is more appropriate because no wage-bracket tables are available for these pay periods. In addition, when wages exceed the amount shown in the last bracket of the wage-bracket tables, use of the percentage method becomes necessary.

The wage-bracket tables are suitable for up to ten allowances. If an employee claims more than ten allowances, the payroll clerk can use a combination of the wage-bracket and percentage methods. To adapt the wage-bracket method to employees with more than ten allowances, follow these steps, using as an example Clarence Davis, personnel interviewer at Jupiter Toys, who earns $680 per week, is married, and claims 12 withholding allowances:

1. Locate in Table 3-1 the allowance value for the number of withholding allowances *over ten* for the appropriate payroll period (two allowances for weekly period).

Allowance Value = $107.70

2. Subtract this amount from the employee's wages.

$680.00 − $107.70 = $572.30

3. Use the wage-bracket tables in Appendix A for the remaining wages with ten allowances.

Withholding for married, weekly, ten allowances = $0 per week

The employer does not have to use the combination method but can continue to withhold the amount shown in the wage-bracket tables for ten allowances. This practice is permissible, provided the employee does not object to having more withheld than may be necessary to meet the income tax liability.

Annualized Wages Method. Although the wage-bracket and percentage methods of withholding are the most popular methods, several other methods have found limited use. One of these is the **annualized wages method**. The percentage method is very adaptable to annualizing wages for withholding. This method allows for the same computation of rates, brackets, and allowances and is convenient when wages by period are the same or average out to a determinable amount. The steps to convert to an annual basis are as follows:

Annualized wages method *A federal income tax withholding method whereby the annual withholding tax is prorated over all payroll periods.*

1. Multiply the wages for a payroll period by the number of payroll periods in the calendar year to get the annualized wages.

2. Find the amount of withholding required on the annualized wages by using Table 7 in the percentage method withholding tables (Exhibit 3-4).

3. Divide the annual withholding amount by the payroll periods to find the amount of withholding for each period.

If Wilma Holden earns $366 a week, her annualized wages are $19,032 ($366 × 52). Using Table 3-1, we find that the value of two withholding allowances for an annual pay period is $5,600. Deducting this amount from the annual wages results in taxable wages of $13,432. Using Table 7 of Exhibit 3-4, the annual withholding tax is $1,617 [($13,432 − $2,650) × .15]. Dividing the tax amount by 52 yields a weekly withholding tax of $31.10, or $31.

Cumulative Wages Method. An employee may request, in writing, to have taxes withheld on cumulative wages. Part-time employees or those on irregular hours may make this request when the amounts withheld with the wage-bracket or percentage methods on widely varying wages are likely to exceed the employee's total tax liability. This method is valid if the type of payroll period (weekly, biweekly, etc.) for the employee has not changed since the beginning of the year. For **cumulative withholding**, the tax is computed as follows:

Cumulative withholding *A federal income tax withholding method whereby the current withholding amount is determined by cumulative wages and the amount that has already been withheld.*

1. Add the wages for the current payroll period to the total wages paid to the employee during the current calendar year.

2. Divide the cumulative wages by the total number of payroll periods represented to determine the average wages.

3. Using the percentage method, calculate the tax that would have been withheld on the average wages. Multiply the average tax amount by the total number of payroll periods represented.

4. Deduct from this amount the total tax already withheld during the calendar year. The excess (if any) is the amount to be withheld for the current payroll period.

EXAMPLE   Jerri Mayne, a Nioga computer programmer who is single with two withholding allowances, earned $512 during the current payroll period. She had previously earned $13,004 for 38 weeks, with a total of $1,050 withheld. Her cumulative wages are $13,516 ($13,004 + $512), and her average wages are $347 ($13,516 ÷ 39). Using Table 3-1 and Table 1 of Exhibit 3-4, the amount to be withheld is $28 ($347 − $107.70 = $239.30 = $239;

$239 − $51 = $188; $188 × .15 = $28.20 = $28). Multiplying the withholding amount by the number of payroll periods ($28 × 39) results in $1,092, the total amount to be withheld for the 39 weeks. After deducting the amount already withheld ($1,092 − $1,050), the amount to be withheld for the current period is determined to be $42.   ▲

Part-Year Employment Method. An employee who works only part of a year may request in writing that the employer use the part-year employment method. To be eligible for the part-year method, the employee must not have worked for more than 245 days during the calendar year including weekends, vacations, and sick days during the period of employment.

The steps to calculate withholding tax by the part-year method are as follows:

1. Add the wages for the current payroll period to the wages, if any, already paid to the employee.

2. Divide the cumulative wages by the total payroll periods for the year to date, including those periods the employee did not work.

3. Locate the tax on this amount in the wage-bracket tables, taking into account the payroll period, marital status, and withholding allowances.

4. Multiply that withholding tax amount by the total payroll periods for the year to date.

5. Deduct the tax already withheld from the total tax liability computed in step four. The excess (if any) is the amount to be withheld for the current payroll period.

EXAMPLE   Dan Frieberg worked the first 21 weeks in the year and earned $7,938. After a layoff of 13 weeks, he worked during week 35 and earned $522. Dividing the cumulative wages of $8,460 by the total payroll periods of 35 yields an average of $242 per week. Using the wage-bracket table from Appendix A (married, weekly, 2 withholding allowances) the amount to be withheld on this average is $2. This amount multiplied by the total payroll periods equals $70. Since the weekly withholdings for the previous 21 weeks totaled $441 ($21 × 21), the latest week's earnings do not require any withholding.   ▲

Nontaxable Fringe Benefits

Fringe benefits are generally taxable and require federal income tax withholding (FITW) and the payment of Social Security and Medicare taxes under the Federal Insurance Contributions Act (FICA) and also unemployment taxes under the Federal Unemployment Tax Act (FUTA). In certain situations, the Internal Revenue Code (Sec. 132) specifies exemptions from taxability, whether benefits are in cash or noncash form. These exemptions under Sec. 132 include:

• no-additional-cost services, e.g., free air trips by airline, free lodging by hotel

- qualified employee discounts—limited to gross margin percentage or 20% of the price for services offered to customers
- working condition fringe benefits, e.g., business use of company car or airplane, professional dues and subscriptions, job related education
- de minimis fringe benefits—insignificant benefits impractical to account for, e.g., occasional typing, telephone, or copier use
- qualified transportation fringe benefits—being a passenger in commuting highway vehicle, transit pass or tokens, on-premises parking, or parking allowance
- qualified moving expense reimbursement
- an on-the-premises gym or athletic facility

TAXABILITY OF OTHER BENEFITS

Certain employer-provided benefits may or may not be subject to FITW, FICA, and FUTA taxes. Let's examine several of the more complex of these benefits.

Noncash Fringe Benefits

Fringe benefits included as wages and provided in cash are subject to FITW, FICA, and FUTA taxes. If the fringe benefits are in a noncash form, special rules apply. These noncash fringe benefits include the use of cars, free or discounted company or commercial flights, vacations, discounts on property or services, memberships in country clubs, and tickets to entertainment or sporting events. In general, the amount included as wages is the amount by which the fair market value of the fringe benefit exceeds the sum of the amount paid by the employee and excluded by law. For example, if Nioga pays $5,500 for Michael Carson's membership in a country club, the full amount constitutes taxable wages. If Nioga pays only $4,000 and Michael the balance, then only $4,000 is taxable wages.

Meals and Lodging

Meals and other payments in kind are not subject to FITW, FICA, and FUTA taxes if furnished on the employer's premises and as a matter of convenience. Lodging furnished under the same conditions and as a condition of employment is also nontaxable. If the employer provides meals as additional compensation, they are taxable. Cash allowances for meals or lodging are taxable compensation.

Employee Business Expense Reimbursements

Payments made to employees for travel and other necessary business expenses are taxable wages if made according to a nonaccountable plan whereby the employee does not have to: (1) substantiate those expenses with receipts or other documentation; or (2) return, after a reasonable period, any unused amount of advance provided by the employer. Examples of nonaccountable plans include per diem and standard mileage plans where the employee receives a fixed rate for travel expenses.

In contrast to the nonaccountable plan, amounts paid under an accountable plan are not taxable wages and are exempt from FITW and payment of FICA and FUTA taxes, providing the reimbursements do not exceed specified government per diem or standard mileage rates. Amounts in excess of the specified rates become taxable wages with the same treatment as a nonaccountable plan and are subject to FITW, FICA, and FUTA taxes for the first payroll period after a reasonable time.

Moving Expenses

Reimbursed and employer-paid nonqualified moving expenses are taxable wages and subject to FITW and payment of FICA and FUTA taxes. Among the generally nondeductible expenses are pre-move house-hunting and temporary living expenses. On the other hand, reimbursed and employer-paid qualified moving expenses are not includible as wages unless the employer has knowledge that the employee deducted the expenses in a prior year, in which case the employer reports them as wages. These deductible moving expenses include transportation and storage of household goods and personal effects and travel and lodging (not meals) for expenses of moving from an old to a new home.

Sick Pay

Sick pay is any amount paid to an employee because of illness or injury under a plan with such benefits. Payments made to an employee under a sick pay or disability plan by the employer or a third party, such as an insurance company, are taxable wages and subject to FICA and FUTA taxes. Federal income tax withholding may be mandatory or voluntary, depending upon who pays the sick pay. The sick pay may be paid by 1) the employer, 2) the employer's agent (bears no insurance risk and is reimbursed by the employer), or 3) a third party that is not the employer's agent.

Sick pay paid by the employer or its agent is subject to mandatory FITW; sick pay paid by an agent is considered supplementary wages, and the agent may choose to withhold federal income tax at the flat rate of 28%; sick pay paid by a third party that is not the employer's agent is not subject to mandatory FITW. An employee may request the third party to withhold income tax by filing Form W-4S, Request for Federal Income Tax Withholding from sick pay. The third party must withhold the employee's portion of the FICA taxes and either pay the employer's portion or transfer the liability to the employer.

If the employee funded the plan with after-tax contributions, then the payments are not taxable wages. However, payments attributable to employee pre-tax contributions are taxable wages and may be subject to FITW, FICA, and FUTA taxes. Under plans where both the employer and employee share the cost, the taxable wages are the sick pay multiplied by the past three-year ratio of employer paid premiums to total premiums.

ADVANCE PAYMENT OF EARNED INCOME CREDIT

Earned income credit *A direct reduction in taxes for employees with incomes below a stipulated level.*

For certain low-income wage earners the federal government provides a subsidy known as the **earned income credit** (EIC). In 2000, workers with annual incomes of less than $27,413 were eligible to receive an earned income credit of up to $2,353 ($3,888 with more than one qualifying child. Employees without a qualifying child may claim an EIC of up to $353 but cannot get advance payments.)

The subsidy for the earned income credit takes two forms. One form represents a refund of the excess of the EIC over the tax liability. The other form is an outright payment to the employee not having income tax withheld. Employers must notify such employees that they may be eligible for the EIC by furnishing them with Copy C of Form W-2 or a copy of IRS Notice 797, "You May Be Eligible for a Refund on Your Federal Income Tax Return Because of the Earned Income Credit." However, employers do not have to notify employees who claim an exemption status from withholding on Form W-4 (rarely do such employees meet the other qualifications for the EIC).

Eligibility Requirements

Employees eligible for the earned income credit may either claim it on their annual federal tax returns or in advance payments during the year. Those who want it in advance must file Form W-5, Earned Income Credit Advance Payment Certificate, with their employer (Exhibit 3-5). Eligible employees who do not file Form W-5 will not receive advance EIC payments but they will still get the full benefit of the EIC on their annual tax returns. To be eligible for the advance EIC, the employee/taxpayer:

1. Expects to have earned income and modified adjusted gross income of less than $27,413.

2. Must, if married, file a joint return or a return as head of household.

3. Maintains a household with a qualifying child. A qualifying child is a son, daughter, adopted child, stepchild, foster child, or descendent. The child must be under age 19, a full-time student under age 24, or permanently and totally disabled and must live in the employee's household for more than 6 months (12 months if a foster child). Temporary absences for school, medical care, or vacation count toward the 6 or 12 months. Special rules apply to a married child claimed as a dependent and to a child of divorced or separated parents.

4. Cannot be a qualifying child of another person who is claiming the credit.

Computing the Advance Payment

A signed Form W-5 becomes effective with the first payroll period ending (or the first wage payment made without regard to a payroll period) on or after the date the employee gives the certificate to the employer; it remains in effect until the end of the calendar year. Eligible employees must

20 Form W-5

Instructions

A Change To Note

Beginning in 2000, new rules apply to determine who is a foster child for purposes of the earned income credit (EIC). See page 3 for details.

Purpose

Use Form W-5 if you are eligible to get part of the EIC in advance with your pay and choose to do so. See **Who Is Eligible To Get Advance EIC Payments?** below. The amount you can get in advance generally depends on your wages. If you are married, the amount of your advance EIC payments also depends on whether your spouse has filed a Form W-5 with his or her employer. However, your employer cannot give you more than $1,412 throughout 2000 with your pay. You will get the rest of any EIC you are entitled to when you file your tax return and claim the EIC.

If you do not choose to get advance payments, you can still claim the EIC on your 2000 tax return.

What Is the EIC?

The EIC is a credit for certain workers. It reduces the tax you owe. It may give you a refund even if you do not owe any tax.

Who Is Eligible To Get Advance EIC Payments?

You are eligible to get advance EIC payments if **all three** of the following apply.

1. You expect to have at least one qualifying child. If you do not expect to have a qualifying child, you may still be eligible for the EIC, but you **cannot** receive advance EIC payments. See **Who Is a Qualifying Child?** on page 2.

2. You expect that your 2000 earned income and modified AGI (adjusted gross income) will each be less than $27,413. Include your spouse's income if you plan to file a joint return. As used on this form, **earned income** does not include amounts inmates in penal institutions are paid for their work or workfare payments (defined on this page). For most people, **modified AGI** is the total of adjusted gross income plus any tax-exempt interest. But see the 1999 revision of **Pub. 596,** Earned Income Credit, for information about how to figure your 2000 modified AGI if you expect to receive nontaxable payments from a pension, annuity, or an IRA; or you plan to file a 2000 Form 1040.

3. You expect to be able to claim the EIC for 2000. To find out if you may be able to claim the EIC, answer the questions on page 2.

Workfare payments. These are cash payments certain people receive from a state or local agency that administers public assistance programs funded under the Federal Temporary Assistance for Needy Families (TANF) program in return for certain work activities such as **(1)** work experience activities (including work associated with remodeling or repairing publicly assisted housing) if sufficient private sector employment is not available, or **(2)** community service program activities.

How To Get Advance EIC Payments

If you are eligible to get advance EIC payments, fill in the 2000 Form W-5 at the bottom of this page. Then, detach it and give it to your employer. If you get advance payments, you **must** file a 2000 Federal income tax return.

You may have only **one** Form W-5 in effect at one time. If you and your spouse are both employed, you should file separate Forms W-5.

(Continued on page 2)

▼ *Give the lower part to your employer; keep the top part for your records.* ▼

-- Detach here --

Form **W-5**	**Earned Income Credit Advance Payment Certificate**	OMB No. 1545-1342
Department of the Treasury Internal Revenue Service	▶ **Use the current year's certificate only.** ▶ **Give this certificate to your employer.** ▶ **This certificate expires on December 31, 2000.**	20

Print or type your full name	Your social security number

Note: *If you get advance payments of the earned income credit for 2000, you **must** file a 2000 Federal income tax return. To get advance payments, you **must** have a qualifying child and your filing status must be any status **except** married filing a separate return.*

		Yes	No
1	I expect to be able to claim the earned income credit for 2000, I do not have another Form W-5 in effect with any other current employer, and I choose to get advance EIC payments		
2	Do you expect to have a qualifying child?		
3	Are you married?		
4	If you are married, does your spouse have a Form W-5 in effect for 2000 with any employer?		

Under penalties of perjury, I declare that the information I have furnished above is, to the best of my knowledge, true, correct, and complete.

Signature ▶   Date ▶

Cat. No. 10227P

EXHIBIT 3-5   Form W-5, Earned Income Credit Advance Payment Certificate

Questions To See if You May Be Able To Claim the EIC for 20XX

⚠ You **cannot** claim the EIC if you plan to file either **Form 2555** or **Form 2555-EZ** (relating to foreign earned income) for 2000. You also **cannot** claim the EIC if you are a nonresident alien for any part of 2000 unless you are married to a U.S. citizen or resident and elect to be taxed as a resident alien for all of 2000.

1   Do you expect to have a qualifying child? Read **Who Is a Qualifying Child?** that starts below before you answer this question. If the child is married, be sure you also read **Married child** on page 3.

☐ **No.** (STOP) You may be able to claim the EIC but you **cannot** get advance EIC payments.

☐ **Yes.** *Continue.*

⚠ If the child meets the conditions to be a qualifying child for both you and another person, you can treat the child as your qualifying child only if you expect your 2000 modified AGI to be **higher** than the other person's modified AGI. If the other person is your spouse and you expect to file a joint return for 2000, this rule does not apply.

2   Do you expect your 2000 filing status to be married filing a separate return?

☐ **Yes.** (STOP) You **cannot** claim the EIC.

☐ **No.** *Continue.*

(TIP) If you expect to file a joint return for 2000, include your spouse's income when answering questions 3 and 4.

3   Do you expect that your 2000 earned income and modified AGI (see page 1) will each be less than: $27,413 if you expect to have 1 qualifying child; $31,152 if you expect to have 2 or more qualifying children?

☐ **No.** (STOP) You **cannot** claim the EIC.

☐ **Yes.** *Continue.* But remember, you **cannot** get advance EIC payments if you expect your 2000 earned income or modified AGI will be $27,413 or more.

4   Do you expect that your 2000 investment income will be more than $2,400? For most people, investment income is the total of their taxable interest and dividends and tax-exempt interest. However, if you plan to file a 2000 Form 1040, see the 1999 Form 1040 instructions to figure your investment income.

☐ **Yes.** (STOP) You **cannot** claim the EIC.

☐ **No.** *Continue.*

5   Do you expect that you, or your spouse if filing a joint return, will be a qualifying child of another person for 2000?
☐ **No.** You may be able to claim the EIC.
☐ **Yes.** You **cannot** claim the EIC.

This Form W-5 expires on December 31, 2000. If you are eligible to get advance EIC payments for 2001, you must file a new Form W-5 next year.

(TIP) You may be able to get a larger credit when you file your 2000 return. For details, see **Additional Credit** on page 3.

Who Is a Qualifying Child?

Any child who meets **all three** of the following conditions is a **qualifying child.**

1. The child is your son, daughter, adopted child, grandchild, stepchild, or foster child.

file a new certificate each year. If an employee has given the employer a signed Form W-5 and later becomes ineligible for the EIC, the employee must revoke the previously filed form within ten days. Marital status and whether or not a spouse receives the earned income credit are important factors in determining the amount of the advance EIC. If the employee's spouse files a Form W-5, the employee must file a new Form W-5. If the spouse's form is no longer in effect, the employee must file a new Form W-5 and certify that the spouse no longer has a Form W-5 in effect.

Reportable wages must include the advance EIC payment to eligible employees who have filed Form W-5. For purposes of the advance EIC payment, wages means amounts subject to income tax withholding, even for those employees who have claimed the exemption from income tax withholding on Form W-4. For household employees, wages means amounts subject to Social Security and Medicare taxes.

To determine the amount of the advance payment, the payroll clerk must take into account (1) wages paid, including tips reported, and (2) whether a married employee's spouse has a Form W-5 in effect with an employer. Use of the appropriate advance EIC payment tables (found in Circular E) gives the exact amount of the credit. Exhibits 3-6 and 3-7 show the advance EIC tables for the wage-bracket and the percentage methods.

EXAMPLE   Helen Moran is single, earns $263.00 a week at Wright's Furniture Store, and is eligible for the advance earned income credit. Using the percentage method tables, her advance EIC is $25.18 weekly ($263.00 − $244.00 = $19.00; $19.00 × .09588 = $1.82; $27.00 − $1.82 = $25.18).   ▲

Making the Advance Payment

The advance EIC payment does not change the amount of federal income, Social Security, or Medicare taxes that the employer withholds from an employee's wages. Advance EIC payments are not subject to payroll taxes because they are not compensation for services rendered.

Generally, employers deduct the amount of the advance EIC payments from the amounts withheld for federal income, Social Security, and Medicare taxes that are periodically paid to the IRS. If for any payroll period the advance EIC payments are more than the total withheld for federal income, Social Security, and Medicare taxes (including the employer's share of Social Security and Medicare taxes), the employer may:

1. Reduce each advance EIC payment by an amount that has the same ratio to the excess as the payment has to the total EIC payments for the payroll period, or

2. Make a full payment of the advance EIC amount and have this full payment be treated as an advance payment of the employer's tax liability. If the employer applies excess EIC payments against any other taxes, an explanation must be added to that tax return on which the employer took the overpayment as a credit.

Tables for Wage Bracket Method of Advance EIC Payments (For Wages Paid in 20XX)

WEEKLY Payroll Period

SINGLE or MARRIED Without Spouse Filing Certificate

Wages— At least	But less than	Payment to be made	Wages— At least	But less than	Payment to be made	Wages— At least	But less than	Payment to be made	Wages— At least	But less than	Payment to be made
$0	$5	$0	$75	$80	$15	$270	$280	$24	$420	$430	$9
5	10	1	80	85	16	280	290	23	430	440	8
10	15	2	85	90	17	290	300	22	440	450	7
15	20	3	90	95	18	300	310	21	450	460	6
20	25	4	95	100	19	310	320	20	460	470	5
25	30	5	100	105	20	320	330	19	470	480	5
30	35	6	105	110	21	330	340	18	480	490	4
35	40	7	110	115	22	340	350	17	490	500	3
40	45	8	115	120	23	350	360	16	500	510	2
45	50	9	120	125	24	360	370	15	510	520	1
50	55	10	125	130	26	370	380	14	520	- - -	0
55	60	11	130	240	27	380	390	13			
60	65	12	240	250	27	390	400	12			
65	70	13	250	260	26	400	410	11			
70	75	14	260	270	25	410	420	10			

MARRIED With Both Spouses Filing Certificate

Wages— At least	But less than	Payment to be made	Wages— At least	But less than	Payment to be made	Wages— At least	But less than	Payment to be made	Wages— At least	But less than	Payment to be made
$0	$5	$0	$35	$40	$7	$120	$130	$13	$190	$200	$6
5	10	1	40	45	8	130	140	12	200	210	5
10	15	2	45	50	9	140	150	11	210	220	4
15	20	3	50	55	10	150	160	10	220	230	3
20	25	4	55	60	11	160	170	9	230	240	2
25	30	5	60	65	12	170	180	8	240	250	1
30	35	6	65	120	13	180	190	7	250	- - -	0

BIWEEKLY Payroll Period

SINGLE or MARRIED Without Spouse Filing Certificate

Wages— At least	But less than	Payment to be made	Wages— At least	But less than	Payment to be made	Wages— At least	But less than	Payment to be made	Wages— At least	But less than	Payment to be made
$0	$5	$0	$140	$145	$29	$505	$515	$52	$785	$795	$25
5	10	1	145	150	30	515	525	51	795	805	24
10	15	2	150	155	31	525	535	50	805	815	23
15	20	3	155	160	32	535	545	49	815	825	22
20	25	4	160	165	33	545	555	48	825	835	21
25	30	5	165	170	34	555	565	47	835	845	20
30	35	6	170	175	35	565	575	46	845	855	19
35	40	7	175	180	36	575	585	45	855	865	18
40	45	8	180	185	37	585	595	44	865	875	17
45	50	9	185	190	38	595	605	43	875	885	16
50	55	10	190	195	39	605	615	42	885	895	15
55	60	11	195	200	40	615	625	41	895	905	14
60	65	12	200	205	41	625	635	40	905	915	13
65	70	13	205	210	42	635	645	39	915	925	12
70	75	14	210	215	43	645	655	38	925	935	11
75	80	15	215	220	44	655	665	37	935	945	10
80	85	16	220	225	45	665	675	36	945	955	10
85	90	17	225	230	46	675	685	35	955	965	9
90	95	18	230	235	47	685	695	34	965	975	8
95	100	19	235	240	48	695	705	34	975	985	7
100	105	20	240	245	49	705	715	33	985	995	6
105	110	21	245	250	50	715	725	32	995	1,005	5
110	115	22	250	255	51	725	735	31	1,005	1,015	4
115	120	23	255	260	52	735	745	30	1,015	1,025	3
120	125	24	260	265	53	745	755	29	1,025	1,035	2
125	130	26	265	485	54	755	765	28	1,035	1,045	1
130	135	27	485	495	54	765	775	27	1,045	- - -	0
135	140	28	495	505	53	775	785	26			

EXHIBIT 3-6 Tables for Wage-Bracket Method of Advance EIC Payments

(Exhibit continues.)

81

BIWEEKLY Payroll Period

MARRIED With Both Spouses Filing Certificate

Wages—At least	But less than	Payment to be made	Wages—At least	But less than	Payment to be made	Wages—At least	But less than	Payment to be made	Wages—At least	But less than	Payment to be made
$0	$5	$0	$70	$75	$14	$250	$260	$26	$390	$400	$12
5	10	1	75	80	15	260	270	25	400	410	11
10	15	2	80	85	16	270	280	24	410	420	10
15	20	3	85	90	17	280	290	23	420	430	9
20	25	4	90	95	18	290	300	22	430	440	8
25	30	5	95	100	19	300	310	21	440	450	7
30	35	6	100	105	20	310	320	20	450	460	6
35	40	7	105	110	21	320	330	19	460	470	5
40	45	8	110	115	22	330	340	18	470	480	5
45	50	9	115	120	23	340	350	17	480	490	4
50	55	10	120	125	24	350	360	16	490	500	3
55	60	11	125	130	26	360	370	15	500	510	2
60	65	12	130	240	27	370	380	14	510	520	1
65	70	13	240		27	380	390	13	520	- - -	0

SEMIMONTHLY Payroll Period

SINGLE or MARRIED Without Spouse Filing Certificate

Wages—At least	But less than	Payment to be made	Wages—At least	But less than	Payment to be made	Wages—At least	But less than	Payment to be made	Wages—At least	But less than	Payment to be made
$0	$5	$0	$150	$155	$31	$545	$555	$56	$845	$855	$28
5	10	1	155	160	32	555	565	55	855	865	27
10	15	2	160	165	33	565	575	54	865	875	26
15	20	3	165	170	34	575	585	53	875	885	25
20	25	4	170	175	35	585	595	52	885	895	24
25	30	5	175	180	36	595	605	52	895	905	23
30	35	6	180	185	37	605	615	51	905	915	22
35	40	7	185	190	38	615	625	50	915	925	21
40	45	8	190	195	39	625	635	49	925	935	20
45	50	9	195	200	40	635	645	48	935	945	19
50	55	10	200	205	41	645	655	47	945	955	18
55	60	11	205	210	42	655	665	46	955	965	17
60	65	12	210	215	43	665	675	45	965	975	16
65	70	13	215	220	44	675	685	44	975	985	15
70	75	14	220	225	45	685	695	43	985	995	14
75	80	15	225	230	46	695	705	42	995	1,005	13
80	85	16	230	235	47	705	715	41	1,005	1,015	12
85	90	17	235	240	48	715	725	40	1,015	1,025	11
90	95	18	240	245	49	725	735	39	1,025	1,035	10
95	100	19	245	250	50	735	745	38	1,035	1,045	9
100	105	20	250	255	51	745	755	37	1,045	1,055	8
105	110	21	255	260	52	755	765	36	1,055	1,065	7
110	115	22	260	265	53	765	775	35	1,065	1,075	6
115	120	23	265	270	54	775	785	34	1,075	1,085	6
120	125	24	270	275	55	785	795	33	1,085	1,095	5
125	130	26	275	280	56	795	805	32	1,095	1,105	4
130	135	27	280	285	57	805	815	31	1,105	1,115	3
135	140	28	285	525	58	815	825	30	1,115	1,125	2
140	145	29	525	535	58	825	835	29	1,125	1,135	1
145	150	30	535	545	57	835	845	29	1,135	- - -	0

MARRIED With Both Spouses Filing Certificate

Wages—At least	But less than	Payment to be made	Wages—At least	But less than	Payment to be made	Wages—At least	But less than	Payment to be made	Wages—At least	But less than	Payment to be made
$0	$5	$0	$45	$50	$9	$90	$95	$18	$135	$140	$28
5	10	1	50	55	10	95	100	19	140	260	29
10	15	2	55	60	11	100	105	20	260	270	29
15	20	3	60	65	12	105	110	21	270	280	28
20	25	4	65	70	13	110	115	22	280	290	27
25	30	5	70	75	14	115	120	23	290	300	26
30	35	6	75	80	15	120	125	24	300	310	25
35	40	7	80	85	16	125	130	26	310	320	24
40	45	8	85	90	17	130	135	27	320	330	23

(continued on next page)

EXHIBIT 3-6   Tables for Wage-Bracket Method of Advance EIC Payments (*cont.*)

SEMIMONTHLY Payroll Period

MARRIED With Both Spouses Filing Certificate

Wages— At least	But less than	Payment to be made	Wages— At least	But less than	Payment to be made	Wages— At least	But less than	Payment to be made	Wages— At least	But less than	Payment to be made
$330	$340	$22	$390	$400	$16	$450	$460	$11	$510	$520	$5
340	350	21	400	410	15	460	470	10	520	530	4
350	360	20	410	420	14	470	480	9	530	540	3
360	370	19	420	430	14	480	490	8	540	550	2
370	380	18	430	440	13	490	500	7	550	560	1
380	390	17	440	450	12	500	510	6	560	- - -	0

MONTHLY Payroll Period

SINGLE or MARRIED Without Spouse Filing Certificate

Wages— At least	But less than	Payment to be made	Wages— At least	But less than	Payment to be made	Wages— At least	But less than	Payment to be made	Wages— At least	But less than	Payment to be made
$0	$5	$0	$250	$255	$51	$500	$505	$102	$1,395	$1,405	$84
5	10	1	255	260	52	505	510	103	1,405	1,415	83
10	15	2	260	265	53	510	515	104	1,415	1,425	82
15	20	3	265	270	54	515	520	105	1,425	1,435	81
20	25	4	270	275	55	520	525	106	1,435	1,445	81
25	30	5	275	280	56	525	530	107	1,445	1,455	80
30	35	6	280	285	57	530	535	108	1,455	1,465	79
35	40	7	285	290	58	535	540	109	1,465	1,475	78
40	45	8	290	295	59	540	545	110	1,475	1,485	77
45	50	9	295	300	60	545	550	111	1,485	1,495	76
50	55	10	300	305	61	550	555	112	1,495	1,505	75
55	60	11	305	310	62	555	560	113	1,505	1,515	74
60	65	12	310	315	63	560	565	114	1,515	1,525	73
65	70	13	315	320	64	565	570	115	1,525	1,535	72
70	75	14	320	325	65	570	575	116	1,535	1,545	71
75	80	15	325	330	66	575	1,055	117	1,545	1,555	70
80	85	16	330	335	67	1,055	1,065	117	1,555	1,565	69
85	90	17	335	340	68	1,065	1,075	116	1,565	1,575	68
90	95	18	340	345	69	1,075	1,085	115	1,575	1,585	67
95	100	19	345	350	70	1,085	1,095	114	1,585	1,595	66
100	105	20	350	355	71	1,095	1,105	113	1,595	1,605	65
105	110	21	355	360	72	1,105	1,115	112	1,605	1,615	64
110	115	22	360	365	73	1,115	1,125	111	1,615	1,625	63
115	120	23	365	370	74	1,125	1,135	110	1,625	1,635	62
120	125	24	370	375	75	1,135	1,145	109	1,635	1,645	61
125	130	26	375	380	77	1,145	1,155	108	1,645	1,655	60
130	135	27	380	385	78	1,155	1,165	107	1,655	1,665	59
135	140	28	385	390	79	1,165	1,175	106	1,665	1,675	58
140	145	29	390	395	80	1,175	1,185	105	1,675	1,685	58
145	150	30	395	400	81	1,185	1,195	104	1,685	1,695	57
150	155	31	400	405	82	1,195	1,205	104	1,695	1,705	56
155	160	32	405	410	83	1,205	1,215	103	1,705	1,715	55
160	165	33	410	415	84	1,215	1,225	102	1,715	1,725	54
165	170	34	415	420	85	1,225	1,235	101	1,725	1,735	53
170	175	35	420	425	86	1,235	1,245	100	1,735	1,745	52
175	180	36	425	430	87	1,245	1,255	99	1,745	1,755	51
180	185	37	430	435	88	1,255	1,265	98	1,755	1,765	50
185	190	38	435	440	89	1,265	1,275	97	1,765	1,775	49
190	195	39	440	445	90	1,275	1,285	96	1,775	1,785	48
195	200	40	445	450	91	1,285	1,295	95	1,785	1,795	47
200	205	41	450	455	92	1,295	1,305	94	1,795	1,805	46
205	210	42	455	460	93	1,305	1,315	93	1,805	1,815	45
210	215	43	460	465	94	1,315	1,325	92	1,815	1,825	44
215	220	44	465	470	95	1,325	1,335	91	1,825	1,835	43
220	225	45	470	475	96	1,335	1,345	90	1,835	1,845	42
225	230	46	475	480	97	1,345	1,355	89	1,845	1,855	41
230	235	47	480	485	98	1,355	1,365	88	1,855	1,865	40
235	240	48	485	490	99	1,365	1,375	87	1,865	1,875	39
240	245	49	490	495	100	1,375	1,385	86	1,875	1,885	38
245	250	50	495	500	101	1,385	1,395	85	1,885	1,895	37

(continued on next page)

(Exhibit continues.)

MONTHLY Payroll Period

SINGLE or MARRIED Without Spouse Filing Certificate

At least	But less than	Payment to be made	At least	But less than	Payment to be made	At least	But less than	Payment to be made	At least	But less than	Payment to be made
$1,895	$1,905	$36	$1,995	$2,005	$27	$2,095	$2,105	$17	$2,195	$2,205	$8
1,905	1,915	35	2,005	2,015	26	2,105	2,115	16	2,205	2,215	7
1,915	1,925	34	2,015	2,025	25	2,115	2,125	15	2,215	2,225	6
1,925	1,935	34	2,025	2,035	24	2,125	2,135	14	2,225	2,235	5
1,935	1,945	33	2,035	2,045	23	2,135	2,145	13	2,235	2,245	4
1,945	1,955	32	2,045	2,055	22	2,145	2,155	12	2,245	2,255	3
1,955	1,965	31	2,055	2,065	21	2,155	2,165	11	2,255	2,265	2
1,965	1,975	30	2,065	2,075	20	2,165	2,175	11	2,265	2,275	1
1,975	1,985	29	2,075	2,085	19	2,175	2,185	10	2,275	- - -	0
1,985	1,995	28	2,085	2,095	18	2,185	2,195	9			

MARRIED With Both Spouses Filing Certificate

At least	But less than	Payment to be made	At least	But less than	Payment to be made	At least	But less than	Payment to be made	At least	But less than	Payment to be made
$0	$5	$0	$150	$155	$31	$545	$555	$56	$845	$855	$28
5	10	1	155	160	32	555	565	55	855	865	27
10	15	2	160	165	33	565	575	54	865	875	26
15	20	3	165	170	34	575	585	53	875	885	25
20	25	4	170	175	35	585	595	52	885	895	24
25	30	5	175	180	36	595	605	52	895	905	23
30	35	6	180	185	37	605	615	51	905	915	22
35	40	7	185	190	38	615	625	50	915	925	21
40	45	8	190	195	39	625	635	49	925	935	20
45	50	9	195	200	40	635	645	48	935	945	19
50	55	10	200	205	41	645	655	47	945	955	18
55	60	11	205	210	42	655	665	46	955	965	17
60	65	12	210	215	43	665	675	45	965	975	16
65	70	13	215	220	44	675	685	44	975	985	15
70	75	14	220	225	45	685	695	43	985	995	14
75	80	15	225	230	46	695	705	42	995	1,005	13
80	85	16	230	235	47	705	715	41	1,005	1,015	12
85	90	17	235	240	48	715	725	40	1,015	1,025	11
90	95	18	240	245	49	725	735	39	1,025	1,035	10
95	100	19	245	250	50	735	745	38	1,035	1,045	9
100	105	20	250	255	51	745	755	37	1,045	1,055	8
105	110	21	255	260	52	755	765	36	1,055	1,065	7
110	115	22	260	265	53	765	775	35	1,065	1,075	6
115	120	23	265	270	54	775	785	34	1,075	1,085	6
120	125	24	270	275	55	785	795	33	1,085	1,095	5
125	130	26	275	280	56	795	805	32	1,095	1,105	4
130	135	27	280	285	57	805	815	31	1,105	1,115	3
135	140	28	285	525	58	815	825	30	1,115	1,125	2
140	145	29	525	535	58	825	835	29	1,125	1,135	1
145	150	30	535	545	57	835	845	29	1,135	- - -	0

DAILY Payroll Period

SINGLE or MARRIED Without Spouse Filing Certificate

At least	But less than	Payment to be made	At least	But less than	Payment to be made	At least	But less than	Payment to be made	At least	But less than	Payment to be made
$0	$5	$0	$15	$20	$3	$45	$55	$5	$75	$85	$2
5	10	1	20	25	4	55	65	4	85	95	1
10	15	2	25	45	5	65	75	3	95	- - -	0

MARRIED With Both Spouses Filing Certificate

At least	But less than	Payment to be made	At least	But less than	Payment to be made	At least	But less than	Payment to be made	At least	But less than	Payment to be made
$0	$5	$0	$10	$20	$2	$30	$40	$1	$40	- - -	$0
5	10	1	20	30	2						

EXHIBIT 3-6 Tables for Wage-Bracket Method of Advance EIC Payments (*cont.*)

Tables for Percentage Method of Advance EIC Payments
(For Wages Paid in 20XX)

Table 1. WEEKLY Payroll Period

(a) SINGLE or MARRIED Without Spouse Filing Certificate

If the amount of wages (before deducting withholding allowances) is:		The amount of payment to be made is:
Over—	But not over—	
$0	$133 . . .	20.40% of wages
$133	$244 . . .	$27
$244	. . . . .	$27 less 9.588% of wages in excess of $244

(b) MARRIED With Both Spouses Filing Certificate

If the amount of wages (before deducting withholding allowances) is:		The amount of payment to be made is:
Over—	But not over—	
$0	$66 . .	20.40% of wages
$66	$122 . .	$13
$122	. . . .	$13 less 9.588% of wages in excess of $122

Table 2. BIWEEKLY Payroll Period

(a) SINGLE or MARRIED Without Spouse Filing Certificate

If the amount of wages (before deducting withholding allowances) is:		The amount of payment to be made is:
Over—	But not over—	
$0	$266 . . .	20.40% of wages
$266	$488 . . .	$54
$488	. . . . .	$54 less 9.588% of wages in excess of $488

(b) MARRIED With Both Spouses Filing Certificate

If the amount of wages (before deducting withholding allowances) is:		The amount of payment to be made is:
Over—	But not over—	
$0	$133 . .	20.40% of wages
$133	$244 . .	$27
$244	. . . .	$27 less 9.588% of wages in excess of $244

Table 3. SEMIMONTHLY Payroll Period

(a) SINGLE or MARRIED Without Spouse Filing Certificate

If the amount of wages (before deducting withholding allowances) is:		The amount of payment to be made is:
Over—	But not over—	
$0	$288 . . .	20.40% of wages
$288	$528 . . .	$59
$528	. . . . .	$59 less 9.588% of wages in excess of $528

(b) MARRIED With Both Spouses Filing Certificate

If the amount of wages (before deducting withholding allowances) is:		The amount of payment to be made is:
Over—	But not over—	
$0	$144 . .	20.40% of wages
$144	$264 . .	$29
$264	. . . .	$29 less 9.588% of wages in excess of $264

Table 4. MONTHLY Payroll Period

(a) SINGLE or MARRIED Without Spouse Filing Certificate

If the amount of wages (before deducting withholding allowances) is:		The amount of payment to be made is:
Over—	But not over—	
$0	$576 . .	20.40% of wages
$576	$1,057 . .	$118
$1,057	. . . . .	$118 less 9.588% of wages in excess of $1,057

(b) MARRIED With Both Spouses Filing Certificate

If the amount of wages (before deducting withholding allowances) is:		The amount of payment to be made is:
Over—	But not over—	
$0	$288 . .	20.40% of wages
$288	$528 . .	$59
$528	. . . .	$59 less 9.588% of wages in excess of $528

EXHIBIT 3-7 Tables for Percentage Method of Advance EIC Payments

(Exhibit continues.)

Tables for Percentage Method of Advance EIC Payments (Continued)
(For Wages Paid in 20XX)

Table 5. QUARTERLY Payroll Period

(a) SINGLE or MARRIED Without Spouse Filing Certificate

If the amount of wages (before deducting withholding allowances) is:

The amount of payment to be made is:

Over—	But not over—	
$0	$1,730	20.40% of wages
$1,730	$3,172	$353
$3,172	. . . .	$353 less 9.588% of wages in excess of $3,172

(b) MARRIED With Both Spouses Filing Certificate

If the amount of wages (before deducting withholding allowances) is:

The amount of payment to be made is:

Over—	But not over—	
$0	$865	20.40% of wages
$865	$1,586	$176
$1,586	. . . .	$176 less 9.588% of wages in excess of $1,586

Table 6. SEMIANNUAL Payroll Period

(a) SINGLE or MARRIED Without Spouse Filing Certificate

Over—	But not over—	
$0	$3,460	20.40% of wages
$3,460	$6,345	$706
$6,345	. . . .	$706 less 9.588% of wages in excess of $6,345

(b) MARRIED With Both Spouses Filing Certificate

Over—	But not over—	
$0	$1,730	20.40% of wages
$1,730	$3,172	$353
$3,172	. . . .	$353 less 9.588% of wages in excess of $3,172

Table 7. ANNUAL Payroll Period

(a) SINGLE or MARRIED Without Spouse Filing Certificate

Over—	But not over—	
$0	$6,920	20.40% of wages
$6,920	$12,690	$1,412
$12,690	. . . .	$1,412 less 9.588% of wages in excess of $12,690

(b) MARRIED With Both Spouses Filing Certificate

Over—	But not over—	
$0	$3,460	20.40% of wages
$3,460	$6,345	$706
$6,345	. . . .	$706 less 9.588% of wages in excess of $6,345

Table 8. DAILY or MISCELLANEOUS Payroll Period

(a) SINGLE or MARRIED Without Spouse Filing Certificate

If the wages divided by the number of days in such period (before deducting withholding allowances) are:

The amount of payment to be made is the following amount multiplied by the number of days in such period:

Over—	But not over—	
$0	$26	20.40% of wages
$26	$48	$5
$48	. . . .	$5 less 9.588% of wages in excess of $48

(b) MARRIED With Both Spouses Filing Certificate

Over—	But not over—	
$0	$13	20.40% of wages
$13	$24	$3
$24	. . . .	$3 less 9.588% of wages in excess of $24

EXHIBIT 3-7   Tables for Percentage Method of Advance EIC Payment (cont.)

Employer's Returns and Penalties

As stated earlier, the amount of the advance EIC payment does not change the amount that the employer withholds from employee's pay for federal income, Social Security, and Medicare taxes. On the employer's tax return (Form 941), the advance EIC payments are treated as having been made from amounts withheld as income tax, employee Social Security tax, and employee Medicare taxes. For deposit purposes, the employer treats the date of an advance EIC payment to an employee as the date of the tax deposit made with the IRS. A similar treatment applies to advance EIC payments also reported on employment tax return Form 943.

The employer must make advance EIC payments to employees who correctly fill out Form W-5. Failure to make such payments subjects the employer to a penalty equal to the amount of the advance EIC payment not made. In addition, the employer must report the total amount of advance EIC payments made during the year on the employee's Form W-2.

WITHHOLDING STATE AND LOCAL INCOME TAXES

Over forty states levy income taxes, and most of these states require the employer to deduct the taxes from employee earnings on a periodic basis. Several metropolitan areas also require the withholding of city income taxes. When these requirements are in effect, the employer determines the withholding amounts by using methods similar to those used for the federal income tax.

Some states provide withholding tables similar to the federal withholding tables. Most businesses use the wage-bracket or percentage withholding methods and base the withholding on the wages earned, marital status, number of allowances claimed, and the payroll period (weekly, biweekly, semimonthly, monthly, and miscellaneous). Many states also allow the use of alternative withholding methods (such as annualizing) that are allowed by the federal government. However, not all states follow the federal guidelines completely. The payroll department of any company must understand clearly the particular rules and regulations involved in payroll deductions for the states or localities in which they do business.

The rules and regulations of New York state are similar to those of the federal government and several other states. New York has its own withholding certificate, Form IT-2104, which employees are not required to fill out. When employees do not file Form IT-2104, the employer follows the federal Form W-4 information—with one exception. The Form IT-2104 does not permit allowances for an employee and spouse, because the income tax tables take into account these exemptions.

Employees may want to file Form IT-2104 because the allowances claimed on this form may differ from those on Form W-4; deductions and credits allowable by one government may not be the same ones allowable by another. Also, unlike the federal rules, each working spouse should file a separate Form IT-2104. Even though each spouse will have an allowance, the couple's withholdings will better match their tax liability if the higher-wage-earning spouse claims all of the couple's allowances and the lower-wage-earning spouse claims no allowances.

The two most commonly used withholding methods in New York state are the wage-bracket and the exact calculation methods, both of which are similar to the federal withholding methods.

Wage-Bracket Method

This method is similar to the method described in *Circular E,* although New York State has its own withholding tables. The employee's marital status and the payroll period determine the table to use. The number of exemptions and wages are used to locate the correct bracket and the applicable tax.

Exact Calculation Method

This method is similar to the percentage method for federal withholding and follows the computation procedure for the state income tax return. Under this method, the tax withheld is the sum of the given accumulated tax for all lower tax brackets and the product of a given percentage multiplied by the portion of wages (after deductions and exemptions) that falls within a wage bracket.

REVIEW QUESTIONS

3–1. Besides wages, what other forms of income are subject to withholding taxes?

3–2. For what forms of payroll taxes is the employer generally liable?

3–3. What is the purpose of the Form W-4?

3–4. List several events for which the employee *may* want to file a new Form W-4 and identify those for which the employee *must* file a new Form W-4.

3–5. For withholding purposes, under what conditions can an employee claim married status if her or his spouse has died?

3–6. What factors affect the number of allowances an employee can claim?

3–7. Under what circumstances would an employer send a copy of the employee's Form W-4 to the Internal Revenue Service for verification?

3–8. When may an employee be exempt from income tax withholding? Name two categories of employees most likely to be eligible for such an exemption.

3–9. What is the simplest and most widely used method of determining the deduction for federal income tax? Explain how this method works.

3–10. Explain briefly the use of the percentage method of income tax withholding.

3–11. Name three alternative methods of computing income tax withholding.

3–12. What is the maximum number of working days permitted under the part-year employment method?

3–13. How is withholding by the part-year method figured?

3–14. Under what circumstances may an employee want to use the cumulative wages method of withholding?

3–15. If the employer makes sick pay payments to employees or pays the insurance company, what taxes must be withheld?

3–16. If the third-party payer is an insurance company, under what condition would it withhold federal income taxes and FICA taxes in sick pay?

3–17. What are the bases of withholding on noncash fringe benefits?

3–18. Describe a nonaccountable expense plan. Does the employee have any tax liability under such a plan?

3–19. What are the eligibility requirements for the advance payment of the earned income credit?

3–20. How does the employer pay the amount of the advance EIC?

DISCUSSION QUESTIONS

3–1. As a stimulant to the economy in times of recession, the government has sometimes advocated changing the income tax withholding tables to decrease the taxes withheld and provide a corresponding increase in employees' take-home pay. As an employee, would you favor this approach? If you disapprove, what can you do about it as an individual? Do you think decreasing income tax withholding might be effective as a short- or long-term economic stimulus?

3–2. Currently, an employee completes a Form W-4 to determine the number of allowances for income tax withholding. These allowances take into account the so-called exemptions to which a taxpayer may be entitled and other factors. Many complain, however, that their withholdings are not close enough to their actual tax liability. What factors may cause this situation to occur? Can you think of a better method for matching income tax withholding to the actual tax liability?

3–3. The flat-tax approach to income taxes is periodically revived and discussed. In its simplest form, this proposal would tax all wages and other forms of income at the same rate. Would this proposal simplify income tax withholding?

3–4. The special withholding rules complicate some of the procedures for withholding. One of the more difficult areas to understand is the taxability of reimbursed expenses. As an employer, would you favor an accountable or nonaccountable reimbursement plan? Why? As an employee, what would be your position? Why?

EXERCISES

3–1. Joanne Klein, the receptionist at Nioga, is single and claims two withholding allowances. Last week she earned $293. Compute her income tax withholding using the

    a. wage-bracket method. $ _____

    b. percentage method. $ _____

3–2. Sallie Foster, the personnel manager at Nioga, is married and claims one withholding allowance. During the last week, she earned $450. Compute Sallie's income tax withholding using the

    a. wage-bracket method. $ _____

    b. percentage method. $ _____

3–3. Michael Carson, a sales manager at Nioga, is married and claims four withholding allowances. During the last month he earned $2,200. Compute his income tax withholding using the

    a. wage-bracket method. $ _____

    b. percentage method. $ _____

3–4. Joe Grady, a Nioga sales analyst, is married and claims two withholding allowances. During the last biweekly period, he earned $860. Compute the income tax withholding using the

    a. wage-bracket method. $ _____

    b. percentage method. $ _____

3–5. Penny Seaver, an institutional salesperson with Nioga, receives a yearly salary of $40,000. Penny is single, and she claims three withholding allowances. Compute Penny's income tax withholding using the percentage method.

    $ _____

3–6. Martin Galley began employment as a sales manager at Nioga in April of the current year. He asked that his income tax withholding be based on cumulative wages. He is married and has four withholding allowances. His wages before the latest weekly payroll period were $12,400 for 20 pay periods with income tax withholding of $820. During the latest week, he earned $630. Compute the correct amount of income tax withholding for the week.

    $ _____

3–7. Cheryl Gordon, a Nioga salesperson, is single and claims one withholding allowance. She earned $412 this past week. Using the annualized method, compute the federal income tax withholding.

    $ _____

3–8. Harold Alston, a married Nioga yard maintenance mechanic with three allowances, did not work for the first 20 weeks of the year, works from May through August, and then is on call for a week at a time. He worked the first week in September, for which he was paid $384. He earned $6,800 for the 17 weeks from May through August with $408 federal income tax withheld. Using the part-year employment method, compute the federal withholding tax for the week in September. (Total: 38 weeks [20 + 17 + 1])

    $ _____

3–9. Sarah White, a Nioga quality control inspector, is married and claims three withholding allowances. During the last weekly payroll period, besides her weekly salary of $420, she received a $300 bonus. Using the flat rate method for supplemental wages, compute the federal withholding tax on Sarah's regular and supplemental wages.

    $ _____

3–10. Bruce Jackson, Nioga's treasurer, is married and claims four withholding allowances. During the year, he received $60,000 in salary with $8,189 federal income tax withheld and a year-end bonus of $15,000. Using the aggregate method for supplemental wages, compute Bruce's total annual federal withholding for both regular and supplemental wages.

    $ _____

PROBLEMS

3–1. Employees of Jupiter Toys, Inc., earned the weekly wages shown in the following table. Using the wage-bracket method and assuming that each employee is single with the number of allowances shown, compute the federal income tax withheld.

Employee	Wages	Withholding Allowances	FITW
Lola Prince	$400	1	$ _____
Howie Rooker	460	3	_____
Bea Quinn	420	4	_____
Clay Pease	350	2	_____

3–2. Production workers at Jupiter Toys, Inc., earned the weekly wages shown in the following table. Using the percentage method and assuming the marital status and number of withholding allowances shown, compute the federal income tax withheld.

Employee	Wages	Marital Status	Withholding Allowances	FITW
Tamara Rome	$420	S	1	$ _____
Christine Craven	440	M	3	_____
Teddy Bunker	410	M	4	_____
Mel Dopson	460	S	2	_____

3–3. Middle managers at Jupiter Toys, Inc., had the weekly salaries shown in the following table. Using the annualized wages method, compute the federal income tax withheld.

Employee	Weekly Salary	Marital Status	Withholding Allowances	FITW
Douglas Finn	$420	M	4	$ _____
Aggie Martin	460	S	2	_____
Bill Rhodes	440	S	1	_____
Meg A. Young	480	M	3	_____

3–4. Salespeople at Jupiter Toys, Inc., earned the commissions for 36 weeks shown in the following table. Using the cumulative wages method, compute the federal income tax to be withheld.

Employee	Commissions 35 wks.	36th wk.	Withholding 35 wks	Marital Status	Withholding Allowances	Tax to be Withheld
Ford Lane	$17,400	$560	$1,081	M	4	$ _____
Terri Klink	18,400	480	2,000	S	2	_____
Win Orton	20,600	580	1,130	M	5	_____
Ann Yount	22,000	620	2,166	S	3	_____

Problems (cont.)

3–5. Homer Harrison, who is single with one withholding allowance, worked only part of the year at Jupiter Toys, Inc. He worked less than 6 months—from January 1 to June 15, when he was laid off. For that 5½-month period, Homer had wages of $12,500 and withholdings of $2,000. Using the part-year employment method, determine the amount of federal income tax to be withheld on wages of $470 earned in the 44th week of the year when Homer returned to work.

$ _____

3–6. Several employees at Jupiter Toys, Inc., have filed W-5 forms, electing to receive advance payment of the earned income credit. For the latest weekly payroll, compute the federal withholding tax and the advance EIC payments of the following employees. All four employees are married with three withholding allowances, and their spouses have not filed Form W-5 certificates. Use the wage-bracket method of withholding.

Employee	Wages	FITW	Advance EIC
Bob Watson	$425	$ _____	$ _____
Diane Drake	375	_____	_____
Joyce Crane	400	_____	_____
Larry Stine	355	_____	_____

3–7. The Discount Appliance Store pays its employees biweekly. From the following data, compute the federal income taxes withheld and the amount of advance EIC payments (where married, both spouses have filed Form W-5 certificates). Use the wage-bracket method for FITW and the percentage method for AEIC.

Employee	Marital Status/ Allowances	Gross Earnings	FITW	Advance EIC
Sue Bunting	M-3	$780	$ _____	$ _____
John Clausen	M-4	460	_____	_____
Gerri Moss	S-2	680	_____	_____
Theo Payne	M-2	660	_____	_____
Roger Thorson	S-1	560	_____	_____

3–8. Spotless Dry Cleaners pays its employees biweekly. From the following data, compute the federal income taxes withheld and the amount of advance EIC payments. For AEIC, use the percentage method, without spouse filing certificate.

Employee	Marital Status/ Allowances	Gross Earnings	FITW	Advance EIC
George Jarrett	S-2	$600	$ _____	$ _____
Heidi Klein	S-3	580	_____	_____
Karen Otto	M-2	620	_____	_____
Lydia Scalia	M-3	640	_____	_____
Bob Weil	M-4	660	_____	_____

Problems (cont.)   **3–9.** The Recycling Process Company pays its employees either weekly or monthly. Using the following data, compute the federal income taxes withheld by each of the methods indicated.

Employee	Marital Status/ Allow.	Payroll Period	Gross Earnings		Withholding Method*	Withholding To Date	Periods Incl. Latest	FITW
			Excl. Latest	Latest				
Glen Abbot	M-3	W	$12,400	$ 620	C/P	$1,140	20	$_____
Harry Dunn	M-3	W	14,000	700	P/B	1,062	28	_____
Jeanne Lyme	M-4	M	13,200	1,640	A/P	NA	NA	_____
Parker Root	S-3	M	16,000	1,780	C/P	1,330	8	_____
Dorothy Haddad	M-2	W	12,800	600	P/B	905	32	_____

*1st letter: (A) = annualized; (P) = part-time; (C) = cumulative; 2nd letter: B = wage-bracket method; P = percentage method.

3–10. The salespersons at Restaurant Supplies receive year-end bonuses. From the following data, compute the federal income taxes to be withheld by the flat rate and aggregate methods.

Employee	Marital Status/ Allow.	Payroll Period	Gross Earnings		Withholding Method	FITW
			Regular	Bonus		
Roy Ghani	M-2	M	$1,620	$400	flat rate	$ _____
Louise Yao	M-3	M	1,580	400	flat rate	_____
Rod Kane	S-2	M	1,490	360	aggregate	_____
Celina Rodriguez	S-1	M	1,640	440	aggregate	_____
Scott Zeal	S-1	M	1,560	500	aggregate	_____

3–11. Stan and Gwenn are husband and wife; both have filed a W-5 form. Stan earns $5.50 an hour for a 40-hour week, while Gwenn earns minimum wage for 16 hours a week. Using the wage-bracket method, calculate the biweekly advance EIC payment for each person.

Stan $ _____

Gwenn $ _____

CONTINUING CASE PROBLEM

We now take another look at Frontier Landscaping, Inc. Some of the eight regular hourly workers it employs have requested different methods of federal income tax withholding. For example, Horace Glenn and Frank Granto work only part of the year, have no other jobs, and do not want their withholding based on the assumption of full-year employment. Harry Fein and Jose Lopez work during the busy season, which lasts 20 weeks, and then work several weeks in the late fall planting shrubs in the greenhouse. Frontier also solicits business in the off-season and pays Carrie Barnes and Melissa Trane a salary and a supplemental amount as a

Continuing Case Problem (cont.) bonus for any customers they sign up for landscaping services. Carrie and Melissa both requested that the withholdings be the lesser of the amounts computed by the flat rate and the aggregate methods.

Based on the following data, calculate the federal withholding tax for each of these employees.

Employee Name	Marital Status/Allow.	Withholding Method*		FITW
Carrie Barnes	M-3	S	Salary: $240 per week; bonus: $200; FITW from salary: none	$_____
Melissa Trane	M-2	S	Salary: $240 per week; bonus: $160; FITW from salary: $4	_____
Horace Glenn	S-2	P	16-week earnings: $5,600; latest week (38th): $220; FITW to date: $113	_____
Frank Granto	M-1	P	16-week earnings: $7,800; latest week (38th): $240; FITW to date: $575	_____
Harry Fein	S-1	C	20-week earnings: $4,000; latest week (21st): $220; FITW to date: $335	_____
Jose Lopez	S-2	C	20-week earnings: $4,200; latest week (21st): $240; FITW to date: $165	_____

*(S) = supplemental; (P) = part-year; (C) = cumulative.

CHAPTER 4

FICA TAXES, NONTAX PAYROLL DEDUCTIONS, AND UNEMPLOYMENT TAXES

LEARNING OBJECTIVES

On completing this chapter, you will be able to:

1. Compute the Social Security and Medicare taxes for various levels of compensation under the Federal Insurance Contributions Act (FICA).
2. Use tables to compute the combined withholding for wages.
3. List the taxable forms of compensation and describe employment relationships that affect FICA taxes.
4. Describe the different methods of computing the self-employment tax and compute the tax.
5. Enumerate and describe other types of deductions: contractual, voluntary, and involuntary.
6. Discuss the different types of voluntary deductions: medical insurance, pension and retirement plan contributions, U.S. Savings Bonds and savings plans, and charitable contributions.
7. Describe the various rules for child support, tax levies, and garnishments as they affect employee wages.
8. List the conditions that give rise to a tax liability under the Federal Unemployment Tax Act (FUTA). Compute, report, and pay the FUTA tax due.
9. Differentiate between covered and noncovered employment and between reportable and nonreportable earnings under the State Unemployment Tax Act (SUTA) of New York.
10. Explain the conditions that initiate and terminate the unemployment tax liability and compute the tax for New York.

95

In addition to withholding federal and state income taxes, employers must calculate and withhold FICA taxes. Clark explains to Lois that the Social Security Act passed by Congress in 1935 and amended several times since calls for three types of insurance in an effort to provide financial security for U.S. workers and their families: (1) old-age, survivors', and disability insurance (commonly referred to as Social Security or sometimes OASDI); (2) hospital insurance (Medicare); and (3) unemployment compensation. Employee and employer contributions mandated by the Federal Insurance Contributions Act (FICA) provide funding for Social Security and Medicare. Employers, through the Federal Unemployment Tax Act (FUTA) and most state unemployment tax acts (SUTA), are the sole funding source for unemployment compensation insurance.

In addition to FICA withholding, a number of other possible payroll deductions may be specified by union contract, legal rulings, or company benefit programs. Clark recalls that at one time additional deductions were the exception rather than the rule and an employee took home almost the entire amount of her or his gross earnings; not so today.

Clark begins with a discussion of FICA withholding methods.

SOCIAL SECURITY AND MEDICARE TAXES

The Federal Insurance Contributions Act (FICA) provides for a federal system of old-age, survivors', disability, and hospital insurance. The Social Security tax funds the old-age, survivors', and disability insurance, and the Medicare tax finances the hospital insurance. Beginning in 1991, the Form W-2 shows each of these taxes separately.

Both employer and employee share these tax contributions. The employer collects and pays the employee's part of the taxes and pays a matching amount.

Tax Rates and Wage Bases

Different tax rates and wage bases apply for the Social Security tax and for the Medicare tax. The wage base is the maximum annual amount that is subject to the tax. Multiplying gross wages for a payroll period by the tax rate or using the tables provided in *Circular E, Employer's Tax Guide* (available at IRS district offices or on the Web at www.irs.gov) provides the amount of taxes to be withheld. The computation of Social Security and Medicare taxes does not depend on withholding allowances.

In 1999 and 2000, the Social Security tax rate was 6.2% each for employer and employee (12.4% total); the wage base was $72,600 in 1999 and $76,200 in 2000. The Medicare tax rate was 1.45% each for employer and employee (2.9% total). All wages were subject to the Medicare tax.

Calculating FICA Withholding

Employers can use one of two methods to determine the amount of Social Security and Medicare taxes to be withheld from the earnings of each employee. The first method involves the use of IRS tax tables that are reproduced in Appendix A in the back of this book. These tables contain Social Security and Medicare tax amounts for wage brackets up to $100 and then amounts ranging up to $1,000. For example, the Social Security tax on wages of $355 would be $22.01 ($18.60 + $3.41) and the Medicare tax would be $5.15 ($4.35 + $.80).

EXAMPLE   Jim Krieg earns $732.00 biweekly as an auto mechanic. The steps taken to calculate the FICA tax to be deducted from Jim's gross pay are as follows:

1. Find, at the bottom of the tables in Appendix A, the amount of Social Security and Medicare taxes on $700.00. They are $43.40 for Social Security tax and $10.15 for Medicare tax.

2. Locate the wage bracket that covers the remaining part of Jim's earnings of $32.00 (see Appendix A). The bracket for the Social Security tax is $31.86 to $32.02, and the tax amount is $1.98. For the Medicare tax (see Appendix A), the bracket is $31.38 to $32.07, and the tax amount is $.46.

3. Add the two amounts from step one. The Social Security tax is $45.38 ($43.40 + $1.98), and the Medicare tax is $10.61 ($10.15 + $.46).

4. Allocate wages in excess of $1,000, into $1,000, a multiple of $100, and an amount under $100, for which you can use the brackets.   ▲

EXAMPLE   Jane O'Reilly earns $1,732 in a biweekly period. Add the tax on $1,000 and the tax on $700. Then use the tables in Appendix A to determine the tax on $32.   ▲

The second method for calculating the Social Security and Medicare tax withholdings is to multiply the employee's gross earnings by the respective tax rates: 6.2% for Social Security tax and 1.45% for Medicare tax. Using this percentage method on gross biweekly earnings of $1,732 results in a Social Security tax of $107.38 and a Medicare tax of $25.11—exactly the amounts determined from the tables. For all wages the percentage method is more convenient than using the tax tables. With constant percentages for FICA taxes, computations are relatively simple.

Like federal income withholding, Social Security and Medicare taxes are deducted from each employee's paycheck and deposited with the Internal Revenue Service along with matching funds for which the employer is liable.

The same two methods can be used to calculate the employer's FICA contribution. However, rather than calculate these amounts for each employee, the payroll clerk can make one computation based on the total wages of all employees. The employer is effectively matching the em-

AVOID OVERWITHHOLDING

A cap has been placed on the amount of income subject to Social Security deductions. You must be careful not to make Social Security deductions for an employee whose wages have passed the maximum taxable amount for the year (for 2000, $76,200 for Social Security taxes.) No limit applies to Medicare taxes. The employee earnings record shows cumulative earnings. Check these records before preparing the payroll to determine whether any employees are near or over the limits for Social Security taxes.

ployee contribution since the employee and employer rates are identical. The same taxable wage base applies to the employee and the employer. Once an employee has reached the Social Security wage base limit, Social Security taxes are no longer withheld from the employee or paid by the employer. (Wages subject to Social Security tax equal $76,200 minus prior cumulative earnings.)

Combined Withholding

To make withholding of the three federal taxes easier to compute, the IRS has provided withholding tables that combine the amounts for federal income tax, employee Social Security tax, and Medicare tax. The tables cover annual wages of $76,200 or less in 2000. The tables are similar to the federal income tax withholding tables in that they are available for weekly, biweekly, semimonthly, monthly, and daily or miscellaneous payroll periods. The payroll period and marital status of the employee determine the table to be used.

An important fact to note, however, is that the combined tables are accurate only if the employee's cumulative wages are $76,200 or less. Employees who earn over $76,200 in 2000 will continue to be taxed for Medicare contributions but not for Social Security once they have reached the wage base limit. Also, the combined tables are not suitable when the wages for income tax withholding, Social Security, and Medicare are not the same.

Taxability for FICA and FUTA Taxes

Several employer-provided payments are subject to FICA and FUTA taxes even though they may be exempt from FITW. These include the following payments:

- Deceased Worker. Wages paid to a beneficiary or estate in the same calendar year as the worker's death.

- Household Employees. Payments made for domestic service in private homes, if $1,000 or more in cash for the year. Exempt from FICA taxes, if performed by an individual under 18 during any portion of the calendar year and is not the principal occupation of the employee. Subject to FUTA tax if the employer paid cash wages of $1,000 or more for all household employees in any quarter in the current or preceding calendar year.

- Retirement and Pension Plans. Elective employee contributions and deferrals to a Section 401(k) plan or employer contributions to a Section 403(b) plan, the latter if paid through a salary reduction agreement.
- Statutory Employees. Payments to statutory employees and other outside salespersons, including full-time life insurance agents, if more than $100 in cash in a year. Also exempt from FUTA tax.

Other employer-provided payments are exempt from FICA and FUTA taxes even though they may be subject to FITW. These include the following payments:

- Retirements and Pension Plans. Distributions from qualified retirement plans and Section 403(b) annuities.
- Sick Pay. Sick pay payments, (1) after the end of six calendar months following the calendar month the employee last worked for the employer; (2) for medical care, workers' compensation, and the employee's contribution to a sick pay plan; (3) to a state or local government employee. The third party payer should contact the state or local government employer for instructions.
- Students, Scholars, and Trainees. Payments to: (1) students enrolled and regularly attending classes and performing services for a private or public school, college, or university or (2) student nurses performing part-time hospital services for nominal earnings as an incidental part of training.
- Supplemental Unemployment Compensation Benefits. Exempt from FICA and FUTA taxes, if the payments are dependent on state unemployment payments. Subject to FICA and FUTA taxes if payment is a lump-sum amount, since such a payment is unrelated to the period of unemployment.

Employment Relationships

Certain employment relationships affect whether or not compensation is equivalent to wages subject to FICA taxes.

Successor Employee. Often a business acquires all or substantially all of the property of another business or a unit of another business. Employees often continue their work—but for a new employer. The new employer may, in determining the wage bases for the employees, take into consideration the wages the previous employer paid to the employees.

EXAMPLE Early in the year, Nioga Gear bought all the assets of Sure Laces, a shoelace company. Lisa Burns, an employee of Sure Laces, had received $3,000 in wages before the date of purchase. She then became an employee of Nioga. Nioga and Lisa Burns are subject to Social Security taxes on the first $73,200 ($76,200 − $3,000) and Medicare taxes on the entire amount of wages Nioga pays her during the rest of the calendar year. ▲

Concurrent Employment by Related Corporations. If two or more related corporations employ the same individual at the same time and pay this individual through a common paymaster that is one of the corporations, the corporations are considered to be a single employer. They have to pay, in total, no more in Social Security and Medicare taxes than a single employer would pay. Each corporation must pay its share of the employer's FICA taxes on that part of the wages it paid. The employer's FICA and also unemployment deductions will not be allowable unless the corporation reimburses the common paymaster for these tax payments as well as the wages paid to the employee.

Spousal and Child Employment. Wages paid to a spouse or child 18 years of age or older for services in one's trade or business are subject to Social Security and Medicare taxes. Wages paid to a child 21 years or older are also subject to FUTA taxes. If the services are not in one's trade or business, such as domestic service in the home, the wages are exempt from Social Security, Medicare, and FUTA taxes.

Self-Employment Income

As described in Chapter 1, the Self-Employment Contribution Act (SECA) extends Social Security and Medicare benefits to self-employed individuals through a tax on net **self-employment income** derived from a trade or business—an activity carried on for a profit. A self-employed person may be a sole proprietor, an independent contractor, a member of a partnership, or an individual otherwise in business for personal benefit. The business does not have to be a regular full-time activity to constitute self-employment. Part-time work, including work on the side while regularly employed, may also be classified as self-employment.

Self-employment income for a member of a partnership that carries on a trade or business is the individual's distributive share of the partnership's income. This self-employment income includes guaranteed payments from the partnership.

Net self-employment income usually includes all business income less all business deductions allowed for income tax purposes. If an individual has more than one trade or business, the net self-employment income is the total net earnings from each business. A loss incurred in one business reduces income overall.

A self-employed person must pay self-employment tax if net earnings from self-employment are $400 or more. A self-employment tax is due if an individual received annual wages of $100 or more as an employee of a church or qualified church-controlled organization that elected exemption from Social Security and Medicare taxes.

Tax Rates. The self-employment tax rate is 12.4% for Social Security tax plus 2.9% for Medicare tax (15.3% total). Thus, a self-employed person pays both the employee and employer portions of these taxes on self-employment earnings. However, the tax laws provide for two adjustments

Self-employment income
The net income of an individual from a business operated as a sole proprietorship or from a partnership to which the individual belongs.

for the self-employed taxpayer in order to make the FICA taxes paid equivalent to those that would be paid by an employee and employer on equivalent wages. The first adjustment reduces the self-employment earnings by the FICA tax rate of 7.65% so that only 92.35% of self-employment earnings is subject to FICA taxes. The second adjustment permits the self-employed taxpayer to take a reduction in total income on the Form 1040, Individual Income Tax Return, of one-half the self-employment tax.

Methods for Calculating the Tax Owed. The amount of self-employment tax owed can be determined by following three steps:

1. Determine net earnings from self-employment.
2. Establish the amount that is subject to the tax.
3. Multiply that amount by the tax rate.

EXAMPLE Leslie Graham has an unincorporated mail-order business selling imported figurines. This year, she earned $32,000 on revenues of $58,000 less expenses of $26,000. The amount subject to tax is $29,552 (.9235 × $32,000), and the self-employment tax is $4,521.46 (.153 × $29,552). The deduction on Leslie's tax return is $2,260.73 (.50 × $4,521.46). ▲

Two optional methods—the farm optional method and the nonfarm optional method—enable a self-employed individual to continue coverage for Social Security and Medicare purposes when net income for the year is small or is even a net loss. These two methods and the regular method differ in the calculation of net earnings. However, the kinds of excluded income and deductions, the wage bases, and the tax rates are the same for all three.

A self-employed individual can use one or both of the optional methods if net self-employment income is less than $1,600 or even a loss and the individual wants to continue Social Security and Medicare benefit coverage, has incurred child and dependent care expenses to be self-employed, or is entitled to the earned income credit. Use of either optional method requires payment of the self-employment tax.

The same wage bases apply for the self-employment tax. The first $76,200 of combined wages, tips, and net earnings in 2000 is subject to the 12.4% Social Security part of the self-employment tax. The wage base for the 2.9% Medicare part of the self-employment tax has no limit and is imposed on all combined wages, tips, and net earnings.

EXAMPLE Joe Blocker owns the Grand Slam Driving Range, an unincorporated business. Joe had revenue of $95,000, and expenses of $35,000, for a net income of $60,000. Joe also had self-employment income from a partnership of $18,500. His total self-employment income is $78,500 ($60,000 + $18,500). The self-employment tax Joe must pay is .124 × .9235 × $76,200 for the Social Security part of the tax, plus .029 × .9235 × $78,500 for the Medicare part of the tax. His total self-employment tax is $10,828.32 ($8,725.97 + $2,102.35). ▲

NONTAX PAYROLL DEDUCTIONS

Contractual deductions
Deductions specified by contract and implicitly or explicitly authorized.

Check-off system   *The authorized withholding of union dues from the gross wages of an employee by an employer.*

Union shop   *A business operating under a labor agreement that requires all new employees to join the union within a certain period.*

Involuntary deductions
Deductions such as child support payments, tax levies, and garnishments requested by legal authorities.

Wage attachments   *Involuntary transfers of funds from gross wages, as required for child support, tax levies, and garnishments.*

In addition to withholding for federal, state, and local income and FICA taxes, the payroll manager is responsible for making many other deductions resulting from contractual, involuntary, and voluntary obligations.

Contractual Deductions

Employers may be required to make **contractual deductions**. For example, in many companies, employees are members of a union that, by contract, requires the withholding of union dues from employees' gross earnings. This arrangement is commonly referred to as a **check-off system**. With written authorization, the employer deducts the amounts for union dues and makes regular payments of the amounts withheld to the union, according to the terms of the employer-union agreement. In a **union shop**, potential employees must provide a written authorization before they can be hired.

Involuntary Deductions

Involuntary deductions—deductions requested by legal authorities other than employees—are called **wage attachments**. Wage attachments include the following, in order of deduction priority:

1. Child support
2. Tax levies—federal, state, and local, in that order
3. Garnishments

Disposable earnings
Earnings less required deductions for taxes, involuntary deductions, and some approved voluntary deductions.

When wages are subject to involuntary deductions, the payroll manager must often first calculate **disposable earnings**, which is the total of all earnings, except tips, after required deductions. Required deductions for all employees include federal and state income tax withholding deductions and FICA tax deductions. Involuntary deductions, if imposed, become required deductions and further reduce disposable earnings in the sequence listed above. The IRS sometimes permits certain voluntary deductions (such as medical insurance) to be included in the calculation of disposable earnings. State regulations usually identify these permissible voluntary deductions, as illustrated in a later example.

Child Support.   Under the Family Support Act of 1988, child support orders issued or modified on or after November 1990 must provide, with some exceptions, for immediate wage withholding, even if the support payments are not overdue. Permissible exceptions occur when one of the parents proves good cause not to require such withholding or when both parents agree, in writing, to an alternative arrangement. Starting in 1994, all support orders will require immediate withholding, regardless of whether a parent has applied for government assistance for child support or welfare. An employer must begin withholding child support payments the next pay period, within 14 days of the mailing date of the support notice, or on the date of the support notice. Furthermore, the employer must send the child support payments to the appropriate agency within 10 days of the employee's payday.

The notice requiring child support payments specifies the amount to be deducted from gross wages. The Consumer Protection Act sets out the maximum amount of an employee's wages that may be attached for child support. The amount of an employee's disposable earnings governs the maximum percentage used in computing the child support payments. Either the state limits or the following federal limits apply, whichever are lower:

- 50% (55% if support is in arrears) or less of the disposable earnings if the employee supports a second family.
- 60% (65% if support is in arrears) or less of the disposable earnings if the employee does not support a second family.

Tax Levies. An involuntary deduction may also be made for unpaid federal, state, or local taxes. If an employee owes back taxes, the IRS can collect the amount due through a levy on the employee's wages. Each state or local tax department may establish its own procedure for collection of tax levies.

A portion of the employee's net pay is exempt from a federal tax levy. To determine the exact exempt amount, the payroll manager divides the annual amount of the standard deduction and the personal exemptions by the number of pay periods in a year. The employee can claim a personal exemption for anyone who receives at least half of her or his total support from the employee, with the exception of that dependent claimed for child support. If the employee does not provide information on the amount of the standard deduction and the personal exemptions, the employer assumes the standard deduction and status as married, filing separately, with one personal exemption.

Calculating the amount to withhold for the federal tax levy requires three computations involving the employee's wages:

1. Disposable earnings, i.e., net pay before the tax levy.
2. Amount exempt from the tax levy.
3. Amount to withhold for the tax levy (line 1 less line 2).

EXAMPLE Biff Hamilton is paid semimonthly by Computer Giants. Besides the required tax withholdings, other deductions from Biff's wages include union dues, medical insurance, and child support payments mandated by court order two years earlier. Computer Giants has just received a federal tax levy against Biff. In a statement of exemptions and filing status, Biff has indicated that he is married, filing jointly, and has three personal exemptions. The state in which Biff lives allows deductions for medical insurance and union dues in the computation of disposable earnings. Calculation of the federal levy and net pay after levy are as follows:

Computation of disposable earnings:

Semimonthly gross wages		$ 2,250.00
Less:		
Federal income tax withholding	$245.00	
FICA tax withholding	172.13	
State income tax withholding	48.75	
Medical insurance deduction	52.00	
Union dues deduction	24.00	
Child support deduction	250.00	$791.88
Disposable earnings		$1,458.12
(Net pay before federal tax levy)		

Computation of amount exempt from levy:

Standard deduction, married, filing jointly	$7,350.00
Personal exemptions ($2,800 × 3)	8,400.00
Total exempt amount	$15,750.00
Exempt amount per pay period (24)	$656.25

Amount to withhold for levy:

Net pay before federal tax levy	$1,458.12
Less exempt amount	$656.25
Amount to withhold for levy	$801.87

Net pay after federal tax levy:

Net pay before federal tax levy	$1,458.12
Amount to withhold for levy	801.87
Net pay after federal tax levy	$656.25 ▲

Standard deduction *An amount fixed by law and subtracted before taxable income. It varies according to tax filing status: single ($4,400), married filing jointly ($7,350) or separately, and head of household.*

Personal exemption *An amount fixed by law and subtracted before taxable income. It is a set amount for a taxpayer, spouse, and qualifying dependent ($2,800).*

The employer must continue to deduct the levy amount until the total tax levy has been paid to the IRS or until the employer receives a release from levy from the IRS.

Garnishment *A legal or equitable process whereby an employer withholds a portion of an employee's gross earnings as payment on a debt.*

Garnishments.   Courts sometimes order an employer to attach gross wages in order to pay off an overdue debt. **Garnishment** refers to the legal process requiring the withholding of part of an employee's earnings. The employer usually receives notice of garnishment in the form of a garnishment summons, a writ of garnishment, or a writ of attachment. Whatever the document, it states the purpose of the garnishment and the amount of indebtedness. The Consumer Credit Protection Act of 1968 limits the amount of disposable earnings subject to garnishment in a week to the lesser of 25% of disposable earnings or the amount by which disposable earnings for the period exceed 30 times the federal minimum wage ($5.15 an hour since September 1, 1997). The employer sends the amounts garnished to the courts or the creditor directly.

EXAMPLE   Margaret Jones earns $400 a week as the office manager for Quik Lube Corp. Her payroll deductions include $55 for federal and state income taxes, $31 for FICA taxes, $70 for medical insurance, and $12 for union dues. Margaret's disposable earnings, assuming deductions for medical insurance and union dues are not permissible, are as follows:

Gross wages		$400.00
Less:		
Federal and state income taxes	$55.00	
FICA taxes	31.00	86.00
Disposable earnings		$314.00

The maximum creditor garnishment is 25% of the disposable earnings, or $78.50 (.25 × $314.00). ▲

Besides placing limits on the amount of an employee's earnings that are available for garnishment in any one week, Title III of the Consumer Protection Act prohibits an employer from discharging an employee because of the garnishment. A second case of garnishment, unless it follows considerably later, could lead to discharge of the employee.

Voluntary Deductions

Many companies allow employees to participate in certain benefits through voluntary payroll deductions, which are held and allocated to a specific fund. **Voluntary deductions**, unless part of a salary reduction program, are applied to after-tax dollars, that is, after taxes have been withheld from gross wages. They are secondary to involuntary deductions, which have prior claims on gross wages, and are thus considered **wage assessments** (as opposed to wage attachments). All such deductions require employee authorization. Some examples of these deductions include:

Voluntary deductions *Optional deductions from gross earnings authorized by an employee for such items as savings plans and medical insurance.*

Wage assessments *Voluntary transfers of funds from gross wages as requested by an employee.*

1. Medical insurance
2. Pension and retirement plan contributions
3. U.S. savings bonds and other savings plans
4. Charitable contributions

Medical Insurance. Practically all companies establish medical plans for their employees, most often providing coverage through private insurance companies. Sometimes the employer pays the entire cost of the medical insurance, but most often the employees share a portion of the cost. In this case, the employee subscribes to the medical insurance plan and indicates whether the coverage is to be single, family, or some other extended coverage. The employer withholds contributions from a participating employee's gross wages and periodically sends the amounts withheld, as well as the employer portion of the premiums, to the insurance provider.

Pension and Retirement Plan Contributions. Many companies establish pension and retirement plans to supplement Social Security benefits. Some plans may be noncontributory and funded entirely by the employer; others may be contributory, where the employees contribute to the plan, often along with the employer but sometimes on their own. The employer must have written authorization from the employee before deducting the employee's contribution from gross wages. Two such salary reduction plans are referred to as 401(k) and 403(b) plans, denoting the Internal Revenue Code sections that describe them.

U.S. Savings Bonds and Savings Plans.   A deduction for U.S. savings bonds or a savings plan is a popular option offered by many employers. Sometimes the companies will match the amounts withheld on behalf of the employees. In any event, the employer is responsible for remitting the amounts deducted from the employees' gross wages. Any bonds or savings certificates are either held on behalf of the employees by the employer until requested or turned over to the employees as issued.

Charitable Contributions.   On occasion, as a community service, a company may decide to act as an agent for a charitable organization. The employer either receives requests for amounts to be withheld or signs up employees for pledges. Employees decide on the amounts to be withheld and the employer deducts these amounts from the employees' gross wages. Periodically, the employer sends the amounts withheld to the various charitable organizations.

UNEMPLOYMENT COMPENSATION TAXES

The Federal Unemployment Tax Act (FUTA) is just one part of the unemployment compensation mandated by the Social Security Act of 1935. The Social Security Act also mandated that each state set up an unemployment compensation program for workers temporarily out of work, including seasonal workers, first-time job seekers, and workers who have lost their jobs. Through **state unemployment tax acts (SUTA)**, the state programs fund the payment of weekly benefits to unemployed workers. Quarterly federal taxes mandated by FUTA and based on the wages of covered employees provide funds primarily for the administration of the program, not for the payment of any worker benefits.

State unemployment tax acts (SUTA) *Laws passed by the various states that impose tax payments on the employer (and sometimes on employees) to cover unemployment insurance.*

The federal-state unemployment compensation programs constitute a far-reaching system of payments. Although the state laws must conform to the federal standard specified in the Social Security and Federal Unemployment Tax acts, states can determine their own rules regarding eligibility requirements, rates of benefits paid, length of paid benefits, etc. Thus, every state is somewhat unique, and an employer must understand the regulations for its particular state, as detailed in Table 4-1. Let's see how these programs work.

Liability Under the Federal Unemployment Tax Act

Based on wages for covered employees, employers must pay a quarterly payroll tax that funds the administration of the FUTA program. Three tests that apply to three separate categories of workers (nonfarm or nonhousehold, household, and farm) determine whether or not a business must pay the FUTA tax. If a test describes an employer's situation either during the current or preceding calendar year, that business is subject to FUTA tax on the wages paid to employees in that category for the current calendar quarter.

Nonfarm or Nonhousehold Workers. A business is subject to federal unemployment tax if, in any calendar quarter, the wages paid to employees totaled $1,500 or more or if in each of 20 different calendar weeks, not necessarily consecutive, the business employed a nonfarm or nonhousehold employee. The employee does not have to be the same individual each week and individuals on sick leave or vacation count as employees.

EXAMPLE   The One-Hour Courier Service hires couriers as needed for the delivery services it provides to lawyers and other businesses. During the last year, it employed three different employees who worked eight, ten, and six weeks, respectively. Since One-Hour employed a nonfarm, nonhousehold employee in each of 20 different calendar weeks, it is subject to federal unemployment tax. ▲

Household Workers. A household or domestic worker is an employee who performs domestic services in a private home, local college club, or local college fraternity or sorority chapter. An employer is subject to FUTA tax if the cash wages paid to employees in this category totaled $1,000 or more in any calendar quarter.

Farm Workers. An employer is subject to federal unemployment tax on the wages paid to farm workers if:

- In any calendar quarter, the cash wages paid for farm labor totaled $20,000 or more.
- In each of 20 different calendar weeks, the number of farm workers was ten or more. The employees do not have to be the same each week, and individuals on sick leave or vacation count as employees. Nor do all ten employees have to work a full day or the same part of the day.

Other Forms of Compensation. Tips, including credit card tips, reported by the employee to the employer for Social Security and Medicare tax purposes are considered wages for federal unemployment tax purposes.

Noncash payments or payments in kind are also wages for federal unemployment tax purposes. Payments in kind may be in the form of goods, lodging, food, clothing, or services. The value of these payments is the fair market value on the payment date.

EXAMPLE   Annie Brown, a student at Mid-Central University, works at Pasquale's Pizzeria. Annie receives a salary of $175 a week and meals with a fair market value of $50 a week. Pasquale's pays unemployment tax on the first $7,000 of Annie's compensation based on wages of $225 per week. ▲

Payments in kind for farm or household workers are not wages for federal unemployment tax purposes. Other exceptions to FUTA are payments under the workers' compensation laws and certain types of employment such as internships for students in cooperative education programs.

HOUSEHOLD EMPLOYEES

The practice of hiring household workers and not paying FICA or unemployment taxes is widespread. In a well-publicized case, the *Wall Street Journal* reported the settlement of a dispute between an elderly woman in Florida and the IRS. The woman had hired a maid and agreed to pay her off the payroll (i.e., in cash). As a result, the woman did not pay any payroll taxes, including unemployment taxes.

After being laid off, the maid tried to collect unemployment compensation and thus revealed to authorities that her employer had not been paying payroll taxes. The IRS imposed on her employer penalties and interest and required the employer to pay back unemployment taxes at the highest rate in Florida.

This case illustrates the potential risk incurred by millions of American families who hire nannies, maids, nurses, gardeners, and other domestic workers. The IRS estimates that, of the two million families who employ household employees, three out of four do not file reports or pay payroll taxes. The problem probably will get worse, because household help of one sort or another has become a necessity for many two-earner families. Getting caught for not complying with the tax laws is a middle-class nightmare. For example, assume a family hired a nanny and paid her under the table for five years at a weekly salary of $250 a week. The back taxes on this arrangement would be almost $5,000 for FICA taxes and could be almost $2,000 for unemployment taxes. These amounts do not include the penalties and interest that could be levied if the IRS found out about the failure to pay taxes.

Most families did not comply with the law because compliance was quite complicated. The simplified new rules specify that (1) cash payments of $1,000 or more during the calendar *year* to any *one* household employee are subject to FICA taxes and (2) cash payments of $1,000 or more during any calendar *quarter* to *all* household employees are subject to FUTA taxes. Payments to an individual under age 18 are exempt from FICA taxes unless household employment is the employee's principal occupation. Household employers report and pay FICA and FUTA taxes on their annual Form 1040 income tax returns.

Calculating and Paying the FUTA Tax

The federal unemployment tax applies to the first $7,000 in wages paid to each employee (current base). An employer pays the tax in its entirety; no amount is deducted from employee wages.

EXAMPLE   Brad Messer earned $27,000 in 20xx. Only the first $7,000 of Brad's 20xx wages are subject to FUTA.   ▲

The current gross federal unemployment tax rate is 6.2%. However, the employer receives a credit of up to 5.4% for the state unemployment tax rate paid. The net tax rate, therefore, can be as low as 0.8% (6.2% − 5.4%) or as high as 6.2% if the state is not subject to a credit reduction.

EXAMPLE   Employees at Butch's Collision Shop receive $36,000 in wages subject to unemployment taxes. The net FUTA tax would be as follows:

Total taxable wages			$36,000
FUTA rate	6.2%	$2,232.00	
State credit	−5.4%	−1,944.00	
Net FUTA tax	0.8%	$ 288.00	

▲

Experience rating   *Method used by states, based on favorable or unfavorable employment history, to determine the percentage to apply to gross wages in the computation of state unemployment taxes.*

The actual SUTA tax paid is based on the **experience rating**. If the experience rating is 2.4%, then the SUTA tax will be $864.00. The state credit against FUTA tax, however, remains at 5.4%.

Even when the SUTA rate is under 5.4% because of a favorable experience rating, the full 5.4% credit applies so that employers reap the reward of favorable employment records. Late payments of the state contributions may result in a reduction of the maximum credit. Also, a reduced credit may result if a state's unemployment fund borrows from the federal government and keeps an outstanding balance for two or more years.

From the previous example, assume that because of late payments, the unemployment state tax credit is 90% of 5.4% or 4.86%, then the net FUTA tax would be as follows:

Total taxable wages		$36,000
FUTA rate	6.20%	$2,232.00
State credit	−4.86%	1,749.60
Net FUTA tax	1.34%	$ 482.40

Form 940, Employer's Annual Federal Unemployment Tax Return   *A tax report filed by an employer at the end of the calendar year to reconcile the employer's unemployment tax liability, the amount paid, and the balance owed.*

Form 940.   A business reports the federal unemployment tax on **Form 940, Employer's Annual Federal Unemployment (FUTA) Tax Return** (Exhibit 4-1). This form covers one calendar year and is generally due one month after the year ends. However, the employer may have to make deposits of the tax before filing the return. An employer may be eligible to file Form 940-EZ (Exhibit 4-2), a simplified version of Form 940, if it paid unemployment taxes to only one state by the due date.

Deposit Due Dates.   If, at the end of any calendar quarter, the employer owes but has not yet deposited more than $100 in federal unemployment tax (FUTA) for the year, the employer must make a deposit by the end of the next month. The due dates are as follows:

If undeposited FUTA tax is more than $100 on	*Deposit the full amount by*
March 31	April 30
June 30	July 31
September 30	October 31
December 31	January 31

If the tax is $100 or less at the end of a quarter, the employer does not have to make a deposit. But that amount must be added to the tax for the next quarter. Then, in the next quarter, if the total undeposited tax is more than $100, the employer must make a deposit. The fourth quarter deposit equals the total FUTA tax liability for the year less the prior amounts deposited.

Additional Liability Under FUTA

If the employer's state is subject to a credit reduction in a given year, the state's name and the amount of the credit reduction must be shown on Form 940. If the state has a reduced credit because of funds owed to the federal government, this reduction creates an additional fourth-quarter

Form **940**

Department of the Treasury
Internal Revenue Service (99)

**Employer's Annual Federal
Unemployment (FUTA) Tax Return**

See separate Instructions for Form 940 for information on completing this form.

OMB No. 1545-0028

20

T	
FF	
FD	
FP	
I	
T	

Name (as distinguished from trade name)   Calendar year

Trade name, if any

Address and ZIP code   Employer identification number

A Are you required to pay unemployment contributions to only one state? (If "No," skip questions B and C.) ☐ Yes ☐ No

B Did you pay all state unemployment contributions by January 31, 2000? ((1) If you deposited your total FUTA tax when due, check "Yes" if you paid all state unemployment contributions by February 10. (2) If a 0% experience rate is granted, check "Yes." (3) If "No," skip question C.) . . . . ☐ Yes ☐ No

C Were all wages that were taxable for FUTA tax also taxable for your state's unemployment tax? . . . . . ☐ Yes ☐ No

If you answered "No" to any of these questions, you must file Form 940. If you answered "Yes" to all the questions, you may file Form 940-EZ, which is a simplified version of Form 940. (Successor employers see **Special credit for successor employers** on page 3 of the instructions.) You can get Form 940-EZ by calling 1-800-TAX-FORM (1-800-829-3676) or from the IRS's Internet Web Site at **www.irs.gov.**

If you will not have to file returns in the future, check here (see **Who Must File** in separate instructions), **and complete and sign the return** . . . . ▶ ☐

If this is an Amended Return, check here. . . . . ▶ ☐

Part I	**Computation of Taxable Wages**

1 Total payments (including payments shown on lines 2 and 3) during the calendar year for services of employees **1**

2 Exempt payments. (Explain all exempt payments, attaching additional sheets if necessary.) ▶ _____ **2**

3 Payments of more than $7,000 for services. Enter only amounts over the first $7,000 paid to each employee. Do not include any exempt payments from line 2. The $7,000 amount is the Federal wage base. Your state wage base may be different. **Do not use your state wage limitation** . **3**

4 Total exempt payments (add lines 2 and 3) **4**

5 **Total taxable wages** (subtract line 4 from line 1) . . . . ▶ **5**

Be sure to complete both sides of this form, and sign in the space provided on the back.

For Privacy Act and Paperwork Reduction Act Notice, see separate instructions.   Cat. No. 11234O   Form **940** (1999)

DETACH HERE

Form **940-V**

Department of the Treasury
Internal Revenue Service

Form 940 Payment Voucher

Use this voucher only when making a payment with your return.

OMB No. 1545-0028

20

Complete boxes 1, 2, 3, and 4. Do not send cash, and do not staple your payment to this voucher. Make your check or money order payable to the "United States Treasury". Be sure to enter your employer identification number, "Form 940", and "20 " on your payment.

1 Enter the amount of the payment you are making

▶ $ _____ . ____

2 Enter the first four letters of your last name (business name if partnership or corporation)

3 Enter your employer identification number

Instructions for Box 2

—Individuals (sole proprietors, trusts, and estates)—Enter the first four letters of your last name.

—Corporations and partnerships—Enter the first four characters of your business name (omit "The" if followed by more than one word).

4 Enter your business name (individual name for sole proprietors)

Enter your address

Enter your city, state, and ZIP code

EXHIBIT 4-1 Form 940, FUTA Tax Return

Form 940 (1999)   Page **2**

Part II   Tax Due or Refund

1 Gross FUTA tax. Multiply the wages from Part I, line 5, by .062	**1**
2 Maximum credit. Multiply the wages from Part I, line 5, by .054 . . **| 2 |**	
3 Computation of tentative credit (**Note:** *All taxpayers must complete the applicable columns.*)	

(a) Name of state	(b) State reporting number(s) as shown on employer's state contribution returns	(c) Taxable payroll (as defined in state act)	(d) State experience rate period		(e) State experience rate	(f) Contributions if rate had been 5.4% (col. (c) x .054)	(g) Contributions payable at experience rate (col. (c) x col. (e))	(h) Additional credit (col. (f) minus col.(g)). If 0 or less, enter -0-.	(i) Contributions paid to state by 940 due date
			From	To					

3a Totals . . . ▶		
3b **Total tentative credit** (add line 3a, columns (h) and (i) only—for late payments also see the instructions for Part II, line 6 . . . . ▶	**3b**	
4		
5		
6 **Credit:** Enter the smaller of the amount from Part II, line 2 or line 3b; or the amount from the worksheet in the Part II, line 6 instructions	**6**	
7 **Total FUTA tax** (subtract line 6 from line 1). If the result is over $100, also complete Part III . .	**7**	
8 Total FUTA tax deposited for the year, including any overpayment applied from a prior year . .	**8**	
9 **Balance due** (subtract line 8 from line 7). Pay to the "United States Treasury". If you owe more than $100, see **Depositing FUTA Tax** on page 3 of the separate instructions . . . . . . ▶	**9**	
10 **Overpayment** (subtract line 7 from line 8). Check if it is to be: ☐ **Applied to next return** or ☐ **Refunded** . . . . ▶	**10**	

Part III   Record of Quarterly Federal Unemployment Tax Liability (Do not include state liability.) **Complete only if line 7 is over $100.** See page 6 of the separate instructions.

Quarter	First (Jan. 1–Mar. 31)	Second (Apr. 1–June 30)	Third (July 1–Sept. 30)	Fourth (Oct. 1–Dec. 31)	Total for year
Liability for quarter					

Under penalties of perjury, I declare that I have examined this return, including accompanying schedules and statements, and, to the best of my knowledge and belief, it is true, correct, and complete, and that no part of any payment made to a state unemployment fund claimed as a credit was, or is to be, deducted from the payments to employees.

Signature ▶   Title (Owner, etc.) ▶   Date ▶

EXHIBIT 4-1   Form 940, FUTA Tax Return   *(cont.)*

liability. Before the fourth quarter, the employer is not liable for depositing any tax owed because of a credit reduction. The credit reduction becomes final on November 10 of each year. To determine the amount of federal unemployment tax owed for the fourth quarter if the business is subject to a credit reduction, an employer follows these steps:

1. Calculate the tax owed on wages paid during the year using an effective tax rate of .062 for the year.

2. Multiply the total wages subject to federal unemployment tax for the year by the amount of the credit reduction.

3. Subtract Step 2 from Step 1. The result is the federal unemployment tax owed for the year.

4. Deduct FUTA payments made for the first three quarters. The balance is the amount owed for the fourth quarter.

Form 940-EZ

Department of the Treasury
Internal Revenue Service   (99)

**Employer's Annual Federal
Unemployment (FUTA) Tax Return**

▶ **See separate Instructions for Form 940-EZ for information on completing this form.**

OMB No. 1545-1110

20

T	
FF	
FD	
FP	
I	
T	

Name (as distinguished from trade name)   Calendar year

Trade name, if any

Address and ZIP code   Employer identification number

*Answer the questions under **Who May Use Form 940-EZ** on page 2. If you cannot use Form 940-EZ, you must use Form 940.*

A   Enter the amount of contributions paid to your state unemployment fund. (See separate instructions.) . . . ▶ $ ....

B   (1) Enter the name of the state where you have to pay contributions . . . . ▶ ....
     (2) Enter your state reporting number as shown on your state unemployment tax return ▶

If you will not have to file returns in the future, check here (see Who Must File in separate instructions), **and complete and sign the return.** ▶ ☐

If this is an Amended Return, check here . . . . ▶ ☐

Part I   Taxable Wages and FUTA Tax

1	Total payments (including payments shown on lines 2 and 3) during the calendar year for services of employees	1
2	Exempt payments. (Explain all exempt payments, attaching additional sheets if necessary.) ▶	2
3	Payments of more than $7,000 for services. Enter only amounts over the first $7,000 paid to each employee. Do not include any exempt payments from line 2. (See separate instructions.) The $7,000 amount is the Federal wage base. Your state wage base may be different. **Do not use your state wage limitation**	3
4	Total exempt payments (add lines 2 and 3)	4
5	**Total taxable wages** (subtract line 4 from line 1) . . . . ▶	5
6	**FUTA tax.** Multiply the wages on line 5 by .008 and enter here. **(If the result is over $100, also complete Part II.)**	6
7	Total FUTA tax deposited for the year, including any overpayment applied from a prior year	7
8	**Balance due** (subtract line 7 from line 6). Pay to the **"United States Treasury"** . . . . . . ▶	8
	If you owe more than $100, see **Depositing FUTA tax** in separate instructions.	
9	**Overpayment** (subtract line 6 from line 7). Check if it is to be: ☐ **Applied to next return or** ☐ **Refunded** ▶	9

Part II   Record of Quarterly Federal Unemployment Tax Liability (Do not include state liability.) **Complete only if line 6 is over $100.**

Quarter	First (Jan. 1 – Mar. 31)	Second (Apr. 1 – June 30)	Third (July 1 – Sept. 30)	Fourth (Oct. 1 – Dec. 31)	Total for year
Liability for quarter					

Under penalties of perjury, I declare that I have examined this return, including accompanying schedules and statements, and, to the best of my knowledge and belief, it is true, correct, and complete, and that no part of any payment made to a state unemployment fund claimed as a credit was, or is to be, deducted from the payments to employees.

Signature ▶   Title (Owner, etc.) ▶   Date ▶

For Privacy Act and Paperwork Reduction Act Notice, see separate instructions.   Cat. No. 10983G   Form **940-EZ** (2000)

DETACH HERE

Form 940-EZ(V)

Department of the Treasury
Internal Revenue Service

Form 940-EZ Payment Voucher

Use this voucher only when making a payment with your return.

OMB No. 1545-1110

20

Complete boxes 1, 2, 3, and 4. Do not send cash, and do not staple your payment to this voucher. Make your check or money order payable to the **"United States Treasury"**. Be sure to enter your employer identification number, "Form 940-EZ", and "20 " on your payment.

1 Enter the first four letters of your last name (business name if partnership or corporation).	2 Enter your employer identification number.	3 Enter the amount of your payment.
		$

Instructions for Box 1

—Individuals (sole proprietors, trusts, and estates)—
Enter the first four letters of your last name.

—Corporations and partnerships—Enter the first four characters of your business name (omit "The" if followed by more than one word).

4 Enter your business name (individual name for sole proprietors)

Enter your address

Enter your city, state, and ZIP code

EXHIBIT 4-2   Form 940-EZ, Simplified FUTA Tax Return

Who May Use Form 940-EZ

The following chart will lead you to the right form to use. However, **do not file Form 940-EZ if you have already filed Form 940 for 20 .**

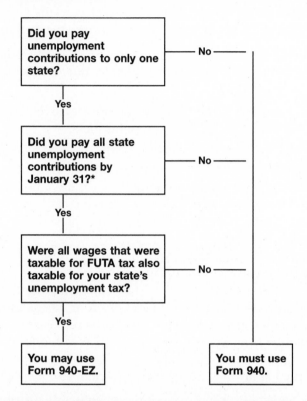

Did you pay unemployment contributions to only one state? — No

Yes ↓

Did you pay all state unemployment contributions by January 31?* — No

Yes ↓

Were all wages that were taxable for FUTA tax also taxable for your state's unemployment tax? — No

Yes ↓

You may use Form 940-EZ.

You must use Form 940.

***If you deposited all FUTA tax when due, you may answer "Yes" if you paid all state unemployment contributions by February 12.**

Also, **do not file Form 940-EZ if—**
• You owe FUTA tax **only for household work** in a private home. See **Schedule H (Form 1040).**
• You are a **successor employer** claiming a credit for state unemployment contributions paid by a prior employer. File Form 940.

☆ U.S. GPO: 2000 435-139

EXHIBIT 4-2 Form 940-EZ, Simplified FUTA Tax Return *(cont.)*

Form 940 or Form 940-EZ is due one month after the end of the calendar year (by January 31). However, if tax deposits have been on time and in full, the business has an extra 10 days to file (until February 10).

Liability Under State Unemployment Tax Acts (SUTA)

All the states, the District of Columbia, Puerto Rico, and the Virgin Islands have established unemployment insurance to complement the federal program provided for in the Social Security Act of 1935. To show how the state program works in partnership with the federal system, let's look at the unemployment insurance program in New York State.

In New York State, a tax on employer payrolls finances the unemployment insurance program. An employer is an individual owner, a partnership, a corporation, or any other enterprise for whom employees perform services. An employer becomes subject to the law and therefore liable for taxes when either of the two following situations occurs.

1. Payment of earnings of $300 or more, including meals, lodging, and rent, to employees in a calendar quarter. Liability begins as of the first day of that quarter.

2. Takeover of a business of a liable employer. Liability begins the day the new owner takes over that business.

The employer must notify the State Department of Labor when it meets either of these conditions for liability. The state issues the business an employer registration number, begins an account in the name and number of the company, and keeps a record of all taxes paid on time and any weekly benefits paid to former employees.

Covered Employment.   An employee in New York State is a worker who performs services for compensation. Coverage extends to all employment whether it is on a part-time, full-time, temporary, seasonal, or casual basis. Employees may perform services on or off the employer's premises or in their own homes. Officers of all corporations, including closely held corporations, who perform services for the corporation are employees of that corporation. Their compensation for these services, whether paid or accrued, is taxable. Covered employment also includes:

1. Agent or commission drivers engaged in distributing meat, vegetables, fruit, bakery products, beverages (except milk), laundry or dry cleaning services.

2. Traveling or city salespersons who work full-time soliciting orders for merchandise for resale or use in the purchaser's business operations.

Noncovered Employment.   The New York State Unemployment Insurance Law excludes certain employees from protection. Their earnings are not counted toward the $300 liability standard, and their employers pay no unemployment tax on their earnings. Excluded are the following:

1. An individual proprietor's child or stepchild under the age of 21 and the proprietor's spouse.
2. Children under age 14.
3. Daytime elementary or high school students employed by a for-profit organization.
4. Students under the age of 22 enrolled in a nonprofit or public educational institution in certain work-study programs that combine academic instruction with work experience.
5. Students in regular attendance in the educational institution that employs them, if their employment is incidental to their course of study.

6. Golf caddies.
7. Freelance shorthand reporters (in some cases).
8. Independent contractors.

Reportable and Nonreportable Earnings under SUTA. Tips are taxable. New York employees have the right to certify to the actual amount of tips they receive, and the employer must advise them of that right. The employee provides the employer with this certification (a signed, written statement) each calendar quarter. If the employee does not complete the certification, the employer can use a schedule of tips provided by the state.

Earnings not subject to SUTA include the following:

1. Reimbursement of travel expenses.

2. Payments to individuals age 65 or older, unless for services performed or vacation or sick pay.

3. Insurance or annuity payments to an employee for retirement.

4. Payments made by an employer to or on behalf of any employee or an employee's dependents under a retirement, sickness, accident, medical, hospital, or death benefit plan covering all or a class of employees.

5. Any other sickness or accident disability payments made more than six calendar months following the last month in which the employee worked.

Termination of Liability. Companies with a payroll of less than $300, including wages and other included forms of compensation, in each of four consecutive calendar quarters may apply for a termination of unemployment liability. Termination will take effect at the end of the calendar quarter in which the employer files the request. When the employer no longer has any employees and does not expect to hire any, the Department of Labor will suspend the account.

Calculating and Paying the SUTA Tax

Tax Rates for Newly Liable Employers. An employer who begins a new business receives an unemployment tax rate of 3.7%, which applies to the first $7,000 of each employee's earnings in a calendar year. An employer who takes over the business of a liable employer inherits the rate of that employer.

Experience Rating. The New York State Unemployment Insurance Law provides for an experience rating system, under which various factors including prior employment and unemployment experience determine the employer's tax rate. Other factors include the length of time the business has been subject to the law, the timeliness of quarterly tax reports, the prompt payment of owed taxes, the amount of benefits paid to former employees based on their employment with the company, and the balance in the State Unemployment Insurance Fund.

Taxable wages *The maximum calendar-year gross wages that are subject to a particular tax.*

Tax rates currently range from 1.5% to 5.4% of **taxable wages**. The state notifies employers of their rate in March of each year, well before the April 30 due date for the first quarter report.

Charging of Benefits. **Unemployment compensation benefits** paid to claimants are charged, in inverse chronological order, to the accounts of the employers for whom they worked in their base periods—the 52 weeks before they file their claims. Generally, the employer's account can be charged for as many weeks of benefits as the claimant worked for the employer in the base period.

Unemployment compensation benefits *Payments under state programs made for a limited time, usually 26 weeks, to workers who are out of a job.*

Employers will receive a notice each time a payment to a former employee is charged to their accounts. Each benefit charge has a potentially adverse effect on the employer's tax rate in future years.

Quarterly and Annual Reporting Under SUTA

A New York employer must report the payroll and pay unemployment insurance taxes each calendar quarter, as follows:

Calendar Quarter	Due Date
January–March	April 30
April–June	July 31
July–September	October 31
October–December	January 31

An employer must file a tax report even for a quarter in which it paid no wages. Only the first $7,000 of each employee's earnings, however, is subject to the unemployment tax in a calendar year.

Payments to elementary and high school students employed by a nonprofit organization and severance or dismissal payments are taxable only if the employer is subject to FUTA. An employer liable under FUTA must report the earnings of elementary and secondary school students, either on the quarterly tax returns or on an Employer's Report of Contributions, Form 1A-5a (Exhibit 4-3). These **contribution reports** are due on or before January 31 for wages paid during the prior calendar year.

Contribution report *Quarterly state unemployment tax return which applies an experience rating percentage to gross wages to compute the quarterly tax.*

Employers with a New York State tax rate of 2.8% or higher may reduce their taxes by reporting the earnings of these students on an annual report using Form 1A-5a. When reported annually, these payments are taxable at a maximum rate of 2.7%. The annual reporting option does not apply to payments to college students. The employer must report their earnings quarterly.

EMPLOYER PAYMENTS FOR OTHER INSURANCE PROGRAMS

Unemployment insurance provides payments to workers who are able but become unemployed. Employers may (or in some cases are required to) participate in two insurance programs that make payments to employees

IA 5a(5-92)

NEW YORK STATE DEPARTMENT OF LABOR
UNEMPLOYMENT INSURANCE DIVISION
EMPLOYER'S REPORT OF CONTRIBUTIONS

For your record, enter your eight-digit Employer Registration Number, as shown on the original, in the space below.
EMPLOYER REGISTRATION NUMBER

COPY TO BE RETAINED
BY EMPLOYER

Your eight-digit Employer Registration Number should always be indicated when corresponding with this division.

IMPORTANT: Read Carefully   ANSWER ALL ITEMS   — See Reverse for Instructions and Information

Report for calendar quarter
FROM-MONTH   DAY   YEAR   THRU   MONTH   DAY   YEAR

	Dollars only
1. Total remuneration paid for employment during this quarter	
2. Remuneration included in Item 1 that exceeds taxable limit of **$7,000** paid each worker during the year	
3. Wages subject to contribution. (Item 1 less 2)	

	Dollars	Cents
4. Contributions due. Your tax rate is Multiply item 3 by		
5. Plus: Amounts previously underpaid		
6. Less: Amounts previously overpaid		
7. Amount of Remittance		

8. Number of employees working during the week which includes the 12th day of each month	FIRST MONTH	
	SECOND MONTH	
	THIRD MONTH	

9. If business or employment in New York State was permanently discontinued or business was sold (other than corporate stock transfer), in whole or in part, during the calendar quarter covered by this report, answer items below:

a. Date of permanent discontinuance in New York State

b. Was all or part of business sold?   ☐ All   ☐ Part

Date of sale: month_____ day_____ year_____

Name of new owner _____

Address _____

10. Has ownership (i.e., partnership, individual ownership) changed during the calendar quarter covered by this report?

☐ Yes   ☐ No   If "YES," enter date and explain:

PLEASE ENTER YOUR EIGHT-DIGIT
EMPLOYER REGISTRATION NUMBER
ON YOUR REMITTANCE.

MAKE REMITTANCES PAYABLE TO:
N.Y.S. UNEMPLOYMENT INSURANCE
Address: P.O. Box 1589, Albany, N.Y. 12201-1589

DO NOT STAPLE
CHECK TO
REPORT

THIS COPY MUST BE RETAINED
FOR A PERIOD OF
NOT LESS THAN THREE YEARS

Requests for additional copies of this form should be
directed to:
New York State Department of Labor
Liability and Determination Section
Governor W. Averell Harriman
State Office Building Campus
Albany, N.Y. 12240-0339

EXHIBIT 4-3   New York State Employer's Report of Contributions

who are unable to continue their jobs: disability insurance and workers' compensation insurance programs.

Disability Insurance

Disability insurance *Insurance paid for by employers and/or employees for protection for employees and their families against loss of wages due to non-job-related accidents or disability.*

Only a few states currently require employers to participate in **disability insurance** programs: California, Hawaii, New Jersey, New York, Rhode Island, and Puerto Rico. However, many employers in other states voluntarily provide disability insurance as an added benefit to their employees. Disability insurance protects against loss of wages by providing payments to employees who are unable to work because of illness, injuries, or non-job-related accidents.

Financing for these benefits comes from taxes imposed on employees, employers, or both. For example, in New York State, the employer may withhold 0.5% of wages or up to $.60 per week from an employee's gross wages; this tax, which is paid to a private insurance company, provides disability benefits to the employee for up to 26 weeks. The employer can elect to pay the entire amount for the insurance or may offer to purchase better coverage through a private insurance company, paying part or all of the cost of this additional insurance.

The contributions to a disability insurance plan by an employer are not taxable. The disability benefits are taxable as wages in whole if the employer paid all the premiums or in part if the employee shared in the cost. The taxable portion is equal to the percentage paid by the employer.

Some companies take advantage of a tax-saving opportunity by treating the premium payments as an increase in wages for their employees (this is most advantageous for employees over FICA limits). Under this arrangement, the employer may fully deduct the payments as wages and the employee must pay income tax on these wages. But any disability benefits received in the future are tax-free to the employee.

Workers' Compensation Insurance

Almost every state has a workers' compensation insurance program. **Workers' compensation insurance** differs from disability insurance in that it provides benefits to employees and their families because of job-related illness, injuries, or death. The employer finances the entire cost of such insurance, which may be purchased from a private insurance company or a state insurance fund. Some states allow companies or certain industries to self-insure.

Workers' compensation insurance *Insurance paid for by employers that provides benefits to employees or their families for loss of wages due to job-related accidents, illness, or injuries.*

The rates for workers' compensation insurance depend on the risk ratings of the various jobs in a company. In most cases, the employer pays estimated premiums based on the estimated wages and rates for each class of worker (type of job). At the end of the year, the insurance company calculates the actual premiums that would have been due based on the actual wages and either credits the employer's account for an overpayment or bills the company for an underpayment.

REVIEW QUESTIONS

4-1. What are the two taxes mandated by the Federal Insurance Contributions Act?

4-2. What are the current tax rates and wage bases that apply to each part of FICA?

4-3. What are the two methods that can be used to compute FICA taxes?

4-4. Name the two situations for which the use of the combined tables for income tax and FICA withholding is not appropriate.

4-5. When might the value of meals be nontaxable?

4-6. What type of employee retirement plan contributions are subject to FICA and FUTA taxes even though exempt from FITW?

4-7. Name three types of sick pay that are not subject to Social Security and Medicare taxes.

4-8. When might supplemental unemployment payments be subject to Social Security and Medicare taxes?

4-9. Under what conditions are special payments to students exempt from FICA and FUTA taxes?

4-10. Explain the effect on FICA taxes when an employer succeeds to a business.

4-11. Describe the tax liability of related corporations that employ the same individual at the same time and pay this individual through a common paymaster.

4-12. Are wages paid for services to a spouse or children in an employer's trade or business taxable? When might these wages not be taxable?

4-13. Define a trade or business according to the Self-Employment Contributions Act.

4-14. Which of the following are considered self-employment income?

    a. Income from a partnership

    b. Loss from a partnership

    c. Guaranteed payments from a partnership

    d. Part-time work in a side business

4-15. Name the three methods that can be used to compute the self-employment tax. In what way do these methods differ?

4-16. When are the optional methods of computing self-employment tax better to use?

4-17. What are the minimum income levels which require payment of self-employment tax? What are the maximum limits?

4-18. Define *disposable earnings* for purposes of wage attachments.

4-19. What are the most common wage attachments? In what order of priority would these amounts be deducted from an employee's earnings?

4-20. When do the state or federal limits apply for child support? What are the federal limits?

4-21. How is the amount of an employee's net pay exempt from a tax levy determined?

4-22. What is the limit on the amount of disposable earnings subject to garnishment?

4-23. Tests to determine liability for unemployment tax may be applied to what three categories of workers? Explain the tests for income and periods of employment for these three categories.

4–24. Besides cash, name two other forms of compensation considered wages for unemployment tax purposes.

4–25. List the tax rates and wage base for unemployment tax purposes.

4–26. Explain how the credit for the state unemployment tax rate affects the federal unemployment tax rate.

4–27. Under what conditions might the state credit for unemployment taxes be reduced?

4–28. By what date must the Annual Federal Unemployment Tax Return be filed?

4–29. How is the amount of the federal unemployment tax owed for the fourth quarter calculated if an employer is subject to a credit reduction?

4–30. Under the New York State unemployment insurance program, when does an employer become liable for taxes?

4–31. Under the New York State unemployment insurance program, explain what is meant by covered employment and noncovered employment.

4–32. Give five examples of nonreportable earnings under the New York State unemployment insurance program.

4–33. What are the four quarterly due dates for the reporting and paying of unemployment insurance taxes?

4–34. What are the factors that determine the experience rating in New York State?

4–35. Against what and in what order are unemployment insurance benefits charged?

4–36. Under what conditions may liability be terminated under the New York State unemployment insurance system?

4–37. How can an employer structure premium payments for disability insurance to the advantage of higher-paid employees?

4–38. What is the basic difference between disability insurance and workers' compensation insurance? Name other possible differences.

DISCUSSION QUESTIONS

4–1. Some employers may have workers who are not officially on the payroll even though this practice is illegal. The existence of this underground economy is a problem the government recognizes and would like to eliminate. Why would a business hire workers and pay them off the books?

4–2. Congress has passed laws to extend the time period for unemployment insurance benefits. Should other factors determine the period of coverage? What factors might be considered on an individual basis to determine the period of coverage?

4–3. In recent years, some employers have set up their own retirement plans for employees in addition to the social security system. What do you think are the advantages and disadvantages of this practice?

4–4. Complaints over the years by self-employed persons have led to changes in the self-employment tax so that it currently equals the combined employer-employee rate. Do you agree that the method is fair or would you set up a different system?

EXERCISES

(Note: Unless otherwise specified, use the tax tables in Appendix A. The FICA taxes are based on the 2000 tax rates and wage base limits.)

4–1. Will Johnson, a Nioga janitor, earned $420 during the last week. Compute the Social Security and Medicare taxes that should be withheld from Mr. Johnson's weekly paycheck using the

	Social Security Tax	Medicare Tax
a. wage-bracket method.	$_____	$_____
b. percentage method.	$_____	$_____

4–2. Scott Martinez, a Nioga salesperson, earned $1,760 during the month of January. Compute the Social Security and Medicare taxes that should be withheld according to the

	Social Security Tax	Medicare Tax
a. wage-bracket method.	$_____	$_____
b. percentage method.	$_____	$_____

4–3. Michele Jasek, a Nioga quality control inspector, earned $720 during the last biweekly payroll period. Compute the employee withholding and employer contribution for Social Security and Medicare taxes for this employee.

	Social Security Tax	Medicare Tax
a. employee withholding:	$_____	$_____
b. employer contribution:	$_____	$_____

4–4. Grace O'Neill, Jupiter's treasurer, earned $78,000 for the year. Compute the Social Security and Medicare taxes for a single paycheck in the month of February if she is paid

	Social Security Tax	Medicare Tax
a. semimonthly.	$_____	$_____
b. monthly.	$_____	$_____

4–5. Rachel Mollone, Nioga's vice president, earns $138,000 per year with $11,500 paid monthly. Compute the employee withholding for Social Security and Medicare taxes for the

	Social Security Tax	Medicare Tax
a. first payroll period.	$_____	$_____
b. seventh payroll period.	$_____	$_____
c. twelfth payroll period.	$_____	$_____

4–6. Terry Whitman is a school teacher who also owns and runs a bookstore. His yearly salary as a teacher was $46,500 and he earned $9,600 from the bookstore. What is his self-employment tax?

Social Security Tax $_____

Medicare Tax $_____

4–7. Mike Corrigan has been ordered to pay child support through payroll withholdings. Mike earns $3,000 a month with federal and state income tax withholdings of $400, FICA taxes of $230, and medical insurance deductions of $250. Mike does not support a second family and the child support is not in arrears. The state and federal limits on the maximum amount that can be deducted are the same. What is the amount of child support if medical insurance (a) is and (b) is not deducted to arrive at disposable earnings?

a. Disposable earnings with medical insurance deduction:

$_____

Maximum Federal and State Percentage ×_____

Maximum Child Support Payment $_____

b. Disposable earnings with *no* medical insurance deduction:

$_____

Maximum Federal and State Percentage ×_____

Maximum Child Support Payment $_____

4–8. Big Lights Videos has just been informed that one of its employees, Vanessa Purdy, has been served with a tax levy and it must begin payroll deductions within the next pay period. Vanessa earns $2,000 biweekly with federal and state income tax withholdings totaling $320 and FICA taxes of $153. She is married and has four withholding allowances. What is the amount the payroll clerk must withhold for the tax levy? (Use $7,350 for the standard deduction and $2,800 for each exemption.)

$_____

4–9. Horace Brody earns $400 per week as a paper finisher with Cullen Paper Company. His withholdings are $55 for federal income taxes, $25 for Social Security taxes, $6 for Medicare taxes, and $60 for child support. What is the maximum amount allowed under federal law for garnishment?

$_____

4–10. Jan's Eatery has a total of three employees who earned $6,000, $15,000, and $21,000, respectively. If Jan's state experience rating for unemployment tax purposes is 4.8%, what are the restaurant's unemployment taxes for the year? The state's taxable wage base is the same as the federal taxable wage base.

FUTA Tax $_____

SUTA Tax $_____

PROBLEMS

(Note: Unless otherwise specified, use the tax tables in Appendix A. The FICA taxes are based on the 2000 tax rates and wage base limits.)

4–1. Judy Chen earned $7,000 a month for the year. Compute the Social Security and Medicare taxes withheld from Judy's paycheck each month, the total amount of her FICA contributions for the year, and the total amount of FICA taxes contributed by Judy's employer for the year.

	Monthly Earnings	Social Security Tax	Medicare Tax
January	$_____	$_____	$_____
February	_____	_____	_____
March	_____	_____	_____
April	_____	_____	_____
May	_____	_____	_____
June	_____	_____	_____
July	_____	_____	_____
August	_____	_____	_____
September	_____	_____	_____
October	_____	_____	_____
November	_____	_____	_____
December	_____	_____	_____
TOTALS	_____	_____	_____

Employer Social Security Tax $_____
(Total Taxable Wages × Social Security Tax Rate)
Employer Medicare Tax $_____
(Total Taxable Wages × Medicare Tax Rate)

4–2. Handley's PC and Fax Shop pays its employees weekly. Compute the Social Security and Medicare taxes for each employee using the wage-bracket tables, the total amounts to be withheld, and the employer's FICA taxes for the same period.

Employee	Weekly Earnings	Social Security Tax	Medicare Tax
Boris Athena	$320	$_____	$_____
Mindy Grace	290	_____	_____
Alex Gregory	260	_____	_____
Samantha Grey	280	_____	_____
Totals	$_____	$_____	$_____

Problems (cont.)   *Employer Social Security Tax* $ _____

                                          Employer Medicare Tax $ _____

4–3. Executives at Bioscreen Waste Management are paid monthly. Compute the Social Security and Medicare taxes for each employee for the month of September, and the employer contribution for the month. Use the percentage method.

Employee	Gross Earnings to Date	Monthly Earnings	Social Security Tax	Medicare Tax
Tom Bolt	$ 74,800	$ 8,400	$_____	$_____
Lisa Asimov	44,160	5,760	_____	_____
Brady Lamb	46,080	5,520	_____	_____
Gail Show	49,280	6,160	_____	_____
Totals	$_____	$_____	$_____	$_____
Employer Contribution (_____ % × totals)			$_____	$_____

4–4. The Greenfield Surveying Company paid wages of $360,000 for the year, of which $28,000 was subject to FUTA and SUTA taxes with the $7,000 limit for each employee. The SUTA experience rating is 3.6%. Because the company has been late in making payments, its state tax credit is 90% of the maximum amount. Compute the FUTA and SUTA taxes.

FUTA Tax $ _____

SUTA Tax $ _____

4–5. Joan Martin, single with no dependents, is under court order to pay back taxes and also has a garnishment against her wages. Joan earns $400 weekly. Her withholdings include federal and state income taxes of $60, FICA taxes of $31, savings of $25, and charitable contributions of $10. What will Joan have to pay on the tax levy and the garnishment?

Tax Levy $ _____

Garnishment $ _____

4–6. Management at Jupiter Toys, Inc., had the yearly earnings shown in the following table. Compute the total Social Security and Medicare taxes for each employee using the percentage method.

Employee	Yearly Earnings	Social Security Tax	Medicare Tax
Steve Adelman	$ 58,000	$_____	$_____
April Arthurs	78,000	_____	_____
Sam Horton	52,000	_____	_____
Cheri Schmidt	140,000	_____	_____

Problems (cont.)

4–7. Using the percentage method, compute the federal income and FICA taxes to be withheld from the following employees at Jupiter Toys, Inc.

Employee	Marital Status	Allow- ances	Gross Earnings	Federal Income Tax	Social Security Tax	Medicare Tax
Alonzo Brown	M	3	$ 540 per wk.	$_____	$_____	$_____
Gerald Gregg	S	0	1,600 per mo.	_____	_____	_____
Clara Lane	S	2	20,000 per yr.	_____	_____	_____
Bette Tocci	M	4	900 per biwk.	_____	_____	_____

4–8. Using the wage-bracket method, compute the federal income and FICA taxes to withhold from the following employees at Jake's Variety Store.

Employee	Marital Status/ Allow.	Gross Earnings	Federal Income Tax	Social Security Tax	Medicare Tax
Andrea Bell	S-1	$1,500 per mo.	$_____	$_____	$_____
Beth Cluny	S-2	1,800 per mo.	_____	_____	_____
Rich Swift	M-2	400 per wk.	_____	_____	_____
Robert Jeter	M-3	700 per wk.	_____	_____	_____

4–9. The employees of Page's Rentals are paid biweekly. Compute the unemployment taxes due in the second quarter based on the following gross earnings to date. Assume a wage base limit of $7,000, a state experience rating of 4.2%, and a federal rate of 0.8%.

Employee	First Quarter Earnings	Second Quarter Earnings to Date
Harold Grove	$ 6,000	$ 6,200
Liam Ryan	8,500	7,000
Chris Blessing	6,500	6,000
Sarah Rogell	4,000	4,500
Totals	$25,000	$23,700

FUTA Tax $ _____

SUTA Tax _____

4–10. Assume the following facts about Harlee Rosen.
   a. Married with five exemptions and supports a second family
   b. Child support is in arrears
   c. Tax levy applied against wages
   d. Garnishment is in effect at 25%
   e. Disposable earnings for the month equal $3,400
Compute the amounts to be deducted for

Child Support $ _____

Tax Levy _____

Garnishment _____

CONTINUING CASE PROBLEM

For a week ending in October, Frontier Landscaping had the following payroll data. The FICA rate is 6.2% for the Social Security tax and 1.45% for the Medicare tax. The state unemployment tax rate is 5.4%, and the federal unemployment tax rate is 0.8%. The taxable wage base for SUTA and FUTA is the same. Compute the FICA taxes and the unemployment taxes for each employee and the totals.

Employee	Cumulative Wages	Wages	FICA Soc. Sec.	Med.	Unemployment SUTA	FUTA
Carrie Barnes	$ 7,800	$ 240	$_____	$_____	$_____	$_____
Julie Brown	8,600	250	_____	_____	_____	_____
Harry Fein	8,200	280	_____	_____	_____	_____
Horace Glenn	6,400	240	_____	_____	_____	_____
Frank Granto	6,800	260	_____	_____	_____	_____
Jose Lopez	8,400	280	_____	_____	_____	_____
Brenda Toomey	8,000	240	_____	_____	_____	_____
Melissa Trane	7,400	240	_____	_____	_____	_____
David Wood	48,000	1,250	_____	_____	_____	_____
Kathy Wood	75,000	1,500	_____	_____	_____	_____
Totals	$_____	$_____	$_____	$_____	$_____	$_____

CHAPTER 5

PREPARING AND DISTRIBUTING THE PAYROLL

LEARNING OBJECTIVES

On completing this chapter, you will be able to:

1. Record employees' wages in the payroll register by payroll period and discuss the uses of the payroll register in relation to other records and reports.
2. Prepare an employee earnings record using data from the Form W-4 and the payroll register and apply the information on this record to the calculation of payroll taxes.
3. Explain the use of a separate payroll account, a bank reconciliation, security measures, and specially designed payroll checks.
4. Discuss the payment of wages by pay envelope, paycheck, and direct deposit.
5. Distinguish the various methods of direct deposit.
6. Describe the legal framework for electronic funds transfer.

The type of payroll system an employer uses depends on the number of its employees, the complexity of the payroll transactions processed each period, and the extent of automation in the company. Clark tells Lois that Nioga still uses a manual system to prepare and distribute the payroll but plans to change to an automated system in the coming year. No matter what the system, however, all companies must keep certain basic records and follow certain procedures to track the payroll and transmit payroll information to the taxing authorities. Clark begins the discussion

127

by describing the two most important types of records: the payroll register and the employee earnings record.

RECORDING PAYROLL DATA

Employers prepare two types of payroll data: permanent and current. A *permanent file,* maintained for each employee, includes such items as the employee's name, address, Social Security number, pay rate, Form W-4 information, other deductions from gross earnings, and year-to-date payroll figures. A *current file* is a record of the latest payroll—the regular and over-time hours worked, bonuses, commissions, sick pay, tips, and vacation pay. The payroll clerk combines permanent and current data to determine net earnings, prepare a payroll check, and update cumulative amounts for gross earnings, various deductions, and net pay. A business usually maintains payroll records on a departmental basis in order to be able to analyze the source of the expenditures later.

A detailed set of payroll records contains information to satisfy the requirements of federal and state laws and to prepare tax reports. These records provide information that helps management control wages and improve operational efficiency. Wages usually are a large, if not the largest, expense in many companies. Management can monitor wages only within a well-organized payroll system that is able to provide timely, accurate information.

The payroll department keeps payroll data in two separate but related records: the payroll register or journal and the employee earnings record. Together, the payroll register and the employee earnings record provide the information needed to complete the payroll, file all the appropriate forms and taxes with the government, and pay the correct amount of taxes when due. Each record provides some information for the other, but each also contains information that can be checked against the other in order to verify the accuracy of the recorded data. Following logical steps in completing these forms and later in proving their accuracy is most important so that other records based on the data compiled from them will also be accurate.

The Payroll Register

Payroll register *A payroll record for a payroll period listing all employees, the gross wages, deductions, and net pay for each, and the totals for all employees.*

The **payroll register** is a sequential listing of every paycheck by payroll period. The payroll register provides a record of payment and a summary of the total payroll for all employees. These data are the basis for calculating quarterly payroll taxes and workers' compensation insurance premiums.

A sample payroll register for a weekly payroll period for Nioga Gear is shown in Figure 5-1. Although the forms used by individual employers may vary slightly, the payroll register must have a space for the payroll period being covered at the top of each page. It generally includes several columns for employee data such as name, an identifying number (such as

Nioga Gear, Inc.

Payroll Register

PAY PERIOD ENDING _____ 20 ____

TIME-CARD NO.	EMPLOYEE	M/S W/H ALLOW.	TIME WORKED			RATE		EARNINGS			FICA		DEDUCTIONS				NET AMOUNT PAID	CHECK NO.	DATE PAID
			REG. HOURS	OVER-TIME	TOTAL HOURS	REG. HOURS	OVER-TIME	REG. WAGES	OVER-TIME	TOTAL	SOC. SEC.	MEDI-CARE	FITW	SITW	MED. INS.	TOTAL			
TOTALS																			

FIGURE 5-1 Payroll Register for Nioga Gear, Inc.

a timecard or employee number), marital status, and the number of withholding allowances (taken from the Form W-4), followed by several columns reflecting rate of pay and time worked. The next two sections cover earnings—both regular and overtime—and the various deductions. A final column lists net pay and may be followed by additional columns for payroll check number and payment date. Each line of the page contains the payroll information for a single employee, with the last line providing the totals for the period. Additional pages may be necessary; some businesses use a separate page for each department.

Accounting and Reporting Uses.   The payroll register provides the basis for

- recording entries in the employee earnings records,
- issuing paychecks for the employees,
- preparing journal entries to record the payroll and the employer's payroll taxes, and
- filing periodic payroll reports with government agencies.

In the payroll journal entry, the payroll clerk records the aggregate amount of wages earned, the deductions made, and the net pay to all employees, as indicated in the Totals line of the payroll register. The entry is recorded in a two-column general journal or a cash payments journal and then posted from the journal to the general ledger. The journal entry reflects the payroll expense, the related payroll liabilities, and the cash paid out. A later chapter discusses this aspect of payroll accounting in more detail.

Completing the Payroll Register.   The steps to complete the payroll register are as follows:

1. List each employee alphabetically or numerically.

2. Transfer to the payroll register information relating to each employee's salary or hourly rate, marital status, and number of withholding allowances claimed as recorded on the employee earnings record (described later).

3. Take hours worked for hourly employees from timecards and time sheets (see Figure 5-2). For nonhourly employees, take information on biweekly or monthly salary from the employee earnings record. Use production and sales records to record gross earnings of employees on piece-rate or commission plans.

EXERCISE   Compare the amounts recorded in the payroll register for Wayne Dean during the week ending November 13 (Figure 5-3) with amounts recorded on his timecard for that same period (Figure 5-2).   ▲

4. Compute each employee's regular, overtime, and gross earnings from the work records examined.

5. Determine each employee's deductions for federal and state income taxes (using the appropriate tax tables based on the marital status and number of withholding allowances) and for FICA taxes.

WEEKLY TIMECARD FROM _11/8/XX_   TO _11/13/XX_
                                    DATE   DATE

(Notice: This card must be turned in to the proper authority before payment can be made)

EMPLOYEE'S NAME   _Dean, Wayne_   S.S. ACCT. NO.   _488-26-5891_
ADDRESS   _402 Pine Avenue, Lockport, NY 14074_
POSITION   _Inspector_   DEPT   _Production_   CLOCK NO.   _265_

| | A.M. | | P.M. | | OVERTIME | | TOTAL HOURS | |
	IN	OUT	IN	OUT	IN	OUT	Regular	Overtime
MONDAY	8:30	12:00	12:30	5:00			8	
TUESDAY	8:25	12:00	12:27	5:00			8	
WEDNESDAY	8:27	12:00	12:28	5:00			8	
THURSDAY	8:30	12:00	12:30	5:00	6:00	7:00	8	1
FRIDAY	8:25	12:00	12:30	5:00	6:00	7:00	8	1
SATURDAY								
SUNDAY								
					WEEKLY TOTAL		40	2

I, the undersigned, certify that this is a true and accurate record of my working time for the period above mentioned.

Signature: _Wayne Dean_

FIGURE 5-2   Weekly Timecard for Wayne Dean

6. Record the medical insurance deduction.

7. Total all the deductions and subtract from gross earnings to determine net amount paid.

Footing *Adding a series of columns vertically to verify the accuracy of the totals.*

Cross-footing *Adding a series of rows horizontally to verify the accuracy of the totals.*

Proving the Totals of the Payroll Register.   The **footing** and **cross-footing** of the columns in the payroll register serve to prove the accuracy of the amounts recorded. Since the totals in the payroll register provide the basis for accounting entries (see Chapter 7), this proof of the payroll register is extremely important. As in any footing and cross-footing test, the vertical totals and horizontal totals must be equal. The specific steps are as follows:

1. Add the totals of the regular and overtime earnings columns. The sum of these columns should equal the total of the Total Earnings column.

2. Add the totals of the various deductions columns. The sum of these columns should equal the total of the Total Deductions column.

3. Subtract the total of the Total Deductions column from the total of the Total Earnings column. The difference should equal the total of the Net Amount Paid column.

If the footings and cross-footings do not total properly, some amount in the payroll register is incorrect. Repeating the process will usually reveal the error; if not, double-check the amounts for each employee.

EXERCISE During the week ending November 13, employees at Nioga Gear worked the hours and had withholdings as follows. Complete the payroll register in Figure 5-3, using this data and assuming an hourly rate of $12.

| Employee | Hours | | FITW | SITW | Medical Insurance |
	Reg.	OT			
Laura Charles	40	—	$46.00	$21.00	$20.00
Wayne Dean	40	2	42.00	24.00	20.00
Fred Moon	40	—	65.00	22.00	20.00
Kate Schmidt	40	4	57.00	23.00	16.00
Robert Wales	40	6	53.00	20.00	20.00

▲

The Employee Earnings Record

As we've seen, the payroll register provides a useful summary of the earnings, deductions, and net pay of all employees for a specific payroll period. Such information is not enough, however, since a business must keep payroll information for each employee from period to period throughout the year. The **employee earnings record**, as shown in Figure 5-4, serves this purpose. The employer updates the employee earnings record, which is maintained on a quarterly and annual basis, by making entries from the payroll register at the end of each payroll period.

Employee earnings record A payroll record for each employee listing the gross wages, deductions, net pay by payroll period, and cumulative earnings.

The top of the employee earnings record contains basic information about the employee, including marital status, number of withholding allowances, and regular rate of pay. This information is needed to compute earnings, deductions, and net pay and is revised when the basic information about the employee changes. For instance, if a single employee gets married or if a married employee requests an increase or decrease in withholding allowances, the payroll clerk makes these changes in the heading section of the employee earnings record. These types of changes require that the employee fill out a new Form W-4. For changes in voluntary deductions, the employee would submit a new authorization form. The employee's pay rate can only be changed on written notification from management. Similarly, written authorization is necessary before adding or deleting an employee.

As Figure 5-4 shows, most of the rest of the information for the employee earnings record comes from the payroll register: hours worked, earnings, deductions, and net pay. The only additional information that the payroll clerk must complete on the employee earnings record is the cumulative earnings. Adding the total earnings for the current payroll period to the previous cumulative earnings yields the latest cumulative earnings total.

Computational and Reporting Uses. The payroll department uses information on the employee earnings record to prepare or determine the following:

1. *Payroll register.* The employee earnings record contains information such as the hourly rate, marital status, and number of withholding allowances claimed—data needed to compute gross earnings and income tax withholding.

Nioga Gear, Inc.

Payroll Register

PAY PERIOD ENDING _____ November 13 _____ 20XX _____

TIME-CARD NO.	EMPLOYEE	M/S W/H ALLOW.	TIME WORKED REG. HOURS	TIME WORKED OVER-TIME	TIME WORKED TOTAL HOURS	RATE REG.	RATE OVER-TIME	EARNINGS REG. WAGES	EARNINGS OVER-TIME	EARNINGS TOTAL	FICA SOC. SEC.	FICA MEDI-CARE	DEDUCTIONS FITW	DEDUCTIONS SITW	DEDUCTIONS MED. INS.	DEDUCTIONS TOTAL	NET AMOUNT PAID	CHECK NO.	DATE PAID
	Laura Charles	MI1	40	—									46 00	21 00	20 00				
	Wayne Dean	MI2	40	2									42 00	24 00	20 00				
	Fred Moon	SI0	40	—									65 00	22 00	20 00				
	Kate Schmidt	MI1	40	4									57 00	23 00	16 00				
	Robert Wales	MI2	40	6									53 00	20 00	20 00				
	TOTALS																		

FIGURE 5-3 Partially Completed Payroll Register for Nioga Gear, Inc.

Nioga Gear, Inc.

Employee Earnings Record

NAME Dean, Wayne

ADDRESS 402 Pine Avenue, Lockport, NY 14074

BIRTHDATE 6/15/56   POSITION Inspector

TIMECARD NO. 265

SOCIAL SECURITY NO. 488-26-5891

DATE EMPLOYED 4/12/86

DATE TERMINATED

MARITAL STATUS Married

WITHHOLDING ALLOWANCES 2

RATE OF PAY $12.00

PERIOD ENDING	TIME WORKED			RATE		EARNINGS			DEDUCTIONS						NET AMOUNT PAID	CHECK NO.	CUMULATIVE EARNINGS
	REG. HOURS	OVER-TIME	TOTAL HOURS	REG. HOURS	OVER-TIME	REG. WAGES	OVER-TIME	TOTAL	FICA SOC. SEC.	FICA MEDI-CARE	FITW	SITW	MED. INS.	TOTAL			
10/9	40		40	12 00		480 00		480 00	29 76	6 96	38 00	18 40	20 00	113 12	366 88	4606	20284 00
10/16	40	2	42	12 00	18 00	480 00	36 00	516 00	31 99	7 48	42 00	24 00	20 00	125 47	390 53	4310	20800 00
10/23	40		40	12 00		480 00		480 00	29 76	6 96	38 00	18 40	20 00	113 12	366 88	4414	21280 00
10/30	40		40	12 00		480 00		480 00	29 76	6 96	38 00	18 40	20 00	113 12	366 88	4518	21760 00
11/6	40	6	46	12 00	18 00	480 00	108 00	588 00	36 46	8 53	53 00	26 30	20 00	144 29	443 71	4622	22348 00
TOTAL																	
ACCUM. TOTALS																	

FIGURE 5-4   Employee Earnings Record for Wayne Dean

2. *Cut-off level of earnings for Social Security, FUTA, and SUTA.* The Cumulative Earnings column signals when an employee has reached the limit of earnings subject to tax (such as the wage base of $72,600 in 1999 and $76,200 in 2000 for Social Security taxes, and the $7,000 applicable wage base limit for unemployment taxes).

3. *Annual employee earnings statement, Form W-2.* The employee earnings record provides information on the annual gross earnings, income and FICA taxes withheld, wages subject to FICA, and other information needed to complete Form W-2.

Proving the Employee Earnings Record. As described earlier, the Cumulative Earnings column in the employee earnings record provides a continuous record of the employee's total earnings for the year. The employer must examine the cumulative total before preparing each payroll to find out whether the employee has reached the annual earnings limit for Social Security taxes or FUTA and SUTA taxes.

EXERCISE Look at the Cumulative Earnings column in Figure 5-4. Has Wayne Dean exceeded the Social Security or FUTA and SUTA limits? ▲

At the end of each quarter and the calendar year, the employer totals the amounts in the employee earnings record. Since these totals are essential to completing the various quarterly tax reports, accuracy is extremely important. The process of footing and cross-footing will make it easier to detect errors.

EXERCISE According to his employee earnings record, Wayne Dean is married with two withholding allowances. Use the tables provided in Appendix A to check the FICA and federal income tax deductions for the payroll period ended November 13. Do you agree with the amounts shown in the employee earnings record? ▲

PAYING EMPLOYEE WAGES

Although payday is probably the favorite day of most employees, it can be a real headache for the payroll manager. Achieving a smooth payday requires a great deal of planning, as well as efficient, well-integrated systems.

Employees get paid in one of three ways: (1) by cash in pay envelopes; (2) by check, either drawn on the company's regular checking account or drawn on a special payroll account; and (3) through direct deposit of funds into an employee's bank account. Each of these payment options has its own set of advantages and disadvantages, and an employer must choose the method or combination of methods that works best for the company and its employees. In addition, as a business grows, it should explore more sophisticated methods for payment of wages. Perhaps the company can justify a separate payroll account; maybe it should abandon the use of pay envelopes and pay by check; or, if circumstances warrant, the company might wish to use direct deposit on a small scale within the geographical area or on a larger scale through electronic funds transfer. The payroll manager must look into the factors involved in making these decisions and evaluate the pros and cons of using more advanced approaches.

Government Regulations Regarding Payment of Wages

State, not federal, regulations control the timing and/or method of the payment of wages to employees. Most states specify the frequency for the payment of wages and also the payment lag period—that is, the number of days by which wages must be paid. This lag period varies from 5 days in Arizona to 30 days for Nebraska and 35 for Oregon. Some states require the use of a local bank for the payroll account although, in most states, the employer is permitted to use a centrally located bank or a centralized account. In some cases, permission depends on the company opening an account with a local bank and having this bank cash any checks presented directly.

Payment by Cash in Pay Envelopes

Although pay envelopes were very popular several decades ago, their use has steadily declined as a method for paying employees. Now only small businesses or those that are far from banking facilities use pay envelopes. Businesses that do use the pay envelope method must follow rather detailed procedures to obtain the correct amount of currency, by denomination and coins, and to stuff the envelopes with the correct pay. The payroll manager or clerk must calculate the exact numbers of each currency denomination and coin from $20 bills to pennies, prepare a requisition to get those specific numbers of denominations from the bank, and deposit a check for the total amount with the bank.

After the payroll manager or clerk obtains the cash, the next step is to fill the pay envelope of each employee with the correct number of bills and coins. Each employee must sign a receipt on picking up the proper pay envelope.

The payroll register provides the basic data for using pay envelopes. Once the net pay for all employees is known, a payroll change sheet is prepared (see Figure 5-5). This form lists the numbers of each denomination of currency or coin needed to equal the net pay of each employee. The proper number of bills and coins of each denomination represents the amounts that, when added, will equal the total payroll check the company exchanges for currency and coins.

EXAMPLE   The Buzzboys Rockabilly Band is continually on the road, so its employees prefer being paid in cash. The payroll change sheet in Figure 5-5 shows the net pay and the specific bills and coins required for each pay envelope.   ▲

The payroll clerk uses the payroll change sheet to complete the currency withdrawal request (see Figure 5-6) in order to receive from the

GREATER NIAGARA BANK

Payroll Change Sheet and Proof, Week Ended October 16, 20XX

		BILLS				COINS			
EMPLOYEE	NET PAY	$20	$10	$5	$1	$.25	$.10	$.05	$.01
Beaton, Greg	$512.25	25	1		2	1			
Kane, Rhonda	480.88	24				3	1		3
Means, Bill	502.60	25			2	2	1		
Reimer, Beverly	473.42	23	1		3	1	1	1	2
Troop, Al	516.27	25	1	1	1	1			2
Totals	$2,485.42	122	3	1	8	8	3	1	7
Multiplied by		$20	$10	$5	$1	$.25	$.10	$.05	$.01
Proof	$2,485.42	$2,440	$30	$5	$8	$2	$.30	$.05	$.07

FIGURE 5-5 Payroll Change Sheet

GREATER NIAGARA BANK

Currency Withdrawal Request

NAME: *Buzzboys Rockabilly Band*
DATE: *October 18, 20XX*

DENOMINATION		NO.	AMOUNT
Bills	$20	122	$2,440.00
	10	3	30.00
	5	1	5.00
	1	8	8.00
Coins	$ .25	8	2.00
	.10	3	.30
	.05	1	.05
	.01	7	.07
			$2,485.42

FIGURE 5-6 Currency Withdrawal Request

bank the proper denomination of currency and coins. The payroll clerk also uses the payroll change sheet to fill the pay envelopes since it lists the correct amount of bills and coins for each pay envelope. A statement of earnings and deductions appears on the face of each pay envelope (see Figure 5-7).

EXAMPLE   For this particular week, the Buzzboys Rockabilly Band will deposit a payroll check for $2,485.42 and submit a currency withdrawal request (see Figure 5-6) to the bank. In exchange, it will receive 122 $20 bills, three $10 bills, one $5 bill, eight $1 bills, eight quarters, three dimes, one nickel, and seven pennies.   ▲

Payment by Check

Internal control *Measures by which a company operates or conducts its activities to safeguard assets, enhance reliability of accounting data, promote operational efficiency, and encourage adherence to company policies.*

From the employer's standpoint, payment by check is preferable to the use of pay envelopes because it involves less work and promotes better **internal control**. The check register serves as a record of all checks issued, de-

NAME	Greg Beaton
Payroll Period	Week 10/16/XX
Hours Worked	40
GROSS EARNINGS	
Salary	$ 600.00
Bonus	198.00
	$ 798.00
DEDUCTIONS	
Federal Income Tax	$ 143.00
Social Security Tax	49.48
Medicare Tax	11.57
State Income Tax	56.10
Medical Insurance	25.60
	$ 285.75
NET PAY	$ 512.25

FIGURE 5-7 Pay Envelope

posits made, and the balance in the account. The payroll checks may be prepared by hand, typed, or computer-generated.

At the top or bottom of most payroll checks is a detachable statement of earnings and deductions (see Figure 5-8). The payroll register provides data for the statement of earnings and deductions and the net pay, which is the amount of the check. The payroll clerk enters the employee's name, the date, the check number, and the amount of the check in the check register; determines the balance of the checking account; and records the check number, amount, and payment date in the payroll register.

On a manually prepared or typed payroll check, the signature line remains blank until all checks have been verified. Then, the treasurer or other authorized paying agent signs all the checks. In a large company, a check-signing machine may imprint an authorized signature on all the checks. The canceled checks serve as receipts and, if the company uses a two-part check, it has a copy of all issued checks, permitting verification for internal or external auditing before the return of the canceled checks.

Use of a Separate Payroll Account. A small employer may issue paychecks from its regular checking account, but many businesses find it advantageous

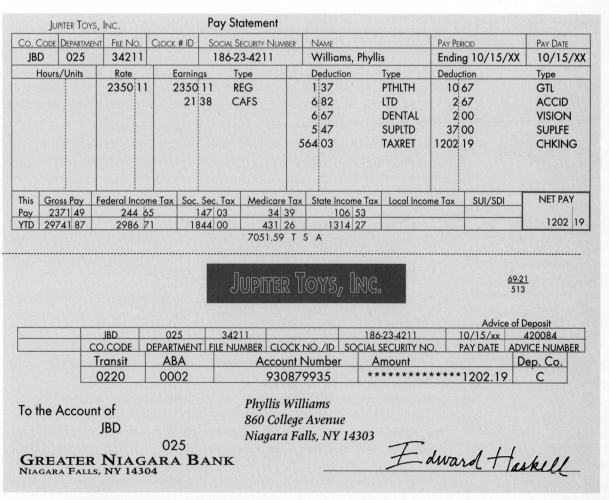

FIGURE 5-8 Payroll Check with Detachable Statement of Earnings and Deductions

to have a separate payroll account. A separate account facilitates mechanical signatures for a large number of payroll checks thus eliminating the need for hand signatures. The most important advantage, however, is the simplification of the reconciliation of the regular and payroll accounts. When payroll checks are cleared through their own account, it is much easier to reconcile the regular account.

Reconciliation of a separate payroll account is also easier. Before payday, the employer transfers the total amount of payroll funds required to meet the payroll from the regular account to the payroll account. After all employees cash their paychecks, the balance in the payroll account should be zero or some fixed or **imprest** amount. Some companies may set up a small balance in the account to cover vacation pay, termination payments, or other special purposes.

Imprest *A term denoting a fixed balance to be maintained at all times.*

Ideally, the accounting department, not the payroll department, should reconcile the payroll account. In any event, the steps in the reconciliation process are as follows:

1. Compare the deposits listed on the bank statement with the deposits shown in the payroll cash account. Add the deposits in transit to the bank balance.

2. Examine all checks returned with the bank statement to make sure they are company checks, properly signed, and charged to the company's account.

3. Compare the canceled checks returned with the bank statement to the payroll cash account. List checks issued but not on the bank statement. Deduct the total of these outstanding checks from the bank statement balance.

4. Add to the payroll cash account balance any interest earned or credit memoranda issued by the bank (such as for the collection of a promissory note) that are listed on the bank statement but not included on the payroll cash account balance.

NSF check *A check returned to the depositor with the amount of the check, if previously deposited, deducted from the depositor's account, because the issuer does not have sufficient funds to cover the check.*

5. Deduct from the payroll cash account balance any debit memoranda issued by the bank (such as for an **NSF check**) and bank service charges.

6. Record in the payroll cash account any other items (such as correction of errors) that the company records do not reflect.

7. Compare the adjusted balance per the bank statement with the adjusted balance per the payroll cash account.

Most bank statements carry a blank reconciliation form that can be used for this purpose. Many companies, however, follow their own form or use a computerized program.

In addition to reconciling the payroll bank account balance, the accounting department should perform reconciliations of payroll account activity. These reconciliations, in which the payroll manager can be of great assistance, consist of the following steps:

1. Review the outstanding checks with the payroll manager to determine why they have not been cashed within a reasonable time.

2. Reconcile the outstanding checks. The total amount of the canceled paychecks (those cashed during the period), less the outstanding payroll checks at the beginning of the period, plus the total amount of payroll checks outstanding at the end of the period should equal the total of all the paychecks written during the period and shown in the cash account.

3. Reconcile the deposits in transit. The amount of deposits reflected during the period, less the deposits in transit at the beginning of the period, plus the amount of deposits in transit at the end of the period should equal the amount of payroll deposits shown in the cash account during the period.

Security Measures. Effective control over checks can help prevent theft, fraud, and other problems. A good internal control measure when paying by check is to use preprinted checks, numbered in sequence; this makes it harder for checks to be lost or stolen and not noticed. The **voided checks** as well as the canceled checks should be kept on file and accounted for during the bank reconciliation. Checks not in the file may be outstanding but also could be lost or stolen. Other security measures include taking additional care in the storage of blank checks and, in particular, the check-signing machine. These items are often stored in vaults or locked facilities as a safeguard. Proper separation of duties—putting the various functions of payroll preparation and distribution in the hands of separate individuals—is essential.

Voided check *A check invalidated or nullified by the issuer at the time of writing or after issuance if the check has been lost or remains uncashed for a relatively long period.*

Direct Deposit of Payroll

Direct deposit *Any of several methods of placing funds directly in an employee's bank account without issuing a paycheck.*

The fastest growing method of paying employees is **direct deposit**. Direct deposit of payroll involves the automatic deposit of an employee's pay into a checking or savings account at a bank or other financial institution. Even with direct deposit, the company must give the employee an earnings and deductions statement.

A number of forms of direct deposit are available. The employer can use:

- one local bank—the employer's bank—with the deposits made by mail or in person.
- several local banks, with the employer making deposits in the banks of the employees either by mail or in person.
- various local and out-of-town banks, with the deposits being made by electronic transfer to the banks of the employees.

The choice of the direct deposit system depends on the size of the company and on the geographic distribution of its employees. A local company with a few employees may use its own bank or two or three local banks. Large companies with employees around the country or in many states may choose one financial institution as the focus of its direct deposit system.

Direct deposit, regardless of the exact method used, has significant advantages for the employer and the employees and a few disadvantages.

For employers, direct deposit reduces the cost of checks, signing, and distribution; makes the bank reconciliation easier with fewer checks to balance; decreases potential loss by theft or fraud; and eliminates the need for trips to the bank, early vacation checks, and the problem of unclaimed checks.

The direct deposit approach has some disadvantages, including the costs associated with setting up the direct deposit system, loss of **float** on payroll funds, the need to handle two payroll systems (checks for some employees and direct deposit for others), and increased difficulty when problems arise (such as issuing stop payment orders). Employers with high turnover may not find direct deposit to be practical because changes are costly to make, particularly in an electronic funds transfer system. Complete or near complete participation by employees helps keep costs down.

For employees, direct deposit is very convenient since they do not have to wait for checks to clear, they can be certain checks will be deposited even if they are sick or out of town, and they do not have to take time for a trip to the bank. Some employees, however, may not be comfortable without a physical check to cash.

Automatic Funds Transfer. One method of direct deposit is automatic funds transfer in which the employer transfers funds automatically from its regular account to those of its employees, at the same bank. In its simplest form, the employer may have its own bank establish checking and savings accounts for all employees. At the end of a payroll period, the employer provides each employee's name, account number, and net pay amount and the bank transfers the net pay amounts from the business checking account of the employer to the accounts of the employees.

An extension of this direct deposit system is to use several local banks where the employees have checking or savings accounts. The employer can deal directly with all the banks involved and send each the appropriate employee information to reflect deposits of the net pay amounts. Or, the employer can give its own bank all the information on the amounts to be deposited in all of the other banks and the employees' accounts to be credited. The employer's bank then coordinates the whole procedure.

Electronic Funds Transfer (EFT). When a company decides to use an **electronic funds transfer** system, it appoints one bank or financial institution to control its direct deposit system. That institution is in charge of transmitting the payroll information to one or more of the banks of the **Automated Clearing House (ACH)** network, which processes and transfers funds from one bank to another across the country.

Under Federal Reserve Regulation E, current employees do not have to sign up for electronic funds transfer but can choose either EFT or regular payroll checks. However, in some states, EFT has become a permissible condition of employment for new employees. Otherwise, the employer needs authorization to deposit the employee's pay and cannot limit employees to accounts at one specific institution but must offer a choice and a check as an alternative.

The steps for establishing an EFT system are as follows:

1. Authorization by the employee.

Float *The period between the date a person presents a check for deposit or payment and the date the bank cashes the check.*

Electronic funds transfer (EFT) *A method whereby financial institutions transfer funds from one account to another instantly and conveniently via computers.*

Automated Clearing House (ACH) *A network of Federal Reserve and private-sector banks that transmit payments and settle accounts between originating and receiving financial institutions.*

EFT ON THE MOVE

The use of direct deposit by electronic funds transfer (EFT) is accelerating and rapidly becoming the payment method of choice. This trend was not always so, however. In fact, for a long time, EFT languished. Developed in the late 1960s, EFT found few converts until the U.S. Treasury Department showed the way in the 1970s by establishing its direct deposit program for Social Security payments. By 1989, 50% of all Social Security recipients and 12% of all U.S. employees were receiving funds by EFT. Today, more than one out of every four U.S. employees gets paid by direct deposit. Over 95% of all U.S. banks, savings and loans, and credit unions are now able to receive EFT transactions.

2. Establishment by the employer of an Automated Clearing House (ACH) file that will electronically transmit payroll payments through an originating financial institution.

3. Forwarding of entries by the originating financial institution to ACH.

4. Distribution of the entries by the ACH to the receiving financial institutions.

5. Posting of the funds by the receiving financial institutions to the employees' bank accounts.

The system requires the use of a specific computer input format, either on magnetic tape or in a file. A direct communications link between the employer's bank and the computers of the originating bank permits transmission of detailed deposit transactions. The originating bank processes information for employees who are customers of that bank and then transmits the remaining transactions through the nationwide ACH network. These ACH banks, which are members of the National Association of Automated Clearing Houses and the Federal Reserve Communications network, transfer electronically the employees' payroll deposits to the designated accounts at their respective financial institutions. In order for direct deposit to work, the payroll system must have three pieces of information for each employee:

Receiving depository financial institution (RDFI) *A financial institution that processes ACH payments by receiving files and posting payments to accounts on the effective date.*

Originating depository financial institution (ODFI) *A financial institution that initiates ACH payments by delivering files to receiving depository financial institutions according to a time schedule and in the proper format.*

- the routing and transit identification number assigned to the employee's receiving financial institution,
- the employee's account number, and
- the type of account (checking or savings).

Receiving depository financial institutions (RDFI) are responsible for crediting employees' accounts with their direct deposits and, according to ACH rules, must make the cash available for withdrawal on the effective date. In order to assure the timely availability of these funds, the **originating depository financial institution (ODFI)** specifies the day it must receive the direct deposit file for delivery.

Processing Schedule of the ACH Network. A successful direct deposit program requires adherence to the processing schedule of the ACH network.

Timely delivery of direct deposit files means that employees will consistently have access to their pay on the effective date. The following standard ACH schedule ensures meeting this goal.

Two days before payday:

1. The company delivers the direct deposit file to the ODFI, generally between noon and 6 P.M.

2. The ODFI combines all customer files and submits the file to the ACH network by 11 P.M.

One day prior to payday:

3. The ACH network sorts the transactions by Federal Reserve district and transmits them to the appropriate ACH entity, which in turn delivers them to the RDFIs.

4. The RDFI posts the transactions to their customers' accounts during the evening.

Payday:

5. The funds are available for the employees' use.

The company should prepare an annual payroll schedule that takes into account that the ACH network does not operate on holidays and weekends. The company provides a copy to the ODFI and also establishes a settlement schedule of when the exchange of funds for the direct deposits and RDFI-returned items is reflected on the books of the Federal Reserve Bank(s). The ACH network delivers and settles for the amount of the direct deposits.

Reconciliation and Accounting for Direct Deposit.   When payroll distribution is by check, reconciliation of the payroll account is a time-consuming process since each check must be accounted for. However, with direct deposit, only the file total appears on the bank statement. The reconciliation for direct deposit requires fewer adjustments than the adjustments for regular payroll checks due to voids, stop payments, and replacements.

To reconcile a direct deposit system, the employer collects information on each direct deposit transmission and any adjustments and verifies the totals against the bank statement. Verification of individual employee transactions is unnecessary.

Additional accounting procedures for a direct deposit system should include:

*   testing for reasonableness by comparing deposit totals of the current year to prior periods,

*   balancing the totals from the direct deposit file and the total net pay from the payroll records, and

*   authorization for release of the direct deposit file into the ACH system.

An inaccurate account number or nonexistent account will generate a return of funds through the ACH network. In this event, the RDFI notifies the ODFI, which in turn informs the employer. The employer can then reimburse the employee with a manual check or bank wire transfer.

PAYROLL IN ACTION

RESPONSES TO EFT OBJECTIONS

Sometimes employees who are used to a weekly or biweekly paycheck resist the change to electronic funds transfer. However, the system works most efficiently when most or all employees participate. Thus, it is often up to payroll management to persuade as many employees as possible to sign up for the program. The following answers to questions most asked by employees may help them achieve that goal.

What about employees who say they want

- to have physical possession of a check? If the employees don't get to the bank on payday, they can lose the interest due on

the funds or immediate access to the funds. In such a case, insistence on physical possession is a distinct disadvantage. Also, many banks offer free checking accounts for direct deposit customers.

- to know how much is being deposited to their accounts? The employer will provide the employees with a statement that is similar to a pay stub and shows the gross earnings, deductions, and net pay amounts.

- to be assured of confidentiality? Electronic funds transfer is as confidential as any other payment method and maybe more so since the transfer is paperless.

Regulations on Electronic Funds Transfer. The Federal Reserve System has established regulations governing EFT under Title IX (the Electronic Funds Transfer Act) and **Regulation E** (the Consumer Credit Protection Act). The federal rules apply to those states that do not have their own regulations concerning EFT direct deposit. Otherwise, the Board of Governors of the Federal Reserve determines where the state laws may be inconsistent and the extent to which the federal laws will prevail.

Besides the federal and state laws, the financial institutions that belong to the ACH have contractually agreed to follow a set of operating rules, as formulated by the National Automated Clearing House Association. These ACH rules define the rights and responsibilities of each of the participants in the direct deposit process and the specifications and requirements of the data files to be transmitted. These rules are binding on all ACH participants (the ODFI, RDFI, and ACH), the company by agreement with the ODFI, and the employee by signed authorization.

Not only must the company have an agreement with the ODFI but must also obtain the employee's authorization to make deposits and correcting entries to the employee's account. The company is also responsible for

Regulation E *The Consumer Credit Protection Act, a Federal Reserve law that provides protection to consumers in disputes involving electronic funds transfers.*

1. sending zero-dollar test entries called **prenotification** at least ten calendar days before the first use of the ACH system,
2. making requested changes before another entry is made to the receiver's account,
3. correcting an erroneous file, and
4. retaining the original or a copy of the original authorization for two years.

Prenotification *A zero-dollar entry sent through the ACH network at least ten days before the real-dollar direct deposit transaction to verify the account and other information.*

The ODFI warrants to each RDFI that each entry is timely, is authorized, and conforms with the ACH rules. In turn, each RDFI verifies that the prenotification account number is valid, must give its receivers access to the transferred funds at the settlement date, and warrants that notification of change made to the ODFI is correct.

REVIEW QUESTIONS

5–1. Distinguish between so-called permanent and current employee payroll data.

5–2. What are the two essential records for an effective payroll system? Describe the basic difference between these records and the need for both types of records.

5–3. List the steps for completing the payroll register.

5–4. What is the process of footing and cross-footing? Why is it important in payroll?

5–5. Name four tasks that depend on information provided by the payroll register.

5–6. How does the data in the payroll register find its way into the accounting system?

5–7. What is the source of the information recorded on the employee earnings record?

5–8. How often is the data on the employee earnings record summarized? Why is this period significant?

5–9. What one column in the employee earnings record is not usually found in the payroll register? How is this one column used in the computation of payroll taxes?

5–10. What is the source of information for changes in an employee's marital status and withholding allowances?

5–11. Name the four uses of the employee earnings record.

5–12. What are the advantages of using a separate payroll account?

5–13. What is the purpose of maintaining a small balance in an imprest bank account?

5–14. What are some of the steps that a payroll manager can take to facilitate a reconciliation of the payroll account?

5–15. List the steps in a bank reconciliation.

5–16. Name two security measures that can be taken for paychecks and the payroll bank account.

5–17. Name the three basic methods for payment of employee wages.

5–18. Describe the procedures involved in paying employees through the use of pay envelopes.

5–19. In what ways is payment by check preferable to pay envelopes?

5–20. Name the various forms of direct deposit and the factors affecting the use of one method over another.

5–21. List the advantages of direct deposits to the employer and the employees. List the disadvantages to the employer and the employees.

5–22. What options must an employer that uses direct deposit by electronic funds transfer offer to employees?

5–23. List the steps for establishing an EFT system.

5–24. What is the Automated Clearing House network?

5–25. What are the responsibilities of the originating depository financial institution (ODFI)?

5–26. What are the responsibilities of the receiving depository financial institution (RDFI)?

5–27. Describe the activities that take place during the three-day EFT direct deposit schedule.

DISCUSSION QUESTIONS

5–1. The employee earnings record provides a yearly summary of data that appears on the employee's wage and tax statement, Form W-2. Information from the payroll register constitutes the basis for payroll accounting.

    a. What information in the employee earnings record do you suppose is pertinent to the Form W-2?

    b. What information in the payroll register is pertinent to accounting for payroll?

5–2. Over a given period of time, the data in the payroll register should give the same basic results as the employee earnings record. If a reconciliation between the two records is not a regular procedure, what payroll errors or irregularities might occur and how might they go undetected?

5–3. Payment by cash in pay envelopes is still the practice in some industries.

    a. Under what circumstances might this payment method still be advisable?

    b. What are the advantages and disadvantages of this payment method?

5–4. Some observers believe payroll fraud is possible on a large scale because of the use of computers, modems, and electronic funds transfer. In what ways might these modern devices increase the risk and the extent of fraud?

5–5. Unintentional errors or mistakes occur in the issuance of payroll checks. In an automatic or electronic funds transfer system, these errors are more difficult to correct. What types of errors might occur and why are they more difficult to correct?

EXERCISES

5–1. Assume that the following table represents the payroll register for Breen's Bagels. Complete the table by filling in the missing amounts. All wages are subject to FICA taxes.

Regular earnings	$_____
Overtime earnings	5,100
Total earnings	_____
Social Security tax (6.2%)	6,200
Medicare tax (1.45%)	1,450
Federal income tax withheld	9,000
State income tax withheld	2,000
Medical insurance	1,400
Total deductions	_____
Net pay	_____

5–2. Assume that the following table represents the employee earnings record for Ryan Adams of Adams' Bakery. Fill in the missing amounts. All wages are subject to FICA taxes.

Regular earnings	$ 1,400
Overtime earnings	40

Exercises (cont.)

Total earnings	_____
Social Security tax (6.2%)	_____
Medicare tax (1.45%)	_____
Federal income tax withheld	240
State income tax withheld	60
Medical insurance	60
Total deductions	_____
Net pay	_____
Cumulative earnings to date	54,000

5–3. Technical Laboratories has five employees who earn $6,000 semi-monthly, as follows:

Employee	Wages	FITW	Wages To Date
Robert Trent	$1,000	$160	$15,000
Harry Black	1,200	192	18,000
Mary Henry	1,400	224	21,000
Gladys O'Brien	1,000	160	15,000
Harriet Ling	1,400	224	21,000
	$6,000	$960	$90,000

Assuming no other withholdings, complete the following lines from the payroll register for all employees.

Payroll Register

Employee	Wages	FICA	FITW	Net Pay
Robert Trent	_____	_____	_____	_____
Harry Black	_____	_____	_____	_____
Mary Henry	_____	_____	_____	_____
Gladys O'Brien	_____	_____	_____	_____
Harriet Ling	_____	_____	_____	_____

5–4. The cumulative earnings of Clarence King, the CEO of Sunrise Health Products, exceeded the wage base limit for the Social Security tax. Prior to the last week of the year, Clarence King had earned $76,500 and had the following deductions: federal income tax withholding of $12,500, state income tax withholding of $4,500, Social Security tax of $4,724.40, Medicare tax of $1,109.25, and medical insurance of $2,500. The last week of the year, Clarence earned $1,500; three of his deductions were for federal income tax withholding of $240, state income tax withholding of $80, and medical insurance of $50. Complete the last week of the employee earnings record and calculate the totals for the year.

Exercises (cont.)

5–5. The Buzzboys Rockabilly Band pays its employees with pay envelopes. During a recent week, its employees had the following net pay.

Greg Beaton	$343.20
Rhonda Kane	325.54
Bill Means	249.67
Beverly Reimer	298.13
Al Troop	312.25

What denominations of currency and coins must the band get from the bank to fill the pay envelopes?

PROBLEMS

(Note: For each of the following problems, assume a FICA tax rate of 6.2% for Social Security and 1.45% for Medicare and a wage base limit of $76,200 for Social Security.)

5–1. Michael Grayson is a CPA with Rio Grande Oil. He is married and claims four withholding allowances. His semimonthly salary is $1,750. Besides federal income tax and FICA tax withholdings, Michael has semimonthly withholdings of 8% of gross wages for state income tax, $75 for health insurance, and $225 for a pension plan. What is Michael's net pay for each semimonthly period?

$ _____

5–2. Emily Carter is an interior decorator with Pauline's Interiors. Her monthly salary is $2,100. She is married and claims three allowances. Her withholdings include the federal income tax and FICA tax withholdings, state income tax withholding at 5% of gross wages, $60 for health insurance, and $100 for a monthly savings plan. What is Emily's net pay each month?

$ _____

5–3. Justin Cooper works as a sales promotion analyst for Greater Outdoor Advertising. Justin is single, claims no withholding allowances, and earns $1,200 biweekly. His withholdings include the federal income tax withholding, FICA taxes, state income tax withholding at 5% of gross wages, $28 for health insurance, and $100 for a pension plan. What is Justin's net pay for the biweekly period?

$ _____

5–4. Dora Caudillo is a market analyst for WXYZ radio station. Dora is single, claims two withholding allowances, and earns $3,000 a month. Her withholdings include federal income tax and FICA tax withholding, state income tax withholding at 5% of gross wages, and $54 for health insurance. What is Dora's net pay per month?

$ _____

5–5. Elaine O'Toole works for Computer Applications, Inc. The following data pertain to her earnings and deductions for the year:

Wages	$58,000
Bonus	4,500

Problems (cont.)

Moving Expenses

Nonqualified, nondeductible	3,500
Personal use of company car	2,800
Pension plan contributions	8,200
Federal income tax withheld	10,800
State income tax withheld	3,600

Compute Elaine's gross wages and net pay.

Gross Wages $ _____

Net Pay $ _____

5–6. Payroll data for the production department at Jupiter Toys during a week in March are as follows:

Employee	Gross Wages	FITW	Medical Insurance
Lori Queen	$320	$48	$16
Harold Rosenberg	340	40	16
Bette Ramsey	280	42	12
Justine Brooks	320	52	12
Terry Drake	260	44	16

The state withholding tax rate is 4% and none of the employees have exceeded the Social Security limit. Complete the blank payroll register provided on page 153.

5–7. Dale Krane is a commission salesperson for Jupiter Toys and earns 5% on sales on the first $5,000 and 6% on any sales over $5,000. Dale is married and has two withholding allowances. Through November, Dale had earned $72,000 and had earnings as shown in the table for the four pay periods in December. Complete the table using the wage-bracket method for federal income tax withholding, 6.2% for Social Security tax, 1.45% for Medicare tax, and 5% for state income tax withholding. After completing the table, add the December amounts by week to the blank employee earnings record on page 154 and answer the following questions.

a. During which week of December were no Social Security taxes withheld on part of the week's earnings?

_____

b. What were Dale's cumulative earnings as of the end of the fourth quarter?

$ _____

	Gross Wages	FITW	SITW	Soc. Sec. Tax	Medicare Tax	Net Pay
1st week	$1,300	$_____	$_____	$_____	$_____	$_____
2nd week	900	_____	_____	_____	_____	_____

Problems (cont.)	Gross Wages	FITW	SITW	Soc. Sec. Tax	Medicare Tax	Net Pay
3rd week	$1,200	$_____	$_____	$_____	$_____	$_____
4th week	1,000	_____	_____	_____	_____	_____

5–8. Jupiter Toys, Inc., has the following salary data for administrative employees for the week ended September 21.

Employee	Gross Wages	SITW	FITW	Medical Insurance	Prior Earnings
Elmer Acker	$ 750	$25	$ 80	$20	$27,000
Jane Blount	1,600	85	200	20	75,500
Takeisha Nichols	700	25	80	25	24,000
Ethel Rogers	800	30	90	15	30,000
Theo Zeale	720	32	84	20	28,000

The FICA tax rates are 6.2% for Social Security tax ($76,200) and 1.45% for Medicare tax. Complete the blank payroll register on page 155 and calculate the company's FICA tax expense for the week.

Social Security Tax $ _____

Medicare Tax $ _____

5–9. The payroll register of Jupiter Toys for the month of December shows gross pay of $220,000 of which $40,000 was exempt from Social Security tax, none was exempt from Medicare tax, and $150,000 was exempt from state and federal unemployment taxes. Compute the employer's payroll tax expense for the month, based on tax rates of 6.2% for Social Security tax, 1.45% for Medicare tax, 5.4% for state unemployment tax, and 0.8% for federal unemployment tax.

Social Security Tax $ _____

Medicare Tax $ _____

SUTA Tax $ _____

FUTA Tax $ _____

5–10. Sarah Schoenle, the receptionist at Jupiter Toys, earns $320 per week for a 40-hour week. She is married and has three withholding allowances. During the month of November, she worked the following hours:

Week	Regular Hours	Overtime Hours
1	40	—
2	40	2
3	36	—
4	40	8

Sarah has $16 per week withheld for health insurance. The state withholding tax rate is 5%. Complete the blank employee earnings record on page 156.

CONTINUING CASE PROBLEM

The months of June, July, and August are the busiest months of the year for Frontier Landscaping. For the week ended July 31 Frontier had the following payroll data.

Employee	Marital Status/ Withholding Allowances	Regular Rate	Hours Worked	Health Insurance
Carrie Barnes	M-3	$5.40 per hr.	48	$16
Melissa Trane	M-2	5.60 per hr.	48	16
Horace Glenn	M-3	5.40 per hr.	44	16
Brenda Toomey	M-3	5.40 per hr.	46	16
Frank Granto	M-3	5.80 per hr.	48	16
Harry Fein	S-1	6.00 per hr.	52	12
Jose Lopez	S-2	6.00 per hr.	48	12
Julie Brown	M-2	5.60 per hr.	52	0
Kathy Wood	M-4	1,500 per wk.	54	16
David Wood	M-2	1,250 per wk.	54	16

None of the employees has exceeded the FICA wage base limits. All employees are subject to state withholding taxes at 5% of gross wages. The company pays overtime at 1½ times the regular hourly rate for all employees except those on salary. For withholding, use the wage bracket method for all employees except Kathy Wood (percentage method).

a. Prepare a payroll register for Frontier using the blank form provided on page 157.

b. Assume that Jose Lopez worked the following schedule for the month of July.

Week	Hours Worked
1	42
2	48
3	44
4	48

Complete the blank employee earnings record provided on page 158.

Payroll Register

PAY PERIOD ENDING _____ 20 ___

TIME-CARD NO.	EMPLOYEE	M/S / W/H ALLOW.	TIME WORKED			RATE		EARNINGS			DEDUCTIONS						NET AMOUNT PAID	CHECK NO.	DATE PAID
			REG. HOURS	OVER-TIME	TOTAL HOURS	REG. HOURS	OVER-TIME	REG. WAGES	OVER-TIME	TOTAL	FICA SOC. SEC.	FICA MEDI-CARE	FITW	SITW	MED. INS.	TOTAL			
TOTALS																			

Payroll Register for use with Problem 5-6.

153

Employee Earnings Record

NAME

ADDRESS

BIRTHDATE

TIMECARD NO.

SOCIAL SECURITY NO.

POSITION

MARITAL STATUS

WITHHOLDING ALLOWANCES

DATE EMPLOYED

RATE OF PAY

DATE TERMINATED

PERIOD ENDING	TIME WORKED			RATE		EARNINGS			DEDUCTIONS						NET AMOUNT PAID	CHECK NO.	CUMULATIVE EARNINGS
	REG. HOURS	OVER-TIME	TOTAL HOURS	REG. HOURS	OVER-TIME	REG. WAGES	OVER-TIME	TOTAL	FICA		FITW	SITW	MED. INS.	TOTAL			
									SOC. SEC.	MEDI-CARE							
TOTAL																	
ACCUM. TOTALS																	

Employee Earnings Record for use with Problem 5-7.

Payroll Register

PAY PERIOD ENDING _____ 20 ___

TIME-CARD NO.	EMPLOYEE	M/S / W/H ALLOW.	TIME WORKED				RATE		EARNINGS			DEDUCTIONS						NET AMOUNT PAID	CHECK NO.	DATE PAID
			REG. HOURS	OVER-TIME	TOTAL HOURS		REG. HOURS	OVER-TIME	REG. WAGES	OVER-TIME	TOTAL	FICA		FITW	SITW	MED. INS.	TOTAL			
												SOC. SEC.	MEDI-CARE							
TOTALS																				

Payroll Register for use with Problem 5-8.

Employee Earnings Record

NAME

ADDRESS

BIRTHDATE

TIMECARD NO.

SOCIAL SECURITY NO.

DATE EMPLOYED

DATE TERMINATED

MARITAL STATUS

WITHHOLDING ALLOWANCES

RATE OF PAY

POSITION

| PERIOD ENDING | TIME WORKED | | | RATE | | EARNINGS | | | | DEDUCTIONS | | | | | | NET AMOUNT PAID | CHECK NO. | CUMULATIVE EARNINGS |
| | REG. HOURS | OVER-TIME | TOTAL HOURS | REG. HOURS | OVER-TIME | REG. WAGES | OVER-TIME | TOTAL | FICA | | FITW | SITW | MED. INS. | TOTAL | | | |
									SOC. SEC.	MEDI-CARE							
TOTAL																	
ACCUM. TOTALS																	

Employee earnings record for use with Problem 5-10.

Payroll Register

PAY PERIOD ENDING _____ 20 _____

TIME-CARD NO.	EMPLOYEE	M/S — W/H ALLOW.	TIME WORKED			RATE		EARNINGS			DEDUCTIONS						NET AMOUNT PAID	CHECK NO.	DATE PAID
			REG. HOURS	OVER-TIME	TOTAL HOURS	REG. HOURS	OVER-TIME	REG. WAGES	OVER-TIME	TOTAL	FICA SOC. SEC.	FICA MEDI-CARE	FITW	SITW	MED. INS.	TOTAL			
TOTALS																			

For use with Continuing Case Problem, question (a).

Employee Earnings Record

NAME

ADDRESS

BIRTHDATE

POSITION

TIMECARD NO.

SOCIAL SECURITY NO.

DATE EMPLOYED

DATE TERMINATED

MARITAL STATUS

WITHHOLDING ALLOWANCES

RATE OF PAY

PERIOD ENDING	TIME WORKED			RATE		EARNINGS			DEDUCTIONS						NET AMOUNT PAID	CHECK NO.	CUMULATIVE EARNINGS
	REG. HOURS	OVER-TIME	TOTAL HOURS	REG. HOURS	OVER-TIME	REG. WAGES	OVER-TIME	TOTAL	FICA		FITW	SITW	MED. INS.	TOTAL			
									SOC. SEC.	MEDI-CARE							
TOTAL																	
ACCUM. TOTALS																	

For use with Continuing Case Problem, question (b).

PART III

PAYROLL REPORTING AND ACCOUNTING PROCEDURES

Clark has now taken Lois through an entire payroll cycle—from timekeeping and computation of gross wages, through calculation of the various taxes and other deductions, to preparation of the payroll register and employee earnings record, and, finally, payroll distribution. He is now ready to discuss the requirements for federal depositing and reporting of payroll taxes withheld and payable and the accounting procedures that integrate the payroll and tax data into the company's overall accounting system.

CHAPTER 6

DEPOSIT AND REPORTING REQUIREMENTS

LEARNING OBJECTIVES

On completing this chapter, you will be able to:

1. Explain the use of deposit coupons for payroll taxes.
2. Explain the requirements for a timely deposit.
3. Describe the methods for making tax deposits by the electronic federal tax payment system (EFTPS) or without a coupon or employer identification number.
4. List the penalties for failure to make tax deposits.
5. Enumerate, with examples, the rules for the timing of tax deposits, based on the amount of taxes owed.
6. Explain the rules for depositing backup withholding and FUTA taxes.
7. Prepare the Employer's Quarterly Federal Tax Return, Form 941 and Employer's Record of Federal Tax Liability, Schedule B, Form 941.
8. Prepare the Annual Return of Withheld Federal Income Tax, Form 945.
9. Complete a Wage and Tax Statement, Form W-2.
10. Review the distinction between employees and independent contractors and explain the requirements for filing Form 1099-MISC, Miscellaneous Income.

Lois has seen how important the payroll register and employee earnings record are to the preparation of the payroll. Without them, the payroll clerk would have no way to verify and summarize gross and net wages and the amounts of various deductions. The payroll register and the employee earnings record are also vital to the reporting of wages and tax

161

data to the government and the timely and accurate payment of payroll taxes. Clark describes to Lois this aspect of payroll accounting.

Clark begins his discussion of deposit and reporting requirements by describing the government's system for collecting tax deposits. He explains that the IRS wants to receive tax payments as employers withhold the taxes; as a result, the system provides for payments that become more frequent as the withheld amounts increase. The liabilities owed and the amount deposited against these liabilities serve as the basis of the quarterly report, Form 941, and the annual report, Form 945.

MAKING TAX DEPOSITS

Depository *A place to put funds for safekeeping; in the case of employment taxes and all other types of taxes, a bank qualified to receive federal tax deposits or a Federal Reserve Bank.*

Federal Reserve Bank *Any of the 12 district banks of the Federal Reserve System, a centralized U.S. banking system with supervisory powers over 12 Federal Reserve Banks, their 25 branches, and all national and state banks that are part of the system.*

Every business must make periodic and timely deposits of employee federal income and FICA taxes, FUTA, and nonpayroll items, such as backup withholdings and withheld taxes on retirement income and gambling winnings. Table 6-1 summarizes the types of taxes payable through periodic deposits. The schedule for deposits depends upon the amounts owed; if the payroll changes often (for example, in a seasonal business), the employer may have to make the payments on a somewhat irregular schedule.

A business must deposit income tax withheld, both the employer and employee FICA taxes, and nonpayroll taxes withheld when the sum of these amounts is $1,000 or more. The total tax liability accumulated for the period, not the total amount of the underpaid taxes on hand at the close of the period, determines an employer's deposit obligation. FUTA taxes are paid on a quarterly basis for any quarter in which they total $100 or more.

Businesses deposit employment taxes and all other types of taxes, except for delinquent taxes, at an authorized federal **depository**, usually a bank qualified to receive federal tax deposits or a **Federal Reserve Bank**.

TABLE 6-1	
Types of Taxes Paid with Form 8109, Federal Tax Deposit Coupon, or EFTPS	
Form 720	Excise Tax
Form 940	Federal Unemployment (FUTA) Tax (Includes Form 940PR)
Form 941	Withheld Income and FICA Taxes (Includes Form 941 series of returns)
Form 943	Agricultural Withheld Income and FICA Taxes (Includes Form 943PR)
Form 945	Backup Withholding and Withholding for Pensions, Annuities, IRAs, and Gambling Winnings
Form 990-C	Farmers' Cooperative Association Income Tax
Form 990-PF	Excise Tax on Private Foundation Net Investment Income
Form 990-T	Exempt Organization Business Income Tax
Form 1042	Withholding at Source
Form 1120	Corporation Income Tax (Includes Form 1120 series of returns and Form 2438)
Form CT-1	Railroad Retirement and Railroad Unemployment Repayment Taxes

Delinquent tax payments are sent directly to the Internal Revenue Service, with a copy of the notice regarding the delinquency.

Deposits Made by Electronic Federal Tax Payment System (EFTPS)

For employers with deposit liabilities above certain levels, electronic funds transfer has replaced the current paper-based (Form 8109) system. Whether an employer must deposit withheld income, employment taxes, and other depository taxes electronically depends on the amount of such taxes the employer deposited during a certain determination period. This threshold amount includes deposits of the following tax returns: Forms 941, 943, 945, and CT-1.

If the employer's total deposits of these taxes was more than $50,000 in 1996 or 1997, the employer must make electronic deposits for all deposit liabilities that occur after December 31, 1997. New rules have raised the threshhold to $200,000 for 1998 and require electronic deposits for such employers after 1999. Prior and all new electronic funds transfer depositors must use the authorized Electronic Federal Tax Payment System (EFTPS). Failure to use this system in a timely and prescribed manner may result in a ten percent penalty. Employees or their payroll service bureaus enroll in EFTPS through a designated Treasury Financial Agent.

Deposit Coupons

When the business applies for an employer **identification number (EIN)**, the IRS supplies the business with a book of preprinted deposit coupons. An employer not making deposits by EFTPS will do so with **Form 8109, Federal Tax Deposit Coupon** (Exhibit 6-1). Each of these coupons has boxes in which to enter the type(s) of tax deposits being made. A completed coupon accompanies each tax payment mailed or hand delivered to an authorized depository. Most states also provide coupons for state tax deposits.

Importance of Depositing on Time

Tax deposits must be made on time to avoid penalties. Late or insufficient payments lead to penalties based on both the number of days the deposit is late and the amount of the late or underpaid portion.

Authorized federal tax depositories must accept cash, a postal money order drawn to the order of the depository, or a check or draft drawn on and made payable to the depository. Some depositories are also willing to accept checks drawn on other financial institutions. Deposits made at an unauthorized financial institution may be subject to the penalty for failure to deposit.

Federal Reserve Banks accept deposits according to the collection schedule and only process immediate credit items. Generally, **immediate credit items** are those with no waiting period to clear; they include checks drawn on commercial banks located in the same city as the Federal Reserve Bank, dated the same day that the commercial bank processes the check. Deposits may be subject to the failure-to-deposit penalty if the check is not an immediate credit item on the day the Federal Reserve Bank

Employer identification number (EIN) *A number assigned by the Internal Revenue Service and used by the employer when making tax deposits or filing tax reports or other documents.*

Form 8109, Federal Tax Deposit Coupon *A form that accompanies each deposit of various federal taxes in an authorized depository and shows the amount being deposited.*

Immediate credit item *A check or other form of payment that the receiving bank accepts for credit at the time of deposit; that is, a deposit with no waiting period to clear.*

receives it. In this situation, the date of recording the payment may not be the date of the deposit.

Taxpayers required to deposit any taxes more than once a month must make the deposit by the due date if the deposit is $20,000 or more. Penalties on deposits not made on time run from the due date to the date of collection, not the date of mailing. The IRS determines if deposits are on time by the date they are received by the authorized depository of the Federal Reserve Bank. However, a deposit received by the authorized depository after the due date will be considered timely if the taxpayer establishes that it was mailed or electronically transferred in the United States at least two days before the due date.

Making Deposits Without a Coupon or Employer Identification Number

A business may be required to make a deposit without a coupon or identification number. This can occur when the business:

1. Has applied for but not yet received an EIN. In this case, the employer should make the deposit with the IRS rather than with a depository or a Federal Reserve Bank. An explanation attached to the check made payable to the IRS indicates the company name, address, type of tax, period covered, and date of EIN application.

2. Hasn't received coupons yet. In this case, the employer should use Form 8109-B, Federal Tax Deposit Coupon (Exhibit 6-2).

Timing of Deposits

The amount of taxes to be paid determines how often deposits must be made. Taxes are due when the employer pays wages, not when the payroll period ends.

If, at the end of the calendar quarter, the total tax liability for the quarter is less than $1,000, the employer does not have to deposit the taxes but may pay them to the IRS with Form 941 at the end of the next month. For making a payment of less than $1,000, the employer completes Form 941-V

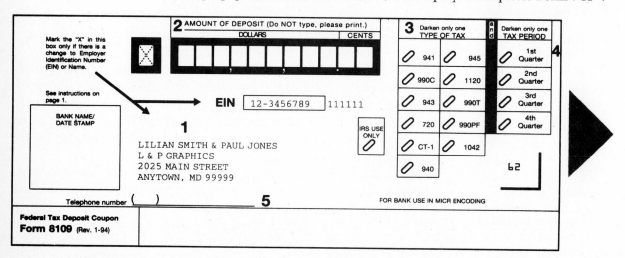

EXHIBIT 6-1 Form 8109, Federal Tax Deposit Coupon

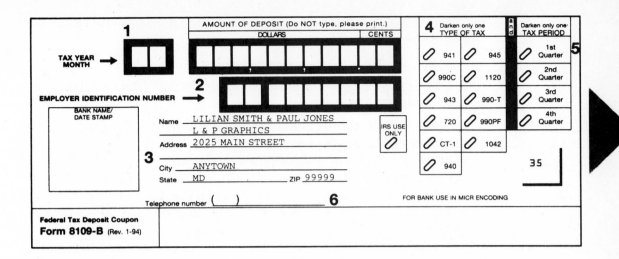

Federal Tax Deposit Coupon
Form 8109-B

1. Enter the month that your tax year ends in this space if you are filling in the 1120, 990-C, 990-PF, or 990-T box; otherwise, leave it blank. For example, if your tax year ends in January, enter 01; if it ends in December, enter 12.

2. Write in your EIN and the money amount. Do not type it in or use dollar signs, commas, decimal points, or leading zeroes. Be sure to enter 00 in the CENTS boxes if your deposit is for whole dollars only.

3. To ensure proper credit to your account, **use the name and address** preprinted on the current business tax forms mailed to you by the IRS, such as Form 940 or 941. This is your correct IRS account identification.

4. To indicate the type of tax, darken the box to the left of the appropriate form. Do not darken the "IRS USE ONLY" box.

5. Darken the box to the left of the quarter that corresponds to the quarter that the deposit is for—not the quarter in which you are making the deposit. For payroll, withholding, and excise tax deposits, the quarters are:

1st quarter - Jan. 1 through Mar. 31   3rd quarter - July 1 through Sept. 30

2nd quarter - Apr. 1 through June 30   4th quarter - Oct. 1 through Dec. 31

For business income tax deposits (this includes the excise tax on net investment income for Form 990-PF filers), darken the 1st Quarter box for deposits made before the end of your tax year. Darken the 4th Quarter box for deposits made after the end of the year.

If you need coupon books and you are not being resupplied automatically, call the IRS or write your Internal Revenue Service Center and provide the following information: business name, address where you want the coupon books sent, number of coupon books, and EIN. Also include the month in which your tax year ends if you have a Form 1120, 990-C, 990-PF (with net investment income), 990-T, or 2438 filing requirement.

6. Be sure to include your daytime telephone number in the space provided.

EXHIBIT 6-2   Form 8109-B, Federal Tax Deposit Coupon (with instructions)

Payment Voucher. The IRS uses the completed voucher to credit the payment to the proper account. If the balance due is $1,000 or more, the employer makes the deposit with Form 8109, Federal Tax Deposit (FTD) coupon, or uses EFTPS, and may be subject to a penalty because the deposit should have been made earlier.

EXAMPLE   The taxes on wages paid by the Record Storage Company for the first quarter of the year are $300. Record Storage does not have to deposit these taxes but can pay them with Form 941 at the end of the next month by filing Form 941-V.   ▲

Under the deposit rules, employers generally must meet two basic deposit schedules:

- Monthly—depositors must make deposits once a month.
- Semiweekly—depositors must make deposits on a set day of the week following each payday.

The deposit rules also include modified quarterly and one-day deposit rules of the old deposit requirements.

Instead of current deposit liabilities, the tax liability of a prior period—the look-back period—determines the employer's deposit category for the coming calendar year. The look-back period is the 12-month period ending June 30 of the prior year. If an employee's payroll taxes were less than $50,000 in the look-back period, the employer uses the monthly schedule; if taxes exceeded $50,000, the employer uses the semiweekly schedule.

The IRS sends out notices by November informing employers which deposit schedule to follow for the coming year, but only if a change in deposit schedule is in order. Let's consider the rules for all categories of employers.

Quarterly Tax Liability.   If, at the end of the calendar quarter, the total tax liability for the quarter is less than $1,000, the employer does not have to deposit the taxes but may pay them to the IRS with Form 941 or Form 945. The change to $1,000 from the previous amount of $500 was effective July 1, 1998 for Form 941, and January 1, 1999 for Form 945.

Monthly Tax Liability.   If the total tax liability for the look-back period is $50,000 or less, the employer uses a monthly schedule and must make deposits once a month on or before the 15th day of the following month. If the tax liability is less than $1,000 for any month, the employer should make the deposit according to its depositor status to avoid any penalties in the event the employer's liability exceeds $1,000 for the quarter.

EXAMPLE   Custom Boats, Inc. filed the following employment tax returns for the four quarters ended June 30, 20xx.

Quarters Ended	Tax Liability
9/30/xx	$12,000
12/31/xx	13,000
3/31/xx	12,000
6/30/xx	12,000
	$49,000

Custom is a monthly depositor for all of the following year since the total deposits for the look-back period are less than $50,000.   ▲

A monthly depositor counts only those payroll taxes accumulated during a calendar month and deposits all accumulated taxes for the month on or before the 15th day of the following month. For example, taxes for all wages paid in April must be deposited by May 15. If a monthly depositor is required to make a next-day deposit at any time during the year, the depositor automatically becomes a semiweekly depositor for the rest of the year and for the next calendar year.

Semiweekly Tax Liability. If the total tax liability for the look-back period is more than $50,000, the employer uses a semiweekly schedule.

EXAMPLE Long Life Batteries had the following employment tax returns for the four quarters ended June 30, 20xx:

Quarters Ended	Tax Liability
9/30/xx	$15,000
12/31/xx	14,000
3/31/xx	14,500
6/30/xx	15,500
	$59,000

Long Life is a semiweekly depositor for all of the following year, since the total deposits for the look-back period are more than $50,000. ▲

With EFTPS deposits, semiweekly depositors can initiate the deposits to be made on a set date of the week following each payday. A semiweekly depositor takes into account only those payroll taxes accumulated during a Wednesday to Friday or Saturday to Tuesday semiweekly period. For paydays on Wednesday, Thursday, or Friday, deposits are due by Wednesday after the payday. For all other paydays, deposits are due by the following Friday.

One-Day Depositors. Employers who accumulate payroll taxes of $100,000 or more must deposit those taxes by the close of the next banking day, regardless of whether the employer is a monthly or semiweekly depositor. In determining the $100,000 threshold, a monthly depositor counts only those payroll taxes accumulated during a calendar month, and a semiweekly depositor takes into account only those payroll taxes accumulated during a Wednesday to Friday or Saturday to Tuesday semiweekly period. Once an employer has hit the $100,000 threshold, additional accumulations in the same semiweekly period are not automatically subject to the one-day rule. A one-day deposit at any time during the year automatically converts a monthly depositor to a semiweekly schedule for the remainder of the year and for the next calendar year.

EXAMPLE Computer Networks and Software Systems are both semiweekly depositors and have the following payroll tax liabilities:

Payday	Computer Networks	Software Systems
Monday	-0-	$55,000
Tuesday	-0-	-0-
Wednesday	$ 55,000	60,000
Thursday	-0-	-0-
Friday	60,000	-0-
Saturday	-0-	-0-
Semiweekly		
Wed.–Fri.	$115,000	$60,000
Sat.–Tues.	-0-	55,000

Computer Networks has exceeded the $100,000 threshold within one semiweekly period (Wednesday to Friday) and must deposit the full $115,000 by the next Monday. On the other hand, Systems Software is not subject to the one-day rule, since the payroll taxes were not accumulated in the same semiweekly period.   ▲

New Employers. In applying the look-back rule for 2000, an employer that was not in business for the entire look-back period of July 1, 1998, through June 30, 1999, uses a zero deposit liability for any quarter before it began business. The same rule applies to the look-back period of any succeeding year when an employer starts a business after June 30 of the preceding year.

EXAMPLE   Handy Tools Corp. and Princess Cosmetics started operations on November 14, 1998, and January 19, 2000, and filed the following employment tax returns for the four quarters ended June 30, 1999, and June 30, 2000.

Handy Tools		*Princess Cosmetics*	
Quarters Ended	*Tax Liability*	*Quarters Ended*	*Tax Liability*
9/30/98	-0-	9/30/99	-0-
12/31/98	$15,000	12/31/99	-0-
3/31/99	14,000	3/31/00	$22,000
6/30/99	16,000	6/30/00	20,000
	$45,000		$42,000

Handy Tools is a monthly depositor for all of 2000 and Princess Cosmetics, a monthly depositor for the remainder of 2000 and all of 2001. Both companies have total tax liability in the look-back period of less than the threshold amount of $50,000.   ▲

Special End-of-Quarter Procedures.   If a semiweekly period spans two calendar quarters of the year, an employer must follow special procedures for its deposit to be credited to the correct quarter. If the deposit is due in the quarter following the payment of the wages, the employer must note on Form 8109, Federal Tax Deposit (FTD) coupon, that the deposit relates to the earlier quarter. If a semiweekly deposit includes taxes for two different quarters, the employer must complete two separate deposit coupons or initiate two separate EFTPS payments, one for each quarter.

EXAMPLE   Mars Connectors is a semiweekly depositor. It pays its employees on Monday, June 26, 20xx. Its payroll tax deposit is due July 3. Since the second quarter ends on June 30, Mars must mark its Form 8109, Federal Tax Deposit (FTD) coupon, to show that its deposit is for the second quarter, not the third quarter, of 20xx.   ▲

EXAMPLE   Assume Mars makes wage payments on Wednesday and Friday. In 20xx, it pays wages on June 29 and July 1. Payroll taxes for both paydays are due on Wednesday, July 6. The second quarter ends on June 30.

Thus, the payroll taxes for the June 30 payroll fall in the second quarter, whereas those for the July 1 payroll fall in the third quarter. Mars should complete two separate Form 8109 coupons to deposit its payroll taxes.   ▲

Safe Harbor (Haven) Rule.   The deposit requirements have a safe harbor provision. When the undeposited taxes are not more than the greater of $100 or 2% of the required deposit, the employer can make up the shortage by a fixed make-up date. For monthly depositors, the make-up date is the due date of the quarterly return. For semiweekly and one-day depositors, the make-up date is the earlier of the first Wednesday or Friday on or after the 15th day of the month following the month of the shortage. For example, if a shortage occurs in September, it must be deposited by the first Wednesday or Friday on or after October 15.

Penalties for Failure to Deposit

The penalties for failure to make deposits of taxes are equal to the amount of the undeposited taxes determined by a percentage based on the number of days the deposit is late. A late deposit of 1 to 5 days entails a 2% penalty, 6 to 15 days, a 5% penalty, and more than 15 days, a 10% penalty.

Delinquency notice *A formal letter from the IRS informing the taxpayer of failure to pay the correct amount of taxes payable by the date when due.*

The 10% penalty also applies to amounts paid to the IRS within ten days of the first IRS **delinquency notice** requesting the tax due. A 15% penalty applies to amounts still unpaid more than ten days after this notice or the day the employer receives the notice and a demand for immediate payment, whichever is earlier.

Depositing Nonpayroll Taxes

Several nonpayroll payments entail federal income tax withholding and, thus, require separate deposits and reporting. These nonpayroll items include pensions, annuities, IRAs, other deferred income, military retirement, gambling winnings, Indian gaming profits, and **backup withholding.** The employer should remit payment for the nonpayroll tax liabilities by filing Form 8109 separately and checking the box for Form 945 (discussed later).

Backup withholding *The federal income tax withheld by payers of taxable interest, dividends, and other non-wage payments when the payee fails to provide a tax identification number or the IRS notifies the payer that the tax identification number (TIN) is incorrect.*

The deposit rules for nonpayroll tax liabilities are the same as those for payroll tax liabilities, except for the time defined as the look-back period. For nonpayroll tax liabilities, the look-back period is the second calendar year preceding the current calendar year. Thus, for the year 2000, the look-back period is the year 1998 while for payroll tax liabilities, it is the four quarters or year ending June 1999.

If the nonpayroll tax liabilities for the look-back period are $50,000 or less, the employer becomes a monthly depositor and at more than $50,000, a semiweekly depositor. The employer then deposits the nonpayroll taxes withheld in the same manner as for payroll taxes.

Depositing FUTA Taxes

For deposit purposes, the employer calculates the FUTA tax quarterly. If the amount due at the end of the quarter, plus any amount not yet deposited

Form 940 (Form 940-EZ), Employer's Annual Federal Unemployment Tax Return   *A tax report filed by an employer at the end of the calendar year to reconcile the employer's tax liability, the amount paid, and the balance owed.*

from prior quarters, is more than $100, the business must deposit these taxes by the last day of the next month. If the amount due is $100 or less, payment is optional, and the amount may be carried over to the next quarter, except for the fourth quarter for which the payment is due. The employer reports the total FUTA tax liability for the year and the amounts deposited on **Form 940** or **Form 940-EZ, Employer's Annual Federal Unemployment Tax Return** (see Exhibits 4-1 and 4-2 in Chapter 4).

For the first three quarters of the year, a business determines whether or not to make a deposit by multiplying that part of the first $7,000 paid to each employee during the quarter by the FUTA tax rate (0.8%).

EXAMPLE   Pierpoint Chocolates has undeposited FUTA taxes of $60 from the first quarter. The company's FUTA wages were $6,000 and the FUTA taxes were $48 ($6,000 × 0.008) for the second quarter. Pierpoint must make a deposit of $108 during the first month of the third quarter ($60 + $48). ▲

For the year-end, if the tax reported on Form 940 or Form 940-EZ (including any credit reductions) minus the amounts deposited for the year is more than $100, the business must remit all of the tax by January 31. If the tax for the year (minus deposits) is $100 or less, the business may choose to deposit it with Form 8109 (the deposit coupon) or use EFTPS, or pay it with Form 940 or Form 940-EZ by January 31.

EMPLOYER WAGE AND TAX REPORTING

The payroll register and the employee earnings record, which are the basis of accounting for payroll within a company (see Chapter 5), are also used for reporting wages and tax data to the government and to employees.

The payroll register provides the data for the reporting of wages and federal income and FICA taxes withheld and payable to the government. The employee earnings record provides similar information on employees. By recording cumulative payroll tax liabilities from the payroll register, the employer is able to meet the deadlines required for tax deposits.

Form 941, Employer's Quarterly Federal Tax Return

Form 941, Employer's Quarterly Federal Tax Return   *A tax report filed by an employer each quarter to reconcile the amount of employees' federal income tax withheld, the employer and employee liabilities for FICA taxes, the amounts paid against these liabilities, and the balance owed.*

The key to the proper reporting and payment of tax liabilities is **Form 941, Employer's Quarterly Federal Tax Return**. This form asks the employer to report:

* All wages, tips, and other compensation, including nontaxable income.
* The amount of federal income tax withheld from wages, tips, and sick pay, or other compensation.
* Total wages and tips subject to Social Security and Medicare taxes.
* Total deposits for the quarter and the balance due or any overpayment.

The due date for Form 941 is the last business day of the month following the end of the quarter. If tax deposits have been on time and for the full amount due, employers can take a ten-day filing extension.

Completing Form 941

Let's complete a Form 941 for Unicorn Construction Corp., as shown in Exhibit 6-3. Unicorn has ten employees and an annual payroll of approximately $280,000 and is a semiweekly depositor. A summary of the company's payroll tax liabilities and deposits is shown in Figure 6-1.

Determination of Deposits Owed.   The first section of Form 941 is completed as follows:

LINE 1   Completed only for first calendar quarter (January–March). Excludes employees who received no pay during the quarter.

LINE 2   Total of all regular and supplemental wages including noncash fringe benefits, reimbursed expenses, sick pay paid by employer or a third party, and tips. Does not include pensions, annuities, supplemental unemployment benefits, or gambling winnings.

LINE 3   Income tax withheld on all items of wages described on line 2.

LINE 4   Used to report corrections in income tax withheld in prior quarters of the same calendar year.

LINE 5   The sum of lines 3 and 4.

LINE 6a,b   The total of all wages and other compensation, including noncash fringe benefits and taxable third-party sick pay, up to wage level base limit multiplied by the Social Security rate (combined 12.4%).

LINE 6c,d   Tips that are subject to the Social Security tax multiplied by the combined rate (12.4%). Tipped employees report tips that total $20 or more in a month to their employer. Employer reports allocated tips on Form 8027.

LINE 7a,b   The total wages and other compensation subject to Medicare taxes multiplied by the combined rate (2.9%).

LINE 8   The sum of lines 6b, 6d, and 7b.

LINE 9   Adjustments to Social Security and Medicare taxes, for example:

1. Errors in credits for overpayments or penalty paid on tax for an earlier quarter (must file Form 941C for correction) and credits against an employer's FICA tax liability for amounts not taken for employee's share of Social Security and Medicare tax withheld and paid over to a third party.

2. Differences in amounts due and collected for Social Security and Medicare taxes and group life insurance premiums paid for former employees and in total Social Security and Medicare tax liability and total amount deducted from employees.

Form **941**
(Rev. October 2000)
Department of the Treasury
Internal Revenue Service

Employer's Quarterly Federal Tax Return
▶ See separate instructions for information on completing this return.
Please type or print.

Enter state code for state in which deposits were made ONLY if different from state in address to the right ▶ (see page 2 of instructions).

Name (as distinguished from trade name)	Date quarter ended
Unicorn Construction Corp.	*March 31, 20xx*
Trade name, if any	Employer identification number
	16-842742
Address (number and street)	City, state, and ZIP code
623 Hazel Avenue	*Sanborn, NY 14094*

OMB No. 1545-0029

T
FF
FD
FP
I
T

If address is different from prior return, check here ▶

IRS Use

1 1 1 1 1 1 1 1 1 1   2   3 3 3 3 3 3 3 3   4 4 4   5 5 5

6   7   8 8 8 8 8 8 8   9 9 9   10 10 10 10 10 10 10 10 10 10

If you do not have to file returns in the future, check here ▶ ☐ and enter date final wages paid ▶

If you are a seasonal employer, see **Seasonal employers** on page 1 of the instructions and check here ▶ ☐

1	Number of employees in the pay period that includes March 12th . ▶	*10*		
2	Total wages and tips, plus other compensation	**2**	*60,344*	*00*
3	Total income tax withheld from wages, tips, and sick pay	**3**	*6,518*	*00*
4	Adjustment of withheld income tax for preceding quarters of calendar year	**4**		
5	Adjusted total of income tax withheld (line 3 as adjusted by line 4—see instructions) . . .	**5**	*6,518*	*00*

6	Taxable social security wages	**6a**	*60,344*	12.4% (.124) =	**6b** *7,482*	*66*
	Taxable social security tips	**6c**		12.4% (.124) =	**6d**	
7	Taxable Medicare wages and tips . . .	**7a**	*60,344*	2.9% (.029) =	**7b** *1,749*	*98*

8	Total social security and Medicare taxes (add lines 6b, 6d, and 7b). Check here if wages are not subject to social security and/or Medicare tax . . . . ▶ ☐	**8**	*9,232*	*64*
9	Adjustment of social security and Medicare taxes (see instructions for required explanation) Sick Pay $ _____ Fractions of Cents $ *.64* Other $ _____ =	**9**		*64*
10	Adjusted total of social security and Medicare taxes (line 8 as adjusted by line 9—see instructions)	**10**	*9,232*	*00*
11	**Total taxes** (add lines 5 and 10)	**11**	*15,750*	*00*
12	Advance earned income credit (EIC) payments made to employees	**12**		
13	Net taxes (subtract line 12 from line 11). **If $1,000 or more, this must equal line 17, column (d) below (or line D of Schedule B (Form 941))**	**13**	*15,750*	*00*
14	Total deposits for quarter, including overpayment applied from a prior quarter	**14**	*15,750*	*00*
15	**Balance due** (subtract line 14 from line 13). See instructions	**15**	*0*	

16   **Overpayment.** If line 14 is more than line 13, enter excess here ▶ $ _____
and check if to be: ☐ Applied to next return   **OR**   ☐ Refunded.

All filers: If line 13 is less than $1,000, you need not complete line 17 or Schedule B (Form 941).
Semiweekly schedule depositors: Complete Schedule B (Form 941) and check here . . . . ▶ ☒
Monthly schedule depositors: Complete line 17, columns (a) through (d), and check here. . . . . . . ▶ ☐

17	**Monthly Summary of Federal Tax Liability.** Do not complete if you were a semiweekly schedule depositor.		
(a) First month liability	**(b)** Second month liability	**(c)** Third month liability	**(d)** Total liability for quarter

Sign Here

Under penalties of perjury, I declare that I have examined this return, including accompanying schedules and statements, and to the best of my knowledge and belief, it is true, correct, and complete.

Signature ▶   Print Your Name and Title ▶   Date ▶

For Privacy Act and Paperwork Reduction Act Notice, see back of Payment Voucher.   Cat. No. 17001Z   Form **941** (Rev. 10-2000)

EXHIBIT 6-3   Completed Form 941, Employer's Quarterly Federal Tax Return

172

	DATE OF LIABILITY	TAXABLE WAGES	FEDERAL INCOME TAX WITHHELD	FICA TAXES	TAX LIABILITY	CUMULATIVE TAX WITHHOLDING	AMOUNT DEPOSITED	DATE OF DEPOSIT	RULE NO.
	JAN								
1	2	578	61	88	149	149	149	1/08/XX	
2	9	3578	451	547	998	998	998	1/15/XX	
3	14	4700	585	719	1304	1304	1304	1/20/XX	
4	16	578	61	88	149	149	149	1/22/XX	
5	23	7500	975	1148	2123	2123	2123	1/29/XX	
6	28	2078	256	318	574	574	574	2/03/XX	
7	30	1078	61	165	226				
8		20090	2450	3073	5523	5297	5297		
9	FEB								
10	1	3000	390	459	849	1075	1075	2/05/XX	
11	6	578	61	88	149	149	149	2/12/XX	
12	13	9500	1170	1454	2624				
13	15	3578	451	547	998	3622	3622	2/19/XX	
14	20	978	61	150	211	211	211	2/26/XX	
15	27	200	—	31	31				
16	28	578	61	88	149				
17		18412	2194	2817	5011	5057	5057		
18	MAR								
19	1	500	—	77	77	257	257	3/05/XX	
20	6	578	61	88	149	149	149	3/12/XX	
21	13	10307	585	1577	2162				
22	15	578	61	88	149	2311	2311	3/19/XX	
23	20	2278	256	349	605	605	605	3/26/XX	
24	27	6000	780	918	1698				
25	28	1601	131	245	376	2074	2074	3/31/XX	
26		21842	1874	3342	5216	5396	5396		
27									
28		60344	6518	9232	15750	15750	15750		
29									
30									
31									

FIGURE 6-1 Payroll Liabilities and Deposits for Unicorn Construction Corp.

LINE 10   The sum of lines 8 and 9.

LINE 11   The total of lines 5 and 10 (the total tax liability).

LINE 12   The amount of advance earned income credit payments an employer made to employees during the quarter.

LINE 13   The difference between lines 12 and 11. This amount represents the quarterly tax liability and, if $1,000 or more, should equal the amounts shown for a monthly depositor (line 17(d)) below or a semiweekly or one-day depositor (line D of Schedule B, Form 941).

LINE 14   Total tax deposits made for the quarter.

LINES 15 and 16   If an employer has been depositing taxes when due, this line should be zero or a slight over- or underpayment. The employer pays any underpayment under $1,000 directly to the IRS and receives a refund of any overpayment or applies it to the next period. Adjustment, if necessary, of the balance due or overpayment to the liability amount in the general ledger ensures that the stated liability is equal to the true liability.

LINE 17   Used to report the monthly tax liabilities for the quarter for a monthly depositor; semiweekly and one-day depositors use Schedule B, Form 941, to provide such liability data.

Schedule B, Form 941

Schedule B of Form 941 (Exhibit 6-4) shows the employer's record of federal tax liability for Unicorn Construction Corp. This form is not a record of tax deposits but, as the name suggests, a listing of the liability for withheld income and FICA taxes by day. A semiweekly or one-day depositor must use Schedule B of Form 941, Employer's Record of Federal Tax Liability. The amounts reported are the actual total liabilities by date incurred, not the amounts from the deposit coupons, or deposited using EFTPS. The total tax liability for the quarter should equal the deposits, plus or minus any adjustments.

Form 945, Annual Return of Withheld Federal Income Tax

Reporting regulations require employers to use Form 941 to report federal income and FICA taxes and Form 945, Annual Return of Withheld Federal Income Tax (Exhibit 6-5), to report all nonpayroll withholdings. The nonpayroll items include backup withholding and withholding for pensions, annuities, IRAs, military retirement pay, and gambling winnings. Form 945 includes all income tax withholding reported on Forms 1099 or W-2G, certain gambling winnings, and has a due date for any year of January 31 of the following year.

Payers of taxable interest, dividends, and certain other payments must generally withhold 31% of the amounts paid, if payees fail to furnish payers with their correct taxpayer identification numbers. Backup withholding does not apply if payees provide payers with a Form W-9, Request for Taxpayer Identification Number and Certification, since the form provides the payer with the correct TIN.

SCHEDULE B (FORM 941)

Department of the Treasury
Internal Revenue Service

5151

Employer's Record of Federal Tax Liability

▶ See Circular E for more information about employment tax returns.

▶ Attach to Form 941 or Form 941-SS.

OMB No. 1545-0029

Name as shown on Form 941 (Form 941-SS)	Employer identification number	Date quarter ended
Unicorn Construction Company	*16-842742*	*March 31, 20xx*

You must complete this schedule if you are required to deposit on a semiweekly basis, or if your tax liability on any day is $100,000 or more. Show tax liability here, not deposits. (The IRS gets deposit data from FTD coupons.)

A. Daily Tax Liability—First Month of Quarter

1	*149*	8		15		22		29	
2		9	*998*	16	*149*	23	*2,123*	30	*226*
3		10		17		24		31	
4		11		18		25			
5		12		19		26			
6		13		20		27			
7		14	*1,304*	21		28	*574*		

A Total tax liability for first month of quarter . . . . ▶ **A** *5,523*

B. Daily Tax Liability—Second Month of Quarter

1	*849*	8		15	*998*	22		29	
2		9		16		23		30	
3		10		17		24		31	
4		11		18		25			
5		12		19		26			
6	*149*	13	*2,624*	20	*211*	27	*31*		
7		14		21		28	*149*		

B Total tax liability for second month of quarter . . . . ▶ **B** *5,011*

C. Daily Tax Liability—Third Month of Quarter

1	*77*	8		15	*149*	22		29	
2		9		16		23		30	
3		10		17		24		31	
4		11		18		25			
5		12		19		26			
6	*149*	13	*2,162*	20	*605*	27	*1,698*		
7		14		21		28	*376*		

C Total tax liability for third month of quarter . . . . ▶ **C** *5,216*

D Total for quarter (add lines **A, B,** and **C**). This should equal line 13 of Form 941 . . . . . ▶ **D** *15,750*

For Paperwork Reduction Act Notice, see page 2.   Cat. No. 11967Q   Schedule B (Form 941)

EXHIBIT 6-4 Schedule B (Form 941), Employer's Record of Federal Tax Liability for Unicorn Construction Corp.

Payers or plan administrators must withhold federal income tax at specified rates on certain periodic, nonperiodic, and eligible rollover distributions from pension, annuity, deferred income, and IRA payments. Recipients may also choose to have additional amounts withheld from periodic payments and nonperiodic distributions or may choose exemption from withholding by submitting to the payer or plan administrator a Form W-4P, Withholding Certificate for Pension or Annuity Payments.

Form **945**

Department of the Treasury
Internal Revenue Service

Annual Return of Withheld Federal Income Tax

▶ For withholding reported on Forms 1099 and W-2G.

▶ See separate instructions. For more information on income tax withholding, see Circular E and Pub. 15-A.
Please type or print.

OMB No. 1545-1430

20

IRS USE ONLY	
T	
FF	
FD	
FP	
I	
T	

Enter state code for state in which deposits were made only if different from state in address to the right (see page 3 of instructions). ▶

Name (as distinguished from trade name)

Employer identification number

Trade name, if any

Address (number and street)

City, state, and ZIP code

If address is different from prior return, check here ▶

IRS Use

1 1 1 1 1 1 1 1 1 1 1   2   3 3 3 3 3 3 3   4 4 4   5 5 5

6   7   8 8 8 8 8 8 8   9 9 9 9   10 10 10 10 10 10 10 10 10

If you do not have to file returns in the future, check here ▶ ☐ and enter date final payments paid ▶ ....

1	Federal income tax withheld from pensions, annuities, IRAs, gambling winnings, etc.	**1**
2	Backup withholding	**2**
3	Adjustment to correct administrative errors (see instructions)	**3**
4	**Total taxes.** If $1,000 or more, this must equal line 8M below or line M of Form 945-A . . .	**4**
5	Total deposits for 20 ___ from your records, including overpayment applied from a prior year .	**5**
6	**Balance due** (subtract line 5 from line 4). See instructions	**6**

7 **Overpayment.** If line 4 is less than line 5, enter overpayment here ▶ $ _____ and check if to be:

☐ Applied to next return   **OR**   ☐ Refunded

- **All filers:** If line 4 is less than $1,000, you need not complete line 8 or Form 945-A.
- **Semiweekly schedule depositors:** Complete Form 945-A and check here . . . . ▶ ☐
- **Monthly schedule depositors:** Complete line 8, entries A through M, and check here . . . . ▶ ☐

8 **Monthly Summary of Federal Tax Liability.** Do not complete if you are a semiweekly schedule depositor.

	Tax liability for month		Tax liability for month		Tax liability for month
A January . . .		**F** June		**K** November. . . .	
B February . .		**G** July		**L** December. . . .	
C March		**H** August . . .		**M** Total liability for year (add entries A through L). . . .	
D April		**I** September . . .			
E May		**J** October . . .			

Under penalties of perjury, I declare that I have examined this return, including accompanying schedules and statements, and to the best of my knowledge and belief, it is true, correct, and complete.

Sign Here

Signature ▶ _____ Date ▶ _____

Print Your Name and Title ▶ _____ Telephone Number (optional) ▶ _____

For Privacy Act and Paperwork Reduction Act Notice, see separate instructions.
Cat. No. 14584B
Form **945** (2000)

✹ *Printed on recycled paper*

EXHIBIT 6-5 Form 945, Annual Return of Withheld Federal Income Tax

Military retirement pay also requires reporting on Form 945 and the retiree receives a Form 1099-R on the amount received. Military retirees use a Form W-4, not Form W-4P, to request income tax withholding.

Periodic payments that are not eligible for rollover are those payable for more than one year and include substantially equal payments made at least once a year over the life of the employee and/or beneficiaries or for 10 years or more. These payments are substantially equivalent to wages and withholding uses the same income tax withholding tables and methods.

Recipients of periodic payments may submit a Form W-4P to claim the number of withholding allowances and any additional amount to withhold or they may also claim an exemption from withholding on Form W-4P. If the recipients do not submit a Form W-4P, employers must figure withholding by treating the recipients as married with three withholding allowances.

Employees must withhold 10% of a non-periodic payment that is not an eligible rollover distribution. Recipients may request additional withholding on Form W-4P or claim exemption from withholding.

Reconciliation of Employer Wages, Tax Liabilities, and Deposits

Form 941 records wages and taxes owed on these wages—federal income withholding and FICA taxes—on a quarterly basis. Quarter-to-quarter and yearly accuracy is essential. At the end of the year, the employer reconciles all quarterly reports to the year-to-date information and completes the Forms W-2. Such a reconciliation proves that the amounts reported on the deposit coupons (Form 8109) and on the Forms 941 balance to the payroll records.

Audit trail *Evidence of the sequence of transactions that allows one to trace the amounts in the financial statements back through the accounting records and to the original source documents (and the reverse).*

The reconciliation should follow certain recommended procedures and provide a clear **audit trail** in the permanent records. All corrections should flow through and change in a consistent manner the payroll register, the employee earnings records, and Form 941. The steps in the reconciliation are as follows:

1. Reconcile the payroll register to the quarter-to-date accumulations of gross wages, income and FICA taxes withheld, and employer-computed FICA taxes (payroll register summary to quarterly reports).

2. Prepare a record of tax liability from the payroll register or tax reports, *not* from the deposit coupons. Reconcile the Schedule B, Form 941, which provides a record of the daily tax liability for semiweekly and one-day depositors, to the payroll register.

3. Balance deposits made with Forms 8109 throughout the quarter to the liability on Form 941 for the same periods to detect late deposits and any remaining liability (Form 8109 to Schedule B, Form 941).

Let's examine how this reconciliation process works in practice for Unicorn Construction Corp.

Look again at the summary of Unicorn's payroll tax liabilities and deposits, Figure 6-1, which shows the taxable wages, the federal income tax withheld, FICA taxes, and the total tax liability for the first quarter of the year. As a semiweekly depositor, Unicorn makes a deposit on Wednesday and Friday for the accumulated tax liabilities incurred during the semiweekly period of Wednesday through Friday and Saturday through Tuesday, respectively.

Unicorn files Form 941, Exhibit 6-3, at the end of the quarter, using the liability information shown in Figure 6-1. The Form 941 then reflects this information by daily tax liability. The first part of Form 941 summarizes the taxable wages and the total liability for federal income tax withheld and Social Security and Medicare taxes. The amount reported on line 13 (net taxes) should equal line D, Schedule B (the sum of the monthly period liabilities).

Exceptions to Form 941 Quarterly Reporting

Generally, all employers who are subject to income tax withholding or Social Security and Medicare taxes must file Form 941 every quarter. However, certain types of employers or employer/employee relationships constitute additions and exceptions to this filing requirement. The most notable exceptions are household employers and agricultural employers.

Household Employers.   Employers of household workers report FICA taxes and federal income tax withheld on Schedule H (Form 1040). Household work includes services by cooks, butlers, housekeepers, maids, cleaning people, baby sitters, janitors, caretakers, handy persons, gardeners, and chauffeurs. Cash wages of $1,000 or more in a calendar year make an employer liable for FICA taxes, a test that applies to each household employee. Noncash items such as food, lodging, clothing, and bus or subway tokens are not subject to the $1,000 test and therefore not taxable for FICA purposes.

Sole proprietors may elect to report applicable wages and taxes for household employees along with their other employees on Form 941. Employers of domestic service employees in a college club, fraternity or sorority house may also use Form 941 while employers of household employees in a private home on a farm operated for profit must file Form 943, Employer's Annual Tax Return for Agricultural Employees (Exhibit 6-6).

Agricultural Employers.   Employers of agricultural workers also report Social Security and Medicare taxes and federal income tax withheld on Form 943, Employer's Annual Tax Return for Agricultural Employees.

Other Exceptions.   Seasonal employers need not file for any quarter in which they have no tax liability and they have not paid any wages. However, they must report their status as a seasonal employer on every quarterly return they do file.

In addition, employers who report only federal income tax withheld or who withheld only the Medicare tax are not required to file Form 941. Such employers include some payers of supplemental unemployment

Form **943**	**Employer's Annual Tax Return for Agricultural Employees**	OMB No. 1545-0035
Department of the Treasury Internal Revenue Service	▶ For more information, see Circular A. ▶ For Paperwork Reduction Act Notice, see page 2.	20

Enter your name, address, employer identification number, and calendar year of return.

Name (as distinguished from trade name)	Calendar year
Trade name, if any	Employer identification number
Address and ZIP code	

	T
	FF
	FD
	FP
	I
	T

If address is different from prior return, check here . . . ▶

If you do not have to file returns in the future, check here . . . . ▶

1	Number of agricultural employees employed in the pay period that includes March 12, 20 ▶	1	
2	Total wages subject to social security taxes (see instructions)	2	
3	Social security taxes (multiply line 2 by 12.4% (.124))	3	
4	Total wages subject to Medicare taxes (see instructions)	4	
5	Medicare taxes (multiply line 4 by 2.9% (.029))	5	
6	Federal income tax withheld (see instructions)	6	
7	Total taxes (add lines 3, 5, and 6)	7	
8	Adjustment to taxes (see instructions)	8	
9	Total taxes as adjusted (line 7 as adjusted by line 8).	9	
10	Advance earned income credit (EIC) payments, if any (see instructions on page 4) .	10	
11	Net taxes (subtract line 10 from line 9)	11	
12	**Total deposits** for 20 , including any overpayment from 20 , as shown in your records	12	
13	**Balance due** (subtract line 12 from line 11—see instructions). Pay to Internal Revenue Service . ▶	13	
14	**Overpayment,** if line 12 is more than line 11, enter here ▶ $ and check if to be: ☐ Applied to next return, or ☐ Refunded		

- **All filers:** If line 13 is less than $500, you need not complete line 15 or Form 943-A.
- **Semiweekly schedule depositors:** Complete Form 943-A and check here . . . . ▶
- **Monthly schedule depositors:** Complete line 15 and check here . . . . ▶

15 Summary of Federal Tax Liability

Deposit period ending	Tax liability for month	Deposit period ending	Tax liability for month	Deposit period ending	Tax liability for month
A January 31 . . .		F June 30 . . .		K November 30 .	
B February 29 . .		G July 31		L December 31 .	
C March 31 . . .		H August 31 . .		M Total liability for year (add lines A through L) . .	
D April 30		I September 30 . .			
E May 31 . . .		J October 31 . .			

Sign Here

Under penalties of perjury, I declare that I have examined this return, including accompanying schedules and statements, and to the best of my knowledge and belief, it is true, correct, and complete.

Signature ▶   Print Your Name and Title ▶   Date ▶

Cat. No. 11252K

DETACH HERE

Form **943-V**	**Form 943 Payment Voucher**	20
Department of the Treasury Internal Revenue Service		

Do not send cash and do not staple your payment to this voucher. Make your check or money order, with your employer identification number clearly written on it, payable to the **Internal Revenue Service.**

1 Enter the amount of the payment you are making	2 Enter the first four letters of your business name	3 Your employer identification number
$		

4 Enter your business name(s)

Enter your address

Do not staple your payment to this voucher.

Enter your city, state, and ZIP code

EXHIBIT 6-6 Form 943, Employer's Annual Tax Return for Agricultural Employees

compensation benefits; churches and church-controlled organizations that have filed Form 8274, *Certification by Churches and Qualified Church-Controlled Organizations Electing Exemption from Employer Social Security Taxes.*

Withholding Adjustments

An employer that does not withhold the proper amount in Social Security, Medicare, or federal income taxes can correct the error by increasing the amounts withheld from later pay to that employee. But it is the employer who owes the underpayment to the IRS; reimbursement is up to the employer and the employee. If the employer withholds *more* than the correct amount of Social Security and Medicare taxes from wages paid, the employer must reimburse the employee for the overpayment. The instructions for Form 941 indicate how to correct mistakes in reporting withheld income, Social Security, and Medicare taxes and include the filing of Form 941C, Supporting Statement To Correct Information (Exhibit 6-7).

For a change in the wage totals reported for a previous year, the employer must also file Forms W-2C, Corrected Wage and Tax Statement, and Form W-3C, Transmittal of Corrected Income and Tax Statements. If the employer cannot adjust Social Security and Medicare taxes that were overwithheld, the employer may be able to claim a refund of these taxes by filing Form 843, Claim for Refund and Request for Abatement.

Form 941-M, Employer's Monthly Federal Tax Return

The IRS may require employers who fail to withhold or deposit taxes or file returns on time to report employment taxes monthly rather than quarterly, using Form 941-M, Employer's Monthly Federal Tax Return (Exhibit 6-8). The employer receives notification from the IRS of its monthly reporting requirements. Monthly filing starts when the employer receives notification from the IRS but it must file for any prior months in the quarter unless the first report covers the first month of the quarter. The Form 941-M reports are due by the 15th of the month following the report month.

In addition to monthly reporting, delinquent employers must conform to a shorter time period for making deposits. Delinquent employers must make deposits into a special government trust fund account within two days of the payroll liability.

PAYROLL WAGE REPORTS

Form W-2, Wage and Tax Statement

Form W-2, Wage and Tax Statement   *A form used to report the wages paid to an employee during a calendar year and the federal income and FICA taxes withheld from those wages.*

An employer must annually furnish each employee with a **Form W-2, Wage and Tax Statement**. This form shows wages received during the calendar year (including tips and other compensation) and the amount of taxes withheld from those wages. For employees with no federal income tax withheld, the employer must still provide a Form W-2 if the wages were subject to Social Security and Medicare taxes. As mentioned earlier,

Form **941c**

Department of the Treasury
Internal Revenue Service

Supporting Statement To Correct Information

Do Not File Separately

▶ File with the employment tax return on which adjustments are made.

OMB No. 1545-0256

Page No.

Name	Employer identification number

Telephone number	A This form supports adjustments to: **Check one box.** ☐ Form 941 ☐ Form 941-SS ☐ Form 945 ☐ Form 941-M ☐ Form 943

B This form is filed with the return for the period ending (month, year) ▶	C Enter the date you discovered the error(s) reported on this form. (If you are making more than one correction and the errors were not discovered at the same time, please explain in Part V.) . . . ▶

Part I — **Signature and Certification** (You **MUST** complete this part for the IRS to process your adjustments for overpayments.)

I certify that **Forms W-2c,** Statement of Corrected Income and Tax Amounts, have been filed (as necessary) with the Social Security Administration, and that (check appropriate boxes):

☐ All overcollected income taxes for the current calendar year and all social security and Medicare taxes for the current and prior calendar years have been repaid to employees. For claims of overcollected employee social security and Medicare taxes in earlier years, a written statement has been obtained from each employee stating that the employee has not claimed and will not claim refund or credit of the amount of the overcollection.

☐ All affected employees have given their written consent to the allowance of this credit or refund. For claims of overcollected employee social security and Medicare taxes in earlier years, a written statement has been obtained from each employee stating that the employee has not claimed and will not claim refund or credit of the amount of the overcollection.

☐ The social security tax and Medicare tax adjustments represent the employer's share only. An attempt was made to locate the employee(s) affected, but the affected employee(s) could not be located or will not comply with the certification requirements.

☐ None of this refund or credit was withheld from employee wages.

Sign Here

Signature ▶	Title ▶	Date ▶

Part II — **Income Tax/Backup Withholding Adjustment**

	(a) Period Corrected (Quarterly returns, enter date quarter ended. Annual returns, enter year.)	(b) Withheld Income Tax Previously Reported for Period	(c) Correct Withheld Income Tax for Period	(d) Withheld Income Tax Adjustment
1				
2				
3				
4				
5	Net withheld income tax/backup withholding adjustment. If more than one page, enter total of all columns (d) on first page only. Enter here and on the **appropriate** line of the return with which this form is filed . . . . ▶ **5**			

Part III — **Social Security Tax Adjustment** (Use the tax rate in effect during the period(s) corrected. You must also complete Part IV.)

	(a) Period Corrected (Quarterly returns, enter date quarter ended. Annual returns, enter year.)	(b) Wages Previously Reported for Period	(c) Correct Taxable Wages for Period	(d) Tips Previously Reported for Period	(e) Correct Taxable Tips for Period	(f) Social Security Tax Adjustment
1						
2						
3						
4						
5	Totals.—If more than one page, enter totals on first page only . ▶					
6	Net social security tax adjustment. If more than one page, enter total of **ALL** columns (f) on first page only. Enter here and on the appropriate line of the return with which this form is filed . . ▶ **6**					
7	Net wage adjustment. If more than one page, enter the total of **ALL** lines 7 on first page only. If 5(c) is smaller than 5(b), enter difference in parentheses . . . . ▶ **7**					
8	Net tip adjustment. If more than one page, enter the total of **ALL** lines 8 on first page only. If 5(e) is smaller than 5(d), enter difference in parentheses . . . . ▶ **8**					

For Paperwork Reduction Act Notice, see page 3.   Cat. No. 11242O   Form **941c**

EXHIBIT 6-7 Form 941C, Statement to Correct Information

Form 941c

| Part IV | Medicare Tax Adjustment | | | | |

(a) Period Corrected (Quarterly returns, enter date quarter ended. Annual returns, enter year.)	(b) Wages and Tips Previously Reported for Period	(c) Correct Taxable Wages and Tips for Period	(d) Medicare Tax Adjustment
1			
2			
3			
4			
5 Totals.—If more than one page, enter totals on first page only . . ▶			
6 Net Medicare tax adjustment. If more than one page, enter total of **ALL** columns (d) on first page only. Enter here and on the appropriate line of the return with which this form is filed . . . . ▶ **6**			
7 Net wage and tip adjustment. If more than one page, enter the totals for **ALL** pages. If 5(c) is smaller than 5(b), enter difference in parentheses . . . . ▶ **7**			

| Part V | Explanation of Adjustments |

EXHIBIT 6-7 Form 941C, Supporting Statement to Correct Information *(cont.)*

the employee earnings record provides all the information required to complete Form W-2. Exhibit 6-9 shows a Form W-2 for Wayne Dean completed by Nioga Gear. Copies of the Form W-2 go to the IRS, to state tax departments, and sometimes to city and local governments. Table 6-2 summarizes the distribution schedule for the six-part form.

Employers must provide employees with Forms W-2 no later than the January 31 following the end of the calendar year. When an employee leaves a company before the end of the calendar year and makes the request, the employer must provide the Form W-2 within 30 days of the request or of the final wages payment, whichever is later. Otherwise, the Form W-2 is due by January 31. If an employee or recipient loses a statement, the employer issues a new one and must write "Reissued Statement" on the new copy. However, the employer does not send Copy A of the reissued form to the Social Security Administration.

The W-2 forms can be obtained from the IRS or purchased from office supply stores in commercially printed versions. Substitute forms or forms supplied by someone other than the IRS must conform to a certain format as explained in IRS Publication 1141.

Completion of Form W-2

Let's take a closer look at the Form W-2 in Exhibit 6-9 to see where the information for Wayne Dean came from.

Box a. The control number is assigned to an employee for internal control purposes; it is not a required item.

Box b. Employer's identification number. Successor employers should use their own number, not that of the prior employer.

Box c. Employer's name, address, and ZIP Code. Employer's legal name should be same as printed on Form 941 or Form 8109.

Form **941-M**
(Rev. January 2000)
Department of the Treasury
Internal Revenue Service

Employer's Monthly Federal Tax Return

OMB No. 1545-0718

Return for (enter month and year) . . . . ▶

Name, address, ZIP code, and employer identification number

For IRS Use Only	
T	
FF	
FD	
FP	
I	
T	

If not correct, please change.

1	**For March Only:** Number of employees (except household) employed in the pay period that includes March 12th . . . . ▶	**1**	
2	Total wages and tips, plus other compensation	**2**	
3	Total income tax withheld from wages, tips, and sick pay.	**3**	
4	Adjustment of withheld income tax for preceding months of calendar year	**4**	
5	Adjusted total of income tax withheld (line 3 as adjusted by line 4)	**5**	

6	Taxable social security wages	**6a**		12.4% (.124) =	**6b**	
	Taxable social security tips	**6c**		12.4% (.124) =	**6d**	
7	Taxable Medicare wages and tips . . .	**7a**		2.9% (.029) =	**7b**	

8	Total social security and Medicare taxes (add lines 6b, 6d, and 7b)	**8**	
9	Adjustment of social security and Medicare taxes (see instructions)	**9**	
10	Adjusted total of social security and Medicare taxes (line 8 as adjusted by line 9)	**10**	
11	Total taxes (add lines 5 and 10)	**11**	
12	Advance earned income credit (EIC) payments made to employees (see instructions) . . .	**12**	
13	Net taxes (subtract line 12 from line 11)	**13**	

14 Record of Federal Tax Liability and Deposits (See instructions on page 4.)

	Tax Liability	Amount Deposited		Tax Liability	Amount Deposited		Tax Liability	Amount Deposited
Overpayment from previous month . . . . ▶								
1			12			23		
2			13			24		
3			14			25		
4			15			26		
5			16			27		
6			17			28		
7			18			29		
8			19			30		
9			20			31		
10			21					
11			22					

a Total tax liability for the month **14a**
b Total deposits for the month (including overpayment from previous month) . . **14b**

15 Undeposited taxes due (subtract line 14b from line 14a). See instructions . . . . ▶ **15**
16 If line 14b is more than line 14a, enter overpayment here ▶ $ _____ and check if to be: ☐ Applied to next return or ☐ Refunded.

Under penalties of perjury, I declare that I have examined this return, including accompanying schedules and statements, and to the best of my knowledge and belief it is true, correct, and complete.

Signature ▶ _____ Print Your Name and Title ▶ _____ Date ▶ _____

For Privacy Act and Paperwork Reduction Act Notice, see page 4.   Cat. No. 17013R   Form **941-M** (Rev. 1-2000)

EXHIBIT 6-8   Form 941M, Employer's Monthly Federal Tax Return

a Control number	22222	Void ☐	For Official Use Only ▶ OMB No. 1545-0008	

b Employer identification number 16-9714606		1 Wages, tips, other compensation 27,640.00	2 Federal income tax withheld 2,444.00
c Employer's name, address, and ZIP code *Nioga Gear, Inc.* *600 Whirlpool Drive* *Niagara Falls, NY 14301*		3 Social security wages 27,640.00	4 Social security tax withheld 1,713.68
		5 Medicare wages and tips 27,640.00	6 Medicare tax withheld 400.78
		7 Social security tips	8 Allocated tips
d Employee's social security number 888-26-5891		9 Advance EIC payment	10 Dependent care benefits
e Employee's name (first, middle initial, last)		11 Nonqualified plans	12 Benefits included in box 1
Wayne Dean *402 Pine Avenue* *Lockport, NY 14074*		13 See instrs. for box 13	14 Other
f Employee's address and ZIP code		15 Statutory employee ☐ Deceased ☐ Pension plan ☐ Legal rep. ☐ Deferred compensation ☐	

16 State Employer's state I.D. no.	17 State wages, tips, etc. 27,640.00	18 State income tax 988.00	19 Locality name	20 Local wages, tips, etc.	21 Local income tax

Form **W-2** Wage and Tax Statement **20**

Department of the Treasury—Internal Revenue Service

For Privacy Act and Paperwork Reduction Act Notice, see separate instructions.

Copy A For Social Security Administration—Send this entire page with Form W-3 to the Social Security Administration; photocopies are **not** acceptable.   Cat. No. 10134D

Do NOT Cut, Fold, or Staple Forms on This Page — Do NOT Cut, Fold, or Staple Forms on This Page

EXHIBIT 6-9   Form W-2, Wage and Tax Statement

Box d.   Employee's Social Security number. An employee can get a Social Security number by filing Form SS-5 with the Social Security Administration.

Box e.   Employee's name (first, middle, last), address, and ZIP Code. The name should be the same as that on the employee's Social Security card. The inclusion of the address permits mailing in a window envelope or self-mailer.

Box 1.   Wages, tips, other compensation. Total of wages; noncash payments (including fringe benefits); tips reported; certain employee business and nonqualified moving expense reimbursements; and all other compensation, including distributions from a nonqualified deferred compensation plan and payments to statutory employees.

Box 2.   Federal income tax withheld. This amount includes any income tax withheld from sick pay paid by a third party.

Box 3.   Social Security wages. Total wages subject to Social Security tax. Amount includes noncash payments, certain employee business expenses,

TABLE 6-2		
Distribution of Form W-2 Copies		
Copy	Who Receives	When Due
Copy A	Social Security Administration	By the end of February following the applicable year.
Copy 1	State, city, or local tax department	Dependent on state law—generally, by the end of January or February.
Copy B	Employee (for filing with federal income tax return)	On or before January 31 following the applicable year.
Copy C	Employee (for personal records)	On or before January 31.
Copy 2	Employee (for filing with state, city, or local income tax return)	On or before January 31.
Copy D	Employer	

employer contributions to a qualified cash or deferred compensation plan, and FICA taxes paid for the employee.

Box 4. Social security tax withheld. Total employee Social Security tax withheld or paid for the employee.

Box 5. Medicare wages and tips. Amount of wages and tips reported regardless of whether employer had sufficient employee funds to collect the Medicare tax.

Box 6. Medicare tax withheld. Total Medicare tax withheld or paid for the employee.

Box 7. Social Security tips. Amount of tips reported regardless of whether employer had sufficient employee funds to collect the Social Security tax.

Box 8. Allocated tips. Share of the excess of 8% of an establishment's gross receipts over the tips reported by employers; applicable to large food and beverage establishments (11 or more employees). Box 1 (wages, tips, other compensation), Box 5 (Medicare wages and tips), and Box 7 (Social Security tips) do not include the amount of allocated tips.

Box 9. Advance EIC payment. Advances of the refundable earned income credit paid out, provided the low-income employee has filed Form W-5 with the employer.

Box 10. Dependent care benefits. Total amount of dependent care benefits paid or incurred for an employee, including any amount in excess of the $5,000 exclusion ($2,500 if married, filing separately) (shown in Box 1).

Box 11. Nonqualified plans. Total amount of distributions to an employee from a nonqualified plan or a Section 457 plan. Box 1 includes this amount.

Box 12. Total value of the taxable fringe benefits included in Box 1 as other compensation.

Box 13. Special taxes and payments.

CODE A Uncollected Social Security tax on tips. Amount of employee Social Security tax on tips not collected because the employee did not have enough funds from which to make the deduction; this amount is not included in Box 4.

CODE B Uncollected Medicare tax on tips. Amount of employee Medicare tax on tips not collected because the employee did not have enough funds from which to make the deduction; this amount is not included in Box 6.

CODE C Cost of group term life insurance provided the employee in excess of $50,000; included in Boxes 1, 3, and 5.

Codes D–H cover contributions to various retirement plans; deferred compensation in Box 15 should have been checked off.

CODE D Section 401(K).

CODE E Section 403(b).

CODE F Section 408(K) (6).

CODE G Section 457(b).

CODE H Section 501(c) (18) (D).

CODE J Sick pay not includible in the employee's income because the plan is contributory. May identify sick pay in Box 13 or a separate Form W-2.

CODE K Tax on excess golden parachute payments. The 20% excise tax is included in Box 2 as income tax withheld.

CODE L Nontaxable part of employee business expense reimbursements. Amounts reimbursed an employee equal to the government-specified amounts with the excess, if any, shown in Box 1.

CODE M Uncollected Social Security tax on the cost of group life insurance over $50,000 provided former employees.

CODE N Uncollected Medicare tax on the cost of group term life insurance over $50,000 provided former employees.

CODE P Excludable moving expense reimbursements.

CODE Q Military employee basic quarters, subsistence and combat pay.

CODE R Employer contributions to Medical Savings Acount (MSA).

CODE S Employee salary reduction contributions to a section 408(p) SIMPLE not included in Box 1.

CODE T Adoption benefits not included in Box 1.

Box 14. Employers can use this box to report any other information they want to give employees such as union dues, health insurance premiums deducted, moving expenses paid, and educational assistance payments.

Box 15. Special categories of employee or compensation.

STATUTORY EMPLOYEE By law, statutory employees are subject to FICA taxes but not federal income tax withholding.

DECEASED Wages paid to a beneficiary or estate in the year after death may be reportable on Form 1099-Misc.

PENSION PLAN An active participant in a retirement plan, including a 401(K) plan, a simplified employee plan (SEP), or a collectively bargained plan.

LEGAL REPRESENTATION Used to indicate that another person is acting on behalf of the employee (who may be a minor) or that the name on the W-4 form is a trust account.

DEFERRED COMPENSATION Contributions made on behalf of the employee to a 401(K), 403(b), 408(K), 457(b), or 501(K) retirement plan.

Box 16. Employer's state I.D. number. Completion is optional; the form provides space for two states.

Boxes 17–21. State and local tax information.

Reconciliation of Employee Wages and Taxes Withheld

The Forms W-2 data should agree with the employee earnings records from which the information comes. A reconciliation proves the Forms W-2 balance to the payroll records. The steps in the reconciliation process are as follows:

1. Reconcile the annual Forms W-2 to the individual gross wages and deductions on the employee earnings record (Form W-2 to employee earnings record).

2. Reconcile the annual Forms W-2 to the total of the Forms 941 for the year. The employer must reconcile the federal income and FICA taxes withheld to the Forms W-2 before issuing them to employees (Form W-2 to Form 941).

3. Reconcile the Forms W-2 information, line by line, to the Form W-3 summaries plus the W-3Cs (Form W-2 to Form W-3).

Form W-3, Transmittal of Wage and Tax Statements

Form W-3 A form that must be filed with the Social Security Administration by February 28 after the end of the previous calendar year and is used for transmittal of copy A of the employees' Forms W-2, summarizing the totals for all employees' wages, taxes withheld, and other wage and tax data.

Employers must use **Form W-3**, Transmittal of Wage and Tax Statements, when filing the Forms W-2 with the Social Security Administration. Form W-3 summarizes the total wages, Social Security and Medicare wages and tips, federal income tax withheld, and FICA taxes withheld from employees during the year and lists the number of Forms W-2 being transmitted. A completed copy of Form W-3 is shown in Exhibit 6-10.

Corrections

Corrections to Forms W-2 are made with Form W-2C, Corrected Wage and Tax Statement (Exhibit 6-11). The Form W-2C must be distributed to

DO NOT STAPLE OR FOLD

a Control number	33333	For Official Use Only ▶ OMB No. 1545-0008		

b Kind of Payer	941 ☒ Military ☐ 943 ☐ CT-1 ☐ Hshld. emp. ☐ Medicare govt. emp. ☐	**1** Wages, tips, other compensation 850,000	**2** Federal income tax withheld 160,000
		3 Social security wages 700,000	**4** Social security tax withheld 43,400
c Total number of Forms W-2 98	**d** Establishment number	**5** Medicare wages and tips 800,000	**6** Medicare tax withheld 11,600
e Employer identification number 16-9714606		**7** Social security tips	**8** Allocated tips
f Employer's name Nioga Gear, Inc.		**9** Advance EIC payments	**10** Dependent care benefits
		11 Nonqualified plans	**12** Deferred compensation
		13	
600 Whirlpool Drive Niagara Falls, NY 14301		**14**	
g Employer's address and ZIP code			
h Other EIN used this year		**15** Income tax withheld by third-party payer	
i Employer's state I.D. no.			

Contact person	Telephone number ( )	Fax number ( )	E-mail address

Under penalties of perjury, I declare that I have examined this return and accompanying documents, and, to the best of my knowledge and belief, they are true, correct, and complete.

Signature ▶ _____ Title ▶ _____ Date ▶ _____

Form **W-3** Transmittal of Wage and Tax Statements 2Ꮰ   Department of the Treasury Internal Revenue Service

Send this entire page with the entire Copy A page of Form(s) W-2 to the Social Security Administration. Photocopies are NOT acceptable. Do NOT send any remittance (cash, checks, money orders, etc.) with Forms W-2 and W-3.

An Item To Note

Separate instructions. See the separate **2000 Instructions for Forms W-2 and W-3** for information on completing this form.

Purpose of Form

Use this form to transmit Copy A of **Form(s) W-2,** Wage and Tax Statement. Make a copy of Form W-3, and keep it with Copy D (For Employer) of Form(s) W-2 for your records. Use Form W-3 for the correct year. **File Form W-3 even if only one Form W-2 is being filed.** If you are filing Form(s) W-2 on magnetic media or electronically, **do not** file Form W-3.

When To File

File Form W-3 with Copy A of Form(s) W-2 by February 28, 2001.

Where To File

Send this entire page with the entire Copy A page of Form(s) W-2 to:

> **Social Security Administration**
> **Data Operations Center**
> **Wilkes-Barre, PA 18769-0001**

Note: *If you use "Certified Mail" to file, change the ZIP code to "18769-0002." If you use an IRS approved private delivery service, add "ATTN: W-2 Process, 1150 E. Mountain Dr." to the address and change the ZIP code to "18702-7997." See* **Circular E,** *Employer's Tax Guide (Pub. 15), for a list of IRS approved private delivery services.*

For Privacy Act and Paperwork Reduction Act Notice, see the 2000 Instructions for Forms W-2 and W-3.

Cat. No. 10159Y

EXHIBIT 6-10 Form W-3, Transmittal of Wage and Tax Statements

everyone who received the original Form W-2. If the employer must correct a Form W-2 before Copy A has been filed with the Social Security Administration (SSA), the employer gives the employee the corrected copies, marks "Void" on the original Copy A, and sends the new Copy A to SSA without writing "corrected" on it.

If correcting more than one Form W-2, the employer must use Form W-3C, Transmittal of Corrected Income and Tax Statements (Exhibit 6-12) when filing the corrected copies with the Social Security Administration.

a Year/Form corrected 20 ..... / W-2	Void ☐	OMB No. 1545-0008	For Official Use Only ▶

b Employee's name, address, and ZIP code ☐ Corrected Name	c Employer's name, address, and ZIP code

d Employee's correct SSN	e Employer's SSA number 69-	f Employer's Federal EIN	g Employer's state I.D. number

h Previously reported ▶ Stat. emp. ☐ De-ceased ☐ Pension plan ☐ Legal rep. ☐ Def'd. comp. ☐ Hshld. emp. ☐	i Corrected ▶ Stat. emp. ☐ De-ceased ☐ Pension plan ☐ Legal rep. ☐ Def'd. comp. ☐ Hshld. emp. ☐	j Employer's use

Complete k and/or l only if **incorrect** on the last form you filed. Show **incorrect** item here. ▶	k Employee's **incorrect** SSN	l Employee's name (as **incorrectly** shown on previous form)

Form W-2 box	(a) As previously reported	(b) Correct information	(c) Increase (decrease)
1 Wages, tips, other comp.			
2 Federal income tax withheld			
3 Social security wages			
4 Social security tax withheld			
5 Medicare wages and tips			
6 Medicare tax withheld			
7 Social security tips			
8 Allocated tips			
State wages, tips, etc.			
State income tax			
Local wages, tips, etc.			
Local income tax			

(CHANGES)

For Privacy Act/Paperwork Reduction Act Notice, see separate instructions.
Form **W-2c** (Rev. 1-99) **Corrected Wage and Tax Statement**
Copy A For Social Security Administration
Department of the Treasury Internal Revenue Service

Do NOT Cut, Staple, or Separate Forms on This Page ± Do NOT Cut, Staple, or Separate Forms on This Page

EXHIBIT 6-11 Form W-2C, Corrected Wage and Tax Statement

Earned Income Credit Notification

An employer must notify any employees who do not have income tax withheld that they may be eligible for an income tax refund because of the earned income credit. They can be notified by

- using the official IRS Form W-2, which contains a statement on the back of Copy C concerning the earned income credit.
- providing the employee with Notice 797, Notice of a Possible Federal Tax Refund due to the Earned Income Credit when it furnishes a non-IRS version of Form W-2 or none at all.

REPORTS ON NONEMPLOYEE COMPENSATION

Information return *A form used to report compensation paid to nonemployees.*

An employer must file **information returns** with the IRS and send copies of those returns to the payees. These information returns report compensation paid to persons other than employees and help the IRS and the payees verify individual income items. Table 6-3, compiled from *Circular E, Employer's Tax Guide,* describes the primary types of information forms.

Form 1099-MISC, Miscellaneous Income

Companies using the services of outside contractors or freelance employees must notify the IRS and these nonemployees of the amounts paid for their services. An employer must file a Form 1099-MISC, Miscellaneous Income for each person (other than a corporation) who either (1) was paid at least $600 in rents, royalties, services, or prizes and awards; or (2) had federal income tax withheld under the backup withholding rules, regardless of the amount of the payment. Employers engaged in a for-profit trade or business are subject to these requirements, as are certain nonprofit organizations. A 1099-MISC is due to the recipient by January 31.

Exhibit 6-13 illustrates a Form 1099-MISC completed for Susan Brainard, who received a free pair of sneakers and $1,000 in cash from Nioga as the winner of a "Name That Shoe" contest.

Form 1096, Annual Summary and Transmittal

Form 1096, Annual Summary and Transmittal of U.S. Information Returns (Exhibit 6-14) summarizes all information returns, including Forms 1099-MISC. An employer must file this transmittal with each type of Form 1099 sent to the IRS. Forms 1099 and the accompanying Form 1096 must be filed by the last day of February in the year following the payments.

a Year/Form corrected 20 .... / W-	OMB No. 1545-0008 For Official Use Only ▶		

b Employer's name, address, and ZIP code	c Number of Forms W-2c ▶
	d Establishment number
	e Employer's Federal EIN

f Kind of payer	941/ 941-SS ☐	Hshld. emp. ☐	943 ☐	CT-1 ☐	Military ☐	Medicare govt. emp. ☐	Sec. 218 ☐	g Employer's state I.D. number
								h Employer's SSA no. (see instructions) 69±

Complete box i, j, and/or k **only** if **incorrect** on the last form you filed. Show the **incorrect** item here.	i Employer's **incorrect** Federal EIN	j **Incorrect** establishment number	k Employer's **incorrect** SSA number

CHANGES

Form W-2c box	Total amounts shown in column (a) on enclosed Forms W-2c	Total amounts shown in column (b) on enclosed Forms W-2c	Total increase (decrease) shown in column (c) on enclosed Forms W-2c
1 Wages, tips, other compensation			
2 Federal income tax withheld			
3 Social security wages			
4 Social security tax withheld			
5 Medicare wages and tips			
6 Medicare tax withheld			
7 Social security tips			
8 Allocated tips			
17 State wages, tips, etc.			
18 State income tax			
20 Local wages, tips, etc.			
21 Local income tax			

22 Explain decreases here

Has an adjustment been made on an employment tax return filed with the Internal Revenue Service? ☐ Yes ☐ No

If "Yes," give date the return was filed ▶

Under penalties of perjury, I declare that I have examined this return, including accompanying documents, and, to the best of my knowledge and belief, it is true, correct, and complete.

Signature ▶   Title ▶   Date ▶

Contact person	Telephone number ( )	Fax number ( )	E-mail address

Form **W-3c** (Rev. 1-99) **Transmittal of Corrected Wage and Tax Statements**

For Privacy Act and Paperwork Reduction Act Notice, see separate instructions. Cat. No. 10164R

Department of the Treasury
Internal Revenue Service

EXHIBIT 6-12 Form W-3C, Transmittal of Corrected Income and Tax Statements

TABLE 6-3 Guide to Information Returns

Form Number	Title	What To Report	Amounts To Report	Due Date — To IRS	Due Date — To Recipient (unless indicated otherwise)
1042S	Foreign Person's U.S. Source Income Subject to Withholding	Payments subject to withholding under Chapter 3 of the Code, including interest, dividends, royalties, pensions and annuities, gambling winnings, and compensation for personal services.	All amounts	March 15	March 15
1098	Mortgage Interest Statement	Mortgage interest (including points) you received in the course of your trade or business from individuals and reimbursements of overpaid interest	$600 or more	February 28	(To Payer/Borrower) January 31
1099-A	Acquisition or Abandonment of Secured Property	Information about the acquisition or abandonment of property that is security for a debt for which you are the lender.	All amounts	February 28	(To Borrower) January 31
1099-B	Proceeds From Broker and Barter Exchange Transactions	Sales or redemptions of securities, futures transactions, commodities, and barter exchange transactions.	All amounts	February 28	January 31
1099-C	Cancellation of Debt	Cancellation of debt owed to a financial institution, credit union, RTC, FDIC, NCUA, or Federal Government agency.	$600 or more	February 28	January 31
1099-DIV	Dividends and Distributions	Distributions, such as dividends, capital gain distributions, or nontaxable distributions, that were paid on stock, and distributions in liquidation.	$10 or more, except $600 or more for liquidations	February 28	January 31
1099-G	Certain Government Payments	Unemployment compensation, state and local income tax refunds, agricultural payments, and taxable grants.	$10 or more for unemployment and tax refunds; $600 or more for all others	February 28	January 31
1099-INT	Interest Income	Interest payments not including interest on an IRA.	$10 or more ($600 or more in some cases)	February 28	January 31
1099-MISC	Miscellaneous Income (Also, use this form to report the occurrence of direct sales of $5,000 or more of consumer goods for resale.)	Rent or royalty payments; prizes and awards that are not for services, such as winnings on TV or radio shows.	$600 or more, except $10 or more for royalties	February 28	January 31
		Payments to crew members by owners or operators of fishing boats. Report payments of proceeds from sale of catch.	All payments		
		Payments to a physician, physicians' corporation, or other supplier of health and medical services. Issued mainly by medical assistance programs or health and accident insurance plans.	$600 or more		
		Payments for services performed for a trade or business by people not treated as its employees. Examples: fees to subcontractors or directors, expenses incurred for use of an entertainment facility treated as compensation to a nonemployee, and golden parachute payments.	$600 or more		
		Substitute dividend and tax-exempt interest payments reportable by brokers.	$10 or more		
		Crop insurance proceeds.	$600 or more		
1099-OID	Original Issue Discount	Original issue discount.	$10 or more	February 28	January 31
1099-PATR	Taxable Distributions Received From Cooperatives	Distributions from cooperatives to their patrons.	$10 or more	February 28	January 31
1099-R	Distributions From Pensions, Annuities, Retirement or Profit-Sharing Plans, IRAs, Insurance Contracts, etc.	Distributions from retirement or profit-sharing plans, IRAs, SEPS, or insurance contracts.	All amounts	February 28	January 31

Form	Title	Reportable item	Amount	Due to IRS	Due to recipient
1099-S	Proceeds From Real Estate Transactions	Gross proceeds from the sale or exchange of real estate.	Generally, $600 or more	February 28	January 31
4789	Currency Transaction Report	Each deposit, withdrawal, exchange of currency, or other payment or transfer by, through, or to financial institutions (other than casinos) that involves a transaction in currency of more than $10,000.	Over $10,000	Within 15 days after the date of the transaction	Not required
5471	Information Return of U.S. Persons With Respect To Certain Foreign Corporations	U.S. persons who are officers, directors, or shareholders in certain foreign corporations report information required by sections 6035, 6038, and 6046, and to compute income under sections 951–964.	See form instructions	Due date of income tax return	None
5472	Information Return of a 25% Foreign-Owned U.S. Corporation or a Foreign Corporation Engaged in a U.S. Trade or Business	Transactions between a 25% foreign-owned domestic corporation or a foreign corporation engaged in a trade or business in the United States and a related party as required by sections 6038A and 6038C.	See form instructions	Due date of income tax return	None
5498	Individual Retirement Arrangement Information	Contributions (including rollover contributions) to an individual retirement arrangement (IRA), and the value of an IRA or simplified employee pension (SEP) account.	All amounts	May 31	(To Participant) (for value of account) January 31 (for contributions) May 31
8027	Employer's Annual Information Return of Tip Income and Allocated Tips	Receipts from food or beverage operations, tips reported by employees, and allocated tips.	See separate instructions.	Last day of February	Allocated tips are shown on Form W-2 due January 31
8300	Report of Cash Payments Over $10,000 Received in a Trade or Business	Payments in cash (including certain monetary instruments) or foreign currency received in one transaction, or two or more related transactions, in the course of a trade or business. Does not apply to banks and financial institutions filing **Form 4789,** Currency Transaction Report, and casinos that are required to report such transactions on **Form 8362,** Currency Transaction Report by Casinos, or, generally, to transactions outside the United States.	Over $10,000	Within 15 days after the date of the transaction	(To Payer) January 31
8308	Report of a Sale or Exchange of Certain Partnership Interests	Sales or exchanges of a partnership interest involving unrealized receivables or substantially appreciated inventory items.	(Transaction only)	Generally, attach to Form 1065	(To Transferor and Transferees) January 31
W-2G	Certain Gambling Winnings	Gambling winnings from horse racing, dog racing, jai alai, lotteries, keno, bingo, slot machines, sweepstakes, and wagering pools.	Generally, $600 or more; $1,200 or more from bingo or slot machines; $1,500 or more from keno	February 28	January 31
926	Return by a U.S. Transferor of Property to a Foreign Corporation, Foreign Estate or Trust, or Foreign Partnership	Transfers of property to a foreign corporation, estate, trust, or partnership; also used to pay excise tax under section 1491 and to report information under section 6038B.	See form instructions	Due date of transfer; for section 6038B, attach to tax return	None
W-2	Wage and Tax Statement	Wages, tips, other compensation, withheld income, Social Security and Medicare taxes, and advance earned income credit (EIC) payments. Include bonuses, vacation allowances, severance pay, moving expense payments, some kinds of travel allowances, and third-party payments of sick pay.	See separate instructions	(To SSA) Last day of February	(To Recipient) January 31
TD F 90-22.1	Report of Foreign Bank and Financial Accounts	Financial interest in or signature or other authority over a foreign bank account, securities account, or other financial account.	Over $10,000	(To Treasury Department) June 30	(To Recipient) None

9595 ☐ VOID ☐ CORRECTED

PAYER'S name, street address, city, state, ZIP code, and telephone no.	1 Rents $	OMB No. 1545-0115	**Miscellaneous Income**
Nioga Gear, Inc. *600 Whirlpool Drive* *Niagara Falls, NY 14301*	2 Royalties $	20	
	3 Other income $ 1,070.00	Form **1099-MISC**	

PAYER'S Federal identification number 16-9714606	RECIPIENT'S identification number 132-58-2683	4 Federal income tax withheld $	5 Fishing boat proceeds $	**Copy A** **For** **Internal Revenue** **Service Center**
RECIPIENT'S name *Susan Brainard*		6 Medical and health care payments $	7 Nonemployee compensation $	**File with Form 1096.** For Privacy Act
Street address (including apt. no.) *842 Walnut Avenue*		8 Substitute payments in lieu of dividends or interest $	9 Payer made direct sales of $5,000 or more of consumer products to a buyer (recipient) for resale ▶ ☐	and Paperwork Reduction Act Notice, see the **20XX General**
City, state, and ZIP code *Niagara Falls, NY 14301*		10 Crop insurance proceeds $	11 State income tax withheld $	**Instructions for Forms 1099, 1098,**
Account number (optional)	2nd TIN Not. ☐	12 State/Payer's state number 16-9714606	13 $	**5498, and W-2G.**

Form **1099-MISC**   Cat. No. 14425J   Department of the Treasury - Internal Revenue Service

Do NOT Cut or Separate Forms on This Page — Do NOT Cut or Separate Forms on This Page

EXHIBIT 6-13 Form 1099-MISC, Miscellaneous Income

DO NOT STAPLE

Form **1096** Department of the Treasury Internal Revenue Service	**Annual Summary and Transmittal of U.S. Information Returns**	OMB No. 1545-0108 20

A
T
T
A
C
H

I
R
S

L
A
B
E
L

H
E
R
E

⌐FILER'S name

Street address (including room or suite number)

City, state, and ZIP code⌐

If you are not using a preprinted label, enter in box 1 or 2 below the identification number you used as the filer on the information returns being transmitted. Do not fill in both boxes 1 and 2.	Name of person to contact if the IRS needs more information Telephone number ( )	**For Official Use Only** ☐☐☐☐☐☐ ☐☐

1 Employer identification number	2 Social security number	3 Total number of forms	4 Federal income tax withheld $	5 Total amount reported with this Form 1096 $

Enter an "X" in only one box below to indicate the type of form being filed.   If this is your FINAL return, enter an "X" here . . ▶ ☐

W-2G 32	1098 81	1098-E 84	1098-T 83	1099-A 80	1099-B 79	1099-C 85	1099-DIV 91	1099-G 86	1099-INT 92	1099-LTC 93	1099-MISC 95	1099-MSA 94	1099-OID 96
☐	☐	☐	☐	☐	☐	☐	☐	☐	☐	☐	☐	☐	☐

1099-PATR 97	1099-R 98	1099-S 75	5498 28	5498-MSA 27
☐	☐	☐	☐	☐

EXHIBIT 6-14 Form 1096, Annual Summary and Transmittal of U.S. Information Returns

REVIEW QUESTIONS

6-1. How and where are tax deposits made? What taxes do these deposits include?

6-2. What are acceptable forms for tax deposits? What are immediate credit items?

6-3. How is the time computed for purposes of the penalty for late tax deposits?

6-4. Under what circumstances should a deposit be made directly with the IRS? What information should accompany the deposit?

6-5. How should an employer make a deposit if it has an EIN but has not received its supply of coupons?

6-6. On what are the penalties for late or insufficient payments based?

6-7. Describe the penalty that may be imposed when the tax deposits are made in response to a delinquency notice.

6-8. What is the basis for the employer's deposit obligation?

6-9. How can an employer handle a tax liability that is less than $1,000 at the end of the quarter?

6-10. What action does an employer take when the tax liability is less than $1,000 at the end of the month?

6-11. How does an employer make a payment of less than $1,000 for a quarterly period? What form is used?

6-12. If the balance due is $1,000 or more at the end of a quarter, how does the employer make the deposit?

6-13. What is the amount of the tax liability that requires a deposit by the close of the next banking day?

6-14. In what way can backup withholding be deposited?

6-15. What are the two basic rules for depositing FUTA taxes?

6-16. Describe the exceptions to the filing of quarterly Form 941 returns.

6-17. What amount of wages paid to a household employee makes the employer liable for Social Security and Medicare taxes? What noncash items are *not* subject to this test?

6-18. Who is responsible for underwithholding of Social Security and Medicare taxes and how can this error be corrected?

6-19. What should an employer do if it has overwithheld Social Security and Medicare taxes?

6-20. How are errors in reporting withheld Social Security and Medicare taxes on a Form W-2 corrected when they are due to (a) incorrect calculations and (b) wage changes?

6-21. List the recipients of the copies of Form W-2. When must the employer provide an employee with a Form W-2?

6-22. How can an employer notify employees who do not have income tax withheld that they may be eligible for an income tax refund because of the earned income credit?

6-23. For whom must a Form 1099-MISC be provided?

6-24. How does an employer making deposits under the deposit rules determine whether it should be a monthly or semiweekly depositor?

6-25. What action is the Internal Revenue Service expected to take to inform employees about which deposit schedule to follow for the coming year?

6-26. What are the deposit dates for a monthly depositor and a semiweekly depositor?

6-27. What are the exceptions to monthly and semiweekly deposit schedules under the deposit rules?

Review Questions
(cont.)

6–28. What happens to the status of a monthly depositor who must make a next-day deposit under the deposit rules?

6–29. How does a new employer determine its deposit liability when it was not in business for purposes of the look-back rule?

6–30. What special precautions should an employer take in making end-of-quarter deposits that overlap two quarters?

DISCUSSION QUESTIONS

6–1. The need for accuracy in all payroll reporting has led to the use of a number of forms designed to facilitate corrections: Form 941C, Form W-2C, Form W-3C. These forms are all used to correct already reported information. Why is it preferable to correct past mistakes rather than carry them over for correction in future reports?

6–2. The rules for depositing and reporting of taxes withheld provide for deposits to be made at authorized depositories and reports to be sent to the Internal Revenue Service. Do you see any problems with this system? Why do you suppose the IRS does not put depositing on the same quarterly basis as reporting?

6–3. The semiweekly period concept facilitates the computation of tax liability. Such periods do not coincide with the normal payroll periods (weekly, biweekly, semimonthly, monthly). Can you think of a deposit system that would be more compatible with the payroll operations of most companies and be as satisfactory to the government?

6–4. The idea of backup withholding is relatively new. Its purpose is to ensure that businesses and individuals who receive nonwage payments will report these amounts and pay the appropriate taxes. What do you think some of the disadvantages of backup withholding might be?

EXERCISES

6–1. The Nu-Age Catalog Company is a monthly depositor and incurred a tax liability for federal income and FICA taxes, including its portion of FICA taxes, during the third quarter of the year as follows:

	Tax Liability
July	$320
August	270
September	290

What are the dates and amounts of tax deposits?

Date Deposit Due	Tax Periods Covered	Amount of Tax
_____	_____	_____
_____	_____	_____
_____	_____	_____

6–2. Universal Solvents Corp. owes a federal tax deposit of $3,400 for the semiweekly period of September 11–14, Saturday to Tuesday. What is the penalty if the tax deposit is made on September 22?

6–3. Two employees of Country Seeds, Inc. have gross earnings in excess of the Social Security base of $76,200.

	Gross Earnings	Federal Income Tax Withheld
Carolyn Boone	$78,000	$12,000
Thomas Cooper	84,000	11,000

Indicate the amounts that will be shown on the Form W-2 for each of the employees.

	Carolyn Boone	Thomas Cooper
Wages, tips, etc.	$_____	$_____
Federal income taxes withheld	$_____	$_____
Social Security wages	$_____	$_____
Medicare wages and tips	$_____	$_____
Social Security tax withheld	$_____	$_____
Medicare tax withheld	$_____	$_____

6–4. Creative Fashions Corp. has ten employees, including its two officers who earn $9,000 and $7,500 per month. Its four salespeople are paid $3,000 per month, and the rest of the employees each earn $1,500 per month. Compute the FUTA tax deposit for the first quarter. Assume the full state credit of 5.4%.

6–5. The Plastic Housewares Corp. is a semiweekly depositor and pays its employees weekly. The company withheld $932.00 in federal income tax and $380 in FICA taxes on Friday June 3, 10, 17, 24. When is Plastic Housewares required to make a federal tax deposit and for what amount?

6–6. The Holsom Bakery Corp, a semiweekly depositor, pays its employees monthly and has made federal tax deposits as follows:

Date of Deposit	Wages Paid	Wages	Federal W/H Tax Liability
November 15	October 30	$16,000	$3,200
December 15	November 30	18,000	4,000
January 15	December 30	17,000	3,600

· Assume that Social Security wages are $6,000 less than total wages, respectively. Complete the following parts of the Form 941:

Total wages and tips   _____

Total income tax withheld   _____

Taxable Social Security wages   _____

Taxable Medicare wages and tips _____

Social Security taxes   _____

Medicare taxes   _____

6–7. The Reader's Warehouse, Inc. has taxable FUTA wages, as follows:

Quarter Ended	Taxable Wages
March	$10,000
June	10,000
September	8,000
December	6,000

At a tax rate of .008% what is the tax owed by Reader's Warehouse and when must it make tax deposits?

Quarter Ended	FUTA Tax	Deposit Amount/Date
March	_____	_____
June	_____	_____
September	_____	_____
December	_____	_____

6–8. Computer Dynamics is a semiweekly depositor and has a biweekly payroll. The tax liability for the payment of wages on Friday, July 2, was $1,600.00. The company pays wages of $5,400 on July 16 and July 30. The federal income tax withheld on these wages is $840 and Social Security and Medicare taxes are withheld at 6.2% and 1.45%, respectively. What amounts must the company make as deposits of payroll taxes and when are they due?

6–9. The executives at Pace Electronics wish to know the extra payroll costs, besides wages, that the company must pay based on the following data:

		Tax Rate %
Gross wages	$250,000	
Social Security wages	210,000	6.20
Medicare wages	250,000	1.45
FUTA wages	90,000	0.8
SUTA wages	90,000	4.00

Compute the extra payroll costs for Pace.

Exercises (cont.)

6–10. The Davidson Radiator Corp. owes $6,400 in payroll taxes due September 1. It makes the following deposits:

September 8	$1,000
September 12	2,000
September 22	3,400

Compute the penalties for failure to deposit in a timely manner.

6–11. Disregarding exceptions, when must the tax deposits be made, if the accumulated tax liability is:

Under $1,000 for quarter _____

Over $1,000 for semiweekly period _____

$100,000 or more on any day
during the month _____

$100,000 or more on any day
during the semiweekly period _____

6–12. Software Systems made a deposit of $82,000 in taxes three days after the semiweekly period when its accumulated tax withholding was $52,000 in federal income taxes and $38,000 in FICA taxes. Ten days later, Software deposited an additional $8,000. What is the penalty, if any, for undeposited taxes?

6–13. Custom Boats, Inc. had the following federal withholding and FICA taxes by month:

	Tax Liability
January	$3,600
February	3,200
March	3,000

If the deposits in each quarter follow the monthly deposit rules, indicate the Form 8109 payments.

Date Deposit Due	Tax Period	Amount of Deposit
_____	_____	_____
_____	_____	_____
_____	_____	_____

6–14. The Rainbow Lighting Corp., a semiweekly depositor, incurred a tax liability for federal income and FICA taxes including its portion of FICA taxes during March as follows:

	Tax Liability	Tax Deposit Date
March 2–4, Wed.–Fri.	$ 95,000	_____
March 5–8, Sat.–Tues.	—	_____
March 9–11, Wed.–Fri.	102,000	_____
March 13–16, Sat.–Tues.	—	_____

What are the dates of the tax deposits?

Exercises (cont.)

6–15. The Pinnacle Theater Chain, a monthly depositor, incurred a federal tax liability for federal income and FICA taxes, including its portion of FICA taxes during the second quarter of the year as follows:

20XX	Tax Liability	Tax Deposit Dates
April 1–30	$ 95,000	_____
May 1–31	102,000	_____
June 1–3, Thurs.–Sat.	10,000	_____

What are the dates of the tax deposits?

PROBLEMS

6–1. Disregarding exceptions, determine when the tax deposits must be made for the following accumulated tax liabilities.

Date of Deposit

a. Under $1,000 for the quarter   _____

b. Over $1,000 but under $100,000 for the month   _____

c. $100,000 for a monthly depositor   _____

d. $100,000 or more for a semiweekly depositor   _____

6–2. Technical Laboratories is a semiweekly depositor and pays its employees $6,000 semimonthly (on the Friday nearest the 15th, and last day of the month) and has total wages during the quarter of $36,000. Income tax withholding on these wages averages 20% and all the employees are subject to FICA taxes. Complete the following schedule of federal tax liability.

Pay Period	First month of Quarter	Second month of Quarter	Third month of Quarter
near 15th	$_____	$_____	$_____
last	_____	_____	_____

When must Technical Laboratories make its tax deposits?

_____

6–3. Aaron Breen of Breen's Bagels had annual wages of $27,000. Aaron also received sick pay of $750 from a plan financed by his employer, was reimbursed for $1,200 of nonqualified moving expenses and had personal use of a company car ($2,400). Aaron's federal and state income tax withholdings were $5,600 and $2,000, respectively. Prepare the W-2 form on page 207 for Aaron Breen. (You need not fill in Aaron Breen's Social Security number and address or Breen's Bagels' address, EIN, state ID number, and state.)

6–4. Graphite Specialties deposited $85,000 in taxes three days after the due date, when its accumulated tax withholding was $56,000 in federal income taxes and $42,000 in FICA taxes. Six days later, Graphite deposited an additional $8,100. What is the penalty, if any, for undeposited taxes?

$ _____

6–5. The Sunrise Health Products Company has two employees whose federal withholding and FICA taxes by quarter were as follows:

	Tax Liability
First Quarter	$420
Second Quarter	430
Third Quarter	440

Assume that Sunrise follows the under $1,000 rule for the quarter. Use the following table to indicate when Sunrise must remit the taxes.

Date Deposit Due	Tax Period	Amount of Deposit
_____	_____	$_____
_____	_____	$_____
_____	_____	$_____

6–6. The Keystone Video Tapes Company had a payroll of $48,000 during a recent quarter with taxable Social Security and Medicare wages of $42,000. Income tax withheld was $7,200. The company paid $1,800 in advance earned income credit. Complete the first page of Form 941 (page 208).

6–7. Quarterly wages for the employees of Estelle Florists are as follows:

	Wages	FITW
Rose Tully	$3,600	$500
Jack Whitfield	4,700	480
Antonio Ruiz	4,200	520
Helen Li	5,000	480

Assume all wages are subject to FICA taxes. Complete the first page of Form 941 (page 209).

6–8. Betty Gomez works for Rialto Cosmetics as a traveling salesperson. Last year her payroll data were as follows. Prepare a Form W-2 (page 210). (You will not be able to fill in Betty Gomez's Social Security number and address or Rialto Cosmetics' address, EIN, state ID number, and state.)

Wages	$59,000
Bonus	6,500
Sick pay—third party	1,500
Deductible moving expenses—qualified	4,000
Pre-tax contributions to pension plan	7,500
Federal income tax withheld	11,000
State income tax withheld	3,000

6–9. Winthrop Corp. has four employees whose wages, shown by quarter, are as follows:

	First Quarter	Second Quarter	Third Quarter	Fourth Quarter	Total
Clara Benton	$2,000	$2,200	$2,000	$2,300	$8,500
Peggy Glasgow	2,400	2,200	2,200	2,400	9,200
John LaMonte	1,800	1,900	2,300	1,800	7,800
Paul Richardson	1,600	1,500	1,400	1,600	6,100

Assume a taxable wage base of $7,000. On the following table, indicate the Form 8109 deposits for FUTA liability.

Problems (cont.)

Date Deposit Due	Tax Period	Amount of Deposit
_____	_____	$_____
_____	_____	$_____
_____	_____	$_____
_____	_____	$_____

6–10. Adams Bakery paid its employees $77,000, of which $53,500 was taxable for federal and state unemployment tax purposes. The FUTA tax liability for each quarter of the year was as follows:

1st quarter	$108
2nd quarter	120
3rd quarter	88
4th quarter	112

Indicate the Form 8109 deposits required during the year.

Date Deposit Due	Tax Period	Amount of Deposit
_____	_____	$_____
_____	_____	$_____
_____	_____	$_____
_____	_____	$_____

6–11. In the second quarter, the Saturn Cable Company paid its employees on Fridays, April 28, May 26, and June 30. Saturn deposits 100% of its tax liabilities; its deposits for the three months were $32,000, $32,500, and $34,000. Saturn also had backup withholding of $1,700. What are the amounts and required dates of the deposits, including the deposit for the backup withholding?

Date Deposit Due	Tax Period	Amount of Deposit
_____	_____	$_____
_____	_____	$_____
_____	_____	$_____
_____	_____	$_____

6–12. Additional second-quarter wage and tax data for Mercury Company are as follows:

Gross wages	$245,000
Social Security wages	238,000
Medicare wages	245,000
Federal income tax withheld	59,000
Sick pay—third-party payer	4,000
FICA taxes withheld from sick pay	306

Complete the blank first page of Form 941 on page 211 using these data.

6–13. Frank's Department Store pays its employees $3,200 biweekly on April 2, 16, and 30, May 14, and 28, June 11, and 25 for total wages of $9,600 in April and $6,400 in May and June. Income tax withholding on these wages averages 15%, and all the employees are subject to FICA taxes. Complete the following schedule of federal tax liability.

Date Wages Paid	First Month of Quarter	Second Month of Quarter	Third Month of Quarter
2	$ _____	$_____	$_____
11	$ _____	$_____	$_____
14	$ _____	$_____	$_____
16	$ _____	$_____	$_____
25	$ _____	$_____	$_____
28	$ _____	$_____	$_____
30	$ _____	$_____	$_____

6–14. The five employees of Hennessey's Collision Shop had the following data for the latest quarter:

Employee	Gross Wages	FITW	FICA Taxes
Brad Andrez	$5,600	$600	$428.40
Lynn Landis	4,400	300	336.60
Pat Malone	5,800	600	443.70
Jan Peters	6,000	620	459.00
B. J. Trent	6,400	620	489.60

Lynn Landis received $434 in advance earned income credit. Backup withholding totaled $1,884 on interest paid to Brad Andrez. Prepare the first page of Form 941 for the quarter (page 212).

6–15. Sky Mountain Amusement Park had FUTA tax liability for the first three quarters of the year as follows:

First quarter	$220.00
Second quarter	96.00
Third quarter	72.00

The company has 8 employees, and all have reached the maximum federal and state unemployment tax wage base of $7,000. The state experience rate is 2.4%.

a. What is the fourth quarter federal unemployment tax?

$ _____

b. Indicate the Form 8109 deposits required during the year.

Date Deposit Due	Tax Period	Amount of Deposit
_____	_____	$_____
_____	_____	$_____
_____	_____	$_____
_____	_____	$_____

CONTINUING CASE PROBLEM

PART A

During the following quarter of the year, Frontier Landscaping paid its ten employees weekly and withheld federal income tax as shown.

	Wages		Federal Inc. Tax Withheld	
	Hourly Employees	Salaried Employees	Hourly Employees	Salaried Employees
July 3	$2,400	$2,750	$360	$550
10	2,800	2,750	420	550
17	2,800	2,750	420	550
24	2,600	2,750	360	550
31	3,000	2,750	450	550
Aug. 7	3,000	2,750	450	550
14	2,800	2,750	420	550
21	2,800	2,750	420	550
28	3,000	2,750	450	550
Sept. 4	2,600	2,750	390	550
11	2,400	2,750	360	550
18	2,400	2,750	360	550
25	2,400	2,750	360	550
	$35,000	$35,750	$5,220	$7,150

All hourly employees are subject to all FICA taxes, but $3,000 of Kathy Wood's salary is exempt from Social Security taxes. The tax rates are: Social Security tax, 6.2%; Medicare tax, 1.45%; FUTA tax, 0.8%; and SUTA tax, 4.2%. Assume none of the hourly employees earned over $7,000 but salaried employees were all over the limit.

Required:
a. Complete the first page of Form 941 provided on page 213, including line 17.
b. Complete the following schedule of Form 8109 deposits:

Schedule of Form 8109 Deposits—semiweekly depositor with a Tuesday payday

Accumulated Liability Requiring Payment

July Date	$	August Date	$	September Date	$
___	___	___	___	___	___
___	___	___	___	___	___
___	___	___	___	___	___
___	___	___	___	___	___

c. Compute the FUTA and SUTA taxes.

FUTA Taxes $ _____

SUTA Taxes $ _____

Continuing Case Problem
(cont.)

PART B

Kathy Wood earned $78,000 in regular wages this year and received a bonus of $8,000. Frontier also contributed $7,800 for her to a pension plan. Kathy's federal income tax withholding was $17,200, and her state income tax withholding was $6,000.

Prepare a Form W-2 for Kathy Wood (page 214). (You will not be able to fill in addresses and identification numbers.)

PART C

Frontier rented some electric garden tools from time to time from an unincorporated business, Agri-Rent. During the year, the total amount paid to Agri-Rent was $3,200.

Complete the Form 1099-MISC provided on page 215.

a Control number	22222	Void ☐	For Official Use Only ▶ OMB No. 1545-0008	

b Employer identification number	1 Wages, tips, other compensation	2 Federal income tax withheld
c Employer's name, address, and ZIP code	3 Social security wages	4 Social security tax withheld
	5 Medicare wages and tips	6 Medicare tax withheld
	7 Social security tips	8 Allocated tips
d Employee's social security number	9 Advance EIC payment	10 Dependent care benefits
e Employee's name (first, middle initial, last)	11 Nonqualified plans	12 Benefits included in box 1
	13 See instrs. for box 13	14 Other

15 Statutory employee ☐	Deceased ☐	Pension plan ☐	Legal rep. ☐	Deferred compensation ☐
f Employee's address and ZIP code				

16 State	Employer's state I.D. no.	17 State wages, tips, etc.	18 State income tax	19 Locality name	20 Local wages, tips, etc.	21 Local income tax

Form **W-2** Wage and Tax Statement **20**

Department of the Treasury—Internal Revenue Service

For Privacy Act and Paperwork Reduction Act Notice, see separate instructions.

Copy A For Social Security Administration—Send this entire page with Form W-3 to the Social Security Administration; photocopies are **not** acceptable.

Cat. No. 10134D

Do NOT Cut, Fold, or Staple Forms on This Page — Do NOT Cut, Fold, or Staple Forms on This Page

For use with Problem 6–3.

Form **941**
(Rev. October 2000)
Department of the Treasury
Internal Revenue Service

Employer's Quarterly Federal Tax Return

▶ See separate instructions for information on completing this return.

Please type or print.

Enter state code for state in which deposits were made ONLY if different from state in address to the right ▶ (see page 2 of instructions).

Name (as distinguished from trade name)	Date quarter ended
Trade name, if any	Employer identification number
Address (number and street)	City, state, and ZIP code

OMB No. 1545-0029

T	
FF	
FD	
FP	
I	
T	

If address is different from prior return, check here ▶

IRS Use

1 1 1 1 1 1 1 1 1 1	2	3 3 3 3 3 3 3	4 4 4	5 5 5
6 7 8 8 8 8 8 8 8	9 9 9 9 9	10 10 10 10 10 10 10 10 10		

If you do not have to file returns in the future, check here ▶ ☐ and enter date final wages paid ▶

If you are a seasonal employer, see **Seasonal employers** on page 1 of the instructions and check here ▶ ☐

1	Number of employees in the pay period that includes March 12th . ▶		
2	Total wages and tips, plus other compensation	**2**	
3	Total income tax withheld from wages, tips, and sick pay	**3**	
4	Adjustment of withheld income tax for preceding quarters of calendar year	**4**	
5	Adjusted total of income tax withheld (line 3 as adjusted by line 4—see instructions) . . .	**5**	

6	Taxable social security wages	**6a**		12.4% (.124) =	**6b**	
	Taxable social security tips	**6c**		12.4% (.124) =	**6d**	
7	Taxable Medicare wages and tips . . .	**7a**		2.9% (.029) =	**7b**	

8	Total social security and Medicare taxes (add lines 6b, 6d, and 7b). Check here if wages are not subject to social security and/or Medicare tax . . . . ▶ ☐	**8**	
9	Adjustment of social security and Medicare taxes (see instructions for required explanation) Sick Pay $ _____ ± Fractions of Cents $ _____ ± Other $ _____ =	**9**	
10	Adjusted total of social security and Medicare taxes (line 8 as adjusted by line 9—see instructions)	**10**	
11	**Total taxes** (add lines 5 and 10)	**11**	
12	Advance earned income credit (EIC) payments made to employees	**12**	
13	Net taxes (subtract line 12 from line 11). **If $1,000 or more, this must equal line 17, column (d) below (or line D of Schedule B (Form 941))**	**13**	
14	Total deposits for quarter, including overpayment applied from a prior quarter	**14**	
15	**Balance due** (subtract line 14 from line 13). See instructions	**15**	

16 Overpayment. If line 14 is more than line 13, enter excess here ▶ $ _____
and check if to be: ☐ Applied to next return **OR** ☐ Refunded.

All filers: If line 13 is less than $1,000, you need not complete line 17 or Schedule B (Form 941).

Semiweekly schedule depositors: Complete Schedule B (Form 941) and check here . . . . ▶ ☐

Monthly schedule depositors: Complete line 17, columns (a) through (d), and check here. . . . . ▶ ☐

17	**Monthly Summary of Federal Tax Liability.** Do not complete if you were a semiweekly schedule depositor.		
(a) First month liability	**(b)** Second month liability	**(c)** Third month liability	**(d)** Total liability for quarter

Sign Here

Under penalties of perjury, I declare that I have examined this return, including accompanying schedules and statements, and to the best of my knowledge and belief, it is true, correct, and complete.

Signature ▶   Print Your Name and Title ▶   Date ▶

For Privacy Act and Paperwork Reduction Act Notice, see back of Payment Voucher.   Cat. No. 17001Z   Form **941** (Rev. 10-2000)

For use with Problem 6–6.

208

Form 941
(Rev. October 2000)
Department of the Treasury
Internal Revenue Service

Employer's Quarterly Federal Tax Return

▶ See separate instructions for information on completing this return.

Please type or print.

Enter state code for state in which deposits were made ONLY if different from state in address to the right ▶

If address is different from prior return, check here ▶

				OMB No. 1545-0029

Name (as distinguished from trade name)

Date quarter ended

Trade name, if any

Employer identification number

Address (number and street)

City, state, and ZIP code

T	
FF	
FD	
FP	
I	
T	

IRS Use

1 1 1 1 1 1 1 1 1 1 1   2   3 3 3 3 3 3 3 3   4 4 4   5 5 5

6   7   8 8 8 8 8 8 8   9 9 9 9   10 10 10Z 10 10 10 10 10 10

If you do not have to file returns in the future, check here ▶ ☐ and enter date final wages paid ▶

If you are a seasonal employer, see **Seasonal employers** on page 1 of the instructions and check here ▶

1	Number of employees in the pay period that includes March 12th . ▶		
2	Total wages and tips, plus other compensation	**2**	
3	Total income tax withheld from wages, tips, and sick pay	**3**	
4	Adjustment of withheld income tax for preceding quarters of calendar year	**4**	
5	Adjusted total of income tax withheld (line 3 as adjusted by line 4—see instructions) . . .	**5**	
6	Taxable social security wages	**6a**	12.4% (.124) =	**6b**	
	Taxable social security tips	**6c**	12.4% (.124) =	**6d**	
7	Taxable Medicare wages and tips . . .	**7a**	2.9% (.029) =	**7b**	
8	Total social security and Medicare taxes (add lines 6b, 6d, and 7b). Check here if wages are not subject to social security and/or Medicare tax . . . . ▶ ☐	**8**	
9	Adjustment of social security and Medicare taxes (see instructions for required explanation) Sick Pay $ _____ ± Fractions of Cents $ _____ ± Other $ _____ =	**9**	
10	Adjusted total of social security and Medicare taxes (line 8 as adjusted by line 9—see instructions)	**10**	
11	**Total taxes** (add lines 5 and 10)	**11**	
12	Advance earned income credit (EIC) payments made to employees	**12**	
13	Net taxes (subtract line 12 from line 11). **If $1,000 or more, this must equal line 17, column (d) below (or line D of Schedule B (Form 941))**	**13**	
14	Total deposits for quarter, including overpayment applied from a prior quarter	**14**	
15	**Balance due** (subtract line 14 from line 13). See instructions	**15**	
16	**Overpayment.** If line 14 is more than line 13, enter excess here ▶ $ _____ and check if to be: ☐ Applied to next return **OR** ☐ Refunded.		

All filers: If line 13 is less than $1,000, you need not complete line 17 or Schedule B (Form 941).

Semiweekly schedule depositors: Complete Schedule B (Form 941) and check here . . . . ▶ ☐

Monthly schedule depositors: Complete line 17, columns (a) through (d), and check here. . . . . ▶ ☐

17	**Monthly Summary of Federal Tax Liability.** Do not complete if you were a semiweekly schedule depositor.		
(a) First month liability	**(b)** Second month liability	**(c)** Third month liability	**(d)** Total liability for quarter

Sign Here

Under penalties of perjury, I declare that I have examined this return, including accompanying schedules and statements, and to the best of my knowledge and belief, it is true, correct, and complete.

Signature ▶   Print Your Name and Title ▶   Date ▶

For Privacy Act and Paperwork Reduction Act Notice, see back of Payment Voucher.   Cat. No. 17001Z   Form **941** (Rev. 10-2000)

For use with Problem 6–7.

a Control number	22222	Void ☐	For Official Use Only ▶ OMB No. 1545-0008		
b Employer identification number				**1** Wages, tips, other compensation	**2** Federal income tax withheld
c Employer's name, address, and ZIP code			**3** Social security wages	**4** Social security tax withheld	
			5 Medicare wages and tips	**6** Medicare tax withheld	
			7 Social security tips	**8** Allocated tips	
d Employee's social security number			**9** Advance EIC payment	**10** Dependent care benefits	
e Employee's name (first, middle initial, last)			**11** Nonqualified plans	**12** Benefits included in box 1	
			13 See instrs. for box 13	**14** Other	

	15 Statutory employee ☐	Deceased ☐	Pension plan ☐	Legal rep. ☐	Deferred compensation ☐
f Employee's address and ZIP code					

16 State	Employer's state I.D. no.	**17** State wages, tips, etc.	**18** State income tax	**19** Locality name	**20** Local wages, tips, etc.	**21** Local income tax

Form **W-2** Wage and Tax Statement **20**

Department of the Treasury—Internal Revenue Service

For Privacy Act and Paperwork Reduction Act Notice, see separate instructions.

Copy A For Social Security Administration—Send this entire page with Form W-3 to the Social Security Administration; photocopies are **not** acceptable.

Cat. No. 10134D

Do NOT Cut, Fold, or Staple Forms on This Page — Do NOT Cut, Fold, or Staple Forms on This Page

For use with Problem 6–8.

Form **941**
(Rev. October 2000)
Department of the Treasury
Internal Revenue Service

Employer's Quarterly Federal Tax Return

▶ See separate instructions for information on completing this return.

Please type or print.

Enter state code for state in which deposits were made ONLY if different from state in address to the right ▶ (see page 2 of instructions).

Name (as distinguished from trade name)

Date quarter ended

Trade name, if any

Employer identification number

Address (number and street)

City, state, and ZIP code

OMB No. 1545-0029

T	
FF	
FD	
FP	
I	
T	

If address is different from prior return, check here ▶

IRS Use

1	1	1	1	1	1	1	1	1	1	2	3	3	3	3	3	3	3	4	4	4	5	5	5
6	7		8	8	8	8	8	8	8		9	9	9	9	9	10	10	10	10	10	10	10	10	10

If you do not have to file returns in the future, check here ▶ ☐ and enter date final wages paid ▶

If you are a seasonal employer, see **Seasonal employers** on page 1 of the instructions and check here ▶

1	Number of employees in the pay period that includes March 12th . ▶		
2	Total wages and tips, plus other compensation	**2**	
3	Total income tax withheld from wages, tips, and sick pay	**3**	
4	Adjustment of withheld income tax for preceding quarters of calendar year	**4**	
5	Adjusted total of income tax withheld (line 3 as adjusted by line 4—see instructions) . .	**5**	
6	Taxable social security wages	**6a**	12.4% (.124) =	**6b**
	Taxable social security tips	**6c**	12.4% (.124) =	**6d**
7	Taxable Medicare wages and tips . . .	**7a**	2.9% (.029) =	**7b**
8	Total social security and Medicare taxes (add lines 6b, 6d, and 7b). Check here if wages are not subject to social security and/or Medicare tax . . . . ▶ ☐	**8**	
9	Adjustment of social security and Medicare taxes (see instructions for required explanation) Sick Pay $ _____ ± Fractions of Cents $ _____ ± Other $ _____ =	**9**	
10	Adjusted total of social security and Medicare taxes (line 8 as adjusted by line 9—see instructions)	**10**	
11	**Total taxes** (add lines 5 and 10)	**11**	
12	Advance earned income credit (EIC) payments made to employees .	**12**	
13	Net taxes (subtract line 12 from line 11). **If $1,000 or more, this must equal line 17, column (d) below (or line D of Schedule B (Form 941))**	**13**	
14	Total deposits for quarter, including overpayment applied from a prior quarter	**14**	
15	**Balance due** (subtract line 14 from line 13). See instructions	**15**	
16	**Overpayment.** If line 14 is more than line 13, enter excess here ▶ $ _____		

and check if to be: ☐ Applied to next return **OR** ☐ Refunded.

All filers: If line 13 is less than $1,000, you need not complete line 17 or Schedule B (Form 941).

Semiweekly schedule depositors: Complete Schedule B (Form 941) and check here . . . . ▶ ☐

Monthly schedule depositors: Complete line 17, columns (a) through (d), and check here . . . . ▶ ☐

17	**Monthly Summary of Federal Tax Liability.** Do not complete if you were a semiweekly schedule depositor.		
(a) First month liability	**(b)** Second month liability	**(c)** Third month liability	**(d)** Total liability for quarter

Sign Here

Under penalties of perjury, I declare that I have examined this return, including accompanying schedules and statements, and to the best of my knowledge and belief, it is true, correct, and complete.

Signature ▶   Print Your Name and Title ▶   Date ▶

For Privacy Act and Paperwork Reduction Act Notice, see back of Payment Voucher.   Cat. No. 17001Z   Form **941** (Rev. 10-2000)

For use with Problem 6–12.

Form **941**
(Rev. October 2000)
Department of the Treasury
Internal Revenue Service

Employer's Quarterly Federal Tax Return

▶ See separate instructions for information on completing this return.

Please type or print.

Enter state code for state in which deposits were made ONLY if different from state in address to the right ▶ ⬚
(see page 2 of instructions).

Name (as distinguished from trade name)	Date quarter ended
Trade name, if any	Employer identification number
Address (number and street)	City, state, and ZIP code

OMB No. 1545-0029

| T |
| FF |
| FD |
| FP |
| I |
| T |

If address is different from prior return, check here ▶ ⬚

IRS Use

| 1 | 1 | 1 | 1 | 1 | 1 | 1 | 1 | 1 | 1 | 2 | 3 | 3 | 3 | 3 | 3 | 3 | 3 | 4 | 4 | 4 | 5 | 5 | 5 |
| 6 | 7 | 8 | 8 | 8 | 8 | 8 | 8 | 8 | 9 | 9 | 9 | 9 | 9 | 10 | 10 | 10 | 10 | 10 | 10 | 10 | 10 | 10 | 10 |

If you do not have to file returns in the future, check here ▶ ⬚ and enter date final wages paid ▶

If you are a seasonal employer, see **Seasonal employers** on page 1 of the instructions and check here ▶ ⬚

1	Number of employees in the pay period that includes March 12th . ▶		
2	Total wages and tips, plus other compensation	**2**	
3	Total income tax withheld from wages, tips, and sick pay	**3**	
4	Adjustment of withheld income tax for preceding quarters of calendar year . .	**4**	
5	Adjusted total of income tax withheld (line 3 as adjusted by line 4—see instructions) . . .	**5**	
6	Taxable social security wages	**6a**		12.4% (.124) =	**6b**	
	Taxable social security tips	**6c**		12.4% (.124) =	**6d**	
7	Taxable Medicare wages and tips . . .	**7a**		2.9% (.029) =	**7b**	
8	Total social security and Medicare taxes (add lines 6b, 6d, and 7b). Check here if wages are not subject to social security and/or Medicare tax . . . . ▶ ⬚	**8**	
9	Adjustment of social security and Medicare taxes (see instructions for required explanation) Sick Pay $ _____ ± Fractions of Cents $ _____ ± Other $ _____ =	**9**	
10	Adjusted total of social security and Medicare taxes (line 8 as adjusted by line 9—see instructions)	**10**	
11	**Total taxes** (add lines 5 and 10)	**11**	
12	Advance earned income credit (EIC) payments made to employees	**12**	
13	Net taxes (subtract line 12 from line 11). **If $1,000 or more, this must equal line 17, column (d) below (or line D of Schedule B (Form 941))**	**13**	
14	Total deposits for quarter, including overpayment applied from a prior quarter	**14**	
15	**Balance due** (subtract line 14 from line 13). See instructions	**15**	
16	**Overpayment.** If line 14 is more than line 13, enter excess here ▶ $ _____		

and check if to be: ⬚ Applied to next return **OR** ⬚ Refunded.

All filers: If line 13 is less than $1,000, you need not complete line 17 or Schedule B (Form 941).

Semiweekly schedule depositors: Complete Schedule B (Form 941) and check here . . . . ▶ ⬚

Monthly schedule depositors: Complete line 17, columns (a) through (d), and check here. . . . . ▶ ⬚

17	**Monthly Summary of Federal Tax Liability.** Do not complete if you were a semiweekly schedule depositor.			
(a) First month liability	**(b)** Second month liability	**(c)** Third month liability	**(d)** Total liability for quarter

Sign Here

Under penalties of perjury, I declare that I have examined this return, including accompanying schedules and statements, and to the best of my knowledge and belief, it is true, correct, and complete.

Signature ▶ _____   Print Your Name and Title ▶ _____   Date ▶ _____

For Privacy Act and Paperwork Reduction Act Notice, see back of Payment Voucher.   Cat. No. 17001Z   Form **941** (Rev. 10-2000)

For use with Problem 6–14.

212

Form 941
(Rev. October 2000)
Department of the Treasury
Internal Revenue Service

Employer's Quarterly Federal Tax Return

▶ See separate instructions for information on completing this return.

Please type or print.

Enter state code for state in which deposits were made ONLY if different from state in address to the right ▶ (see page 2 of instructions).

Name (as distinguished from trade name)	Date quarter ended
Trade name, if any	Employer identification number
Address (number and street)	City, state, and ZIP code

OMB No. 1545-0029

T	
FF	
FD	
FP	
I	
T	

If address is different from prior return, check here ▶

IRS Use

1 1	1 1 1 1 1 1 1 1	2	3 3 3 3 3 3 3	4 4 4	5 5 5
6	7 8 8 8 8 8 8 8		9 9 9 9 9	10 10 10 10 10 10	10 10 10 10

If you do not have to file returns in the future, check here ▶ ☐ and enter date final wages paid ▶

If you are a seasonal employer, see **Seasonal employers** on page 1 of the instructions and check here ▶ ☐

1	Number of employees in the pay period that includes March 12th . ▶		
2	Total wages and tips, plus other compensation	**2**	
3	Total income tax withheld from wages, tips, and sick pay	**3**	
4	Adjustment of withheld income tax for preceding quarters of calendar year	**4**	
5	Adjusted total of income tax withheld (line 3 as adjusted by line 4—see instructions) . . .	**5**	
6	Taxable social security wages	**6a**	12.4% (.124) =	**6b**	
	Taxable social security tips	**6c**	12.4% (.124) =	**6d**	
7	Taxable Medicare wages and tips . . .	**7a**	2.9% (.029) =	**7b**	
8	Total social security and Medicare taxes (add lines 6b, 6d, and 7b). Check here if wages are not subject to social security and/or Medicare tax . . . . ▶ ☐	**8**	
9	Adjustment of social security and Medicare taxes (see instructions for required explanation) Sick Pay $ _____ ± Fractions of Cents $ _____ ± Other $ _____ =	**9**	
10	Adjusted total of social security and Medicare taxes (line 8 as adjusted by line 9—see instructions)	**10**	
11	**Total taxes** (add lines 5 and 10)	**11**	
12	Advance earned income credit (EIC) payments made to employees	**12**	
13	Net taxes (subtract line 12 from line 11). **If $1,000 or more, this must equal line 17, column (d) below (or line D of Schedule B (Form 941))**	**13**	
14	Total deposits for quarter, including overpayment applied from a prior quarter	**14**	
15	**Balance due** (subtract line 14 from line 13). See instructions	**15**	
16	**Overpayment.** If line 14 is more than line 13, enter excess here ▶ $ _____ and check if to be: ☐ Applied to next return **OR** ☐ Refunded.		

All filers: If line 13 is less than $1,000, you need not complete line 17 or Schedule B (Form 941).

Semiweekly schedule depositors: Complete Schedule B (Form 941) and check here . . . . ▶ ☐

Monthly schedule depositors: Complete line 17, columns (a) through (d), and check here. . . . . ▶ ☐

17	**Monthly Summary of Federal Tax Liability.** Do not complete if you were a semiweekly schedule depositor.			
	(a) First month liability	**(b)** Second month liability	**(c)** Third month liability	**(d)** Total liability for quarter

Sign Here

Under penalties of perjury, I declare that I have examined this return, including accompanying schedules and statements, and to the best of my knowledge and belief, it is true, correct, and complete.

Signature ▶ _____ Print Your Name and Title ▶ _____ Date ▶ _____

For Privacy Act and Paperwork Reduction Act Notice, see back of Payment Voucher.   Cat. No. 17001Z   Form **941** (Rev. 10-2000)

For use with Continuing Case Problem, Part A.

213

a Control number	22222	Void ☐	For Official Use Only ▶ OMB No. 1545-0008		
b Employer identification number			1 Wages, tips, other compensation	2 Federal income tax withheld	
c Employer's name, address, and ZIP code			3 Social security wages	4 Social security tax withheld	
			5 Medicare wages and tips	6 Medicare tax withheld	
			7 Social security tips	8 Allocated tips	
d Employee's social security number			9 Advance EIC payment	10 Dependent care benefits	
e Employee's name (first, middle initial, last)			11 Nonqualified plans	12 Benefits included in box 1	
			13 See instrs. for box 13	14 Other	
f Employee's address and ZIP code			15 Statutory employee ☐	Deceased ☐	Pension plan ☐	Legal rep. ☐	Deferred compensation ☐

16 State	Employer's state I.D. no.	17 State wages, tips, etc.	18 State income tax	19 Locality name	20 Local wages, tips, etc.	21 Local income tax

Form **W-2** **Wage and Tax Statement** **20**

Copy A For Social Security Administration—Send this entire page with Form W-3 to the Social Security Administration; photocopies are **not** acceptable.

Cat. No. 10134D

Department of the Treasury—Internal Revenue Service

For Privacy Act and Paperwork Reduction Act Notice, see separate instructions.

Do NOT Cut, Fold, or Staple Forms on This Page — Do NOT Cut, Fold, or Staple Forms on This Page

For use with Continuing Case Problem, Part B.

9595 ☐ VOID ☐ CORRECTED

PAYER'S name, street address, city, state, ZIP code, and telephone no.		**1** Rents $	OMB No. 1545-0115	**Miscellaneous Income**
		2 Royalties $	20	
		3 Other income $	Form **1099-MISC**	
PAYER'S Federal identification number	RECIPIENT'S identification number	**4** Federal income tax withheld $	**5** Fishing boat proceeds $	**Copy A**
RECIPIENT'S name		**6** Medical and health care payments $	**7** Nonemployee compensation $	**For Internal Revenue Service Center**
Street address (including apt. no.)		**8** Substitute payments in lieu of dividends or interest $	**9** Payer made direct sales of $5,000 or more of consumer products to a buyer (recipient) for resale ▶ ☐	**File with Form 1096.** For Privacy Act and Paperwork Reduction Act Notice, see the
City, state, and ZIP code		**10** Crop insurance proceeds $	**11** State income tax withheld $	**20XX General Instructions for Forms 1099, 1098,**
Account number (optional)	2nd TIN Not. ☐	**12** State/Payer's state number	**13** $	**5498, and W-2G.**

Form **1099-MISC**   Cat. No. 14425J   Department of the Treasury - Internal Revenue Service

Do NOT Cut or Separate Forms on This Page — Do NOT Cut or Separate Forms on This Page

For use with Continuing Case Problem, Part C.

CHAPTER 7

ACCOUNTING FUNDAMENTALS AND PROCEDURES

LEARNING OBJECTIVES

On completing this chapter, you will be able to:

1. Explain the basic accounting fundamentals and procedures for payroll accounting.
2. Identify the specific accounts used to record payroll and payroll taxes.
3. Describe the use of payroll records in recording payroll and the segments of payroll transactions.
4. Reconcile the various payroll records with deposit and reporting requirements.
5. Understand the objectives of the external auditor in the audit of payroll.

Clark explains to Lois that payroll accounting is really a subset of general accounting—a specialized application of the double-entry system. The employer records an expense, wages, and at the same time records the liabilities related to that expense, namely payroll deductions and wages to be paid. Then the employer pays these liabilities by issuing checks to the employees for wages, to the government in the form of deposits for taxes withheld, and to others for other payroll deductions. In addition, Clark explains, the employer incurs other payroll tax liabilities to cover the employer part of FICA taxes and federal and state unemployment taxes.

Basic accounting knowledge is essential to obtaining a better understanding of payroll operations and management. Many payroll man-

216

agers have studied accounting in business school or college, and their knowledge of accounting procedures helps in many ways, particularly in complying with payroll regulations regarding tax deposits and report filing. Clark reviews with Lois some of these accounting fundamentals.

ACCOUNTING BASICS

Accounting *The process of analyzing and recording business transactions and reporting and interpreting the results.*

Business transactions *Economic activities affecting the resources a business owns or controls.*

Accounting is the system of summarizing and recording business transactions and the process of analyzing, verifying, reporting, and interpreting the results. **Business transactions** are events, expressed in terms of money, that affect the resources a business owns or controls and that may lead to obligations to other parties or claims by the owner(s) of the business. In the language of accounting, the resources are assets, the obligations to other parties are liabilities, and those claims by the owner(s) of the business are owner's equity. Each of these is described in more detail in the following section.

Fundamental Accounting Equation

Accounting equation *Assets equal liabilities plus owner's equity.*

The relationship of assets, liabilities, and owner's equity can be expressed using what is often referred to as the **accounting equation:**

$$\text{Assets} = \text{Liabilities} + \text{Owner's Equity}$$

Assets *Resources a business owns or controls for the future benefit or value they possess.*

Liabilities *Obligations or future sacrifices of assets.*

In the accounting equation, **assets** are resources or items of value or future benefit owned or controlled by a business. Assets include cash, land, equipment, automobiles, and accounts receivable. Examples of assets in the payroll department include the payroll checking account, computer equipment, and furniture. **Liabilities** are obligations or future sacrifices of assets. Liabilities include accounts payable, notes payable, and unearned revenues when a business owes product, time, or services to a customer who has paid in advance. Examples of payroll liabilities include wages not yet paid, taxes withheld but not yet deposited, pension plan contributions not yet made, and other payroll tax liabilities and deductions not yet remitted.

Owner's equity *The net worth or ownership of a business; the difference between assets and liabilities.*

Owner's equity, the third part of the accounting equation, is the owner's net worth or ownership in the business. It represents the difference between assets and liabilities. For instance, if a business has no liabilities (it has no obligations against its assets), then the value of owner's equity is equal to the value of its assets.

EXAMPLE Margaret O'Toole invested $6,000 (owner's equity) in furniture and equipment for her hair salon, HairLights. HairLights currently owes no money to creditors, so it has no liabilities. The assets of the business are thus equal to the claims against them, or owner's equity, as follows:

$$\text{Assets} = \text{Liabilities} + \text{Owner's Equity}$$
$$\$6,000 = \quad \$0 \quad + \quad \$6,000$$

▲

Creditor   *A person or company that provides cash or other assets with the expectation of repayment.*

Another way to look at the accounting equation is to view it as a business entity with the right side representing the **creditors** and owners who have claims against the left side, which represents the assets of the business. Offsetting changes can occur in the accounts representing assets, liabilities, and owner's equity.

EXAMPLE

In the case of Margaret's hair salon above, let's suppose she decides to invest $2,000 more into the business in its first year and to borrow $1,000 from her parents in order to make some future equipment purchases. According to the equation, she would have added $2,000 more in owner's equity, and $1,000 in liabilities, which would result in the following change in assets:

Assets	=	Liabilities	+	Owner's Equity
$6,000 =		$ 0	+	$6,000
+2,000				+2,000
+1,000		+1,000		
$9,000 =		$1,000	+	$8,000

▲

Balance sheet   *The financial statement that reports the financial position of a company at a point in time.*

The accounting equation forms the basis for one of the primary financial statements prepared for a business—the balance sheet. The **balance sheet** summarizes the balances of the business's assets, liabilities, and owner's equity on a given date.

Revenue and Expense Accounts

Revenue   *The value of products sold or services rendered to customers.*

Expenses   *The value of assets surrendered or liabilities incurred to obtain revenue.*

Often, the changes in the accounts representing assets, liabilities, and owner's equity result from business transactions with outside sources—revenue and expense accounts. An increase in assets or a decrease in liabilities may come about from revenues. **Revenues** represent the value of products or services sold or rendered to customers; they are the monetary amounts earned by a business. A decrease in assets or an increase in liabilities may result from **expenses**, expenditures made or to be made in obtaining revenue. Examples of expenses are rent, salaries, the cost of employer-paid benefit programs, the employer's share of payroll taxes, and advertising.

Revenues and expenses are considered part of owner's equity. An increase in revenues increases owner's equity; an increase in expenses decreases owner's equity. Including revenues and expenses makes the accounting equation look like this:

Assets = Liabilities + Owner's Equity + Revenue – Expenses

Income statement   *The financial statement that reports on the ability of a business to conduct profitable operations over a period of time.*

Transactions involving revenue and expense accounts form the basis for a company's **income statement**, which shows the results of business transactions over time, its total revenue minus its total expenses.

Business Transactions

As we've seen, business transactions affect one or more of the categories of assets, liabilities, owner's equity, revenues, and expenses. The specific

Account *An asset, liability, or owner's equity item and the debits and credits affecting each.*

items affected within these categories are called the accounts. **Accounts** contain all the information in an accounting system; they are the records of each asset, liability, owner's equity, revenue, or expense item. For instance, an asset account called *Cash* contains information about cash, whereas a liability account called *Medicare Taxes Payable* stores information about Medicare tax liabilities, and an expense account called *Rent Expense* has accumulated information about rent expense. In order to keep track of all these accounts, every business has an official listing of accounts covering all possible transactions called the **chart of accounts.**

Chart of accounts *An orderly listing of accounts, with every account having its own unique number.*

Although the chart of accounts is always tailored to the needs of a specific company, most are organized according to the company's financial statements, which include the balance sheet (assets, liabilities, and owner's equity) and the income statement (revenues and expenses). A chart of accounts for Nioga Gear, a manufacturing business, appears in Figure 7-1. Each account in the chart of accounts has an assigned code number and title.

RECORDING BUSINESS TRANSACTIONS

T account *A form of account shaped like the letter T used in recording business transactions, with the left side for debit entries and the right side for credit entries.*

Every business transaction must be recorded in a way that maintains the balance of the accounting equation. We can visualize this effect by using a T account form when recording transactions in the accounts. A **T account** has two sides: a left side called the *debit side* and a right side called the *credit side.* Thus, to debit an account is to record a dollar amount on the left side of the account and to credit an account is to record a dollar amount on the right side. **Debits always go on the left; credits always go on the right.** Whenever we debit one or more accounts, we must credit one or more other accounts in order to keep the accounting equation balanced.

Double-entry system *An accounting system where a business transaction is recorded in two or more accounts with equal debits and credits.*

With the **double-entry system**, increases to an account go on one side and decreases to the account go on the other side. However, the rules for determining on which sides to place the increases and decreases depend on the type of account. It is important to learn these rules before trying to record transactions. The **debit and credit rules** are summarized in Figure 7-2. By using these debit and credit rules, each business transaction contains equal debits and credits. The proper recording of these transactions then ensures the balancing of the accounting equation, which is the essence of the double-entry concept of accounting.

Debit and credit rules *Rules that state the effect debits and credits have on asset, liability, owner's equity, expense, and revenue accounts. Debits increase assets and expenses and decrease liabilities, owner's equity, and revenue. Credits increase liabilities, owner's equity, and revenues and decrease assets and expenses.*

Journals and Ledgers

The accounting system revolves around two basic types of records: journals and ledgers. A **journal** is a chronological record of the daily transactions of a business. The most commonly used journals are the sales journal, purchases journal, cash receipts journal, cash disbursements journal, and the general journal. For each transaction, the journal lists the date, the accounts affected, the debit and credit amounts, and a description of the transaction. The **ledger** is a group of accounts. It provides a chronological record of the business transactions affecting each account.

Journal *A chronological record of the daily transactions of a business.*

Ledger *A group of accounts.*

Nioga Gear, Inc.

Chart of Accounts

BALANCE SHEET ACCOUNTS		INCOME STATEMENT ACCOUNTS

1000	ASSETS	2000	LIABILITIES	4000	REVENUES
1100	Current Assets	2100	Current Liabilities	4100	Sales
1110	Cash	2110	Notes Payable	4100-1	Sales Discounts
1120	Trading Securities		(current portion)	4100-2	Sales Returns and
1130	Accounts Receivable	2120	Accounts Payable		Allowances
1130-1	Allowance for	2130	Accrued Liabilities	4200	Dividends
	Uncollectible Accounts	2131	Wages Payable	4300	Interest Earned
1140	Inventories	2132	Social Security Taxes		
1141	Raw Materials		Payable	5000	EXPENSES
1142	Work in Progress	2133	Medicare Taxes	5100	Purchases
1143	Finished Goods		Payable	5100-1	Purchase Discounts
1150	Prepaid Expenses	2134	Federal Withholding	5100-2	Purchase Returns and
1200	Investments		Taxes Payable		Allowances
1210	Long-term Investments	2135	State Withholding Taxes	5110	Freight-In
1300	Property, Plant, and		Payable	5140	Interest Expense
	Equipment	2136	FUTA Taxes Payable	5200	Wages and Salaries
1310	Building	2137	SUTA Taxes Payable	5210	Direct Factory Labor
1310-1	Accumulated	2138	State Disability	5210	Technical Labor
	Depreciation — Building		Insurance Payable	5220	Craft Labor
1320	Production Equipment	2140	Federal Income Tax	5230	Apprentice Labor
1320-1	Accumulated		Payable	5300	Indirect Factory Labor
	Depreciation —	2141	State Income	5400	Administrative Expenses
	Product Equipment		Tax Payable	5410	Officers' Salaries
1330	Office Equipment	2200	Long-term Liabilities	5420	Management Salaries
1330-1	Accumulated	2210	Notes Payable	5430	Office Salaries
	Depreciation — Office	2220	Bonds Payable	5440	Other Administrative
	Equipment				Expenses
1340	Furniture and Fixtures	3000	STOCKHOLDERS'	5442	Social Security Taxes
1340-1	Accumulated		EQUITY	5443	Medicare Taxes
	Depreciation —	3100	Preferred Stock —	5444	FUTA Taxes
	Furniture and Fixtures		par value	5445	SUTA Taxes
1400	Intangible Assets	3110	Paid in Capital —	5500	Selling Expenses
1410	Trademarks and		Preferred Stock	5510	Sales Salaries
	Tradenames	3200	Common Stock —	5520	Advertising Expenses
			par value	5530	Other Selling Expenses
		3210	Paid in Capital —	5540	Interest Expense
			Common Stock		
		3300	Retained Earnings		

FIGURE 7-1   Chart of Accounts for Nioga Gear

Asset Accounts		Liability Accounts		Owner's Equity Accounts	
debit increases	credit decreases	debit decreases	credit increases	debit decreases	credit increases

Expense Accounts		Revenue Accounts	
debit increases	credit decreases	debit decreases	credit increases

1. Debits *increase* assets and expenses and *decrease* liabilities, owner's equity, and revenues.
2. Credits *increase* liabilities, owner's equity, and revenues and *decrease* assets and expenses.
3. Assets and expenses normally have debit balances.
4. Liabilities, owner's equity, and revenues normally have credit balances.

FIGURE 7-2 Debit and Credit Rules

Accounting Process (or Cycle)

Accounting process (or cycle) *Sequence of steps in accounting, from recording transactions in journals, to posting to a general ledger, to making adjustments, to preparing financial statements.*

The **accounting process (or cycle)** starts with a transaction. The transaction is recorded in the journal and then posted (transferred) to the ledger accounts. Periodically, the financial data in the ledger are used to prepare the financial statements.

To illustrate the application of the debit and credit rules and the use of the journal and ledger, let's look at Nioga Gear's purchase on June 1 of a specialized personal computer. The transaction would be recorded in the general journal as follows:

20xx		*Debit*	*Credit*
June 1	Office Equipment	3,600	
	Accounts Payable		3,600
	Bought Apex Model 31		
	computer from MicroWorld.		

This entry is posted to the ledger accounts as follows:

Office Equipment			Accounts Payable	
Debit	*Credit*		*Debit*	*Credit*
Bal. 54,000				Bal. 24,000
6/1 3,600				6/1 3,600

FINANCIAL STATEMENTS

Generally, a business prepares and issues financial statements—such as the balance sheet and the income statement—at the end of each accounting period, which is usually one year. It may also prepare the financial statements at the end of a half-year or a quarter. By showing the financial position of the business at a particular point in time, the balance sheet reveals the financial strength or weakness of the business. The income statement presents the revenues, expenses, and net income of a business during a period of time, indicating the ability of the business to conduct profitable operations over time. Both the balance sheet and income statement follow more or less standard formats.

Current assets *Assets that a business expects to convert into cash within a relatively short period, usually one year or less.*

Long-term assets *Assets that a business expects to use for more than one year.*

Depreciation *The process of recognizing as an expense a portion of the original cost of property, plant, and equipment.*

Intangible assets *Long-term assets having no physical substance.*

Current liabilities *Obligations due within the next year.*

Long-term liabilities *Obligations that a business expects to pay off over a period of more than one year.*

Common stock *The ownership interest in a corporation, with voting rights and often rights to receive dividends.*

Paid-in capital *The additional capital represented by cash or other assets being contributed or invested in a corporation in excess of the par or stated value of the capital stock.*

Retained earnings *The profits accumulated in the business rather than paid out to stockholders.*

Dividends *A distribution of cash or other assets of a corporation with a corresponding reduction in the accumulated earnings and profits or retained earnings.*

Balance Sheet

The balance sheet reports the balances of all asset, liability, and owner's (or stockholders') equity accounts as of a specific date. Typically, the balance sheet is classified into current, long-term, and intangible assets; current and long-term liabilities; and owner's or stockholders' equity. **Current assets** are those that a business expects to convert into cash or consume within a relatively short period, usually one year or less. **Long-term assets** are those that a business expects to use or have for more than one year. Property, plant, and equipment assets wear out or become obsolete and, therefore, are subject to **depreciation**, a process that periodically recognizes as an expense a portion of the original cost of the asset. Investments consist of securities or other forms of ownership that the business expects to hold over an indefinite long-term period. **Intangible assets** (such as patents, trademarks, and goodwill) generally are also long term but have no physical substance. The cost of these assets is amortized (written off as an expense) over a period of time.

Liabilities are also classified as current or long-term. **Current liabilities** represent obligations due within one year or less. All payroll liabilities (taxes, accrued wages) are current liabilities. **Long-term liabilities** are those that a business expects to pay back over a period of more than one year.

The balance sheet also presents the accounts representing the claims of the owners or stockholders. A typical balance sheet might report the value of **common stock**, usually listed at par or stated value of the outstanding stock; **paid-in capital**, the amount received for shares of stock above the par or stated value; and **retained earnings**, the accumulated profits left in the business rather than paid out in the form of **dividends**.

Nioga's most recent balance sheet appears in Figure 7-3.

Income Statement

The income statement shows the results of business transactions involving revenue and expense accounts over a period of time. The income statement may be in a single-step or multi-step format. In the single-step format, total expenses are subtracted from total revenues to arrive at net income before taxes. The multi-step format gives more detail. A multi-step

Nioga Gear, Inc.

Balance Sheet December 31, 20XX

Assets
  Current Assets:

Cash		$ 50,000
Accounts Receivable (net)		400,000
Inventories		600,000
Prepaid Expenses		20,000
Total Current Assets		$1,070,000
Property, Plant, and Equipment	$490,000	
Less Accumulated Depreciation	160,000	330,000
Total Assets		$1,400,000

Liabilities and Stockholders' Equity
  Current Liabilities:

Notes Payable		$ 40,000
Accounts Payable		200,000
Accrued Liabilities		35,000
Wages Payable		20,000
Payroll Taxes Payable		5,000
Total Current Liabilities		$ 300,000

Stockholders' Equity

Common Stock, no par value		$ 120,000
(200,000 shares authorized, 120,000 outstanding)		
Retained Earnings		980,000
Total Stockholders' Equity		$1,100,000
Total Liabilities and Stockholders' Equity		$1,400,000

FIGURE 7-3 Nioga Gear's Balance Sheet

income statement shows net sales less cost of goods sold, which yields gross profit. Operating expenses are then deducted and nonoperating items such as interest earned or paid out are added or subtracted to determine the net income before taxes. After deducting corporate income taxes, the statement reports net income for the period.

The income statement for Nioga Gear for the most recent year is shown in Figure 7-4.

Nioga Gear, Inc.

Income Statement For the Year Ended December 31, 20XX

Net Sales		$2,800,000
Cost of Goods Sold		1,300,000
Gross Profit		$1,500,000
Operating Expenses:		
Administrative Expenses	$600,000	
Selling Expenses	450,000	
Total Operating Expenses		1,050,000
Operating Income		$ 450,000
Other Income (Expenses):		
Interest Earned	$ 10,000	
Interest Expense	(40,000)	(30,000)
Net Income Before Taxes		$ 420,000
Federal and State Corporate Income Taxes		100,000
Net Income		$ 320,000

FIGURE 7-4 Nioga Gear's Income Statement

PAYROLL ACCOUNTING

With an understanding of accounting fundamentals and the accounting cycle, a payroll manager can handle payroll operations more efficiently and effectively.

Every business transaction, including those involving payroll, finds its way into the accounting system. Payroll accounting then is an important part of a general accounting system in a company. The various payroll schedules and reports provide the data entered into this system.

The payroll register summarizes the payroll data for a given period and is a source of data for the journal entry. The employer enters the data for each employee—gross wages, various deductions, and net pay—and then determines the totals for the entire payroll. These totals are the amounts entered into the accounting system.

The accounts used in payroll accounting range from the expense accounts used to record gross earnings to the various liability accounts used to record the different deductions. Figure 7-5 illustrates how Nioga Gear's

Nioga Gear, Inc.

General Journal Entries for Payroll Period Ended October 14

Date 20xx	DESCRIPTION	POST REF.	DEBIT	CREDIT
OCT. 18	Direct Factory Labor		9,000	
	Indirect Factory Labor		3,000	
	Officers' Salaries		3,500	
	Management Salaries		2,500	
	Office Salaries		1,500	
	Sales Salaries		3,500	
	Social Security Taxes Payable			1,426
	Medicare Taxes Payable			334
	Federal Withholding Taxes Payable			4,250
	State Withholding Taxes Payable			1,850
	Wages Payable			15,140
	Payroll for period ended October 14			
18	Social Security Taxes Expense		1,426	
	Medicare Taxes Expense		334	
	Social Security Taxes Payable			1,426
	Medicare Taxes Payable			334
	To record employer's FICA payroll taxes			
18	FUTA Taxes Expense		64	
	SUTA Taxes Expense		160	
	FUTA Taxes Payable			64
	SUTA Taxes Payable			160
	To record employer's federal and state unemployment taxes			

FIGURE 7-5   General Journal Entries for Nioga Gear's Payroll Period Ended October 14

weekly payroll for the period ending October 14 is recorded in a general journal.

Wages and Salaries Expense

The gross earnings of all employees comprise the wages and salaries expense. A small company may have only one wage expense account. In a large company, the total wages may be divided among several expense accounts, as shown in Figure 7-5. Some companies have separate accounts for overtime and other special premiums. Nioga Gear divides its total wages among six expense accounts (see lines 1–6 of Figure 7-5).

Usually, some time elapses between the date of the payroll entry and the actual payment of employees. Until the employees are paid, the Wages Payable account reflects the amount owed to employees. The entry for payment of the wages debits Wages Payable and credits Cash.

EXAMPLE The entry made at Nioga to pay the October 18 payroll is as follows:

20xx—		Debit	Credit
Oct. 18	Wages Payable	15,140	
	Cash		15,140
	To record payment of October 18 payroll		

This entry reduces the company's liability for wages to zero. ▲

Income and FICA Taxes Payable

Liability accounts for federal, state, and local withholding taxes are credited for the total amount withheld from the employees' earnings, as shown in Figure 7-5. When the taxes are deposited, the accounts are debited. Any balance represents the as-yet-undeposited taxes.

An employer is responsible for making periodic deposits not only of the amounts withheld from employee earnings for federal income and FICA taxes but also of its own share of FICA taxes. The sums owed determine when the deposit must be made.

EXAMPLE On October 18 Nioga owed $7,770 for employer's and employees' FICA and federal withholding taxes and made a deposit using EFT. An entry is made to decrease (debit) the liability accounts and decrease (credit) the Cash account.

20xx—		Debit	Credit
Oct. 18	Social Security Taxes Payable	2,852	
	Medicare Taxes Payable	668	
	Federal Withholding Taxes Payable	4,250	
	Cash		7,770
	To record payment of FICA and federal withholding taxes		

▲

A similar entry is prepared to record the deposits of the state and local taxes withheld from employee earnings.

Employer Payroll Taxes

At the end of each payroll period, an employer must also record its share of FICA taxes and the federal and state unemployment taxes. These payroll taxes are operating expenses and represent liabilities until the employer pays the amounts to the government.

The liability account FUTA Taxes Payable represents the accumulations of the employer's federal unemployment taxes payable to the federal government. The liability account SUTA Taxes Payable shows the amounts payable to the state unemployment insurance fund. Separate accounts are necessary if the employer owes taxes to more than one state. The FUTA and SUTA taxes are determined by multiplying gross wages (up to a specified amount for each employee) by the appropriate tax rates.

EXAMPLE The taxable wages of Nioga employees for the October 18 payroll for FICA tax purposes are $23,000. To determine the Social Security taxes, that amount is multiplied by 6.2% (the current rate): $23,000 × 0.062 = $1,426. The employer's Medicare taxes are determined by multiplying the taxable wages by 1.45% (the current rate): $23,000 × 0.0145 = $333.50 = $334. This entry appears in Figure 7-5. ▲

Nioga incurs tax liabilities periodically throughout each month and makes deposits using the EFT system. The typical entry (without amounts) to record these payments is as follows:

	Debit	Credit
Federal Withholding Taxes Payable	xx	
Social Security Taxes Payable	xx	
Medicare Taxes Payable	xx	
Cash		xx

Of the $23,000 payroll, $8,000 represents the earnings of those employees who have not yet reached the $7,000 FUTA wage base. Assuming a FUTA rate of 0.8%, Nioga owes $64 for the period ($8,000 × .008). The SUTA tax rate is 2%, and Nioga owes $160 for the period ($8,000 × .02). This journal entry appears in Figure 7-5.

Nioga deposits FUTA and SUTA taxes on a quarterly basis. At the end of each quarter, it prepares a Form 8109 and issues a check for the amount of FUTA taxes owed. A journal entry is recorded debiting FUTA Taxes Payable and crediting Cash. Likewise, Nioga issues checks for the federal and state unemployment taxes for the fourth quarter in January of the following year.

	Debit	Credit
FUTA Taxes Payable	384	
Cash		384
SUTA Taxes Payable	1,140	
Cash		1,140

Accrual *An increase in the revenue or expense, resulting from revenue being earned or expense being incurred. Adjusting journal entries at the end of a period reflect accrual of unrecorded revenues and expenses.*

Despite depositing unemployment taxes quarterly, the employer records a journal entry for the taxes at the end of each payroll period. Thus, the accounts reflect the up-to-date expenses and liabilities for payroll taxes.

The **accrual** of wages and payroll tax liabilities may occur within an accounting period, and payment within the period satisfies these liabilities.

EXAMPLE   Jupiter has a $60,000 payroll on the 24th of September. Taxes owed are:

	Date Payable	Amount
Federal Income Taxes Withheld	9/29	9,000
Employee Social Security Taxes Withheld	9/29	3,720
Employee Medicare Taxes Withheld	9/29	870
Employer Social Security Taxes Payable	9/29	3,720
Employer Medicare Taxes Payable	9/29	870
State Income Taxes Withheld	9/30	3,000
SUTA Taxes Payable	10/31	1,200

The accounting entry on September 24 is as follows:

	Debit	Credit
Wages and Salaries Expense	60,000	
Social Security Taxes Expense	3,720	
Medicare Taxes Expense	870	
SUTA Taxes Expense	1,200	
Federal Withholding Income Taxes Payable		9,000
Social Security Taxes Payable		7,440
Medicare Taxes Payable		1,740
State Withholding Income Taxes Payable		3,000
SUTA Taxes Payable		1,200
Wages Payable		43,410

Payment of the accrued amounts satisfies the liabilities. In the example, assume Jupiter makes the required deposits of federal income and FICA taxes on September 29. The debit part of the entry decreases liabilities, and the credit part of the entry decreases cash.

The accounting entry on September 29 is as follows:

	Debit	Credit
Federal Withholding Taxes Payable	9,000	
Social Security Taxes Payable	7,440	
Medicare Taxes Payable	1,740	
Cash		18,180

On September 30, the company pays the state income taxes and a month later, the SUTA taxes. The accounting entries to reflect these payments are as follows:

	Debit	Credit
State Withholding Taxes Payable	3,000	
Cash		3,000
SUTA Taxes Payable	1,200	
Cash		1,200

▲

Other Deductions

If the employees have any voluntary deductions from their wages (such as for health insurance, life insurance, pension plan, savings bonds, or charitable contributions) or any involuntary deductions (such as for child support, tax levies, or garnishments), the amounts for these deductions are recorded as liabilities for payment at a later date.

EXAMPLE Jupiter Toys deducts medical insurance premiums from its employees' gross wages and sends the amounts deducted to the insurance company monthly. For September, Jupiter deducted $8,400 from employees' gross wages and remits this amount to Acme Health Insurance Company.

	Debit	Credit
Medical Insurance Payable	8,400	
Cash		8,400

▲

Review of Payroll Transactions

Let's review the sequence of transactions for the October 18 payroll of Nioga Gear, Inc. The transactions in general journal form are summarized as follows:

a. Recording of payroll from the payroll register

Wages and Salaries Expense	23,000	
Social Security Taxes Payable		1,426
Medicare Taxes Payable		334
Federal Withholding Taxes Payable		4,250
State Withholding Taxes Payable		1,850
Wages Payable		15,140

b. Recording of employer's share of FICA taxes

Social Security Taxes Expense	1,426	
Medicare Taxes Expense	334	
Social Security Taxes Payable		1,426
Medicare Taxes Payable		334

c. Payment of net payroll to employees

Wages Payable	15,140	
Cash		15,140

PAYROLL IN ACTION

ACCOUNTING FOR COMPENSATED ABSENCES

An increasingly important employment expense involves compensated absences or time off from work for which employees expect to be paid, such as vacations, sick days, holidays, and other absences. With paid vacations of two, three, and four weeks rather common and sick pay allowances extending from several days to 10 or more, the payment for compensated absences can be substantial.

The Financial Accounting Standards Board issued guidelines on the recording of compensated absences. According to FASB No. 43, employees earn rights to receive compensation based on the time employed, and at the end of an accounting period, an employer has a liability for earned, but unused compensated absences. Statement No. 43 requires the recognition of the liability if the amount of the accrual is estimable and probable.

In practice, it is difficult to estimate the amount to accrue for most compensated absences, except vacation pay. When the amount cannot reasonably be estimated, as is generally true for sick pay, the potential liability should be disclosed. Sick pay is accrued only if it vests with the employee, i.e., the employee is entitled to compensation whether absent from work or not.

---

   d. Deposit of employer's and employees' FICA and federal withholding
      taxes by EFT

Social Security Taxes Payable	2,852	
Medicare Taxes Payable	668	
Federal Withholding Taxes Payable	4,250	
Cash		7,770

  e. Payment of other liabilities when due

State Withholding Taxes Payable	1,850	
Cash		1,850

These transactions flow through the ledger accounts as shown in the following T accounts.

Cash			Wages and Salaries Expense			Social Security Taxes Expense	
Debit	*Credit*		*Debit*	*Credit*		*Debit*	*Credit*
	c. 15,140		a. 23,000			b. 1,426	
	d. 7,770						
	e. 1,850						

Medicare Taxes Expense			Wages Payable			Social Security Taxes Payable	
Debit	*Credit*		*Debit*	*Credit*		*Debit*	*Credit*
b. 334			c. 15,140	a. 15,140		d. 2,852	a. 1,426
							b. 1,426

Medicare Taxes Payable			Federal Withholding Taxes Payable			State Withholding Taxes Payable	
Debit	*Credit*		*Debit*	*Credit*		*Debit*	*Credit*
d. 668	a. 334		d. 4,250	a. 4,250		e. 1,850	a. 1,850
	b. 334						

End-of-Quarter Reporting

A payroll manager follows these same steps for each payroll period. At the end of a quarter, the manager summarizes this information for Form 941, as described in Chapter 6.

EXAMPLE   Lois summarizes Nioga Gear's total wages for the fourth quarter in Table 7-1. Clark retrieves the payroll liabilities information from the general ledger (Table 7-2). They work together to prepare and file Form 941 at the end of the fourth quarter (Exhibit 7-1). ▲

TABLE 7-1			
Nioga Gear's Fourth Quarter Wages			
Date	Total Wages	Social Security Wages	Medicare Wages
10/05/XX	$ 23,000	$ 23,000	$ 23,000
10/12/XX	23,000	23,000	23,000
10/19/XX	23,000	23,000	23,000
10/26/XX	18,000	18,000	18,000
11/02/XX	18,000	18,000	18,000
11/09/XX	18,000	18,000	18,000
11/16/XX	18,000	18,000	18,000
11/23/XX	20,500	20,500	20,500
11/30/XX	20,500	20,500	20,500
12/07/XX	20,500	10,500	20,500
12/14/XX	20,500	10,500	20,500
12/21/XX	23,000	8,000	23,000
12/28/XX	23,000	8,000	23,000
	$269,000	$219,000	$269,000

Accounting for Accrued Wages and Salaries

A number of transactions overlap accounting periods. For example, the end of a payroll period may not coincide with the end of the accounting period. The ledger accounts, however, must accurately reflect expenses for wages, taxes, benefits, or other items. Adjusting entries should be recorded when the employer accrues wages and salaries, payroll taxes on these amounts, and vacation pay. In each instance, the expenses have been incurred in one fiscal period, but not paid until the next fiscal period.

Vacation Pay Accrual

Paid vacation time is an almost universal benefit offered to employees as a benefit of employment. The vacation time may not begin to accrue until an employee has worked for a period of time and may be for 2 weeks or more.

To reflect the proper vacation pay expense, an employer accrues the amount according to various formulas. Under one formula, an employer accrues vacation pay for 52 weeks less the number of vacation weeks. Thus, for a two-week vacation, the vacation pay covers 50 weeks accrual; for three weeks, 49 weeks accrual; and for four weeks, 48 weeks accrual. Another formula grants each employee a day's vacation for every five weeks worked. Regardless of the specific accrual method used, the company makes payment to the employee for the vacation days.

EXAMPLE Eric Beverage Company had a March payroll of $200,000 and vacation pay related to the payroll, as shown at the top of page 234.

TABLE 7-2
Nioga Gear's Fourth Quarter Tax Liabilities

Week Ended	Social Security Taxes Payable Dr	Cr	Balance	Medicare Taxes Payable Dr	Cr	Balance	Federal Withholding Taxes Payable Dr	Cr	Balance	Total Liabilities Cr	(Dr)
10/05/XX		1426			334						
		1426	2852		334	668		4250	4250	7770	
10/12/XX	2852			668			4250				(7770)
		1426			333						
		1426	2852		334	667		4250	4250	7769	
10/19/XX	2852			667			4250				(7769)
		1426			333						
		1426	2852		334	667		4250	4250	7769	
10/26/XX	2852			667			4250				(7769)
		1116			261						
		1116	2232		261	522		3500	3500	6254	
11/02/XX	2232			522			3500				(6254)
		1116			261						
		1116	2232		261	522		3500	3500	6254	
11/09/XX	2232			522			3500				(6254)
		1116			261						
		1116	2232		261	522		3500	3500	6254	
11/16/XX	2232			522			3500				(6254)
		1116			261						
		1116	2232		261	522		3500	3500	6254	
11/23/XX	2232			522			3500				(6254)
		1271			297						
		1271	2542		297	594		3875	3875	7011	
11/30/XX	2542			594			3875				(7011)
		1271			297						
		1271	2542		297	594		3875	3875	7011	
12/07/XX	2542			594			3875				(7011)
		651			297						
		651	1302		297	594		3875	3875	5771	
12/14/XX	1302			594			3875				(5771)
		651			297						
		651	1302		297	594		3875	3875	5771	
12/21/XX	1302			594			3875				(5771)
		496			333						
		496	992		334	667		4250	4250	5909	
12/28/XX	992			667			4250				(5909)
		496			333						
		496	992		334	667		4250	4250	5909	
12/31/XX	992		-0-	667		-0-	4250		-0-		(5909)
	27,156	27,156		7800	7800		50,750	50,750		50,750	

Form **941**
(Rev. October 2000)
Department of the Treasury
Internal Revenue Service

Employer's Quarterly Federal Tax Return

▶ See separate instructions for information on completing this return.

Please type or print.

Enter state code for state in which deposits were made ONLY if different from state in address to the right ▶ ☐
(see page 2 of instructions).

Name (as distinguished from trade name)	Date quarter ended
Nioga Gear, Inc.	*12/31/XX*
Trade name, if any	Employer identification number
	16-9714606
Address (number and street)	City, state, and ZIP code
600 Whirlpool Drive	*Niagara Falls, NY 14301*

OMB No. 1545-0029

T
FF
FD
FP
I
T

If address is different from prior return, check here ▶ ☐

IRS Use

```
1  1  1  1  1  1  1  1  1  1    2    3  3  3  3  3  3  3    4  4  4    5  5  5
6     7     8  8  8  8  8  8  8         9  9  9  9    10  10 10Z  10  10 10  10 10 10
```

If you do not have to file returns in the future, check here ▶ ☐ and enter date final wages paid ▶ _____

If you are a seasonal employer, see **Seasonal employers** on page 1 of the instructions and check here ▶ ☐

1	Number of employees in the pay period that includes March 12th . ▶	*85*	
2	Total wages and tips, plus other compensation	2	*269,000*
3	Total income tax withheld from wages, tips, and sick pay	3	*50,750*
4	Adjustment of withheld income tax for preceding quarters of calendar year	4	
5	Adjusted total of income tax withheld (line 3 as adjusted by line 4—see instructions)	5	*50,750*

6	Taxable social security wages	6a	*219,000*	12.4% (.124) =	6b	*27,156*
	Taxable social security tips	6c		12.4% (.124) =	6d	
7	Taxable Medicare wages and tips . . .	7a	*269,000*	2.9% (.029) =	7b	*7,801*

8	Total social security and Medicare taxes (add lines 6b, 6d, and 7b). Check here if wages are not subject to social security and/or Medicare tax . . . . ▶ ☐	8	*34,957*
9	Adjustment of social security and Medicare taxes (see instructions for required explanation) Sick Pay $ _____ ± Fractions of Cents $ *-1.00* ± Other $ _____ =	9	*(1)*
10	Adjusted total of social security and Medicare taxes (line 8 as adjusted by line 9—see instructions)	10	*34,956*
11	**Total taxes** (add lines 5 and 10)	11	*85,706*
12	Advance earned income credit (EIC) payments made to employees	12	
13	Net taxes (subtract line 12 from line 11). **If $1,000 or more, this must equal line 17, column (d) below (or line D of Schedule B (Form 941))**	13	*85,706*
14	Total deposits for quarter, including overpayment applied from a prior quarter	14	*85,706*
15	**Balance due** (subtract line 14 from line 13). See instructions	15	*0*
16	**Overpayment.** If line 14 is more than line 13, enter excess here ▶ $ _____ and check if to be: ☐ Applied to next return **OR** ☐ Refunded.		

All filers: If line 13 is less than $1,000, you need not complete line 17 or Schedule B (Form 941).

Semiweekly schedule depositors: Complete Schedule B (Form 941) and check here . . . . ▶ ☒

Monthly schedule depositors: Complete line 17, columns (a) through (d), and check here. . . . . ▶ ☐

17	**Monthly Summary of Federal Tax Liability.** Do not complete if you were a semiweekly schedule depositor.		
(a) First month liability	**(b)** Second month liability	**(c)** Third month liability	**(d)** Total liability for quarter

Sign Here

Under penalties of perjury, I declare that I have examined this return, including accompanying schedules and statements, and to the best of my knowledge and belief, it is true, correct, and complete.

Signature ▶ *Clark Barr* Print Your Name and Title ▶ *Clark Barr, Mur.* Date ▶ *1/31/XX*

For Privacy Act and Paperwork Reduction Act Notice, see back of Payment Voucher. Cat. No. 17001Z Form **941** (Rev. 10-2000)

EXHIBIT 7-1 Nioga Gear's Fourth Quarter Form 941

233

	Related Weeks	*Estimate of Past*
Payroll	*Vacation*	*Vacations Taken*
$110,000	2	.75
70,000	3	.84
20,000	4	.96
$200,000		

The estimated vacation pay liability for March is as follows:

Payroll   × Accrual Ratio × Vacations Taken = Liability

$110,000 ×	2/50	×	.75	= $3,300
70,000 ×	3/49	×	.84	= 3,600
20,000 ×	4/48	×	.96	= 1,600
$200,000				$8,500

Eric records the estimated vacation pay liability for March as follows:

Vacation Pay Expense	8,500	
Estimated Vacation Pay Liability		8,500

When the employees take their vacations, the actual payroll liabilities take the place of the estimated vacation pay liability, as follows:

Estimated Vacation Pay Liability	9,000	
Social Security Taxes Payable		558
Medicare Taxes Payable		131
Federal Withholding Taxes Payable		1,224
State Withholding Taxes Payable		633
Wages Payable		6,454

The actual vacation pay expense more than likely will not be the same as the estimated amount. An adjusting entry takes care of any difference—a debit to vacation pay expense if the actual exceeds the estimated and a credit to this account for the reverse.   ▲

Account Reconciliation

The payroll manager must ensure that the various accounts affecting payroll are accurate and in balance, that employee paychecks are correct, and that taxes are withheld, deposited, and reported accurately and on time. It is important to periodically verify the accuracy of the general ledger and compare the accounts to records of payroll, payroll taxes, and other deductions. We discussed the reconciliation process in Chapter 6. Let's take another look from the point of view of timing. A reconciliation should be done at each of these stages:

Every payroll period. Review the payroll register to be sure that, for each employee, gross wages minus deductions equal the net pay. Recompute the amounts withheld for FICA taxes by multiplying the taxable FICA wages by the current tax rates.

When making a tax deposit. Reconcile the quarter-to-date and year-to-date amounts recorded in the ledger accounts with the accumulated totals generated by the payroll system.

At the end of each quarter and at year-end. Reconcile all accounts before filing quarterly Forms 941 and the annual Form 940. The FICA deposits for the quarter should equal the current rate multiplied by the taxable FICA wages. Also, the liabilities shown on Form 941 should agree with the total deposits for the period. The total gross wages on Form 940 should equal that shown on Form 941.

At year-end. Reconcile the totals for the four quarters on the quarterly Form 941 with those on the annual Form W-2.

Accounting for Workers' Compensation Insurance

Besides an equal share of FICA taxes and payments for unemployment insurance, an employer must also provide workers' compensation insurance to protect employees against loss of income from job-related injuries, illness, or death. An employer may obtain coverage by buying the insurance from a private company or contributing to a state-operated insurance fund. In some states, employees may share in the cost of the insurance, as in Oregon and Washington.

The cost of workers' compensation insurance depends on the risk inherent in the types of work done by the employees and the company's history of claims. The premium rates are higher for jobs considered dangerous than for relatively safe jobs—for example, a company would pay more for its production workers than for its office staff. The insurance companies state the risk in terms of percentages of $100 of wages or salaries—for example, the employer would pay .15 or 15¢ per $100 of office wages and may pay $2.25 per $100 of production wages.

Although some employers charge the workers' compensation expense when paid, the usual practice is to pay an estimated premium at the beginning of a period and then adjust the expense according to the actual payroll at the end of the period.

EXAMPLE   Process Associates estimates its workers' compensation insurance as follows:

Work Classification	Estimated Total Wages	Rate per $100	Estimated Premium
Office	$ 80,000	.0015	$ 120
Production	300,000	.0225	6,750
Total	$380,000		$6,870

The company records the transaction as follows:

	Debit	Credit
Prepaid Workers' Comp. Insurance	6,870	
Cash		6,870

At the end of the period, an audit of the actual payroll by work classification indicates an overpayment or underpayment of the estimated premium paid. An adjusting journal entry then reflects the actual expense.

Assuming that the actual premium should have been $8,200, then the entry would be as follows:

	Debit	Credit
Workers' Compensation Expense	8,200	
Prepaid Workers' Comp. Insurance		6,870
Cash		1,330

▲

AUDITING PAYROLL

Extensive records are essential for accurate earnings, tax reports, and statements and for timely tax deposits. As a result, accounting for payroll is more complex than accounting for most of the other expenses incurred by a business. Besides the usual approval and disbursement procedures necessary for most expenses, payroll requires numerous calculations for timekeeping, compensation methods, wage rates, tax withholding, and other data. An external auditor can help provide assurance that the methods and systems yield accurate results.

One task of the external auditor is to establish that the company being audited has certain control procedures in place. Proper controls should provide reasonable assurance that the recipients of paychecks actually exist, are employees of the company, have worked for the period indicated, and have earned the wages they receive.

If the internal control is satisfactory, the auditor seeks to verify the accuracy of the amounts in the financial statements that relate to payroll. The payroll manager can assist the auditor in this examination by recording payroll transactions in compliance with applicable laws and agreements, maintaining adequate documentation, and being attentive to the details that go along with payroll operations.

The process of auditing the payroll accounts is the reverse of the recording of the original transactions. The auditor selects several of the individual wage payments from the company's payroll records. Then the auditor traces these amounts back through the accounting records and vouches them to the original documents. The accounts and transactions examined by the auditor and the procedures performed are as follows:

Wages and Salaries
- Verifies gross pay for each individual selected by referring to timecards, salary authorizations, union contracts, or other wage records.
- Establishes that all officers are paid in accordance with the plan approved by the corporation's board of directors.

Payroll Tax Liabilities
- Determines that deductions from gross pay have been properly authorized and calculated correctly.
- Verifies footings and extensions on selected payroll listings and traces postings to the general ledger.

Other Payroll-Related Liabilities
• Reviews computations related to vacation pay, pensions, and profit-sharing plans.

REVIEW QUESTIONS

7–1. Define assets, liabilities, and owner's equity.

7–2. Explain why business transactions do not disturb the equality of the accounting equation.

7–3. State the rules of debits and credits.

7–4. What are the two most important financial statements? What does each report?

7–5. What is the accounting process (or cycle)?

7–6. Name the accounts used in payroll accounting.

7–7. Explain the need for recording payroll accruals and give examples of situations where accruals are in order.

7–8. Describe the sequence of payroll transactions and the accounts affected.

7–9. Explain how the payroll register is used in accounting for payroll.

7–10. Name the employer's payroll taxes.

7–11. How are FUTA and SUTA taxes recorded and paid?

7–12. Why is reconciliation of the payroll records important?

7–13. Name each payroll record or report and describe how they are reconciled to each other.

7–14. How can a payroll manager help the accounting department reconcile the payroll bank account?

7–15. Of what payroll objectives does an external audit provide reasonable assurance?

7–16. What is the general audit approach taken by the auditor?

7–17. What accounts and transactions does an outside auditor examine?

DISCUSSION QUESTIONS

7–1. *Fund accounting* is a type of accounting used for governments and non-profit organizations. According to this system of accounting, a fund consists of resources to be used for a particular purpose; those in charge of the fund are accountable for its effective and efficient operation. Some theorists think that fund accounting may be preferable to current accounting systems for business enterprises. In your opinion, would fund accounting be a concept that might be useful in payroll accounting? How?

7–2. Many companies issue conventional annual reports with the standard financial statements and also issue supplementary statements that follow the rules of so-called social accounting. *Social accounting* shows the use that a corporation makes of its resources—that is, where it spends its money to serve social purposes. One of these uses is the payment of wages and salaries, which provides the means for workers to support their families. The social accountants think corporations should spend a higher percentage of their available resources on environmental improvement, community projects, scientific research, and wages to improve the standard of living of their employees. What is your view of social accounting?

7–3. Many employees invest in the companies they work for and are therefore vitally interested in the companies' operations from the standpoint of

Discussion Questions
(cont.)

investors as well as of workers. If you enjoyed your status as an employee for a company, would you invest in its securities, if available? What are the advantages and disadvantages of such an investment?

7–4. A popular employee benefit of recent years is the employee stock ownership plan, or ESOP. With an ESOP, a company makes tax-deductible contributions to a trust, either of the company's stock or cash that is used to purchase the company's stock. Employees purchase stock in the trust and, at retirement, receive shares of the company based on their contributions and those of the company. How would you record the contributions of the company to the trust?

EXERCISES

7–1. Cal Torey, a technician, is the only employee for Ray's Exterminating Service and earns a salary of $540 a week. Through payroll deductions, Cal donates $2 a week to the United Way and pays $5 a week for medical insurance. Tax rates on Cal's salary are 12% for federal income tax, 5% for state income tax, 6.2% for Social Security taxes, and 1.45% for Medicare taxes. Record in general journal form the weekly payroll of Ray's Exterminating Service.

7–2. The Rambler Company has the following payroll information for the week ended June 15.

Gross earnings	$42,500
Federal income tax withheld	8,000
State income tax withheld	3,600
Medical insurance premiums	500

The Social Security tax rate is 6.2%, the Medicare tax rate is 1.45%, the FUTA tax rate is 0.8%, and the SUTA rate is 5.0%. All wages are subject to employer's payroll taxes except for $6,000 not subject to FUTA and SUTA taxes. Record Rambler's payroll tax expense and payments of each in general journal form.

7–3. Hogan's Carpet Cleaning Service incurred salary expenses of $48,000 for November. The employer's payroll expense includes Social Security taxes of 6.2%, Medicare taxes of 1.45%, a state unemployment tax of 5.4%, and federal unemployment tax of 0.8%. Of the total wages, $42,000 is subject to Social Security taxes and $7,000 is subject to the unemployment taxes. In addition, the company pays medical insurance of $1,200 for its employees. Record Hogan's payroll taxes and its medical insurance expense in general journal form.

7–4. Wages of the Fix-It Home Improvement Company subject to FUTA taxes for the four quarters of the year are listed in the following table. Compute the FUTA tax liability for each quarter (using a rate of 0.8%), the amount deposited, and the total amount owed at the end of the year.

	Wages Subject to FUTA	FUTA Tax Liability	Amount Deposited
First quarter	$ 9,500	$_____	$_____

Exercises (cont.)

	Wages Subject to FUTA	FUTA Tax Liability	Amount Deposited
Second quarter	10,000	_____	_____
Third quarter	12,000	_____	_____
Fourth quarter	-0-	_____	_____

7–5. Wedding Accessories Company incurred a $120,000 salary expense for the week ending October 15. Of this amount, $20,000 was not subject to Social Security taxes, and $45,000 was not subject to state and federal unemployment taxes. The Social Security tax rate is 6.2%, the Medicare tax rate is 1.45%, the state unemployment tax rate is 2.8%, and the federal unemployment tax rate is 0.8%. Compute the company's payroll tax expenses for the period.

7–6. Grana's Fruit Baskets had the following payroll data for its employees for the week ended September 25.

	Weekly Earnings	Accumulated Earnings	Weekly Social Security Taxes	Weekly Medicare Taxes	FITW	SITW
Virginia Blue	$400	$16,000	$24.80	$5.80	$40.00	$20.00
Ted Lamson	420	17,500	26.04	6.09	42.00	21.00
Jeff Kane	380	15,200	23.56	5.51	38.00	19.00
Karen Garfield	440	18,200	27.28	6.38	44.00	22.00

Assume a FUTA rate of 0.8% and a SUTA rate of 3.0%. Record the
a. Weekly payroll information in general journal form.
b. Employer's payroll taxes in general journal form.

7–7. The annual payroll of Helio Lighting Company is $420,000, of which $60,000 is not subject to Social Security taxes, and $200,000 is not subject to unemployment taxes. The applicable tax rates are as follows:

	Tax Rate (%)
Social Security taxes	6.20
Medicare taxes	1.45
FUTA taxes	0.80
SUTA taxes	2.80

Compute the amounts the company owes for payroll taxes for the year.

Annual Social Security taxes expense $ _____

Annual Medicare taxes expense   _____

Annual FUTA taxes expense   _____

Annual SUTA taxes expense   _____

7–8. The latest biweekly payroll of the HiTech Engineering Company was $70,000, all of which was subject to FICA taxes and $64,000 of which was subject to unemployment taxes. HiTech withheld from employees' gross wages $12,000 for federal income taxes, $4,000 for state income taxes, $2,800

Exercises (cont.)

for medical insurance premiums, and $880 for union dues. The applicable tax rates are as follows:

	Tax Rate (%)
Social Security taxes	6.20
Medicare taxes	1.45
FUTA taxes	0.80
SUTA taxes	3.60

Prepare journal entries to record the payroll and payroll deductions and to record the employer's payroll tax expense.

7–9. Genre Art Galleries issued its yearly income statement, which showed wages expense of $82,500. The related balance sheet account Wages Payable had a beginning balance of $5,000 and a year-end balance of $10,000. Assume that wages are accrued at year-end. Compute the cash paid for wages during the year.

7–10. The balance sheets for Keller Instruments for the previous year and the current year showed a year-end balance in the Wages Payable account of $6,500 and $3,600, respectively. The accounting records show that cash paid out for wages during the year was $54,000. Assume the accrual of wages at year-end. Compute the amount of wages expense for the year.

PROBLEMS

7–1. The payroll records of Sports Cards Unlimited for the week ended October 15 show the following data (rounded to the nearest dollar):

Gross earnings	$12,000
Social Security earnings	9,290
Medicare earnings	12,000
Unemployment taxable earnings	8,000 (FUTA and SUTA)
Social Security taxes withheld	576
Medicare taxes withheld	174
Federal income taxes withheld	900
Medical insurance premiums	250

Assume the Social Security tax rate is 6.2%, the Medicare tax rate is 1.45%, the SUTA tax rate is 5.2%, and the FUTA tax rate is 0.8%. Prepare the entries to record the
  a. Payroll totals
  b. Employer's payroll taxes

7–2. Video Shoppe has four employees with the following earnings data.

Name	Gross Earnings	Year-to-Date Earnings
Linda Como	$1,500	$56,500
Tim Morrison	350	25,000
Judy Phan	280	18,000
Bruce Stein	1,200	50,000

Assume a Social Security tax rate of 6.2% on the first $76,200 of earnings, a Medicare tax of 1.45% on the entire amount of earnings, a state unemployment tax rate of 2.8% and a federal unemployment tax rate of 0.8% on the first $7,000. Prepare the journal entry to record the company's payroll taxes.

Problems (cont.)

7–3. Payroll data from the July 15 payroll period for Beau's Men's Store are as follows (rounded to the nearest dollar):

Gross earnings	$9,000
Federal income taxes withheld	1,100
Social Security taxes withheld	558
Medicare taxes withheld	131
State income taxes withheld	200
Medical insurance premiums	150

The following transactions occurred in July:

July 15   Recorded the July 15 payroll.

15   Recorded the employer's payroll taxes. All earnings were taxable for FICA, FUTA, and SUTA.

18   Issued paychecks for the July 15 payroll.

20   Issued check for payroll taxes withheld plus employer's share for deposit with Form 8109.

22   Completed Form 8109 and issued a check for $180 to deposit the FUTA tax owed for the second quarter.

25   Filed the quarterly state unemployment tax return and sent a check for $780 to pay the SUTA tax for the second quarter.

Prepare journal entries for these transactions. Use 6.2% for Social Security taxes, 1.45% for Medicare taxes, 0.8% for FUTA, and 5.2% for SUTA.

7–4. Bill Smedley began a souvenir manufacturing business. The Keepsake Company recorded the following payroll data in the first two months of operations. Journalize the payroll and payroll tax entries.

July 15 and 31   Recorded and paid employees their semimonthly salaries. Payroll data were as follows (rounded to the nearest dollar):

Gross earnings	$4,500
Taxable FICA earnings	4,500
Unemployment taxable earnings	4,500
Social Security taxes withheld	279
Medicare taxes withheld	65
Federal income tax withheld	520
Net pay	3,636

July 15 and 31   Recorded employer's payroll taxes as follows:

Social Security tax rate	6.20%
Medicare tax rate	1.45%
SUTA tax rate	5.00%
FUTA tax rate	0.80%

July 20 and August 3   Made deposits for the July FICA and federal taxes withheld.

7–5. Ceil's Ceramics has two employees and recorded the following payroll information for the month ended March 31 (rounded to the nearest dollar):

Salaries	$850
Deductions:	
Employees' federal income tax	140
Social Security taxes	53
Medicare taxes	12
Medical insurance premiums	40
Net pay	605

Problems (cont.)

Employer payroll taxes:

Social Security taxes	53
Medicare taxes	12
Federal unemployment taxes	7
State unemployment taxes	36

    a. Prepare the journal entries to record the payroll for the month of March and the employer's payroll taxes.

    b. Prepare the journal entry to record the monthly deposit of federal and state taxes if Ceil's Ceramics is a monthly depositor.

7–6. Gloria Benson is a purchasing agent for Airlift Express and earns $3,200 a month, with a year-end bonus of 10% of her salary. During the year, Gloria's wages were subject to the following monthly deductions and employer's payroll taxes.

	Per Month	Rate (%)
Federal income tax withheld	$620	
State income tax withheld	48	
Social Security taxes (employee and employer)		6.2
Medicare taxes (employee and employer)		1.45
Health insurance withheld	200	
FUTA taxes		0.8
SUTA taxes		3.2

    a. Compute

        (1) Gloria Benson's yearly gross wages, payroll deductions, and net pay. The federal income tax rate on the bonus is 28%. State rate is 5%.

        (2) Total payroll cost to Airlift Express.

    b. Prepare summary general journal entries for Airlift for

        (1) Yearly gross wages, payroll deductions, and net pay of Gloria Benson.

        (2) Airlift's payroll taxes on the compensation paid to Gloria Benson.

7–7. Payroll data for Strikes and Spares for the latest weekly payroll period ended September 8 are as follows:

Salaries	$12,000
Deductions:	
Federal income tax withheld	2,400
Social Security taxes withheld	744
Medicare taxes withheld	174
State income taxes withheld	700
Health insurance premiums withheld	50
Savings plan contributions	40
Employer's Taxes:	
Social Security taxes	744
Medicare taxes	174
FUTA taxes (0.8%)	96
SUTA taxes (2.2%)	264

Prepare the general journal entries to record the

    a. Payroll for the week, including the employer's payroll taxes.

    b. Payment of federal taxes withheld (based on no liability before the week recorded above for a semiweekly depositor).

Problems (cont.)

7–8. The Party Time Supplies Company pays its four employees weekly. Payroll data for the latest week were as follows:

	Wages	FITW	Cumulative Gross Wages
Albert Parker	$240	$40	$8,400
Carol Trane	240	44	6,400
Sarah Linden	280	50	7,400
Ellen Bragg	280	54	6,800

The Social Security tax rate is 6.2% and the Medicare tax rate is 1.45%. The federal unemployment tax rate is 0.8% and the state unemployment tax rate is 4.8% on the first $7,000 of wages.
Record the:
  a. Payroll for the week.
  b. Employer's tax expense.

7–9. Vox Advertising had the following payroll data for February for its monthly employees.

	Gross Wages	FITW	SITW	Medical Insurance	Cumulative Wages
Bruce Farmer	$2,400	$360	$100	$40	$4,800
Regina Garth	3,600	480	120	50	7,200
Ralph Brady	4,000	440	110	50	8,000
Henrietta Dunn	2,800	300	80	40	5,600

The applicable tax rates and taxable wage base limits are as follows:

	Tax Rate (%)	Taxable Wage Base
Social Security taxes	6.20	$ 76,200
Medicare taxes	1.45	no limit
FUTA taxes	0.80	7,000
SUTA taxes	4.00	7,000

  a. Compute the Social Security and Medicare taxes withheld.
  b. Prepare general journal entries to record at March 4 the
    (1) Payroll for the month.
    (2) Employer's payroll tax expense.

7–10. Morgan Furniture Makers has four employees with the following bi-weekly payroll data:

	Wages	FITW
Harry Negron	$1,200	$200
Pat Torrey	2,000	360
Greg Hale	1,600	220
Carrie Acker	1,800	240

Assume all employees are subject to all FICA taxes. The following tax rates apply.

Social Security taxes	6.20%
Medicare taxes	1.45%

Problems (cont.)

Record at August 22 the
   a. Payroll for the biweekly period and the payroll tax liabilities.
   b. Payment of the payroll.
   c. Payment with Form 8109 of the payroll tax liability.

CONTINUING CASE PROBLEM

On June 30, certain payroll accounts in the general ledger of Frontier Landscaping had the following balances:

Social Security Taxes Payable	$ 670
Medicare Taxes Payable	156
Federal Withholding Taxes Payable	1,080
State Withholding Taxes Payable	360
Medical Insurance Payable	400
Charitable Contributions Payable	200

The following transactions occurred during July:

July 1 Prepared a journal entry to record the weekly payroll (rounded to the nearest dollar):

Gross wages	$5,600
Social Security taxes withheld	347
Medicare taxes withheld	81
Federal income taxes withheld	1,120
State income taxes withheld	380
Medical insurance premiums withheld	400
Charitable contributions withheld	200

July 1 Wrote a check on the company's general checking account at Suburbia Bank to transfer the net amount of the weekly payroll to the payroll account at Metropolis Bank.

July 3 Issued paychecks to all employees of the company.

July 3 Prepared a general journal entry to record the employer's payroll tax expense. The Social Security tax rate is 6.2% and the Medicare tax rate is 1.45%. The FUTA tax rate is 0.8% and the SUTA tax rate is 4.4%. Gross wages in excess of the taxable unemployment base of $7,000 were $2,600.

July 7 Issued a check to Suburbia Bank with Form 8109 in payment of federal withholding and FICA taxes payable.

July 31 Issued checks in payment of the company's FUTA and SUTA taxes for the second quarter.

July 31 Issued checks to the following:

State Tax Department	$740
Acme Insurance Company	800
United Way	400

Record the above transactions in general journal form.

PART IV

PAYROLL SYSTEMS AND POLICIES

Lois Arruda has learned a lot about payroll accounting. She understands the laws that govern payroll compensation and recordkeeping; she knows how to run the payroll so that employees are paid accurately and on time; she is able to complete and make use of the various forms involved in payroll and goes back and forth between the payroll register and employee earnings records with ease; she understands the importance of meeting federal and state tax deposit and report filing deadlines based on wages paid; and she is able to analyze and journalize payroll transactions.

Clark believes that in order to be an effective payroll manager, Lois must learn two more important components of the payroll accounting process: methods for internal control of the payroll system and policies for cost-saving in payroll operations. While the latter topic covers some techniques that are available only to upper management, Clark thinks that it is important for Lois to understand how a company that pays attention to its employee and payroll patterns can achieve substantial savings. And he wants to stress that a knowledgeable payroll department that communicates important payroll information efficiently to management can prove invaluable.

To start, Clark focuses on the concept of internal control of payroll, first describing the various types of payroll systems available and then focusing on techniques applicable to all systems that ensure accurate and efficient payroll operations. Such internal control measures are also necessary to ensure compliance with all federal and state government regulations. In the process, these internal control measures make the payroll and the company less vulnerable to error and/or fraud.

245

CHAPTER 8

PAYROLL SYSTEMS AND CONTROL PROCEDURES

LEARNING OBJECTIVES

On completing this chapter, you will be able to:

1. Review the various payroll systems.
2. State the internal control objectives relating to payroll and measures taken to achieve these objectives.
3. Enumerate the various internal control principles.
4. Describe the four functions in the payroll and personnel cycle and the duties of the two separate departments that comprise this cycle.
5. Describe various payroll documents and records and their use in an effective internal control system.
6. Follow the flow of documents through the payroll and personnel cycle.
7. Explain the use of an imprest payroll account and its advantages.
8. Discuss various types of payroll fraud and various methods that can be used to detect and prevent them.

Nioga eventually plans to use a computerized system for processing the payroll but will still prepare checks manually for a while. The company plans to upgrade the entire payroll system in the coming year. Lois is concerned that the control procedures and systems now in place be maintained through this transition. She wants to know how she can make

247

*sure that Nioga's payroll operations always conform to the law and that
systems exist to prevent or at least detect fraudulent payroll distributions.*

*Clark assures Lois that careful systems planning and the segregation
of key payroll responsibilities at Nioga help to achieve these goals. Nioga
is large enough to have separate personnel and payroll departments and
to segregate the payroll functions of timekeeping, payroll preparation,
and payroll distribution. This segregation of duties is the framework for
effective internal control over payroll. When it is necessary to share payroll functions, however, other methods make for a logical division of responsibilities. Clark explains that these methods can help all businesses
maintain control over the operations required by law and at the same
time protect the company from fraud.*

*Clark begins the discussion of internal control by describing the types
of payroll systems a business might use, reviewing the objectives of internal control measures appropriate for all systems, and discussing ways to
implement effective control techniques.*

PAYROLL SYSTEMS

In most organizations, the payroll function is the largest operating system
both in terms of paperwork volume and dollar expenditures. It could also
be argued that payroll operations are the most important, or at least the
most sensitive, in an organization. Failure to meet production deadlines or
to take advantage of vendor discounts creates management problems but
nothing stirs up as much trouble and ill will as an incorrect or late payroll
check.

Payroll systems may be manual, mechanized, or computerized. Regardless of the type of system, it must be well integrated with overall business operations. Sometimes it is necessary to adapt the system in place or
change systems entirely, such as when a company outgrows an existing
system.

The important factors to consider in designing a payroll system are:

1. Method of compensation: fixed salary or wages on an hourly, piece
   work, or incentive plan.
2. Length of pay period: weekly, biweekly, semimonthly, or monthly.
3. Size of payroll: number of employees and total amount of compensation.
4. Type of supplementary payroll services needed: the information that
   must be provided to other departments such as personnel, production,
   or cost accounting.

Manual and Pegboard Systems

A manual system is probably sufficient for a small company with relatively
few (1–20) employees. With this method, the designated employee pre-

pares by hand the payroll register, employee earnings records, the Forms W-2, and the Forms 940 and 941.

To simplify the procedures and avoid duplication of work, some companies use a board or a device that holds and aligns several documents so they can be prepared at the same time. On a **pegboard (one-write) payroll system**, the payroll clerk aligns the payroll register, employee earnings record, and the employee paycheck in a step-wise fashion. Pegs along the edge of the board hold these documents in place. When the payroll clerk, using a ball-point pen, inserts the gross earnings, payroll deductions, and net pay on the employee check, the same data are entered on the payroll register and the employee earnings record.

The documents are layered on a pegboard as follows:

1. Position the payroll register for the period on the board, using the pegs to hold it in place. Enter the date of the payroll.

2. Place the employee earnings record over the payroll register so that the first blank line on the earnings record is over the first blank line of the payroll register.

3. Put the payroll check on top so that the pay stub aligns with the blank lines in the earnings record and the payroll register.

After writing the first check, the payroll clerk removes the employee earnings record and the payroll check for that employee and replaces them with the next employee earnings record and a blank payroll check. The payroll register stays on the pegboard until the payroll clerk has written payroll checks for all employees.

The pegboard system saves time and promotes accuracy since the payroll amounts are written only one time.

Mechanized Systems

The first step toward the automatic data processing of payroll involved electromechanical machines that used cards punched with alphabetic and numeric data. These machines could read the cards and perform arithmetic calculations. One type of machine punched input data onto cards, and a variety of other machines sorted, collated, and printed completed forms, paychecks, payroll records, and tax reports. This simple input-output system served as the forerunner to the computer systems of today. But this **mechanized payroll system** was not fast enough to survive the computer age, and is chiefly of interest to show the development of more advanced systems.

Computerized Systems

Computer technology has provided an important tool for organizing payroll systems in businesses of all sizes. Currently, a wide variety of **computerized payroll accounting systems** are available, but all require a payroll clerk or manager to set up a file on each employee with data on the name, address, pay rate, marital status, withholding allowances, and other deductions. Most programs allow updating of the file when the status of an employee changes as in the case of a promotion, transfer, or pay raise.

Pegboard (one-write) payroll system *A one-write system whereby proper alignment of forms permits the recording of payroll data to several records at the same time.*

Mechanized payroll system *A system that uses electromechanical machines and punch cards to process payroll data.*

Computerized payroll accounting system *A system that uses computers and tape or disk input devices to process payroll data.*

For each pay period, the payroll department inputs the current period information: number of regular hours worked, bonuses, or commissions to be received. Current tax tables are part of the computer's data base. The computer automatically calculates each employee's paycheck: regular pay, overtime pay, gross pay, deductions, and net pay. The computer also calculates year-to-date earnings and taxes for each employee.

Many payroll or accounting software programs can print the payroll register and the paychecks with accompanying stubs. Some programs can also record the payroll journal entry, post the amounts to the general ledger accounts, and update the employee earnings records. At the end of the calendar year, the system can print out the Form W-2, Wage and Tax Statement for each employee using the information in the computer files.

Choosing the Right System. A company must make several basic decisions before purchasing a computer system. Although a number of departments may use the system, the importance of meeting the payroll usually places the responsibility for the computer system on the payroll department. The payroll department must be assured that the system will meet its needs and be flexible enough to cope with new regulations and tax rates. A number of factors can have a profound effect on payroll operations, and the department must consider these factors when selecting a computer system and software.

Backup. Another program-compatible system should be available in case the selected system breaks down. Backup files should record all data and programs of permanent or continuing interest.

Technical support. The provider of the software should be accessible and able to assist in the specialized payroll problems of a particular business.

Cost. The costs of running the computer and software should reflect both variable and fixed costs so that total costs are in direct proportion to the volume of work.

Data security. The payroll system must have safeguards to protect the confidential payroll data against unauthorized access.

Service expandability. The expandability of the computer should be convenient and cost effective.

Processing speed. The computer should have the capability of processing data so that they are available as needed.

Ease of installation and maintenance. The problems of installation and maintenance should be minimal, and the vendor should respond quickly to service calls.

In looking for a reliable vendor, the company should be wary of vendors new to the market or those who are underfinanced. Expertise in the payroll area is also an especially desirable characteristic of a vendor. Some vendors offer a variety of products but lack specialized knowledge in payroll. A vendor who agrees with the company about the importance of payroll is more likely to treat payroll with the same attention.

A small vendor may not be able to handle a large account, and a large vendor may have trouble servicing a small account. The size of the vendor should be relative to the size of the payroll operations. When the fit is right, a vendor is usually more responsive to the company's needs.

Applications Software. An in-house computer system gives the company complete control over the payroll. A well-organized computer department includes data-entry operators, network managers, and accounting information system managers. Even with the best computer system and an efficient staff, however, the computer processing of payroll is only as good as the application software used. Application software consists of programs developed to perform specific jobs on the computer. In accounting, software programs are available for general ledger, accounts payable, accounts receivable, and payroll. The application program for payroll may be generalized or custom-made. Regardless of the type of application program, the ultimate result should be a program that meets the needs of the company's payroll operations. The company should also try to choose software that balances present and future needs. General ledger programs with payroll functions may be ideal for small organizations.

Other features to look for in the computer system and software are the ability

- to share information with benefits administration and human resource departments, including information on such areas as child support payments, garnishments, and direct deposit.
- to generate frequent tax updates, including recent tax tables and schedules.
- to be compatible with various computer types or to run on different system sizes (mainframe, minicomputers, or microcomputers).

Maintaining Security. The computer hardware and software can be an important part of effective internal control by enhancing security. The company must avoid mistakes that can compromise the security of the computer system. The company should try to create an awareness of the need for security. For example, the company can have new employees sign a statement acknowledging their responsibility to protect their passwords and to inform management whenever they suspect a security breach. Other security measures include periodically running a virus detection and eradication program on all systems and backing up all critical data on a daily or even hourly basis.

Data Processing Service Bureau

Some companies opt to send their raw payroll data for each payroll period to a data processing service bureau or a bank that offers payroll services. The service bureau or bank runs the data on its computer system and returns payroll records and paychecks to the company for signing, often overnight, or it directly deposits paychecks to employees' accounts. Sometimes, the raw data can be sent by modem from a business's computer directly to the payroll service's computer.

With the growing complexity of laws and payroll procedures, service bureaus are becoming very popular with both small and large businesses. Service bureaus cater to different needs; some specialize in small business tasks, others are especially suited for very large payrolls. These preparation services can do any or all of the payroll accounting functions, including check preparation, maintenance of employee payroll records, tax filing, and other accounting functions.

INTERNAL CONTROL WITHIN PAYROLL SYSTEMS

Whether manual, mechanized, or computerized, a company's payroll accounting system must be governed by certain internal control principles in order to accomplish the goals of the company as they relate to employees and others. Requirements for accuracy and timeliness make for strict deadlines on all payroll activities; governmental reporting for payroll taxes complicates the process. The design of the payroll system must take all of these elements into account in order to accomplish several crucial objectives. A company's payroll system must provide for:

- an *accurate* computation of employees' gross earnings, based on appropriate methods and pay rates.
- withholding from employees' earnings the amounts required by the government and requested by the employees.
- *timely* remittance of the amounts withheld to the government and others in compliance with regulations and authorizations.
- *timely* filing of quarterly and annual tax reports and the preparation of employees' annual wage and tax statements.
- issuing *timely* and *accurate* paychecks to all employees.
- recording in the general accounting system on a *timely* and *accurate* basis the journal entries for payroll and tax liabilities, the payment of employees, and the payment of tax and other payroll-related liabilities.

As the preceding list reveals, timeliness and accuracy are the epitome of an effective payroll system. An employer can achieve these objectives through management policies, monitoring of functions, a well-integrated system of communication and documentation, and independent verification.

Responsibilities of Management

Internal control of payroll begins with the selection of one department or person from the company's management to supervise and monitor payroll operations. In other words, management should be in control of all payroll transactions. Management must provide general or specific authorization for all hiring or firing actions, promotions, rates and methods of pay, hours of work, overtime allowed, withholding of payroll taxes and other deductions, and issuing of payroll checks. Thus, if an individual is on the payroll or works overtime, has earned a level of gross wages, and receives a certain net pay, management has given either general or implicit authorization for such events to have occurred. In other words, an individual, being paid as an employee, is one who belongs on the payroll and is receiving the amount that is proper for the time worked. If any person is not entitled to a paycheck by virtue of not being an employee or is receiving more pay than earned, the responsibility rests with management.

Management should institute specific internal control measures to achieve segregation of payroll functions. For example, timekeeping should be a function separate from personnel, payroll preparation, and payroll distribution. A separate timekeeping department, together with proper documentation and independent verification, promotes accuracy and provides an assurance that the recorded payroll represents payments for work actually performed by existing employees.

Separation of Key Functions

The payroll system is actually part of a payroll and personnel cycle. This cycle begins with the hiring of employees and ends with the payment of employees for services performed and the payment of the amounts withheld for taxes and other benefits. This cycle consists of four functions, as shown in Figure 8-1: personnel and employment, timekeeping, payroll preparation, and payroll distribution.

The key ingredient in effective control over payroll procedures is a separation of these four functions. Even in a small business where one employee may carry out two or more functions, some separation of these functions is necessary. By separating the various duties involved in the payroll system, no one person has complete responsibility, thus limiting the possibility of fraud. Employers must, however, be aware of the possibility of collusion (two or more people joining together in payroll fraud).

Personnel Functions. In the payroll and personnel cycle, the personnel or human resources department performs the first function. Its work begins with interviewing and hiring job applicants. Establishing the competence and honesty of prospective employees is crucial. The department is also responsible for providing a new employee with a full job description and information on the rate and method of pay and company policies on overtime and benefits. The personnel department prepares the employee roster that lists the date of employment, the authorized rate of pay, withholding allowances (as specified by the employee on Form W-4), and payroll deductions, including union and/or voluntary deductions authorized by the employee.

Deduction authorization form *Another name for Form W-4, Employee's Withholding Allowance Certificate.*

The personnel department may use many types of forms such as job applications, change of status forms, work performance reviews, employee injury reports, **deduction authorization forms**, and employee counseling and termination notices. The personnel department is also responsible for verifying that the employee's Form I-9, Employment Eligibility Verification is complete and valid (see Chapter 1) and that a new employee has filled out Form W-4, Employee's Withholding Allowance Certificate, which authorizes payroll deductions for the withholding of income taxes (see Chapter 3). Other deductions, such as those required by union contracts or

PERSONNEL AND EMPLOYMENT
- Interview and hire job applicants.
- Prepare, maintain, and update employee records.
- Notify payroll department to place new employee on payroll.
- Forward employee work information to timekeeping department.

TIMEKEEPING
- Review and verify time records (by supervising managers).
- Submit timecards or sheets to payroll department for data processing.

PAYROLL PREPARATION
- Provide independent verification of all data from timekeeping.
- Compute gross earnings, deductions, and net pay.
- Prepare payroll registers and employee earnings records and send to accounting department for preparation of checks.

PAYROLL DISTRIBUTION
- Sign checks (should be someone who does not have access to timekeeping or payroll preparation).
- Distribute checks (should be someone who is not involved in other payroll preparation functions).

FIGURE 8-1   Payroll or Personnel Cycle

voluntary deductions for health insurance, pension plans, purchase of savings bonds or company stock, or charitable contributions, are as authorized by the employee in writing. Thus the personnel department maintains up-to-date master records to support the payment of wages, salaries, commissions, and the various deductions.

The personnel department sends a written notice to the payroll department to place the new employee on the payroll. It maintains responsibility for transmitting routine changes in an employee's status to the payroll department. Such changes may result from promotion or demotion, transfers, or pay rate increases or decreases. When terminating an employee, the personnel department should conduct an exit interview and notify the payroll department to remove the employee's name from the payroll.

The most important internal control within the personnel department is to restrict personnel workers' access to timecards, payroll records, or paychecks. These records go directly from timekeeping to payroll preparation.

Timekeeping Functions. Employers use timecards or time sheets to record hours and minutes on the job, and a supervisor approves these time records. The manager responsible for the related work activity is in charge of the timecards or sheets. At the end of each payroll period, the supervising managers review the time records to verify their accuracy and then transmit them to the payroll department for data processing. In many businesses, the time records then go to cost accounting where the labor costs are allocated to individual jobs.

For employees who use timecards, control measures are necessary to ensure that employees punch only their own cards and do not submit a fictitious timecard.

Payroll Preparation Functions. The payroll department should maintain internal controls that provide for automatic cross-checking of records and for independent internal verification of all important data. This all-encompassing approach requires competent, independent people to:

1. Recalculate actual hours worked on timecards and job order tickets.
2. Review approvals of all overtime.

IN THE NEWS

AUTOMATED TIME AND ATTENDANCE SYSTEMS REPLACING OLD-STYLE TIMEKEEPING

Emphasis by employers on cost-cutting methods has led to increasing use of new state-of-the-art timekeeping systems. Automated time and attendance systems are making headway in industries where cost savings on payroll preparation costs are vital. The hospital industry has turned to these systems to help keep down health care costs. The beleaguered steel industry also has increasingly converted to automated timekeeping.

Current payroll systems operate on a batch basis, but the new time and attendance systems provide an on-line approach. The sequence of transactions flows automatically from timekeeping right through to paycheck preparation. The new systems record hours worked; calculate earnings from the hours, deductions based on the earnings, and the final net pay; and prepare the Forms W-2. In addition, the systems generate analyses and permit data entry and query.

Data entry is the key to the automated system. The employee enters the identification and transaction date either through a badge reader or telephone. The employees run their badges through a badge reading device or, if using a telephone, enter a PIN (personal identification number) on the telephone push button key pad.

The major benefits of the new system are faster payroll processing and improved report generation, with all payroll operations under the control of the payroll department. The bar-coded identification cards or PINs permit the rapid accumulation and processing of data. Even though the functions of timekeeping and payroll preparation are combined, the internal control is enhanced because the timekeeping data cannot be altered once it enters the system. However, independent verification is necessary to ensure the integrity of the original data.

3. Reconcile payroll hours with independent production records.

4. Examine timecards and job order tickets for alterations.

5. Compare (a) batch control totals calculated from payroll cards to computer-processed hours and (b) the computer printout of wage and withholding rates to authorized rates in the personnel files.

6. Determine that labor hours, particularly for manufacturing, are allocated to proper account classifications.

Payroll department personnel prepare the payroll registers and employee earnings records, which are sent to accounting. The accounting department prepares the paychecks or one check that transfers the exact amount of the net payroll to a special payroll account. The accounting department then issues the paychecks using the payroll account.

In the preparation of the payroll checks, the most important internal control is to prevent those responsible for preparing the payroll checks from having access to timecards, from signing or distributing the payroll checks, or from independently verifying payroll output. The use of prenumbered checks and verifying check amounts during the reconciliation process are also very important activities.

Payroll Distribution.   Distribution of the payroll checks is the final step in the payroll and personnel cycle. The paymaster should be someone independent of the payroll department and the supervision of employees. Internal controls for payroll distribution should include:

1. Limiting the authority to sign payroll checks to a responsible employee who does not have access to timekeeping or preparation of the payroll.

2. Assigning the distribution of the payroll to someone who is not involved in the other payroll functions.

3. Requiring the immediate return of unclaimed checks for redeposit.

4. Restricting access to the check-signing machine or stamp.

5. Using an imprest payroll account to prevent the issuance of unauthorized payroll checks.

Use of an Imprest Payroll Account.   An imprest payroll account is a separate payroll cash account that always carries a fixed, predetermined balance. Before the distribution of the payroll, a check drawn on the general cash account is used to transfer the exact amount of the net pay to the payroll cash account. With a separate imprest account, an employer saves time with preprinted signatures on checks. A separate payroll cash account also makes it easier to reconcile the regular checking account because payroll checks flow through a controlled account.

Use of an imprest account also simplifies the reconciliation of the payroll account itself, since the balance on the bank statement should equal the imprest amount plus the total of any outstanding payroll checks.

Other advantages of an imprest account are that it (1) allows the delegation of payroll check-signing duties, (2) separates payment of net pay from other business payments, and (3) facilitates cash management.

Use of Direct Deposit. A direct deposit system, as discussed in Chapter 5, also enhances internal control. Instead of issuing checks on payday, the company gives the employee an earnings statement; the funds go directly to the employee's bank account.

Direct deposit results in significant savings to the employer since the payroll department does not have to write or distribute as many checks or replace lost or stolen checks. Employees have immediate access to their money, even while on vacation, without having to make a trip to the bank.

In many states, the employer needs the employee's written authorization for direct deposit. Usually, an employer cannot restrict direct deposit to one specific institution. If a choice of banks is not available, the employer must offer a regular paycheck as an alternative. In any event, the employer must give all employees an earnings statement at the time of payroll distribution.

Escheat laws *Laws on the disposition of unclaimed wages.*

Uncashed and Unclaimed Paychecks. Every state has **escheat laws** that require employers to hold uncashed and unclaimed checks for a certain period of time. After an employer has attempted to contact the employee, it must turn over unclaimed paychecks to the state tax department. Despite this requirement, the amounts reported on the employee earnings record and the Form W-2 generally must include the unclaimed checks. The employer records the uncashed and unclaimed checks as a liability.

Some states have reduced the time period employers must hold unclaimed wages before turning them over to the state. In some states, however, the holding period may be several years. Accurate recordkeeping procedures are, therefore, essential. These procedures require that all undelivered checks be returned to payroll, that a list be prepared of the employees and the amounts of the checks, that a certified letter be mailed to the employees stating that wages are available for pickup, and that a record be kept of any claim on the funds. If the employees fail to claim their checks, the employer should file all returned and unclaimed checks in a reference file. If the employees claim their checks, the employer should monitor all reissued payments to ensure that the accounting system has reflected the transactions.

Importance of Accurate and Thorough Recordkeeping

Failure to record all payroll transactions weakens the company's internal control. A strong documentation system promotes accuracy and provides assurance that payroll transactions are complete. Prenumbering of payroll checks and the checks used to pay tax and other liabilities makes it easier to track the checks and reconcile the bank accounts.

Independent verification enhances the accuracy of recorded payroll transactions. A chart of accounts also facilitates accuracy, in addition to providing useful information to management.

Careful recordkeeping can also deter lawsuits over back pay or termination wages by providing evidence of hours spent at work and actual pay rates.

Claims for Back Pay.   Maintaining complete and accurate records is a vital safeguard against back-pay claims. Back-pay claims may arise when an employee claims nonexempt status and asks for back pay for overtime hours worked. Complete records may provide essential evidence to support or disprove the employee's claim.

Disputes over Termination Wages.   When a dispute arises over the amount of a terminated employee's final wages, the employer should act quickly and pay any wages that are not in dispute. This precaution is necessary because most states penalize employers for late payment of wages, doubling the amount, in some cases. If the employer pays the uncontested wages, a lesser amount is subject to penalty.

The late-payment penalty usually applies only to wages, but commissions, bonuses, and other forms of compensation may qualify as wages. If the company computes a bonus based on profit at mid-year and year-end and an employee earns a mid-year bonus before termination, the employer must pay the bonus within the prescribed time after termination. It cannot postpone the payment until reporting of the year-end profit.

Whether the termination is voluntary or involuntary may affect the deadline for termination pay. The deadline may also be more stringent if the employee provided advance notice of intent to leave the company.

Evaluation of Control Procedures

The payroll manager should evaluate and develop procedures to ensure that the payroll department operates effectively. The approach to an evaluation of the payroll department can be routine or imaginative. The routine approach includes rather typical steps.

1. Examine internal controls designed to
   a. prevent improper additions of newly hired employees to the payroll and ensure prompt deletions of terminated employees from the payroll.
   b. assure the accuracy of hours worked and the calculations of gross and net pay, in accordance with authorized wage rates.
   c. protect against the misuse of signature plates.

2. Review legislation concerning various deductions.

Job order ticket or cost card   *A time record listing the hours worked by an employee by job.*

3. Analyze **job order tickets and cost cards** to distribute labor costs to operating or overhead areas.

The imaginative approach might include some of the following steps.

1. Examine the organizational plan of the payroll department, the assignment of duties, staffing, and work flow, devoting particular attention to peaks and valleys of activity.

2. Evaluate overtime payments, labor turnover, and shift differentials to improve scheduling and even out the flow of work and employee requirements.

PREVENTION AND DETECTION OF FRAUD

Despite efforts to maintain internal control of payroll, employees can and do commit payroll fraud. The most common types of fraud involve fictitious employees, fraudulent hours, and duplicate payroll checks.

Fictitious Employees

Issuing payroll checks to individuals who are no longer employed occurs when an individual remains on the payroll as an employee after termination. The individual most likely to perpetuate this crime is a payroll clerk, supervisor, fellow employee, or former employee. For instance, where internal control is weak, a supervisor could punch in for an employee and approve the timecard at the end of the pay period. If the supervisor also distributes paychecks, detection of the fraud becomes less likely.

To avoid this padding of the payroll, the paymaster should pay the employees directly and be aware of new hires and terminations. The paymaster should not turn over paychecks for absent employees to another person for delivery. Instead, the paymaster should retain those paychecks for later retrieval by the absent employees with proper identification and signature. The personnel department should inform the payroll and computer departments of changes in employment.

The payroll department can also try to detect fictitious employees by:

1. Checking to be sure the endorsement on the canceled paycheck matches the authorized signature on the Form W-4.

2. Scanning endorsements on canceled checks for unusual or recurring second endorsements.

3. Examining checks recorded as voided to make sure no one has fraudulently cashed them.

4. Tracing selected transactions in the payroll register to personnel records to establish whether the individuals are bona fide employees.

5. Reviewing personnel files to determine whether terminated employees have received termination pay and then examining subsequent payroll records to make sure that terminated employees have not received a payroll check.

6. Conducting a surprise payroll distribution, where employees actually pick up their paychecks. Any check that goes unclaimed may indicate a fictitious employee.

Fraudulent Hours

One way to detect discrepancies in the number of hours worked versus the number of hours recorded is to reconcile the total hours paid according to the payroll records with an independent record of the hours worked, if available from production control. Discrepancies may result from:

1. Improper reporting of time by employees. Timekeeping can detect this practice by observing the use of time clocks and enforcing strict rules

requiring employees to punch their own timecards. In addition, time-keeping should make periodic floor checks of employees on duty.

2. Employees working unauthorized overtime hours. The company should have an overtime authorization procedure that timekeeping can use to verify when employees have been requested to work overtime.

3. Wasting time on the job and assigning excess hours to other jobs. Employees should use a time clock to report hours by job. The supervisor should explore this policy and should review and approve job order tickets. Timekeeping should verify these approvals.

4. Charging an overtime rate for regular hours. Timekeeping must note the overtime hours authorized and verify that only those hours count for the overtime rate.

5. Failure to reconcile job order tickets and timecards. Differences may occur but should fall within reasonable limits. If not, timekeeping should resolve them or bring exceptions to the attention of the payroll department.

Duplicate Paychecks

Another type of payroll fraud involves the issuance of duplicate payroll checks. To prevent this, the employer should require an independent party to compare canceled paychecks with initial payroll disbursement records or should monitor the activities of those participating in either payroll disbursements or the reconciliation of payroll bank accounts.

REVIEW QUESTIONS

8–1. Which internal control objective is achieved through the use of time clocks?

8–2. What authorizations are required for payroll transactions?

8–3. Why should all payroll checks be prenumbered?

8–4. How are the following personnel records used?
a. Deduction authorization form
b. Rate authorization form

8–5. Describe the flow of transactions and documents in the payroll and personnel cycle—from employment to issuance of a payroll check.

8–6. Name several events that can cause a change in an employee's status.

8–7. What are the two most important internal control measures to have in effect for timekeeping?

8–8. Name the principal areas where independent internal verification of hours worked should be used.

8–9. What organizational and documentation controls should be in effect with respect to payroll checks?

8–10. How should unclaimed payroll checks be handled?

8–11. What is an imprest payroll account? What are its advantages? How are payroll disbursements controlled through such an account?

8–12. What are the most common types of payroll-related fraud?

8–13. Name situations that lead to fictitious employees. How can this fraud be prevented?

8–14. What actions can be taken to detect fictitious employees?

8–15. Name one way to detect whether employees have been paid for more hours than they actually worked.

8–16. How can the issuance of duplicate paychecks be prevented?

DISCUSSION QUESTIONS

8–1. Businesses whose employees handle cash extensively (such as retail stores) frequently require lie detector tests as a condition of employment. Do you think lie detector tests are a good screening device? Why or why not?

8–2. Most businesses with more than twenty employees use a computerized accounting system or a payroll service to process their payroll. What are the primary advantages of a computerized payroll system? What are the advantages of using an outside payroll service? Of what significance is the size of the user company?

8–3. An old story tells the tale of Ernest Loyal, a faithful cashier-bookkeeper who worked for his company for 25 years, arrived early for work and stayed late, and never took a vacation or any time off. One day Ernest became ill and missed a week of work. During this week, the replacement employee found that, over his 25 years of service, Ernest had embezzled $250,000. How can this type of fraud be prevented?

8–4. Some companies require all employees from the chairman of the board and president down to the janitor to punch in; other companies rely entirely on the honor system and have employees complete their own timecards. Which system do you think makes more sense? Why? Would yet another approach be better in your opinion?

EXERCISES

8–1. The Village Cinemas, like most other organizations, maintains a separate payroll cash account and uses a general account for such other disbursements as purchases, equipment, and investments. Explain the advantages of maintaining separate accounts for payroll and for other disbursements.

8–2. Explain why the paymaster should list unclaimed payroll checks and turn them over to the payroll department for later distribution to the employee rather than hold them until requested by the unpaid employees.

8–3. The office staff of BlackTop Sealer Company consists of a bookkeeper, a typist, and the owner Jim Malone. In addition, the company employs six service persons who are paid by the hour. The service persons submit weekly time reports on which they record the hours devoted to each job. How would you set up the organization and duties of the office staff to have the best possible internal control over payroll?

8–4. Laboratory Devices has the following payroll control procedures. At the end of each workweek, the supervisor distributes payroll checks for the preceding workweek, notes the regular and overtime hours worked by each employee, and initials the timecards signifying approval. The supervisor then delivers all timecards and unclaimed payroll checks to the payroll clerk. List the deficiencies in the company's internal controls.

8–5. The control procedures for the Perfect Cravat Company are as follows. At the start of each week, the payroll clerk reviews the payroll department files to determine the employment status of the factory employees and distributes timecards as each individual arrives for work. The payroll clerk also has custody of the signature stamp machine, verifies the identity of each payee, and delivers signed paychecks to the supervisor. List the deficiencies in this internal control system.

8–6. The Waste Away Corp. plans to use an outside payroll service, providing a local bank with a list of its employees and the hours worked during the pay period. The bank will prepare the payroll records, deposit each employee's pay directly to her or his bank account, and prepare all tax reports and wage statements. Identify any problem areas with this arrangement and suggest solutions.

8–7. Renata Higgins has asked her accountant to evaluate the internal control in her business, Country General Store. Higgins has two employees. One employee orders inventory, receives goods, and pays suppliers. The other employee maintains the accounting records, collects cash, and makes all deposits. Evaluate the internal control procedures—the organization and division of duties.

8–8. Cash registers in stores and gasoline pumps in service stations provide locked-in totals of transactions. Name two comparable devices used in payroll operations and describe how they provide the same sort of protection. (*Hint:* Consider timekeeping methods.)

8–9. Computer program controls can be effective in preventing payroll fraud. Such controls include limit tests, which assess the reasonableness of data, and validity tests, which verify authenticity. Describe how these tests may detect errors or irregularities in payroll data.

8–10. Amy Bok, the bookkeeper at Bowen Electric, noted that most employees did not reconcile total federal income tax withheld on their Forms W-2 with amounts deducted from their weekly paychecks. For the current year, Amy understated the FITW in the final employee earnings records of several employees and overstated the amounts withheld for herself by the same amount. The Forms W-2 were issued accordingly, showing the understatement of FITW for several employees and an overstatement for Amy, permitting her to claim a tax refund. How can the payroll manager or auditor detect this fraud?

PROBLEMS

8–1. The Quik-Clic Company manufactures promotional pens and employs about 50 production workers. The company has the following payroll procedures:

a. The factory supervisor interviews applicants for jobs and has the final say on hiring.

b. On starting work, a new employee completes the Form W-4, Employee's Withholding Allowance Certificate and gives it to the factory supervisor.

c. The factory supervisor writes the employee's hourly rate of pay on the Form W-4 and gives it to a payroll clerk as notice of hiring. The supervisor verbally notifies the payroll department of any rate adjustments.

d. Each worker takes a timecard at the beginning of the week from a supply of cards kept in a box near the factory entrance. The employee

Problems (cont.)

fills out the card in pencil with his or her name and daily arrival and departure times.

e. At the end of the week, the employees drop the timecards in a box near the factory door where a payroll clerk collects them.

f. The payroll clerk computes gross pay, deductions, and net pay; records the details on each employee earnings record; and prepares the payroll checks.

g. The chief accountant manually signs the payroll checks, reconciles the payroll bank account, and prepares the various quarterly and annual payroll tax reports.

h. The factory supervisor, who receives the signed checks from the chief accountant, distributes the checks to the employees.

Indicate the control weakness and recommend procedures that Quik-Clic should put into effect to improve its internal control system for hiring and payroll.

8–2. The internal control procedures relating to payroll for the Exclusive Hair Salon are as follows:

a. The assistant manager thoroughly checks and verifies important information in an employment application before offering an employment contract.

b. The employee roster or personnel file for each employee contains current information on authorized pay rates.

c. Updated procedures manuals contain the latest personnel and payroll procedures.

d. All paychecks over $1,200 require two signatures.

e. Charging direct labor hours to appropriate jobs follows specified procedures.

For each procedure, indicate the control weakness that the procedure prevents.

8–3. A recent review of the internal control procedures relating to payroll of the Advance Computer Corp. indicates that a number of weaknesses may exist.

a. A few recent hirings violated equal opportunity laws.

b. Employees in the shipping department received a pay raise that was not approved by management.

c. An employee cashed an excessively large paycheck. The check was for hours neither authorized nor worked.

d. Labor summaries or payroll tax accruals do not agree with the payroll register and employee earnings records.

e. Timecards are available from an open bin outside the payroll office if an employee does not have one.

For each weakness, indicate an internal control procedure that management could implement to prevent it.

8–4. A questionnaire relating to the payroll functions of the Style-Rite Building Products Co. revealed that a number of control procedures are in effect.

a. The operating department supervisors, along with the personnel department, approve all employee changes (hirings, transfers, promotions, terminations).

b. Employee personnel records include authorizations for all deductions and withholdings.

c. Timekeeping is separate from payroll preparation and distribution.

d. An employee who is independent of payroll preparation and distribution reconciles the payroll bank account monthly.

e. A responsible officer independent of payroll preparation approves the payroll distribution.

For each procedure, indicate the test that provides evidence of the reliability of the internal control procedures.

8–5. Fireside Supplies used a computer to process personnel and payroll operations. Some of the procedures are as follows:

a. The personnel department hires new employees, assigns them ID numbers, and places them on the payroll. It also terminates employees and removes them from the payroll.

b. Timekeepers keep a daily record of the hours worked by employees in each department.

c. The payroll department keeps the Form W-4 deduction authorizations for all employees.

d. The computer department prepares the entire payroll, the payroll checks, and the withholding stubs accompanying the checks.

Explain how these controls might prevent overpayment to current employees or payment to fictitious employees.

CONTINUING CASE PROBLEM

Three years ago when it began business, Frontier Landscaping hired a number of students during the summer as part-time workers. All employees were paid in cash with pay envelopes as a convenience to employees and to save on clerical expenses.

On several occasions, employees failed to pick up their pay envelopes. Kathy Wood, who was in charge of payroll, would put the unclaimed wages in the petty cash fund so the cash could be used for disbursements. When the unpaid employees later asked for their wages, the money was taken from the petty cash fund.

Does this system provide proper internal control of unclaimed wages? If not, what procedures do you think Frontier should have used, even while continuing to use pay envelopes?

CHAPTER 9

COST-SAVING POLICIES AND TECHNIQUES

LEARNING OBJECTIVES

On completing this chapter, you will be able to:

1. Explain four policies for payroll and payroll tax savings.
2. Describe three approaches to payroll tax savings.
3. Discuss the unemployment tax-savings techniques.
4. List reasons for tax penalties and the monetary amounts involved.

While learning about payroll procedures and practices, Lois Arruda has become very aware of the tremendous possibilities for cost savings in payroll. With so many labor hours and dollars at stake, including payroll taxes, even a small percentage improvement can lead to significant cost savings overall.

Clark points out that the best approach for achieving savings is to reduce payroll directly insofar as possible because this approach also saves on payroll taxes. Reducing payroll taxes directly is the next most desirable strategy. Although many techniques involve decision making at higher levels of management, Lois realizes that the payroll department could play an important role in carrying out cost-saving measures by providing accurate and up-to-date payroll records to management, by paying close attention to tax- and report-filing deadlines in order to avoid penalties, and by suggesting possible areas for savings. She and Clark discuss the specific techniques available to the payroll department and to the company's management team.

265

EMPLOYMENT POLICIES FOR PAYROLL SAVINGS

An employer can reduce payroll costs through efficient personnel management policies regarding the retention of employees, the use of nonconventional workers, the control of overtime, and, when applicable and state-approved, implementation of work-sharing plans.

Retention of Employees

An employer derives substantial direct and indirect benefits from long-term employee retention. Keeping employees satisfied with their jobs and their compensation packages is the first step toward this goal. While employees expect periodic raises for good work, an employer can offer a number of nonwage payments to employees to increase their job satisfaction and assist them in keeping up with rising costs. An added advantage is that these payments are not taxable wages and are exempt from payroll taxes. Examples of such nonwage payments are fringe benefits, meals furnished by the employer, employment agency fees, and prizes and awards.

Fringe Benefits.   Some fringe benefits a company can offer its employees and their dependents are not wages and are therefore not subject to payroll taxes. These excludable fringe benefits include de minimus fringe benefits, qualified employee discounts, no-additional-costs services, working condition fringes, and merchandise gifts.

De minimus fringe benefits *De minimus fringe benefits* are of such minimal value or infrequent occurrence that keeping account of them is impractical. Examples include such occasional privileges extended to or taken by employees as occasional typing or copying of personal correspondence, use of the telephone for personal calls, parties, tickets for theatrical or athletic events, and traditional holiday gifts.

Benefits that are not taxable because they are of such minimal value or infrequent occurrence that keeping account of them is impractical.

EXAMPLE   Amalia's, a women's clothing store, offers its buyers theater tickets when they travel to New York on buying excursions.   ▲

Qualified employee discounts on goods cannot exceed the profit margin on sales to customers. Employee discounts on services cannot exceed 20% of the customer's price.

EXAMPLE   Nioga offers its employees a 35% discount off the retail price of all shoes sold at the company store.   ▲

No-additional-costs services are those that the company normally offers to customers. The company makes these services available to employees without a substantial additional cost to the employer, generally because of excess capacity. Examples include discounted or free railroad or airline tickets or hotel accommodations.

Working condition fringes *Working condition fringes* are services or property provided to employees in connection with the employer's business—business expenses that would be deductible if the employees had paid for them. Examples in-

Benefits that are not taxable because the employer provides them in connection with its business.

clude employer-provided vehicles, flights on company-provided aircraft, qualified use of a demonstration automobile, and parking on or near the employer's premises.

EXAMPLE   Jupiter Toys provides free parking adjacent to its plant for its employees. ▲

Merchandise gifts of nominal value (such as turkeys, hams, or champagne) are not wages and not subject to payroll taxes.

Meals. Meals furnished by the company for its convenience are also not considered wages and are exempt from payroll taxes. The value of a free meal meets the "convenience of the employer" test if the employer furnishes the meal for a substantial noncompensatory business reason. Meals furnished during working hours where the employee cannot be expected to eat elsewhere meet this test. The employer should set up conditions that must be met to receive supper money, such as working a minimum number of hours after regular closing hours or working after a certain time, say, 6 P.M. or 7 P.M.

Prizes and Awards. An employer can exclude from an employee's taxable wages the value of an award made for length of service or safety achievement if the employer can deduct the cost of the award. The award, to be deductible, must be in the form of tangible, personal property. Also not taxable is an employer's policy of rewarding employees for perfect attendance as with an extra vacation day or an extra paid day.

Use of Nonconventional Workers

Judicious planning of the employee work force by management can result in substantial payroll savings. This technique can be especially useful to businesses that have seasonal peaks and fluctuating work-force needs. Use of independent contractors, part-time workers, temporary agency help, and leased employees can all contribute to substantial payroll and payroll tax savings.

Independent Contractors. An employer can slash payroll costs by using independent contractors. Except for employees earning over the Social Security wage base, every $100 an employer spends on wages requires an additional payment of $7.65 in FICA taxes. By using independent contractors, the employer can save not only on FICA taxes but also on unemployment taxes and workers' compensation costs.

As discussed in Chapter 1, the determining factor for status as an independent contractor is control over the work done or product created. Often, the distinction is not clear-cut, however, and the facts of each case must govern the determination. An employer has the legal right to control the methods and results of its employees' services. If a business is paying wages to someone who is not controlled in this way, it may be making unnecessary FICA and unemployment tax payments.

EXAMPLE Bertha Ryan cleans a doctor's office once a week. Since she has 15 other customers whose offices she cleans, she is an independent contractor. ▲

Temporary agency help
Employees of a temporary help agency who work for clients of the agency.

Temporary Agency Help. If a business has fluctuating workloads, use of **temporary agency help** may cut payroll costs. An employer can hire temporary workers on a daily or weekly basis to do extra work during the busiest times. The employer issues a single check to the temporary help organization. The fees paid to the agency are not wages and are not subject to payroll taxes. The payroll savings result from:

1. Reduced state unemployment tax. An employer's unemployment tax rate depends on employee turnover. Using agency help rather than hiring and later laying off employees may prevent the company's experience rating from increasing the following year.

2. No federal FICA and unemployment taxes. The temporary help agency pays these taxes, not the employer.

3. No fringe benefits. Again, the temporary help agency is responsible for fringe benefit payments, not the employer.

4. No time off with pay. An employer is not responsible for time off taken by the temporaries, as might be the case for its own employees. Thus, an employer will not have to pay for time taken for vacations, holidays, sick days, jury duty or voting, or personal reasons.

Employee leasing *The situation when a company transfers employees to a leasing company, which leases the employees back to the original company.*

Leased Employees. **Employee leasing** occurs when an employer transfers its employees to a third party, which takes over all or a portion of the employer's responsibilities. The employer, or subscriber, officially releases its employees, who then become employees of the leasing company, which, in turn, leases these employees back to the subscriber. The leasing company is legally the employer of the leased employees and as such pays their wages, payroll taxes, and benefits.

The leasing company provides its workers with a benefit package in place of the one they previously had. The benefits can include medical, dental, and vision plans; life, accidental death, and dismemberment insurance; long-term disability coverage; and retirement plan benefits.

With employee leasing, an employer/subscriber does not need to get involved in the details of being an expert in human resources, payroll, or benefits administration. An employer should consider employee leasing if it is having problems with delinquent payroll taxes and increasing liabilities from discrimination.

Leasing is especially suitable for companies with fewer than 100 workers since they are too small to qualify for low group insurance rates and usually do not have pension benefits. Even larger companies may find it worthwhile to lease segments of their work force, particularly as an interim measure until a new division comes on board.

EXAMPLE Jupiter Toys is starting a new baby furniture division and expects its employees now making wooden toys to work in this division. During the training and startup period for the new division, Jupiter has decided to lease workers from Crafts for Hire Leasing Agency to work in its wooden toys division. ▲

Generally, the cost of leasing is about 25% above the wages paid to employees. Thus, for this one-quarter addition, an employer enjoys relief from payroll taxes, benefit contributions, and various administrative headaches.

Part-time Employees. Homemakers' shifts and part-time summer employment are two programs that involve the hiring of nonconventional employees. The so-called homemakers' shift coincides with school hours and permits mothers to work on the same schedule as their children's attendance at school. They also have the same vacation schedule as their children and may take time off from work for their children's illnesses. Sometimes college students replace the mothers during the summer.

Offering temporary employment to high school and college students gives employers extra help during vacation periods (such as during the summer or the Christmas season) as well as the chance to train young people for possible future full-time jobs. The students acquire knowledge of the company operations and the company establishes closer contact with the community and area schools.

Work-sharing Plans

Work sharing permits employers to cut their payrolls without cutting their work force. Through work sharing, an employer can withstand a recession, yet avoid the later costs of a layoff—the expense of hiring and training new workers when business improves. Work sharing is in effect in over 15 states.

Work-sharing plan *A plan for reducing workers' hours during a slowdown; employees receive less pay from the employer and the state covers part of the reduction.*

Under a **work-sharing plan**, an employer can reduce employee hours during a slowdown instead of eliminating jobs. The employees share the reduced hours and receive less pay, but the state makes up part of the reduction. The state payments come from the employer's unemployment tax account. Benefits paid equal the percentage reduction in wages multiplied by the weekly unemployment benefit the person would receive if unemployed.

California's plan, a model for other states, requires at least a 10% participation in work sharing by the work force of the entire company or a distinct unit and a reduction in wages of 10% or more. The state certifies the work-sharing plan for periods of six months.

EXAMPLE Mike Anson normally receives $400 a week at Caltron Graphics. During a downturn in business, Caltron reduces Mike's hours and earnings by 20% under a work-sharing plan. The maximum California weekly unemployment benefit is $230. Mike is eligible to receive 20% of the maximum. His total receipts consist of wages and unemployment benefits as follows:

$$(\$400 \times .80) + (\$230 \times .20) = \$320 + \$46 = \$366$$ ▲

The employee benefits from work-sharing through continued employment and the employer saves on payroll costs and unemployment insurance taxes.

Control of Overtime

The right amount of overtime—not too little and not too much—is the best policy for saving on wages. The company that doesn't pay any overtime often has more employees than it actually needs. Likewise, the company that pays a high percentage of its total payroll in overtime pay often needs to hire more employees.

Strategy for Overtime. An employer should periodically analyze its work force in terms of numbers and types of jobs performed. Good recordkeeping can make later analysis much easier and more useful. If the payroll is growing fast, the employer might look at the differences in regular and overtime costs. If overtime is a significant portion of the total payroll, the employer might consider varying the number of employees to solve the problem. Certain periods when business is booming may justify overtime, but the employer must watch for the overtime pitfall and develop a strategy for getting the job done at various levels of production and sales.

Guaranteed wage plan *A work arrangement, agreed to in writing, whereby an employee agrees to complete a job in an indeterminate number of hours and receives straight-time for all hours worked with only an extra half-hour premium for hours over 40.*

Guaranteed Wage Plan. A **guaranteed wage plan** or irregular workweek permits the employer to control and anticipate weekly labor cost. If working hours vary greatly, the plan serves as an effective way to keep overtime costs at a minimum. The Fair Labor Standard Act permits a guaranteed wage plan for workers who spend irregular hours each week on the job.

The employer guarantees an employee a fixed wage each week for a specified number of hours, but no more than sixty. The employee receives the same fixed pay regardless of the number of hours worked in any one week and, if nonexempt, a decreased overtime rate.

This overtime control technique works well with employees whose duties force them to work widely varying hours, such as on-call service people, insurance adjusters, and newspaper reporters. The plan is impractical if the employee works at least 40 hours a week and only overtime hours are irregular.

The guaranteed wage plan must be in writing as part of a bona fide employment or collective bargaining contract. The contract must specify a regular pay rate of at least the legal minimum rate per hour, plus overtime pay of at least time and a half for hours over 40 a week.

EXAMPLE Replace-It-Fast, an on-call windshield replacement company, has five replacement specialists available around-the-clock in different locations throughout a large metropolitan area. If the company wants to guarantee each replacement specialist $385 a week for an average workweek of 50 hours, the basic hourly rate must be $7.00 and the overtime rate $10.50. The employee receives $385 per week regardless of whether the hours worked are 30, 40, or 50, but the employer must pay overtime for any hours over 40. In one month, Janet Wheeler, the replacement specialist on the south side of the city, worked the following hours for a total compensation of $1,631.00 for the month.

Week	Hours Worked	Guaranteed Wages	Overtime Wages	Total Wages
1	50	$ 385.00	$38.50	$ 423.50
2	30	385.00		385.00
3	39	385.00		385.00
4	55	385.00	52.50	437.50
		$1,540.00	$91.00	$1,631.00

Computations for

Week 1: Average Hourly Rate = $385 ÷ 50 hours = $7.70 per hour

Overtime Rate = $7.70 ÷ 2 = $3.85 per hour

Overtime Wages = $3.85 × 10 hours = $38.50

Week 4: Average Hourly Rate= $385 ÷ 55 hours = $7.00 per hour

Overtime Rate = $7.00 ÷ 2 = $3.50

Overtime Wages = $3.50 × 15 hours = $52.50 ▲

Dual or Multiple Duties. An employer can keep some overtime payments to a minimum if workers have dual or multiple job responsibilities. If overtime is necessary, the employer makes an agreement with the employee to pay overtime based on the type of work being done. Then, the employer can try to arrange the overtime for work that has the lowest hourly rate.

EXAMPLE Harry Ryan works 48 hours a week for Paragon Cleaners. He works the first 40 hours as a pick-up and delivery driver at $6.00 an hour and the next 8 hours as a presser at $5.50 an hour. Harry receives $240.00 for regular hours (40 × $6.00) and $66.00 for the overtime hours (8 hours × $8.25). ▲

Selection of Workweek. Changing the workweek can cut overtime. The law says an employer must pay time-and-a-half when an employee works more than 40 hours in any one workweek. A workweek is any period of 168 hours or seven consecutive 24-hour periods. It can start at any hour of the day and any day of the week and does not have to coincide with the payroll period. The employer should set up a workweek that will include no more than 40 hours in one of two weeks.

EXAMPLE Employees at Whittaker Corp., a package and parcel delivery service, worked for ten consecutive days and then had four days off. The workweek started on Monday and ended on Sunday, resulting in a 56-hour workweek the first week and a 24-hour workweek the second week. Every two weeks, the company paid 16 hours overtime to each employee. If Whittaker Corp. changed the workweek to begin on Saturday and end on Friday, only five of the ten consecutive workdays would fall in any one week. The result is no overtime. ▲

Obviously, an employer can't change the workweek to evade the wage and hour laws. But a legitimate change, if permanent, is permissible.

TECHNIQUES FOR ACHIEVING SAVINGS ON PAYROLL TAXES

Not only can an employer save substantial sums on payroll taxes by reducing payroll, but the business can also save on payroll taxes directly. One technique is to pay wages, insofar as possible, that are exempt from FICA taxes and another is to make payments not classified as wages.

Special Payments Exempt from FICA and FUTA Taxes

For FICA and FUTA purposes, taxable compensation generally means all wages, including the fair value of noncash payments for services performed by employees working in covered employment. Not all wages are subject to FICA and FUTA, only those wages received in covered employment. Although FICA and FUTA coverage applies to most professions and industries, notable exceptions include:

- certain agricultural and domestic workers
- family members, under 18 years of age (21 years of age for FUTA), employed by a parent, spouse, son, or daughter
- students working for a private school
- ministers and members of religious orders under a vow of poverty
- newspaper carriers under 18 or newspaper and magazine vendors buying at fixed prices
- railroad workers (they have their own federal retirement system)
- employer contributions to a qualified retirement plan
- sickness or injury payments under workers' compensation

Payments Not Classified as Taxable Wages or Compensation

An employer cannot do much about wages or other compensation subject to FICA tax because these payments result from covered employment. But one strategy that can help reduce both FICA and FUTA taxes is to make payments that are not taxable wages and therefore are exempt from FICA and FUTA taxes. Here are some payments of that nature.

1. Reimbursement of payments for dependent care assistance plans under a written, nondiscriminatory program for the care of children under age 13 or any dependent who is incapable of self-care. Such dependent care assistance payments are not wages since the employee will be able to exclude the assistance from income. The tax law provides that employees can exclude amounts up to $5,000 ($2,500 if married filing separately) paid or incurred by their employer for furnishing dependent care assistance to them under a dependent care assistance plan, with any excess included in the employee's gross income.

2. Qualified educational assistance plans are not wages up to $5,250 and therefore not subject to payroll taxes. This tax-favored status applies to undergraduate courses beginning before June 1, 2000. The program does not cover graduate courses started after June 30, 1996. In any event, employer-paid tuition for job-related courses will remain tax-free as a working condition fringe benefit. A job-related course is one that must maintain or improve skills required for the job or be required by the employer or by law as a condition of continuing employment in the employee's current job.

EXAMPLE   Moreland Business Forms reimburses its employees for business courses, provided the employees get at least a B grade.   ▲

3. Group term life insurance premiums on coverage up to $50,000 under a nondiscriminatory plan are not wages and are not subject to payroll taxes.

4. Medical and accident claims and medical expense reimbursements are not wages and are not subject to payroll taxes.

5. Reimbursed and employer-paid qualified moving expenses for tax purposes are excludible as wages unless the employee deducted the expenses in a prior year. Nonqualified moving expenses are includible as wages and are subject to FITW, FICA, and FUTA taxes.

EXAMPLE   Jupiter Toys transfers toy designers to other plants for one-year assignments. It pays the designers' nonqualified moving expenses, which are included in their wages and are subject to withholding and FICA and FUTA taxes.   ▲

6. In general, pension distributions and retirement pay are wages subject to withholding unless the recipient elects not to have tax withheld by completing Form W-4P, Withholding Certificate for Pension or Annuity Payments. Amounts paid in the form of annuities to a retired employee are exempt from withholding and payroll taxes.

7. An allowance paid under an accountable travel and entertainment expense plan is not wages and is exempt from payroll taxes. Payments made under a nonaccountable plan, such as per diem allowances, are wages subject to withholding and payroll taxes. To qualify as an accountable plan, expenses under the plan must have a business connection and the employees must document the expenses and return unspent amounts.

EXAMPLE   The D. F. Cavell Public Accounting Firm pays its employees the standard government per diem allowance. The CPAs who travel provide no documentation for this reimbursement, so expenses are not deductible.   ▲

8. Amounts paid to employees as advances or reimbursement for uniforms are not wages and are exempt from payroll taxes, if the expenses have a business connection. The employees must document the expenses and return any advanced funds they cannot document.

EXAMPLE   Doctors Grana and Whiteman reimburse their dental assistants for uniforms purchased for wear in their orthodontic practice. The uniforms are therefore considered expenses deductible by the employer and are not considered wages.   ▲

9. A successor employer can count wages paid by the old employer toward the taxable wage base for the year for each employee who continues to work for the successor, provided the employee immediately begins working for the successor and received wages from the predecessor. Thus, when the employee's wages for the year reach the cut-off points for Social Security and FUTA taxes, the employer is no longer responsible for their payment.

10. Loans are not taxable wages when made whereas drawing account advances—that is, advances against future commissions—are taxable. If the employee signs a written acknowledgement of the debt and the business carries the advance in its records as a loan, it is exempt from payroll taxes.

Use of a Common Paymaster

When an employee works for two or more corporations, each employer must pay Social Security and FUTA taxes on the wages it pays to that employee, up to the taxable wage limits. If the employers qualify as related corporations, they can save on these payroll taxes by using a **common paymaster.** Use of a common paymaster permits each corporation to pay payroll taxes only on the total wages up to the Social Security and FUTA limits.

Common paymaster *In a group of two or more related companies, the company that acts as paymaster for the group.*

Corporations are considered related if they pass either the 50% test or the 30% test. The 50% test states that if one corporation has a 50% or more relationship in the other corporation, then the corporations are related. The relationships are possession of common stock or voting power, membership on the board of directors, and serving as officers of the corporation. The 30% test states that the corporations are related if 30% or more of one corporation's employees are employees of the other corporation.

The common paymaster is responsible for keeping payroll records, filing information and tax returns, issuing Forms W-2 on wages paid, and paying the taxes on compensation it pays out as a common paymaster. The law assumes that the common paymaster is the sole employer of the employee. Regardless of this arrangement, each related corporation is responsible for its share of the taxes and each is entitled to any applicable deductions.

EXAMPLE   Alex Crane works equally for Able, Inc., and Baker Corp., which are related corporations, and receives an annual salary of $80,000, with $40,000 from each corporation. If either Able or Baker acts as a common paymaster, the total tax liability for the two corporations will be as follows:

Employer's share of FICA taxes (limit of $76,200):
6.20% × $76,200 = $4,724.40
1.45% × $80,000 = <u>1,160.00</u>
$5,884.40

FUTA taxes:
0.8% × $7,000   56.00
                    $5,940.40

If neither corporation is a common paymaster, then the total tax liability for *each* corporation would be as follows:

Employer's share of FICA taxes:
6.20% × $40,000 = $2,480.00
1.45% × $40,000 =   580.00
                 $3,060.00

FUTA taxes:
0.8% × $7,000   56.00
                   $3,116.00

The total tax liability for both corporations would be as follows:

Able, Inc. $3,116.00
Baker Corp.   3,116.00
                  $6,232.00

The tax savings in using a common paymaster:
Employer taxes without common paymaster $6,232.00
Employer taxes with common paymaster   −5,940.40
                                          $ 291.60

Multiplying this amount by the number of employees employed by both corporations shows how the use of a common paymaster could result in very substantial savings.   ▲

TECHNIQUES FOR ACHIEVING SAVINGS ON UNEMPLOYMENT TAXES

A good understanding of unemployment insurance can lead to significant cost savings. Unemployment insurance provides compensation to employees during periods of temporary unemployment. A joint federal-state program funds unemployment insurance. Employers, and in some states employees, fund the program.

The employer contributions for unemployment taxes result from the following calculations:

- SUTA taxes = Assigned State Rate × Taxable Wage Base
- FUTA taxes = Fixed Federal Rate × Taxable Wage Base

Significant cost savings result from control of the taxable wage base or the **assigned state rate,** since FUTA taxes depend on a fixed federal rate.

Assigned state rate *The experience rating, a percentage, that indicates the state unemployment insurance rate.*

Limiting Taxable Wages

Knowledge of the definitions of employer, employees, and wages may help in keeping down taxable wages. Certain taxable wages as discussed previously are not subject to either FICA or FUTA taxes. Also, an employee may be exempt from SUTA taxes.

For FUTA purposes, an employer is one who has, on each of 20 days (each in a different calendar week) during the preceding or current calendar year, hired at least one employee for some portion of the day or who pays wages of $1,500 or more during any calendar quarter in the current or preceding calendar year.

Just as an employer may not qualify as a FUTA employer, some workers may not be employees for FUTA purposes. Controlling unemployment taxes is a procedure that requires two steps. The employer must make sure that it is

- paying taxes only on workers classified as employees
- examining payments to employees to determine whether or not they are taxable wages.

Reducing the Number of Covered Employees. One method that leads to savings on unemployment taxes is to reduce the number of covered employees. Many types of workers are exempt from FUTA and most SUTA taxes including

- independent contractors
- temporary agency employees
- partners or sole proprietors of a business
- members of boards of directors
- life insurance salespeople paid solely on commission
- religious, educational, and charitable organization employees
- agricultural, fishing industry, and domestic service employees.

Since temporary help and independent contractors are not subject to unemployment taxes, they are particularly useful for seasonal businesses, such as summer camping equipment retailers and agricultural or landscaping companies. Likewise, if the workload is variable, use of temporary agency employees may help keep an employer's experience rating low since such workers cannot make claims against the company's account.

Reducing the Amount of Taxable Wages. Another way to save on unemployment taxes is to reduce taxable wages. The following payments are exempt from FUTA and SUTA taxes:

- reimbursements for business expenses or moving expenses
- allowances for tools or equipment and laundry or uniforms
- benefit plans, such as qualified pension plans, profit-sharing plans or simplified employee pensions
- tips of less than $20 per month
- qualifying child care or dependent care plans.

Controlling the Assigned Rate

The unemployment taxes paid by an employer go into a pooled unemployment insurance fund. In effect, all the employers in a particular state contribute to the cost of unemployment insurance. State unemployment

Experience rating *Method used by states, based on favorable or unfavorable employment history, to determine the percentage to apply to gross wages in the computation of unemployment taxes.*

taxes depend on the **experience rating** as determined by the number of claims filed. The fewer the claims made against an employer's account, the lower the experience rating. The monetary effect of even a small reduction in the experience rating may be substantial when applied to the total taxable wages. For example, on a payroll of $400,000, an experience rating of 1% versus 2% will save $4,000.

As described in Chapter 4, the assigned rate depends on the employer's previous experience with employment and unemployment, and specifically the prior 12 months. A favorable record in hiring and keeping employees translates to a lower assigned rate. Sound management policies and practices are vital to maintaining such a rate.

States assign an initial experience rating to newly covered employers until they can establish their own experience rating. To keep this rating as low as possible, a company should challenge any claims they believe to be based on false and inaccurate statements.

The experience ratings serve as percentage multipliers for the calculation of unemployment insurance taxes. The rating system attempts to adjust unemployment insurance taxes with the amount of benefits charged against the employer's account. Generally, the experience rating depends on the balance in the reserve account. States may use one of four different methods to establish the experience rating used to calculate an employer's tax liability. To illustrate the four methods, we'll apply each method to the payroll of Jupiter Toys. Jupiter Toys has 80 employees with a total taxable payroll for FUTA and SUTA purposes of $560,000. During the year, the company laid off 7 workers who collected $4,200 in benefits.

Reserve ratio *A method used to compute the unemployment experience rating that takes into account the taxes paid and the amount of benefits charged to the employer's account.*

Reserve Ratio. This method, used by most states, applies a long-term perspective to an employer's experience. The **reserve ratio** formula balances taxes paid against the amount of benefits charged to an employer's account. The formula is as follows:

$$\text{Reserve ratio (RR)} = \frac{\text{Reserve end of year (Re)}}{\text{Taxable payroll (TP)}}$$

The reserve at the end of the year equals the reserve at the beginning of the year plus taxes paid minus benefits charged.

EXAMPLE

Jupiter has a reserve account balance at the beginning of the year of $64,000. It paid taxes of $10,200 and had benefits charged against its account of $4,200. Its reserve ratio is:

$$RR = Re \div TP = (\$64,000 + \$10,200 - \$4,200) \div \$560,000$$
$$RR = \$70,000 \div \$560,000 = 12.5\% \qquad \blacktriangle$$

The reserve ratio of 12.5% is then compared to a specific table of equivalencies established by the state to determine the **experience rating**, which can be anywhere from 0% to the maximum allowed in each state. The maximum allowable rate in New York State is 5.4%.

Benefit ratio *A method used to compute the unemployment experience rating that takes into account the benefits charged against an employer's taxable payroll, usually for a period of one to three years.*

Benefit Ratio. The **benefit ratio** measures the relationship between benefits charged against an employer's account and the taxable payroll. The benefit ratio considers only a short-term experience (usually one to three years).

$$\text{Benefit ratio (BR)} = \frac{\text{Total benefits charged (B)}}{\text{Taxable payroll (TP)}}$$

EXAMPLE Benefits charged against Jupiter total $4,200 on a taxable payroll of $560,000. The benefit ratio is as follows:

$$\text{BR} = \$4,200 \div \$560,000 = 0.75\% \qquad \blacktriangle$$

Again, comparing this ratio to a table of benefit ratio equivalencies would yield an experience rating somewhere between 0% and the maximum allowable.

Benefit-wage ratio *A method used to compute the unemployment experience rating that takes into account the incidence rather than the severity of unemployment.*

Benefit-Wage Ratio. The **benefit-wage ratio** is a method, also based on short-term experience of one to three years, that measures the incidence rather than the severity of unemployment. A claim reduces the employer's account by the amount of wages earned by the claimant up to the state's taxable wage base limit.

$$\text{Benefit-wage ratio (BWR)} = \frac{\text{Total benefit wages charged (BW)}}{\text{Taxable payroll (TP)}}$$

EXAMPLE The seven workers laid off by Jupiter earned $80,000 in base period wages. Its benefit-wage ratio is:

$$\text{BWR} = \$80,000 \div \$560,000 = 14.3\% \qquad \blacktriangle$$

Comparing this benefit-wage ratio to the state's benefit-wage ratio table of equivalencies would translate to an experience rating between 0% and the maximum allowable.

Payroll variation *A method used to compute the unemployment experience rating that takes into account the employer's experience by measuring and comparing the period to period changes in payroll.*

Payroll Variation. This method does not consider the incidence and severity of unemployment claims. This method, unlike the reserve ratio method, calculates the employer's experience by measuring and comparing the period-to-period **payroll variations**.

EXAMPLE If Jupiter Toys maintains a taxable payroll at $560,000 or above, then its experience rating will be favorable. ▲

Reducing the Assigned Rate

Effective payroll management means hiring, managing, and discharging employees to minimize unemployment insurance claims against the company. The best overall policy is to achieve a low employee turnover since a high turnover means a higher experience rating. Lowering this rate by even a small amount can result in significant savings. Some effective strategies for achieving low employee turnover and thus reducing the tax liability of the company include:

1. Hiring qualified long-term personnel. Underqualified or overqualified personnel usually result in problems, terminations, and increased SUTA taxes. Before hiring, an employer should know the job requirements and the conditions and terms of employment. A complete job description is essential. The employer should check references, particularly those from the most recent employer. A good idea is to have a supervisor talk to the applicant's direct supervisor. Testing an applicant's competence will help ensure that only those with the skills needed for the job are hired, thereby reducing the possibility of having to discharge an unsatisfactory employee.

2. Managing employees effectively. When employees know exactly what their employer expects of them, they tend to have higher job satisfaction.

3. Discharging unsatisfactory employees. Policies for disciplining or firing employees should include documentation on performance and immediate action, when required.

An employer can also take some important steps to keep a low experience rating when employees do leave, either on their own or through discharge. These approaches include:

1. Assisting laid-off employees to find jobs with other companies to reduce the unemployment benefits charged to the employer's account.

2. Verifying that only eligible claimants receive payments. An employee may be ineligible to receive benefits if he or she is unavailable for work, is unemployed due to a labor dispute or refusal to accept suitable work, was fired for misconduct or quit without good cause, is self-employed and receiving some form of compensation, or misrepresented facts to receive benefits.

When the employer receives the statement of benefits charged against the reserve account, it should verify from its records that each claimant had actually worked for the company and was not working while collecting benefits. The employer should also verify that the statement accurately lists the amount of the contributions paid for all past years and the amount of charges against the account.

3. Saving the documentation if a worker is discharged for misconduct. Documentation consists of attendance reports, records of violations of rules, and other misconduct reports.

4. Conducting an exit interview. This technique may prove to be a surprising means for holding down unemployment taxes. An employer may acquire information useful in preventing or lessening the payment of benefits. For instance, the employee may reveal a previously undisclosed skill needed by the company. The employer may then rehire the employee or notify the local employment office of this skill. In either event, if the employee gets a suitable job and doesn't draw unemployment benefits, the employer's experience rate will not suffer.

IN THE NEWS

COPING WITH RIGHTS TO DISCHARGE

According to newspaper reports, some companies have given up the right to discharge employees at will. For instance, a *Wall Street Journal* article reported that Federal Express and the Donnelly Corp. have turned firing authority over to independent panels as a way to build employee trust and reduce the threat of wrongful discharge lawsuits. At Federal Express, the discharged employee picks three members from a company-established pool to sit on a five-member board.

Other companies, such as Northrop Corp., use outside arbitrators when they can't resolve appeals internally. Employees discharged by CIGNA have access to appeals panels made up of a cross section of employees, including one member selected by the discharged employee.

The American Civil Liberties Union supports legislation to eliminate the employer's right to fire at will and to provide arbitration. According to the ACLU, the average jury verdict in wrongful discharge cases is now over $500,000.

Fighting for the right to fire employees can be costly in other ways. Companies may be so wary of lawsuits that they may end up retaining mediocre workers, using overtime or temporaries to make up for inadequate work, offering overly generous severance payments, or going overboard on employee screening and performance reviews.

TECHNIQUES FOR ACHIEVING SAVINGS BY AVOIDING PENALTIES

The Internal Revenue Service and the various state tax departments impose penalties for violations of the rules and regulations governing the payment of all types of taxes, including income taxes. The various procedures for reconciliation of payroll records to reporting and deposit requirements help ensure that the employer will pay all payroll taxes, as required and when due, thereby avoiding tax penalties. Unless justified by reasonable cause, the employer is subject to penalties for failure to file, to pay, and to make deposits. First, we'll quickly look at the required tax documents; then we'll look at the penalties for missing deadlines and other specific violations of the rules and regulations.

Tax Documents

As discussed in earlier chapters, particularly Chapter 6, payroll regulations require the completion of a number of government forms. The completed forms demonstrate compliance with payroll regulations. Let's review some of these forms.

Form 940, Employer's Annual Federal Unemployment (FUTA) Tax Return, filed with the IRS annually, shows the quarterly and the total federal unemployment tax liabilities, both before and after the state unemployment tax credit, and the tax deposits made against these liabilities (see Chapter 4).

Form 941, Employer's Quarterly Federal Tax Return, filed with the IRS, shows the quarterly gross earnings, the federal income tax and FICA taxes withheld and due, and the federal deposits made using Form 8109 or electronically against the total tax liability. Some states and local governments may require a similar form for tax reporting (see Chapter 3).

Form 945, Annual Return of Withheld Federal Income Tax, filed with the IRS annually, shows the federal income tax withheld from nonpayroll payments (pensions, annuities, IRAs, other deferred income, military retirement, gambling winnings, backup withholding) and the federal deposits made (Form 8109) against the total tax liability.

Form 8109, Federal Tax Deposit Coupon, filed with an authorized federal depository, accompanies the payment of tax liabilities not only for payroll taxes (Forms 940 and 941) but also for corporate income tax (Form 1120) and other taxes (Form 945) (see Chapter 6).

Form W-2, Wage and Tax Statement, sent annually to employees, the IRS, and other tax authorities, shows the annual regular and supplemental wages and tips, the federal income tax and FICA taxes withheld, state income taxes withheld, and data relating to other receipts and payments.

Form W-4, Employee's Withholding Allowance Certificate, completed by the employee and filed with the employer, lists the number of allowances claimed by the employee for the purpose of withholding federal income tax from the employee's gross earnings (see Chapter 3).

Form W-5, Earned Income Credit Advance Payment Certificate, completed by the employee and filed with the employer, states the expected eligibility and election by the employee to receive advance payment of the earned income credit (see Chapter 3).

Tax Penalties

Penalties may be assessed not only for late or delinquent tax deposits and returns but also for late filing of information returns and wage statements.

Failure to File Tax Returns.   The penalty for failure to file a tax return applies to returns that require tax payments. The penalty for failure to file tax returns is 5% of the tax for up to one month, with an extra 5% of each additional month or fraction thereof, up to a maximum of 25%. The minimum penalty for failure to file a return within 60 days of the due date is the lesser of $100 or 100% of the tax due. The failure to file penalty applies to all returns that require tax payments (Form 1040, Form 1120, etc.) but, for payroll purposes, the penalty refers mainly to Form 941.

The penalty for failure to pay the tax is 0.5% of the unpaid tax shown on the return, less credits for each month or fractional month of delinquency, up to a maximum of 25%. The interest rate for delinquent payment is the federal short-term rate plus 3%, adjusted quarterly. This penalty is not levied until 11 days after the IRS demand notice.

Failure to Make Deposits.   The penalty for failure to make timely deposits in an authorized depository is equal to the applicable percentage of the amount of the underpayment. The applicable percentage is 2% if the payment is no more than 5 days late, 5% if more than 5 days but not more than 15 days late; 10% if more than 15 days late; and 15% in cases of jeopardy, that is, if the employer does not deposit the taxes by the date given in the notice and demand for payment.

Payment with a Bad Check.   The penalty for submitting a bad check in payment of taxes is 2% of the amount of the check. If the check is for less than $750, the penalty is the lesser of $15 or the amount of the check. No penalty is imposed if the check is tendered in good faith. Any penalty is in addition to the liability for the full payment of the amount of the check.

Failure to File Information Returns.   The penalty for failure to file an information return (such as Form 1099) on or before the due date and for any failure to include all the information required on the return is $50 for each failure, up to a maximum of $250,000 for all failures during the calendar year. Correction of the failure within a specified period of time reduces the penalty as follows:

1. $15 a return (maximum $7,500 reduction) if filed within 30 days after the due date
2. $30 a return (maximum $150,000 reduction) if filed later than 30 days after the due date but before August 1
3. $50 a return (maximum $250,000 reduction) if not filed by August 1.

Failure to Furnish Wage Statements.   The penalty for failure to give an employee a Wage and Tax Statement (Form W-2) by the due date or failure to include all information required on the statement is $50 for each failure, but not more than $100,000 a year. If the failure is an intentional disregard of the requirements to furnish the statement, the penalty is the greater of $100 a statement or 10% of the amount required to be shown on the statement with no limit on the maximum penalty in a calendar year. For willful failure to furnish a proper statement or for willfully providing a false or fraudulent statement, the penalty is $50 for each violation, in addition to possible criminal penalties.

REVIEW QUESTIONS

9–1. What are some fringe benefits deductible as business expenses by the employer and not taxable to the employee?

9–2. What other noncash payments may help employers retain employees with little or no cost to the employer.

9–3. Describe two employment programs that use nonconventional employees.

9–4. What is meant by a strategy for overtime?

9–5. Explain how the guaranteed wage plan or irregular workweek may save overtime costs.

9–6. Explain how having workers with dual or multiple job responsibilities can save on overtime.

9–7. In what way may adjusting the workweek cut down on overtime?

9–8. Explain the difference between an independent contractor and an employee.

9–9. In what ways does the use of temporary agency help save on payroll and payroll taxes?

9–10. How does the leasing of employees work? What circumstances would make leasing of employees advisable?

9–11. What is work-sharing and when is it especially suitable?

9–12. Name at least five types of wages not subject to FICA taxes.

9–13. List at least five payments (made to or on behalf of employees) that are not considered wages and are therefore exempt from FICA and FUTA taxes.

Review Questions
(cont.)

9–14. What are the rules that govern whether loans are taxable wages?

9–15. Under what circumstances will reimbursement or payments for dependent care assistance plans not be considered wages?

9–16. With respect to tax withholding, how do medical expenses and moving expenses differ and how are they similar?

9–17. Under what conditions are group term life insurance and retirement plan distributions subject to withholding?

9–18. Explain the difference between accountable and nonaccountable travel and entertainment expense plans.

9–19. Under what circumstances are uniform allowances exempt from wage and payroll tax liability?

9–20. How can a successor employer save on payroll taxes?

9–21. Explain how the use of a common paymaster saves on payroll taxes.

9–22. How is the employer's contribution to state unemployment tax calculated?

9–23. List two ways that employers can reduce taxable wages for FUTA.

9–24. What is meant by the assigned rate for SUTA purposes? What determines it?

9–25. Name the four methods most states use to calculate the employer's tax liability for state unemployment insurance.

9–26. Name at least four steps an employer can take to lower its experience rating even when employees leave the company.

9–27. Name five types of workers ineligible for unemployment benefits.

9–28. Name the actions that lead to the imposition of penalties with regard to the payment of payroll taxes. What are the penalties for each of these actions?

DISCUSSION QUESTIONS

9–1. The Cascade Paper Corporation hired a group of engineers for a six-month period to redesign its production line to incorporate new paper forming machines and computerized techniques. Under what circumstances would these engineers be considered employees? Independent contractors?

9–2. Some women's rights organizations regard special employment arrangements made for mothers as job discrimination. These groups feel that the so-called mommy track is simply an excuse to hold back promotions for women on the basis of their lesser commitment to the success of the business. Do you agree or disagree?

9–3. The training wage permitted some employers to hire students and save on costs. However, some groups look upon it as a way for businesses to take advantage of employees with low wages. Do you agree or disagree?

9–4. The Hammer Construction Company is going through difficult times and has reduced its payroll of construction workers. To assist its former long-time employees to find work, Hammer has agreed to reimburse those employees for college courses related to their work. Under what circumstances are these amounts paid by the employer not wages?

9–5. Two techniques for saving on payroll are the guaranteed wage plan or irregular workweek schedule and the dual or multiple duties arrangement. Opponents believe that under these plans employees subject themselves to unfair overtime compensation. Explain this point of view and list reasons why employees might accept these plans under particular circumstances.

EXERCISES

Where applicable in the following exercises, assume the following tax rates: Social Security, 6.20%; Medicare, 1.45%; FUTA, 0.8%; and SUTA, 4.2%.

9–1. Jupiter Toys provides the following employee benefits, with the average cost or value per year as indicated.

	Value per Year
Parking near the plant	$1,050
Meals if employee works 2 hours overtime	400
Expense reimbursement (accountable plan)	1,600
Use of telephone for personal calls	1,050
Contribution to pension plan	1,500
Qualified educational assistance payments	2,000
Vacation pay	1,200
Discount at company store	200
Medical insurance	2,000
Moving expense reimbursements—nonqualified	500

Which of these benefits are considered wages?

9–2. James Husek, a dentist, has hired two part-time workers at 20 hours per week each to serve as his dental assistants. Beth Greer, a housewife, works from 8 A.M. to 12 noon and Debra Brown, a college student, works from 1 P.M. to 5 P.M. Beth receives $6.50 an hour while Debra gets $6.00 an hour. Neither Beth nor Debra is eligible for any benefits except medical insurance paid by Dr. Husek.

If the dentist hired a full-time worker instead of the two part-time employees, he would have to pay $7.00 per hour and cover that person on his self-employment retirement plan at 15% of wages. How much has Dr. Husek saved with his current situation?

$ _____

9–3. The Seneca Pickle Farm has a choice of hiring two new employees or increasing the overtime of its current staff of eight employees by an average of 10 hours a week. The current employees are paid $8.00 an hour; the new employees would be hired at $7.00 an hour. The current employees receive approximately 18% of wages in benefits; during the first year, the new employees would receive about 12% of wages in benefits. Which course of action would be the most cost effective for Seneca? What is the monetary difference on a weekly basis?

Most cost-effective approach   _____

Weekly monetary difference $ _____

9–4. Aries Tool Works has decided to hire independent contractors to design a new tool-making machine rather than hire its own engineers. It is estimated that this job will take 240 hours. The Aries engineers would be paid $10,000 for the job. All earnings are subject to FICA taxes (disregard unemployment and workers' compensation). The rate for the independent contractors is $60 per hour. Compare the cost of employees versus independent contractors for this design job.

9–5. Lucinda Fabrics needs to increase production to keep up with the demand for its new polyester blend. It can either hire four new employees or engage four temporary agency workers. Lucinda pays its employees $7 per hour

Exercises (cont.)

and they receive approximately 20% in fringe benefits (such as medical insurance, sick pay, pension plan, etc.). Temporary workers would be paid $9 per hour with no benefits. Compare the cost of employees versus temporary workers for a 40-hour week.

9–6. Cataract Abrasives is considering transferring employees in its grain division to a leasing company and then leasing these workers. The leased workers would receive wages that are 22.5% above those paid to regular employees. Besides payroll taxes, estimated at 11%, other costs that the company would not have to pay on a percentage basis are vacation pay (3%) and other benefits (11%). The payroll of the grain division is $80,000 a year. What is the extra cost or savings in using leased workers?

$ _____

9–7. At the beginning of the year, Banner Bottling Works has a reserve balance of $120,000 in its state unemployment account. During the year, Banner paid additional taxes of $18,200 and benefits charged against its account were $9,200. The taxable payroll was $840,000.

a. What is Banner's reserve ratio?   _____

b. What is its benefit ratio?   _____

9–8. During the course of the year, Banner Bottling Works laid off two employees who earned a total of $30,000 in base-period wages. The taxable payroll in the current year was $840,000 and in the previous year was $780,000.

a. What is the benefit-wage ratio?   _____

b. Is the payroll variation favorable or not?   _____

9–9. NuTime Fashions had accumulated tax liabilities consisting of federal income tax withholding of $56,000, Social Security taxes of $34,205, and Medicare taxes of $8,000. Three days after the due date, NuTime deposited $85,000 and five days later, an additional $8,295 and three weeks later, the balance owed. Must NuTime pay a penalty? If so, how much?

$ _____

9–10. Jupiter Toys failed to file its Form 941 on time and also failed to pay a tax deposit owed of $46,000 until nine days after it was due. What are the tax penalties charged for the amount not reported nor paid on time?

$ _____

PROBLEMS

9–1. Wilhem Stein is a repair and maintenance mechanic at the Speedee Car Wash Service. He works on a guaranteed wage plan of $451 a week for an average workweek of 44 hours. One week, Wilhem worked 50 hours. Complete the following items to calculate Wilhem's gross wages for the week.

a. Guaranteed wage $ _____

b. Actual hours worked if over 40   _____

c. Hourly rate (a ÷ b) $ _____

d. Overtime rate (c × .5) $ _____

e. Overtime hours (b − 40) $ _____

Problems (cont.)

f. Overtime pay (d × e) $_____

g. Gross wages (a + f) $_____

9–2. Susan Garrett has multiple duties for the Monaco Dress Shop. She acts as a hostess for fashion shows and special showings and also as a buyer of new lines for the store. One week she worked 22 hours as a hostess and 26 hours as a buyer. She receives $10 an hour as a hostess and $12 an hour as a buyer. If Monaco pays Susan the overtime rate for the time she worked as a hostess, calculate her gross earnings for the week. (Complete the following items to calculate Susan's gross wages.)

	1 Lower-Paying Job	2 Higher-Paying Job	3 Total
a. Hours worked	_____	_____	_____
b. Hourly rate	_____	_____	_____
c. Regular pay	_____	_____	_____
d. Overtime hours (a3 − 40)	_____	_____	_____
e. Overtime rate (1.5 × b1 − b1)	_____	_____	_____
f. Overtime pay (d1 × e1)	_____	_____	_____
g. Gross wages (c + f)	_____	_____	_____

9–3. Employees at the Napa Valley Winery are on a work-sharing plan. Jose Perez normally receives $360 a week, but Napa Valley has reduced his hours and earnings by 25%. Jose receives unemployment benefits (maximum $230) to make up for part of his lost wages. What are his total receipts? (Use the following formula.)

Receipts = [(1.00 − fractional reduction in wages) × (Regular wages)] + [(Fractional reduction in wages) × (Unemployment benefits)].

9–4. Eastern Machine Shop and the Glendale Tool Works are related corporations. Charlene Mayne works equally for the two corporations and receives an annual salary of $84,000. If the FICA rates are 6.2% for Social Security taxes and 1.45% for Medicare taxes and the FUTA rate is 0.8%, what are the total FICA and FUTA taxes with and without using a common paymaster?

	Without Common Paymaster	With Common Paymaster
a. Annual salary	_____	_____
b. Social Security wages (up to wage base limit)	_____	_____
c. Medicare wages	_____	_____
d. Social Security tax (0.062 × b)	_____	_____
e. Medicare tax (0.0145 × c)	_____	_____

Problems (cont.)

	Without Common Paymaster	With Common Paymaster
f. FUTA wages (up to wage base limit)	_____	_____
g. FUTA tax (0.008 × f)	_____	_____
h. Total taxes (d + e + g)	_____	_____
i. Additional taxes	_____	_____
j. Gross taxes	_____	_____

9–5. Tardee Corp. failed to file its quarterly tax report for payment of FICA taxes for a period of three months. It deposited the tax liability of $5,000 due on its late report at the time of filing. What penalties must Tardee pay when it files its return?

CONTINUING CASE PROBLEM

Frontier Landscaping has recently made the following payroll decisions.

PART A

a. Placed its chief landscape designer on a guaranteed wage plan. D. J. Stewart will receive wages of $540 per week for a 48-hour week.

b. Assigned sales duties in the garden store to Oscar Storey, one of its newest employees, in addition to landscaping work. Oscar will receive $8 an hour for sales work and $12 an hour for landscaping work, with overtime to be paid based on the sales rate.

c. Began a work-sharing plan for Cliff Hardy, one of its employees who works a reduced work load in the winter. Part of Cliff's lost wages (regular wages $400) will be covered by unemployment insurance (maximum $240).

During one week in the winter, these employees worked the following hours:

1. D. J. Stewart: 54 hours
2. Oscar Storey: sales hours, 32; landscaping hours, 12
3. Cliff Hardy: 32 hours (regular hours, 40)

What are the gross wages and/or receipts for these employees?

PART B

As a seasonal business, Frontier has an erratic payroll and above average lay-offs followed by rehiring with relatively high unemployment tax payments. What policies and procedures can Frontier put into effect to reduce its unemployment taxes?

FEDERAL TAX WITHHOLDING TABLES

Allowance Table for Percentage Method of Withholding

Allowance Table	And wages are paid-							
	Weekly	Biweekly	Semi-monthly	Monthly	Quarterly	Semi-annually	Annually	Daily or Misc.
If the number of withholding allowances is:	The total amount of withholding allowances for the payroll period is:							
0	$ 0	$ 0	$ 0	$ 0	$ 0	$ 0	$ 0	$ 0
1	53.85	107.95	116.67	233.33	700.00	1,400.00	2,800.00	10.77
2	107.70	215.38	233.34	466.66	1,400.00	2,800.00	5,600.00	21.54
3	161.55	323.07	350.01	699.99	2,100.00	4,200.00	8,400.00	32.31
4	215.40	430.76	466.68	933.32	2,800.00	5,600.00	11,200.00	43.08
5	269.25	538.45	583.35	1,166.65	3,500.00	7,000.00	14,000.00	53.85
6	323.10	646.14	700.02	1,399.98	4,200.00	8,400.00	16,800.00	64.62
7	376.95	752.83	816.69	1,633.31	4,900.00	9,800.00	19,600.00	75.39
8	430.80	861.52	933.36	1,866.64	5,600.00	11,200.00	22,400.00	86.16
9	484.65	969.21	1,050.03	2,099.97	6,300.00	12,600.00	25,200.00	96.93
10	538.50	1,076.90	1,166.70	2,333.30	7,000.00	14,000.00	28,000.00	107.70

Tables for Percentage Method of Withholding
(For Wages Paid in 20XX)

TABLE 1—WEEKLY Payroll Period

(a) SINGLE person (including head of household)—

If the amount of wages (after subtracting withholding allowances) is:
The amount of income tax to withhold is:

Not over $51 . . . . . . $0

Over—	But not over—		of excess over—
$51	—$536	. . 15%	—$51
$536	—$1,152	. . $72.75 plus 28%	—$536
$1,152	—$2,581	. . $245.23 plus 31%	—$1,152
$2,581	—$5,576	. . $688.22 plus 36%	—$2,581
$5,576	. . . . . .	. $1,766.42 plus 39.6%	—$5,576

(b) MARRIED person—

If the amount of wages (after subtracting withholding allowances) is:
The amount of income tax to withhold is:

Not over $124 . . . . $0

Over—	But not over—		of excess over—
$124	—$931	. . 15%	—$124
$931	—$1,942	. . $121.05 plus 28%	—$931
$1,942	—$3,192	. . $404.13 plus 31%	—$1,942
$3,192	—$5,633	. . $791.63 plus 36%	—$3,192
$5,633	. . . . . .	. $1,670.39 plus 39.6%	—$5,633

TABLE 2—BIWEEKLY Payroll Period

(a) SINGLE person (including head of household)—

If the amount of wages (after subtracting withholding allowances) is:
The amount of income tax to withhold is:

Not over $102 . . . . $0

Over—	But not over—		of excess over—
$102	—$1,071	. . 15%	—$102
$1,071	—$2,304	. . $145.35 plus 28%	—$1,071
$2,304	—$5,162	. . $490.59 plus 31%	—$2,304
$5,162	—$11,152	. . $1,376.57 plus 36%	—$5,162
$11,152	. . . . . .	. $3,532.97 plus 39.6%	—$11,152

(b) MARRIED person—

If the amount of wages (after subtracting withholding allowances) is:
The amount of income tax to withhold is:

Not over $248 . . . . $0

Over—	But not over—		of excess over—
$248	—$1,862	. . 15%	—$248
$1,862	—$3,885	. . $242.10 plus 28%	—$1,862
$3,885	—$6,385	. . $808.54 plus 31%	—$3,885
$6,385	—$11,265	. . $1,583.54 plus 36%	—$6,385
$11,265	. . . . . .	. $3,340.34 plus 39.6%	—$11,265

TABLE 3—SEMIMONTHLY Payroll Period

(a) SINGLE person (including head of household)—

If the amount of wages (after subtracting withholding allowances) is:
The amount of income tax to withhold is:

Not over $110 . . . . $0

Over—	But not over—		of excess over—
$110	—1,160	. . 15%	—$110
$1,160	—$2,496	. . $157.50 plus 28%	—$1,160
$2,496	—$5,592	. . $531.58 plus 31%	—$2,496
$5,592	—$12,081	. . $1,491.34 plus 36%	—$5,592
$12,081	. . . . . .	. $3,827.38 plus 39.6%	—$12,081

(b) MARRIED person—

If the amount of wages (after subtracting withholding allowances) is:
The amount of income tax to withhold is:

Not over $269 . . . . $0

Over—	But not over—		of excess over—
$269	—$2,017	. . 15%	—$269
$2,017	—$4,208	. . $262.20 plus 28%	—$2,017
$4,208	—$6,917	. . $875.68 plus 31%	—$4,208
$6,917	—$12,204	. . $1,715.47 plus 36%	—$6,917
$12,204	. . . . . .	. $3,618.79 plus 39.6%	—$12,204

TABLE 4—MONTHLY Payroll Period

(a) SINGLE person (including head of household)—

If the amount of wages (after subtracting withholding allowances) is:
The amount of income tax to withhold is:

Not over $221 . . . . $0

Over—	But not over—		of excess over—
$221	—$2,321	. . 15%	—$221
$2,321	—$4,992	. . $315.00 plus 28%	—$2,321
$4,992	—$11,183	. . $1,062.88 plus 31%	—$4,992
$11,183	—$24,163	. . $2,982.09 plus 36%	—$11,183
$24,163	. . . . . .	. $7,654.89 plus 39.6%	—$24,163

(b) MARRIED person—

If the amount of wages (after subtracting withholding allowances) is:
The amount of income tax to withhold is:

Not over $538 . . . . $0

Over—	But not over—		of excess over—
$538	—$4,033	. . 15%	—$538
$4,033	—$8,417	. . $524.25 plus 28%	—$4,033
$8,417	—$13,833	. . $1,751.77 plus 31%	—$8,417
$13,833	—$24,408	. . $3,430.73 plus 36%	—$13,833
$24,408	. . . . . .	. $7,237.73 plus 39.6%	—$24,408

Source: The tables on pages A-4 through A-25 are from *Circular E, Employer's Tax Guide.*

A-4

TABLE 5—QUARTERLY Payroll Period

(a) SINGLE person (including head of household)—

If the amount of wages (after subtracting withholding allowances) is: The amount of income tax to withhold is:

Not over $663 . . . . $0

Over—	But not over—		of excess over—
$663	—$6,963	. 15%	—$663
$6,963	—$14,975	. $945.00 plus 28%	—$6,963
$14,975	—$33,550	. $3,188.36 plus 31%	—$14,975
$33,550	—$72,488	. $8,946.61 plus 36%	—$33,550
$72,488	. . . . . .	. $22,964.29 plus 39.6%	—$72,488

(b) MARRIED person—

If the amount of wages (after subtracting withholding allowances) is: The amount of income tax to withhold is:

Not over $1,613 . . . . $0

Over—	But not over—		of excess over—
$1,613	—$12,100	. 15%	—$1,613
$12,100	—$25,250	. $1,573.05 plus 28%	—$12,100
$25,250	—$41,500	. $5,255.05 plus 31%	—$25,250
$41,500	—$73,225	. $10,292.55 plus 36%	—$41,500
$73,225	. . . . . .	. $21,713.55 plus 39.6%	—$73,225

TABLE 6—SEMIANNUAL Payroll Period

(a) SINGLE person (including head of household)—

If the amount of wages (after subtracting withholding allowances) is: The amount of income tax to withhold is:

Not over $1,325 . . . . $0

Over—	But not over—		of excess over—
$1,325	—$13,925	. 15%	—$1,325
$13,925	—$29,950	. $1,890.00 plus 28%	—$13,925
$29,950	—$67,100	. $6,377.00 plus 31%	—$29,950
$67,100	—$144,975	. $17,893.50 plus 36%	—$67,100
$144,975	. . . . .	. $45,928.50 plus 39.6%	—$144,975

(b) MARRIED person—

If the amount of wages (after subtracting withholding allowances) is: The amount of income tax to withhold is:

Not over $3,225 . . . . $0

Over—	But not over—		of excess over—
$3,225	—$24,200	. 15%	—$3,225
$24,200	—$50,500	. $3,146.25 plus 28%	—$24,200
$50,500	—$83,000	. $10,510.25 plus 31%	—$50,500
$83,000	—$146,450	. $20,585.25 plus 36%	—$83,000
$146,450	. . . . .	. $43,427.25 plus 39.6%	—$146,450

TABLE 7—ANNUAL Payroll Period

(a) SINGLE person (including head of household)—

If the amount of wages (after subtracting withholding allowances) is: The amount of income tax to withhold is:

Not over $2,650 . . . . $0

Over—	But not over—		of excess over—
$2,650	—$27,850	. 15%	—$2,650
$27,850	—$59,900	. $3,780.00 plus 28%	—$27,850
$59,900	—$134,200	. $12,754.00 plus 31%	—$59,900
$134,200	—$289,950	. $35,787.00 plus 36%	—$134,200
$289,950	. . . . .	. $91,857.00 plus 39.6%	—$289,950

(b) MARRIED person—

If the amount of wages (after subtracting withholding allowances) is: The amount of income tax to withhold is:

Not over $6,450 . . . . $0

Over—	But not over—		of excess over—
$6,450	—$48,400	. 15%	—$6,450
$48,400	—$101,000	. $6,292.50 plus 28%	—$48,400
$101,000	—$166,000	. $21,020.50 plus 31%	—$101,000
$166,000	—$292,900	. $41,170.50 plus 36%	—$166,000
$292,900	. . . . .	. $86,854.50 plus 39.6%	—$292,900

TABLE 8—DAILY or MISCELLANEOUS Payroll Period

(a) SINGLE person (including head of household)—

If the amount of wages (after subtracting withholding allowances) divided by the number of days in the payroll period is: The amount of income tax to withhold per day is:

Not over $10.20 . . . . $0

Over—	But not over—		of excess over—
$10.20	—$107.10	. 15%	—$10.20
$107.10	—$230.40	. $14.54 plus 28%	—$107.10
$230.40	—$516.20	. $49.06 plus 31%	—$230.40
$516.20	—$1,115.20	. $137.66 plus 36%	—$516.20
$1,115.20	. . . . . .	. $353.30 plus 39.6%	—$1,115.20

(b) MARRIED person—

If the amount of wages (after subtracting withholding allowances) divided by the number of days in the payroll period is: The amount of income tax to withhold per day is:

Not over $24.80 . . . . $0

Over—	But not over—		of excess over—
$24.80	—$186.20	. 15%	—$24.80
$186.20	—$388.50	. $24.21 plus 28%	—$186.20
$388.50	—$638.50	. $80.85 plus 31%	—$388.50
$638.50	—$1,126.50	. $158.35 plus 36%	—$638.50
$1,126.50	. . . . . .	. $334.03 plus 39.6%	—$1,126.50

A-5

SINGLE Persons—WEEKLY Payroll Period

(For Wages Paid in 20XX)

If the wages are—		And the number of withholding allowances claimed is—										
At least	But less than	0	1	2	3	4	5	6	7	8	9	10
		The amount of income tax to be withheld is—										
$0	$55	0	0	0	0	0	0	0	0	0	0	0
55	60	1	0	0	0	0	0	0	0	0	0	0
60	65	2	0	0	0	0	0	0	0	0	0	0
65	70	2	0	0	0	0	0	0	0	0	0	0
70	75	3	0	0	0	0	0	0	0	0	0	0
75	80	4	0	0	0	0	0	0	0	0	0	0
80	85	5	0	0	0	0	0	0	0	0	0	0
85	90	5	0	0	0	0	0	0	0	0	0	0
90	95	6	0	0	0	0	0	0	0	0	0	0
95	100	7	0	0	0	0	0	0	0	0	0	0
100	105	8	0	0	0	0	0	0	0	0	0	0
105	110	8	0	0	0	0	0	0	0	0	0	0
110	115	9	1	0	0	0	0	0	0	0	0	0
115	120	10	2	0	0	0	0	0	0	0	0	0
120	125	11	3	0	0	0	0	0	0	0	0	0
125	130	11	3	0	0	0	0	0	0	0	0	0
130	135	12	4	0	0	0	0	0	0	0	0	0
135	140	13	5	0	0	0	0	0	0	0	0	0
140	145	14	6	0	0	0	0	0	0	0	0	0
145	150	14	6	0	0	0	0	0	0	0	0	0
150	155	15	7	0	0	0	0	0	0	0	0	0
155	160	16	8	0	0	0	0	0	0	0	0	0
160	165	17	9	1	0	0	0	0	0	0	0	0
165	170	17	9	1	0	0	0	0	0	0	0	0
170	175	18	10	2	0	0	0	0	0	0	0	0
175	180	19	11	3	0	0	0	0	0	0	0	0
180	185	20	12	4	0	0	0	0	0	0	0	0
185	190	20	12	4	0	0	0	0	0	0	0	0
190	195	21	13	5	0	0	0	0	0	0	0	0
195	200	22	14	6	0	0	0	0	0	0	0	0
200	210	23	15	7	0	0	0	0	0	0	0	0
210	220	25	17	8	0	0	0	0	0	0	0	0
220	230	26	18	10	2	0	0	0	0	0	0	0
230	240	28	20	11	3	0	0	0	0	0	0	0
240	250	29	21	13	5	0	0	0	0	0	0	0
250	260	31	23	14	6	0	0	0	0	0	0	0
260	270	32	24	16	8	0	0	0	0	0	0	0
270	280	34	26	17	9	1	0	0	0	0	0	0
280	290	35	27	19	11	3	0	0	0	0	0	0
290	300	37	29	20	12	4	0	0	0	0	0	0
300	310	38	30	22	14	6	0	0	0	0	0	0
310	320	40	32	23	15	7	0	0	0	0	0	0
320	330	41	33	25	17	9	1	0	0	0	0	0
330	340	43	35	26	18	10	2	0	0	0	0	0
340	350	44	36	28	20	12	4	0	0	0	0	0
350	360	46	38	29	21	13	5	0	0	0	0	0
360	370	47	39	31	23	15	7	0	0	0	0	0
370	380	49	41	32	24	16	8	0	0	0	0	0
380	390	50	42	34	26	18	10	2	0	0	0	0
390	400	52	44	35	27	19	11	3	0	0	0	0
400	410	53	45	37	29	21	13	5	0	0	0	0
410	420	55	47	38	30	22	14	6	0	0	0	0
420	430	56	48	40	32	24	16	8	0	0	0	0
430	440	58	50	41	33	25	17	9	1	0	0	0
440	450	59	51	43	35	27	19	11	3	0	0	0
450	460	61	53	44	36	28	20	12	4	0	0	0
460	470	62	54	46	38	30	22	14	6	0	0	0
470	480	64	56	47	39	31	23	15	7	0	0	0
480	490	65	57	49	41	33	25	17	9	0	0	0
490	500	67	59	50	42	34	26	18	10	2	0	0
500	510	68	60	52	44	36	28	20	12	3	0	0
510	520	70	62	53	45	37	29	21	13	5	0	0
520	530	71	63	55	47	39	31	23	15	6	0	0
530	540	73	65	56	48	40	32	24	16	8	0	0
540	550	75	66	58	50	42	34	26	18	9	1	0
550	560	78	68	59	51	43	35	27	19	11	3	0
560	570	81	69	61	53	45	37	29	21	12	4	0
570	580	84	71	62	54	46	38	30	22	14	6	0
580	590	87	72	64	56	48	40	32	24	15	7	0
590	600	89	74	65	57	49	41	33	25	17	9	1

A-6

(For Wages Paid in 20XX)

If the wages are—		And the number of withholding allowances claimed is—										
At least	But less than	0	1	2	3	4	5	6	7	8	9	10
		The amount of income tax to be withheld is—										
$600	$610	92	77	67	59	51	43	35	27	18	10	2
610	620	95	80	68	60	52	44	36	28	20	12	4
620	630	98	83	70	62	54	46	38	30	21	13	5
630	640	101	85	71	63	55	47	39	31	23	15	7
640	650	103	88	73	65	57	49	41	33	24	16	8
650	660	106	91	76	66	58	50	42	34	26	18	10
660	670	109	94	79	68	60	52	44	36	27	19	11
670	680	112	97	82	69	61	53	45	37	29	21	13
680	690	115	99	84	71	63	55	47	39	30	22	14
690	700	117	102	87	72	64	56	48	40	32	24	16
700	710	120	105	90	75	66	58	50	42	33	25	17
710	720	123	108	93	78	67	59	51	43	35	27	19
720	730	126	111	96	81	69	61	53	45	36	28	20
730	740	129	113	98	83	70	62	54	46	38	30	22
740	750	131	116	101	86	72	64	56	48	39	31	23
750	760	134	119	104	89	74	65	57	49	41	33	25
760	770	137	122	107	92	77	67	59	51	42	34	26
770	780	140	125	110	95	79	68	60	52	44	36	28
780	790	143	127	112	97	82	70	62	54	45	37	29
790	800	145	130	115	100	85	71	63	55	47	39	31
800	810	148	133	118	103	88	73	65	57	48	40	32
810	820	151	136	121	106	91	76	66	58	50	42	34
820	830	154	139	124	109	93	78	68	60	51	43	35
830	840	157	141	126	111	96	81	69	61	53	45	37
840	850	159	144	129	114	99	84	71	63	54	46	38
850	860	162	147	132	117	102	87	72	64	56	48	40
860	870	165	150	135	120	105	90	74	66	57	49	41
870	880	168	153	138	123	107	92	77	67	59	51	43
880	890	171	155	140	125	110	95	80	69	60	52	44
890	900	173	158	143	128	113	98	83	70	62	54	46
900	910	176	161	146	131	116	101	86	72	63	55	47
910	920	179	164	149	134	119	104	88	73	65	57	49
920	930	182	167	152	137	121	106	91	76	66	58	50
930	940	185	169	154	139	124	109	94	79	68	60	52
940	950	187	172	157	142	127	112	97	82	69	61	53
950	960	190	175	160	145	130	115	100	85	71	63	55
960	970	193	178	163	148	133	118	102	87	72	64	56
970	980	196	181	166	151	135	120	105	90	75	66	58
980	990	199	183	168	153	138	123	108	93	78	67	59
990	1,000	201	186	171	156	141	126	111	96	81	69	61
1,000	1,010	204	189	174	159	144	129	114	99	84	70	62
1,010	1,020	207	192	177	162	147	132	116	101	86	72	64
1,020	1,030	210	195	180	165	149	134	119	104	89	74	65
1,030	1,040	213	197	182	167	152	137	122	107	92	77	67
1,040	1,050	215	200	185	170	155	140	125	110	95	80	68
1,050	1,060	218	203	188	173	158	143	128	113	98	82	70
1,060	1,070	221	206	191	176	161	146	130	115	100	85	71
1,070	1,080	224	209	194	179	163	148	133	118	103	88	73
1,080	1,090	227	211	196	181	166	151	136	121	106	91	76
1,090	1,100	229	214	199	184	169	154	139	124	109	94	79
1,100	1,110	232	217	202	187	172	157	142	127	112	96	81
1,110	1,120	235	220	205	190	175	160	144	129	114	99	84
1,120	1,130	238	223	208	193	177	162	147	132	117	102	87
1,130	1,140	241	225	210	195	180	165	150	135	120	105	90
1,140	1,150	243	228	213	198	183	168	153	138	123	108	93
1,150	1,160	246	231	216	201	186	171	156	141	126	110	95
1,160	1,170	249	234	219	204	189	174	158	143	128	113	98
1,170	1,180	252	237	222	207	191	176	161	146	131	116	101
1,180	1,190	256	239	224	209	194	179	164	149	134	119	104
1,190	1,200	259	242	227	212	197	182	167	152	137	122	107
1,200	1,210	262	245	230	215	200	185	170	155	140	124	109
1,210	1,220	265	248	233	218	203	188	172	157	142	127	112
1,220	1,230	268	251	236	221	205	190	175	160	145	130	115
1,230	1,240	271	254	238	223	208	193	178	163	148	133	118
1,240	1,250	274	257	241	226	211	196	181	166	151	136	121

$1,250 and over   Use Table 1(a) for a **SINGLE person** on page 34. Also see the instructions on page 32.

MARRIED Persons—WEEKLY Payroll Period

(For Wages Paid in 20XX)

If the wages are—		And the number of withholding allowances claimed is—										
At least	But less than	0	1	2	3	4	5	6	7	8	9	10
		The amount of income tax to be withheld is—										
$0	$125	0	0	0	0	0	0	0	0	0	0	0
125	130	1	0	0	0	0	0	0	0	0	0	0
130	135	1	0	0	0	0	0	0	0	0	0	0
135	140	2	0	0	0	0	0	0	0	0	0	0
140	145	3	0	0	0	0	0	0	0	0	0	0
145	150	4	0	0	0	0	0	0	0	0	0	0
150	155	4	0	0	0	0	0	0	0	0	0	0
155	160	5	0	0	0	0	0	0	0	0	0	0
160	165	6	0	0	0	0	0	0	0	0	0	0
165	170	7	0	0	0	0	0	0	0	0	0	0
170	175	7	0	0	0	0	0	0	0	0	0	0
175	180	8	0	0	0	0	0	0	0	0	0	0
180	185	9	1	0	0	0	0	0	0	0	0	0
185	190	10	1	0	0	0	0	0	0	0	0	0
190	195	10	2	0	0	0	0	0	0	0	0	0
195	200	11	3	0	0	0	0	0	0	0	0	0
200	210	12	4	0	0	0	0	0	0	0	0	0
210	220	14	6	0	0	0	0	0	0	0	0	0
220	230	15	7	0	0	0	0	0	0	0	0	0
230	240	17	9	0	0	0	0	0	0	0	0	0
240	250	18	10	2	0	0	0	0	0	0	0	0
250	260	20	12	3	0	0	0	0	0	0	0	0
260	270	21	13	5	0	0	0	0	0	0	0	0
270	280	23	15	6	0	0	0	0	0	0	0	0
280	290	24	16	8	0	0	0	0	0	0	0	0
290	300	26	18	9	1	0	0	0	0	0	0	0
300	310	27	19	11	3	0	0	0	0	0	0	0
310	320	29	21	12	4	0	0	0	0	0	0	0
320	330	30	22	14	6	0	0	0	0	0	0	0
330	340	32	24	15	7	0	0	0	0	0	0	0
340	350	33	25	17	9	1	0	0	0	0	0	0
350	360	35	27	18	10	2	0	0	0	0	0	0
360	370	36	28	20	12	4	0	0	0	0	0	0
370	380	38	30	21	13	5	0	0	0	0	0	0
380	390	39	31	23	15	7	0	0	0	0	0	0
390	400	41	33	24	16	8	0	0	0	0	0	0
400	410	42	34	26	18	10	2	0	0	0	0	0
410	420	44	36	27	19	11	3	0	0	0	0	0
420	430	45	37	29	21	13	5	0	0	0	0	0
430	440	47	39	30	22	14	6	0	0	0	0	0
440	450	48	40	32	24	16	8	0	0	0	0	0
450	460	50	42	33	25	17	9	1	0	0	0	0
460	470	51	43	35	27	19	11	3	0	0	0	0
470	480	53	45	36	28	20	12	4	0	0	0	0
480	490	54	46	38	30	22	14	6	0	0	0	0
490	500	56	48	39	31	23	15	7	0	0	0	0
500	510	57	49	41	33	25	17	9	1	0	0	0
510	520	59	51	42	34	26	18	10	2	0	0	0
520	530	60	52	44	36	28	20	12	4	0	0	0
530	540	62	54	45	37	29	21	13	5	0	0	0
540	550	63	55	47	39	31	23	15	7	0	0	0
550	560	65	57	48	40	32	24	16	8	0	0	0
560	570	66	58	50	42	34	26	18	10	2	0	0
570	580	68	60	51	43	35	27	19	11	3	0	0
580	590	69	61	53	45	37	29	21	13	5	0	0
590	600	71	63	54	46	38	30	22	14	6	0	0
600	610	72	64	56	48	40	32	24	16	8	0	0
610	620	74	66	57	49	41	33	25	17	9	1	0
620	630	75	67	59	51	43	35	27	19	11	2	0
630	640	77	69	60	52	44	36	28	20	12	4	0
640	650	78	70	62	54	46	38	30	22	14	5	0
650	660	80	72	63	55	47	39	31	23	15	7	0
660	670	81	73	65	57	49	41	33	25	17	8	0
670	680	83	75	66	58	50	42	34	26	18	10	2
680	690	84	76	68	60	52	44	36	28	20	11	3
690	700	86	78	69	61	53	45	37	29	21	13	5
700	710	87	79	71	63	55	47	39	31	23	14	6
710	720	89	81	72	64	56	48	40	32	24	16	8
720	730	90	82	74	66	58	50	42	34	26	17	9
730	740	92	84	75	67	59	51	43	35	27	19	11

A-8

(For Wages Paid in 20XX)

If the wages are–		And the number of withholding allowances claimed is—										
At least	But less than	0	1	2	3	4	5	6	7	8	9	10
		The amount of income tax to be withheld is—										
$740	$750	93	85	77	69	61	53	45	37	29	20	12
750	760	95	87	78	70	62	54	46	38	30	22	14
760	770	96	88	80	72	64	56	48	40	32	23	15
770	780	98	90	81	73	65	57	49	41	33	25	17
780	790	99	91	83	75	67	59	51	43	35	26	18
790	800	101	93	84	76	68	60	52	44	36	28	20
800	810	102	94	86	78	70	62	54	46	38	29	21
810	820	104	96	87	79	71	63	55	47	39	31	23
820	830	105	97	89	81	73	65	57	49	41	32	24
830	840	107	99	90	82	74	66	58	50	42	34	26
840	850	108	100	92	84	76	68	60	52	44	35	27
850	860	110	102	93	85	77	69	61	53	45	37	29
860	870	111	103	95	87	79	71	63	55	47	38	30
870	880	113	105	96	88	80	72	64	56	48	40	32
880	890	114	106	98	90	82	74	66	58	50	41	33
890	900	116	108	99	91	83	75	67	59	51	43	35
900	910	117	109	101	93	85	77	69	61	53	44	36
910	920	119	111	102	94	86	78	70	62	54	46	38
920	930	120	112	104	96	88	80	72	64	56	47	39
930	940	122	114	105	97	89	81	73	65	57	49	41
940	950	125	115	107	99	91	83	75	67	59	50	42
950	960	128	117	108	100	92	84	76	68	60	52	44
960	970	131	118	110	102	94	86	78	70	62	53	45
970	980	133	120	111	103	95	87	79	71	63	55	47
980	990	136	121	113	105	97	89	81	73	65	56	48
990	1,000	139	124	114	106	98	90	82	74	66	58	50
1,000	1,010	142	127	116	108	100	92	84	76	68	59	51
1,010	1,020	145	130	117	109	101	93	85	77	69	61	53
1,020	1,030	147	132	119	111	103	95	87	79	71	62	54
1,030	1,040	150	135	120	112	104	96	88	80	72	64	56
1,040	1,050	153	138	123	114	106	98	90	82	74	65	57
1,050	1,060	156	141	126	115	107	99	91	83	75	67	59
1,060	1,070	159	144	128	117	109	101	93	85	77	68	60
1,070	1,080	161	146	131	118	110	102	94	86	78	70	62
1,080	1,090	164	149	134	120	112	104	96	88	80	71	63
1,090	1,100	167	152	137	122	113	105	97	89	81	73	65
1,100	1,110	170	155	140	125	115	107	99	91	83	74	66
1,110	1,120	173	158	142	127	116	108	100	92	84	76	68
1,120	1,130	175	160	145	130	118	110	102	94	86	77	69
1,130	1,140	178	163	148	133	119	111	103	95	87	79	71
1,140	1,150	181	166	151	136	121	113	105	97	89	80	72
1,150	1,160	184	169	154	139	123	114	106	98	90	82	74
1,160	1,170	187	172	156	141	126	116	108	100	92	83	75
1,170	1,180	189	174	159	144	129	117	109	101	93	85	77
1,180	1,190	192	177	162	147	132	119	111	103	95	86	78
1,190	1,200	195	180	165	150	135	120	112	104	96	88	80
1,200	1,210	198	183	168	153	137	122	114	106	98	89	81
1,210	1,220	201	186	170	155	140	125	115	107	99	91	83
1,220	1,230	203	188	173	158	143	128	117	109	101	92	84
1,230	1,240	206	191	176	161	146	131	118	110	102	94	86
1,240	1,250	209	194	179	164	149	134	120	112	104	95	87
1,250	1,260	212	197	182	167	151	136	121	113	105	97	89
1,260	1,270	215	200	184	169	154	139	124	115	107	98	90
1,270	1,280	217	202	187	172	157	142	127	116	108	100	92
1,280	1,290	220	205	190	175	160	145	130	118	110	101	93
1,290	1,300	223	208	193	178	163	148	133	119	111	103	95
1,300	1,310	226	211	196	181	165	150	135	121	113	104	96
1,310	1,320	229	214	198	183	168	153	138	123	114	106	98
1,320	1,330	231	216	201	186	171	156	141	126	116	107	99
1,330	1,340	234	219	204	189	174	159	144	129	117	109	101
1,340	1,350	237	222	207	192	177	162	147	131	119	110	102
1,350	1,360	240	225	210	195	179	164	149	134	120	112	104
1,360	1,370	243	228	212	197	182	167	152	137	122	113	105
1,370	1,380	245	230	215	200	185	170	155	140	125	115	107
1,380	1,390	248	233	218	203	188	173	158	143	128	116	108

$1,390 and over   Use Table 1(b) for a **MARRIED person** on page 34. Also see the instructions on page 32.

SINGLE Persons—BIWEEKLY Payroll Period

(For Wages Paid in 20XX)

If the wages are—		And the number of withholding allowances claimed is—										
At least	But less than	0	1	2	3	4	5	6	7	8	9	10
		The amount of income tax to be withheld is—										
$0	$105	0	0	0	0	0	0	0	0	0	0	0
105	110	1	0	0	0	0	0	0	0	0	0	0
110	115	2	0	0	0	0	0	0	0	0	0	0
115	120	2	0	0	0	0	0	0	0	0	0	0
120	125	3	0	0	0	0	0	0	0	0	0	0
125	130	4	0	0	0	0	0	0	0	0	0	0
130	135	5	0	0	0	0	0	0	0	0	0	0
135	140	5	0	0	0	0	0	0	0	0	0	0
140	145	6	0	0	0	0	0	0	0	0	0	0
145	150	7	0	0	0	0	0	0	0	0	0	0
150	155	8	0	0	0	0	0	0	0	0	0	0
155	160	8	0	0	0	0	0	0	0	0	0	0
160	165	9	0	0	0	0	0	0	0	0	0	0
165	170	10	0	0	0	0	0	0	0	0	0	0
170	175	11	0	0	0	0	0	0	0	0	0	0
175	180	11	0	0	0	0	0	0	0	0	0	0
180	185	12	0	0	0	0	0	0	0	0	0	0
185	190	13	0	0	0	0	0	0	0	0	0	0
190	195	14	0	0	0	0	0	0	0	0	0	0
195	200	14	0	0	0	0	0	0	0	0	0	0
200	205	15	0	0	0	0	0	0	0	0	0	0
205	210	16	0	0	0	0	0	0	0	0	0	0
210	215	17	0	0	0	0	0	0	0	0	0	0
215	220	17	1	0	0	0	0	0	0	0	0	0
220	225	18	2	0	0	0	0	0	0	0	0	0
225	230	19	3	0	0	0	0	0	0	0	0	0
230	235	20	3	0	0	0	0	0	0	0	0	0
235	240	20	4	0	0	0	0	0	0	0	0	0
240	245	21	5	0	0	0	0	0	0	0	0	0
245	250	22	6	0	0	0	0	0	0	0	0	0
250	260	23	7	0	0	0	0	0	0	0	0	0
260	270	24	8	0	0	0	0	0	0	0	0	0
270	280	26	10	0	0	0	0	0	0	0	0	0
280	290	27	11	0	0	0	0	0	0	0	0	0
290	300	29	13	0	0	0	0	0	0	0	0	0
300	310	30	14	0	0	0	0	0	0	0	0	0
310	320	32	16	0	0	0	0	0	0	0	0	0
320	330	33	17	1	0	0	0	0	0	0	0	0
330	340	35	19	3	0	0	0	0	0	0	0	0
340	350	36	20	4	0	0	0	0	0	0	0	0
350	360	38	22	6	0	0	0	0	0	0	0	0
360	370	39	23	7	0	0	0	0	0	0	0	0
370	380	41	25	9	0	0	0	0	0	0	0	0
380	390	42	26	10	0	0	0	0	0	0	0	0
390	400	44	28	12	0	0	0	0	0	0	0	0
400	410	45	29	13	0	0	0	0	0	0	0	0
410	420	47	31	15	0	0	0	0	0	0	0	0
420	430	48	32	16	0	0	0	0	0	0	0	0
430	440	50	34	18	2	0	0	0	0	0	0	0
440	450	51	35	19	3	0	0	0	0	0	0	0
450	460	53	37	21	5	0	0	0	0	0	0	0
460	470	54	38	22	6	0	0	0	0	0	0	0
470	480	56	40	24	8	0	0	0	0	0	0	0
480	490	57	41	25	9	0	0	0	0	0	0	0
490	500	59	43	27	11	0	0	0	0	0	0	0
500	520	61	45	29	13	0	0	0	0	0	0	0
520	540	64	48	32	16	0	0	0	0	0	0	0
540	560	67	51	35	19	3	0	0	0	0	0	0
560	580	70	54	38	22	6	0	0	0	0	0	0
580	600	73	57	41	25	9	0	0	0	0	0	0
600	620	76	60	44	28	12	0	0	0	0	0	0
620	640	79	63	47	31	15	0	0	0	0	0	0
640	660	82	66	50	34	18	1	0	0	0	0	0
660	680	85	69	53	37	21	4	0	0	0	0	0
680	700	88	72	56	40	24	7	0	0	0	0	0
700	720	91	75	59	43	27	10	0	0	0	0	0
720	740	94	78	62	46	30	13	0	0	0	0	0
740	760	97	81	65	49	33	16	0	0	0	0	0
760	780	100	84	68	52	36	19	3	0	0	0	0
780	800	103	87	71	55	39	22	6	0	0	0	0

If the wages are—		And the number of withholding allowances claimed is—										
At least	But less than	0	1	2	3	4	5	6	7	8	9	10
		The amount of income tax to be withheld is—										
$800	$820	106	90	74	58	42	25	9	0	0	0	0
820	840	109	93	77	61	45	28	12	0	0	0	0
840	860	112	96	80	64	48	31	15	0	0	0	0
860	880	115	99	83	67	51	34	18	2	0	0	0
880	900	118	102	86	70	54	37	21	5	0	0	0
900	920	121	105	89	73	57	40	24	8	0	0	0
920	940	124	108	92	76	60	43	27	11	0	0	0
940	960	127	111	95	79	63	46	30	14	0	0	0
960	980	130	114	98	82	66	49	33	17	1	0	0
980	1,000	133	117	101	85	69	52	36	20	4	0	0
1,000	1,020	136	120	104	88	72	55	39	23	7	0	0
1,020	1,040	139	123	107	91	75	58	42	26	10	0	0
1,040	1,060	142	126	110	94	78	61	45	29	13	0	0
1,060	1,080	145	129	113	97	81	64	48	32	16	0	0
1,080	1,100	151	132	116	100	84	67	51	35	19	3	0
1,100	1,120	156	135	119	103	87	70	54	38	22	6	0
1,120	1,140	162	138	122	106	90	73	57	41	25	9	0
1,140	1,160	167	141	125	109	93	76	60	44	28	12	0
1,160	1,180	173	144	128	112	96	79	63	47	31	15	0
1,180	1,200	179	149	131	115	99	82	66	50	34	18	2
1,200	1,220	184	154	134	118	102	85	69	53	37	21	5
1,220	1,240	190	160	137	121	105	88	72	56	40	24	8
1,240	1,260	195	165	140	124	108	91	75	59	43	27	11
1,260	1,280	201	171	143	127	111	94	78	62	46	30	14
1,280	1,300	207	177	146	130	114	97	81	65	49	33	17
1,300	1,320	212	182	152	133	117	100	84	68	52	36	20
1,320	1,340	218	188	158	136	120	103	87	71	55	39	23
1,340	1,360	223	193	163	139	123	106	90	74	58	42	26
1,360	1,380	229	199	169	142	126	109	93	77	61	45	29
1,380	1,400	235	205	174	145	129	112	96	80	64	48	32
1,400	1,420	240	210	180	150	132	115	99	83	67	51	35
1,420	1,440	246	216	186	155	135	118	102	86	70	54	38
1,440	1,460	251	221	191	161	138	121	105	89	73	57	41
1,460	1,480	257	227	197	167	141	124	108	92	76	60	44
1,480	1,500	263	233	202	172	144	127	111	95	79	63	47
1,500	1,520	268	238	208	178	148	130	114	98	82	66	50
1,520	1,540	274	244	214	183	153	133	117	101	85	69	53
1,540	1,560	279	249	219	189	159	136	120	104	88	72	56
1,560	1,580	285	255	225	195	164	139	123	107	91	75	59
1,580	1,600	291	261	230	200	170	142	126	110	94	78	62
1,600	1,620	296	266	236	206	176	145	129	113	97	81	65
1,620	1,640	302	272	242	211	181	151	132	116	100	84	68
1,640	1,660	307	277	247	217	187	157	135	119	103	87	71
1,660	1,680	313	283	253	223	192	162	138	122	106	90	74
1,680	1,700	319	289	258	228	198	168	141	125	109	93	77
1,700	1,720	324	294	264	234	204	173	144	128	112	96	80
1,720	1,740	330	300	270	239	209	179	149	131	115	99	83
1,740	1,760	335	305	275	245	215	185	155	134	118	102	86
1,760	1,780	341	311	281	251	220	190	160	137	121	105	89
1,780	1,800	347	317	286	256	226	196	166	140	124	108	92
1,800	1,820	352	322	292	262	232	201	171	143	127	111	95
1,820	1,840	358	328	298	267	237	207	177	147	130	114	98
1,840	1,860	363	333	303	273	243	213	183	152	133	117	101
1,860	1,880	369	339	309	279	248	218	188	158	136	120	104
1,880	1,900	375	345	314	284	254	224	194	164	139	123	107
1,900	1,920	380	350	320	290	260	229	199	169	142	126	110
1,920	1,940	386	356	326	295	265	235	205	175	145	129	113
1,940	1,960	391	361	331	301	271	241	211	180	150	132	116
1,960	1,980	397	367	337	307	276	246	216	186	156	135	119
1,980	2,000	403	373	342	312	282	252	222	192	161	138	122
2,000	2,020	408	378	348	318	288	257	227	197	167	141	125
2,020	2,040	414	384	354	323	293	263	233	203	173	144	128
2,040	2,060	419	389	359	329	299	269	239	208	178	148	131
2,060	2,080	425	395	365	335	304	274	244	214	184	154	134
2,080	2,100	431	401	370	340	310	280	250	220	189	159	137

$2,100 and over   Use Table 2(a) for a **SINGLE person** on page 34. Also see the instructions on page 32.

MARRIED Persons—BIWEEKLY Payroll Period

(For Wages Paid in 20XX)

If the wages are—		And the number of withholding allowances claimed is—										
At least	But less than	0	1	2	3	4	5	6	7	8	9	10
		The amount of income tax to be withheld is—										
$0	$250	0	0	0	0	0	0	0	0	0	0	0
250	260	1	0	0	0	0	0	0	0	0	0	0
260	270	3	0	0	0	0	0	0	0	0	0	0
270	280	4	0	0	0	0	0	0	0	0	0	0
280	290	6	0	0	0	0	0	0	0	0	0	0
290	300	7	0	0	0	0	0	0	0	0	0	0
300	310	9	0	0	0	0	0	0	0	0	0	0
310	320	10	0	0	0	0	0	0	0	0	0	0
320	330	12	0	0	0	0	0	0	0	0	0	0
330	340	13	0	0	0	0	0	0	0	0	0	0
340	350	15	0	0	0	0	0	0	0	0	0	0
350	360	16	0	0	0	0	0	0	0	0	0	0
360	370	18	1	0	0	0	0	0	0	0	0	0
370	380	19	3	0	0	0	0	0	0	0	0	0
380	390	21	4	0	0	0	0	0	0	0	0	0
390	400	22	6	0	0	0	0	0	0	0	0	0
400	410	24	7	0	0	0	0	0	0	0	0	0
410	420	25	9	0	0	0	0	0	0	0	0	0
420	430	27	10	0	0	0	0	0	0	0	0	0
430	440	28	12	0	0	0	0	0	0	0	0	0
440	450	30	13	0	0	0	0	0	0	0	0	0
450	460	31	15	0	0	0	0	0	0	0	0	0
460	470	33	16	0	0	0	0	0	0	0	0	0
470	480	34	18	2	0	0	0	0	0	0	0	0
480	490	36	19	3	0	0	0	0	0	0	0	0
490	500	37	21	5	0	0	0	0	0	0	0	0
500	520	39	23	7	0	0	0	0	0	0	0	0
520	540	42	26	10	0	0	0	0	0	0	0	0
540	560	45	29	13	0	0	0	0	0	0	0	0
560	580	48	32	16	0	0	0	0	0	0	0	0
580	600	51	35	19	3	0	0	0	0	0	0	0
600	620	54	38	22	6	0	0	0	0	0	0	0
620	640	57	41	25	9	0	0	0	0	0	0	0
640	660	60	44	28	12	0	0	0	0	0	0	0
660	680	63	47	31	15	0	0	0	0	0	0	0
680	700	66	50	34	18	2	0	0	0	0	0	0
700	720	69	53	37	21	5	0	0	0	0	0	0
720	740	72	56	40	24	8	0	0	0	0	0	0
740	760	75	59	43	27	11	0	0	0	0	0	0
760	780	78	62	46	30	14	0	0	0	0	0	0
780	800	81	65	49	33	17	1	0	0	0	0	0
800	820	84	68	52	36	20	4	0	0	0	0	0
820	840	87	71	55	39	23	7	0	0	0	0	0
840	860	90	74	58	42	26	10	0	0	0	0	0
860	880	93	77	61	45	29	13	0	0	0	0	0
880	900	96	80	64	48	32	16	0	0	0	0	0
900	920	99	83	67	51	35	19	2	0	0	0	0
920	940	102	86	70	54	38	22	5	0	0	0	0
940	960	105	89	73	57	41	25	8	0	0	0	0
960	980	108	92	76	60	44	28	11	0	0	0	0
980	1,000	111	95	79	63	47	31	14	0	0	0	0
1,000	1,020	114	98	82	66	50	34	17	1	0	0	0
1,020	1,040	117	101	85	69	53	37	20	4	0	0	0
1,040	1,060	120	104	88	72	56	40	23	7	0	0	0
1,060	1,080	123	107	91	75	59	43	26	10	0	0	0
1,080	1,100	126	110	94	78	62	46	29	13	0	0	0
1,100	1,120	129	113	97	81	65	49	32	16	0	0	0
1,120	1,140	132	116	100	84	68	52	35	19	3	0	0
1,140	1,160	135	119	103	87	71	55	38	22	6	0	0
1,160	1,180	138	122	106	90	74	58	41	25	9	0	0
1,180	1,200	141	125	109	93	77	61	44	28	12	0	0
1,200	1,220	144	128	112	96	80	64	47	31	15	0	0
1,220	1,240	147	131	115	99	83	67	50	34	18	2	0
1,240	1,260	150	134	118	102	86	70	53	37	21	5	0
1,260	1,280	153	137	121	105	89	73	56	40	24	8	0
1,280	1,300	156	140	124	108	92	76	59	43	27	11	0
1,300	1,320	159	143	127	111	95	79	62	46	30	14	0
1,320	1,340	162	146	130	114	98	82	65	49	33	17	1
1,340	1,360	165	149	133	117	101	85	68	52	36	20	4
1,360	1,380	168	152	136	120	104	88	71	55	39	23	7

A-12

MARRIED Persons—BIWEEKLY Payroll Period
(For Wages Paid in 20XX)

If the wages are—		And the number of withholding allowances claimed is—										
At least	But less than	0	1	2	3	4	5	6	7	8	9	10
		The amount of income tax to be withheld is—										
$1,380	$1,400	171	155	139	123	107	91	74	58	42	26	10
1,400	1,420	174	158	142	126	110	94	77	61	45	29	13
1,420	1,440	177	161	145	129	113	97	80	64	48	32	16
1,440	1,460	180	164	148	132	116	100	83	67	51	35	19
1,460	1,480	183	167	151	135	119	103	86	70	54	38	22
1,480	1,500	186	170	154	138	122	106	89	73	57	41	25
1,500	1,520	189	173	157	141	125	109	92	76	60	44	28
1,520	1,540	192	176	160	144	128	112	95	79	63	47	31
1,540	1,560	195	179	163	147	131	115	98	82	66	50	34
1,560	1,580	198	182	166	150	134	118	101	85	69	53	37
1,580	1,600	201	185	169	153	137	121	104	88	72	56	40
1,600	1,620	204	188	172	156	140	124	107	91	75	59	43
1,620	1,640	207	191	175	159	143	127	110	94	78	62	46
1,640	1,660	210	194	178	162	146	130	113	97	81	65	49
1,660	1,680	213	197	181	165	149	133	116	100	84	68	52
1,680	1,700	216	200	184	168	152	136	119	103	87	71	55
1,700	1,720	219	203	187	171	155	139	122	106	90	74	58
1,720	1,740	222	206	190	174	158	142	125	109	93	77	61
1,740	1,760	225	209	193	177	161	145	128	112	96	80	64
1,760	1,780	228	212	196	180	164	148	131	115	99	83	67
1,780	1,800	231	215	199	183	167	151	134	118	102	86	70
1,800	1,820	234	218	202	186	170	154	137	121	105	89	73
1,820	1,840	237	221	205	189	173	157	140	124	108	92	76
1,840	1,860	240	224	208	192	176	160	143	127	111	95	79
1,860	1,880	244	227	211	195	179	163	146	130	114	98	82
1,880	1,900	250	230	214	198	182	166	149	133	117	101	85
1,900	1,920	256	233	217	201	185	169	152	136	120	104	88
1,920	1,940	261	236	220	204	188	172	155	139	123	107	91
1,940	1,960	267	239	223	207	191	175	158	142	126	110	94
1,960	1,980	272	242	226	210	194	178	161	145	129	113	97
1,980	2,000	278	248	229	213	197	181	164	148	132	116	100
2,000	2,020	284	253	232	216	200	184	167	151	135	119	103
2,020	2,040	289	259	235	219	203	187	170	154	138	122	106
2,040	2,060	295	265	238	222	206	190	173	157	141	125	109
2,060	2,080	300	270	241	225	209	193	176	160	144	128	112
2,080	2,100	306	276	246	228	212	196	179	163	147	131	115
2,100	2,120	312	281	251	231	215	199	182	166	150	134	118
2,120	2,140	317	287	257	234	218	202	185	169	153	137	121
2,140	2,160	323	293	262	237	221	205	188	172	156	140	124
2,160	2,180	328	298	268	240	224	208	191	175	159	143	127
2,180	2,200	334	304	274	244	227	211	194	178	162	146	130
2,200	2,220	340	309	279	249	230	214	197	181	165	149	133
2,220	2,240	345	315	285	255	233	217	200	184	168	152	136
2,240	2,260	351	321	290	260	236	220	203	187	171	155	139
2,260	2,280	356	326	296	266	239	223	206	190	174	158	142
2,280	2,300	362	332	302	272	242	226	209	193	177	161	145
2,300	2,320	368	337	307	277	247	229	212	196	180	164	148
2,320	2,340	373	343	313	283	253	232	215	199	183	167	151
2,340	2,360	379	349	318	288	258	235	218	202	186	170	154
2,360	2,380	384	354	324	294	264	238	221	205	189	173	157
2,380	2,400	390	360	330	300	269	241	224	208	192	176	160
2,400	2,420	396	365	335	305	275	245	227	211	195	179	163
2,420	2,440	401	371	341	311	281	250	230	214	198	182	166
2,440	2,460	407	377	346	316	286	256	233	217	201	185	169
2,460	2,480	412	382	352	322	292	262	236	220	204	188	172
2,480	2,500	418	388	358	328	297	267	239	223	207	191	175
2,500	2,520	424	393	363	333	303	273	243	226	210	194	178
2,520	2,540	429	399	369	339	309	278	248	229	213	197	181
2,540	2,560	435	405	374	344	314	284	254	232	216	200	184
2,560	2,580	440	410	380	350	320	290	259	235	219	203	187
2,580	2,600	446	416	386	356	325	295	265	238	222	206	190
2,600	2,620	452	421	391	361	331	301	271	241	225	209	193
2,620	2,640	457	427	397	367	337	306	276	246	228	212	196
2,640	2,660	463	433	402	372	342	312	282	252	231	215	199
2,660	2,680	468	438	408	378	348	318	287	257	234	218	202

$2,680 and over   Use Table 2(b) for a **MARRIED person** on page 34. Also see the instructions on page 32.

A-13

SINGLE Persons—SEMIMONTHLY Payroll Period

(For Wages Paid in 20XX)

If the wages are—		And the number of withholding allowances claimed is—										
At least	But less than	0	1	2	3	4	5	6	7	8	9	10
		The amount of income tax to be withheld is—										
$0	$115	0	0	0	0	0	0	0	0	0	0	0
115	120	1	0	0	0	0	0	0	0	0	0	0
120	125	2	0	0	0	0	0	0	0	0	0	0
125	130	3	0	0	0	0	0	0	0	0	0	0
130	135	3	0	0	0	0	0	0	0	0	0	0
135	140	4	0	0	0	0	0	0	0	0	0	0
140	145	5	0	0	0	0	0	0	0	0	0	0
145	150	6	0	0	0	0	0	0	0	0	0	0
150	155	6	0	0	0	0	0	0	0	0	0	0
155	160	7	0	0	0	0	0	0	0	0	0	0
160	165	8	0	0	0	0	0	0	0	0	0	0
165	170	9	0	0	0	0	0	0	0	0	0	0
170	175	9	0	0	0	0	0	0	0	0	0	0
175	180	10	0	0	0	0	0	0	0	0	0	0
180	185	11	0	0	0	0	0	0	0	0	0	0
185	190	12	0	0	0	0	0	0	0	0	0	0
190	195	12	0	0	0	0	0	0	0	0	0	0
195	200	13	0	0	0	0	0	0	0	0	0	0
200	205	14	0	0	0	0	0	0	0	0	0	0
205	210	15	0	0	0	0	0	0	0	0	0	0
210	215	15	0	0	0	0	0	0	0	0	0	0
215	220	16	0	0	0	0	0	0	0	0	0	0
220	225	17	0	0	0	0	0	0	0	0	0	0
225	230	18	0	0	0	0	0	0	0	0	0	0
230	235	18	1	0	0	0	0	0	0	0	0	0
235	240	19	2	0	0	0	0	0	0	0	0	0
240	245	20	2	0	0	0	0	0	0	0	0	0
245	250	21	3	0	0	0	0	0	0	0	0	0
250	260	22	4	0	0	0	0	0	0	0	0	0
260	270	23	6	0	0	0	0	0	0	0	0	0
270	280	25	7	0	0	0	0	0	0	0	0	0
280	290	26	9	0	0	0	0	0	0	0	0	0
290	300	28	10	0	0	0	0	0	0	0	0	0
300	310	29	12	0	0	0	0	0	0	0	0	0
310	320	31	13	0	0	0	0	0	0	0	0	0
320	330	32	15	0	0	0	0	0	0	0	0	0
330	340	34	16	0	0	0	0	0	0	0	0	0
340	350	35	18	0	0	0	0	0	0	0	0	0
350	360	37	19	2	0	0	0	0	0	0	0	0
360	370	38	21	3	0	0	0	0	0	0	0	0
370	380	40	22	5	0	0	0	0	0	0	0	0
380	390	41	24	6	0	0	0	0	0	0	0	0
390	400	43	25	8	0	0	0	0	0	0	0	0
400	410	44	27	9	0	0	0	0	0	0	0	0
410	420	46	28	11	0	0	0	0	0	0	0	0
420	430	47	30	12	0	0	0	0	0	0	0	0
430	440	49	31	14	0	0	0	0	0	0	0	0
440	450	50	33	15	0	0	0	0	0	0	0	0
450	460	52	34	17	0	0	0	0	0	0	0	0
460	470	53	36	18	1	0	0	0	0	0	0	0
470	480	55	37	20	2	0	0	0	0	0	0	0
480	490	56	39	21	4	0	0	0	0	0	0	0
490	500	58	40	23	5	0	0	0	0	0	0	0
500	520	60	42	25	7	0	0	0	0	0	0	0
520	540	63	45	28	10	0	0	0	0	0	0	0
540	560	66	48	31	13	0	0	0	0	0	0	0
560	580	69	51	34	16	0	0	0	0	0	0	0
580	600	72	54	37	19	2	0	0	0	0	0	0
600	620	75	57	40	22	5	0	0	0	0	0	0
620	640	78	60	43	25	8	0	0	0	0	0	0
640	660	81	63	46	28	11	0	0	0	0	0	0
660	680	84	66	49	31	14	0	0	0	0	0	0
680	700	87	69	52	34	17	0	0	0	0	0	0
700	720	90	72	55	37	20	2	0	0	0	0	0
720	740	93	75	58	40	23	5	0	0	0	0	0
740	760	96	78	61	43	26	8	0	0	0	0	0
760	780	99	81	64	46	29	11	0	0	0	0	0
780	800	102	84	67	49	32	14	0	0	0	0	0
800	820	105	87	70	52	35	17	0	0	0	0	0
820	840	108	90	73	55	38	20	3	0	0	0	0

If the wages are—		And the number of withholding allowances claimed is—										
At least	But less than	0	1	2	3	4	5	6	7	8	9	10
		The amount of income tax to be withheld is—										
$840	$860	111	93	76	58	41	23	6	0	0	0	0
860	880	114	96	79	61	44	26	9	0	0	0	0
880	900	117	99	82	64	47	29	12	0	0	0	0
900	920	120	102	85	67	50	32	15	0	0	0	0
920	940	123	105	88	70	53	35	18	0	0	0	0
940	960	126	108	91	73	56	38	21	3	0	0	0
960	980	129	111	94	76	59	41	24	6	0	0	0
980	1,000	132	114	97	79	62	44	27	9	0	0	0
1,000	1,020	135	117	100	82	65	47	30	12	0	0	0
1,020	1,040	138	120	103	85	68	50	33	15	0	0	0
1,040	1,060	141	123	106	88	71	53	36	18	1	0	0
1,060	1,080	144	126	109	91	74	56	39	21	4	0	0
1,080	1,100	147	129	112	94	77	59	42	24	7	0	0
1,100	1,120	150	132	115	97	80	62	45	27	10	0	0
1,120	1,140	153	135	118	100	83	65	48	30	13	0	0
1,140	1,160	156	138	121	103	86	68	51	33	16	0	0
1,160	1,180	160	141	124	106	89	71	54	36	19	1	0
1,180	1,200	166	144	127	109	92	74	57	39	22	4	0
1,200	1,220	171	147	130	112	95	77	60	42	25	7	0
1,220	1,240	177	150	133	115	98	80	63	45	28	10	0
1,240	1,260	183	153	136	118	101	83	66	48	31	13	0
1,260	1,280	188	156	139	121	104	86	69	51	34	16	0
1,280	1,300	194	161	142	124	107	89	72	54	37	19	2
1,300	1,320	199	167	145	127	110	92	75	57	40	22	5
1,320	1,340	205	172	148	130	113	95	78	60	43	25	8
1,340	1,360	211	178	151	133	116	98	81	63	46	28	11
1,360	1,380	216	184	154	136	119	101	84	66	49	31	14
1,380	1,400	222	189	157	139	122	104	87	69	52	34	17
1,400	1,420	227	195	162	142	125	107	90	72	55	37	20
1,420	1,440	233	200	168	145	128	110	93	75	58	40	23
1,440	1,460	239	206	173	148	131	113	96	78	61	43	26
1,460	1,480	244	212	179	151	134	116	99	81	64	46	29
1,480	1,500	250	217	184	154	137	119	102	84	67	49	32
1,500	1,520	255	223	190	157	140	122	105	87	70	52	35
1,520	1,540	261	228	196	163	143	125	108	90	73	55	38
1,540	1,560	267	234	201	169	146	128	111	93	76	58	41
1,560	1,580	272	240	207	174	149	131	114	96	79	61	44
1,580	1,600	278	245	212	180	152	134	117	99	82	64	47
1,600	1,620	283	251	218	185	155	137	120	102	85	67	50
1,620	1,640	289	256	224	191	158	140	123	105	88	70	53
1,640	1,660	295	262	229	197	164	143	126	108	91	73	56
1,660	1,680	300	268	235	202	170	146	129	111	94	76	59
1,680	1,700	306	273	240	208	175	149	132	114	97	79	62
1,700	1,720	311	279	246	213	181	152	135	117	100	82	65
1,720	1,740	317	284	252	219	186	155	138	120	103	85	68
1,740	1,760	323	290	257	225	192	159	141	123	106	88	71
1,760	1,780	328	296	263	230	198	165	144	126	109	91	74
1,780	1,800	334	301	268	236	203	170	147	129	112	94	77
1,800	1,820	339	307	274	241	209	176	150	132	115	97	80
1,820	1,840	345	312	280	247	214	182	153	135	118	100	83
1,840	1,860	351	318	285	253	220	187	156	138	121	103	86
1,860	1,880	356	324	291	258	226	193	160	141	124	106	89
1,880	1,900	362	329	296	264	231	198	166	144	127	109	92
1,900	1,920	367	335	302	269	237	204	171	147	130	112	95
1,920	1,940	373	340	308	275	242	210	177	150	133	115	98
1,940	1,960	379	346	313	281	248	215	183	153	136	118	101
1,960	1,980	384	352	319	286	254	221	188	156	139	121	104
1,980	2,000	390	357	324	292	259	226	194	161	142	124	107
2,000	2,020	395	363	330	297	265	232	199	167	145	127	110
2,020	2,040	401	368	336	303	270	238	205	172	148	130	113
2,040	2,060	407	374	341	309	276	243	211	178	151	133	116
2,060	2,080	412	380	347	314	282	249	216	184	154	136	119
2,080	2,100	418	385	352	320	287	254	222	189	157	139	122
2,100	2,120	423	391	358	325	293	260	227	195	162	142	125
2,120	2,140	429	396	364	331	298	266	233	200	168	145	128

$2,140 and over   Use Table 3(a) for a **SINGLE person** on page 34. Also see the instructions on page 32.

A-15

MARRIED Persons—SEMIMONTHLY Payroll Period

(For Wages Paid in 20XX)

If the wages are—		And the number of withholding allowances claimed is—										
At least	But less than	0	1	2	3	4	5	6	7	8	9	10
		The amount of income tax to be withheld is—										
$0	$270	0	0	0	0	0	0	0	0	0	0	0
270	280	1	0	0	0	0	0	0	0	0	0	0
280	290	2	0	0	0	0	0	0	0	0	0	0
290	300	4	0	0	0	0	0	0	0	0	0	0
300	310	5	0	0	0	0	0	0	0	0	0	0
310	320	7	0	0	0	0	0	0	0	0	0	0
320	330	8	0	0	0	0	0	0	0	0	0	0
330	340	10	0	0	0	0	0	0	0	0	0	0
340	350	11	0	0	0	0	0	0	0	0	0	0
350	360	13	0	0	0	0	0	0	0	0	0	0
360	370	14	0	0	0	0	0	0	0	0	0	0
370	380	16	0	0	0	0	0	0	0	0	0	0
380	390	17	0	0	0	0	0	0	0	0	0	0
390	400	19	1	0	0	0	0	0	0	0	0	0
400	410	20	3	0	0	0	0	0	0	0	0	0
410	420	22	4	0	0	0	0	0	0	0	0	0
420	430	23	6	0	0	0	0	0	0	0	0	0
430	440	25	7	0	0	0	0	0	0	0	0	0
440	450	26	9	0	0	0	0	0	0	0	0	0
450	460	28	10	0	0	0	0	0	0	0	0	0
460	470	29	12	0	0	0	0	0	0	0	0	0
470	480	31	13	0	0	0	0	0	0	0	0	0
480	490	32	15	0	0	0	0	0	0	0	0	0
490	500	34	16	0	0	0	0	0	0	0	0	0
500	520	36	19	1	0	0	0	0	0	0	0	0
520	540	39	22	4	0	0	0	0	0	0	0	0
540	560	42	25	7	0	0	0	0	0	0	0	0
560	580	45	28	10	0	0	0	0	0	0	0	0
580	600	48	31	13	0	0	0	0	0	0	0	0
600	620	51	34	16	0	0	0	0	0	0	0	0
620	640	54	37	19	2	0	0	0	0	0	0	0
640	660	57	40	22	5	0	0	0	0	0	0	0
660	680	60	43	25	8	0	0	0	0	0	0	0
680	700	63	46	28	11	0	0	0	0	0	0	0
700	720	66	49	31	14	0	0	0	0	0	0	0
720	740	69	52	34	17	0	0	0	0	0	0	0
740	760	72	55	37	20	2	0	0	0	0	0	0
760	780	75	58	40	23	5	0	0	0	0	0	0
780	800	78	61	43	26	8	0	0	0	0	0	0
800	820	81	64	46	29	11	0	0	0	0	0	0
820	840	84	67	49	32	14	0	0	0	0	0	0
840	860	87	70	52	35	17	0	0	0	0	0	0
860	880	90	73	55	38	20	3	0	0	0	0	0
880	900	93	76	58	41	23	6	0	0	0	0	0
900	920	96	79	61	44	26	9	0	0	0	0	0
920	940	99	82	64	47	29	12	0	0	0	0	0
940	960	102	85	67	50	32	15	0	0	0	0	0
960	980	105	88	70	53	35	18	0	0	0	0	0
980	1,000	108	91	73	56	38	21	3	0	0	0	0
1,000	1,020	111	94	76	59	41	24	6	0	0	0	0
1,020	1,040	114	97	79	62	44	27	9	0	0	0	0
1,040	1,060	117	100	82	65	47	30	12	0	0	0	0
1,060	1,080	120	103	85	68	50	33	15	0	0	0	0
1,080	1,100	123	106	88	71	53	36	18	1	0	0	0
1,100	1,120	126	109	91	74	56	39	21	4	0	0	0
1,120	1,140	129	112	94	77	59	42	24	7	0	0	0
1,140	1,160	132	115	97	80	62	45	27	10	0	0	0
1,160	1,180	135	118	100	83	65	48	30	13	0	0	0
1,180	1,200	138	121	103	86	68	51	33	16	0	0	0
1,200	1,220	141	124	106	89	71	54	36	19	1	0	0
1,220	1,240	144	127	109	92	74	57	39	22	4	0	0
1,240	1,260	147	130	112	95	77	60	42	25	7	0	0
1,260	1,280	150	133	115	98	80	63	45	28	10	0	0
1,280	1,300	153	136	118	101	83	66	48	31	13	0	0
1,300	1,320	156	139	121	104	86	69	51	34	16	0	0
1,320	1,340	159	142	124	107	89	72	54	37	19	2	0
1,340	1,360	162	145	127	110	92	75	57	40	22	5	0
1,360	1,380	165	148	130	113	95	78	60	43	25	8	0
1,380	1,400	168	151	133	116	98	81	63	46	28	11	0
1,400	1,420	171	154	136	119	101	84	66	49	31	14	0

A-16

If the wages are—		And the number of withholding allowances claimed is—										
At least	But less than	0	1	2	3	4	5	6	7	8	9	10
		The amount of income tax to be withheld is—										
$1,420	$1,440	174	157	139	122	104	87	69	52	34	17	0
1,440	1,460	177	160	142	125	107	90	72	55	37	20	2
1,460	1,480	180	163	145	128	110	93	75	58	40	23	5
1,480	1,500	183	166	148	131	113	96	78	61	43	26	8
1,500	1,520	186	169	151	134	116	99	81	64	46	29	11
1,520	1,540	189	172	154	137	119	102	84	67	49	32	14
1,540	1,560	192	175	157	140	122	105	87	70	52	35	17
1,560	1,580	195	178	160	143	125	108	90	73	55	38	20
1,580	1,600	198	181	163	146	128	111	93	76	58	41	23
1,600	1,620	201	184	166	149	131	114	96	79	61	44	26
1,620	1,640	204	187	169	152	134	117	99	82	64	47	29
1,640	1,660	207	190	172	155	137	120	102	85	67	50	32
1,660	1,680	210	193	175	158	140	123	105	88	70	53	35
1,680	1,700	213	196	178	161	143	126	108	91	73	56	38
1,700	1,720	216	199	181	164	146	129	111	94	76	59	41
1,720	1,740	219	202	184	167	149	132	114	97	79	62	44
1,740	1,760	222	205	187	170	152	135	117	100	82	65	47
1,760	1,780	225	208	190	173	155	138	120	103	85	68	50
1,780	1,800	228	211	193	176	158	141	123	106	88	71	53
1,800	1,820	231	214	196	179	161	144	126	109	91	74	56
1,820	1,840	234	217	199	182	164	147	129	112	94	77	59
1,840	1,860	237	220	202	185	167	150	132	115	97	80	62
1,860	1,880	240	223	205	188	170	153	135	118	100	83	65
1,880	1,900	243	226	208	191	173	156	138	121	103	86	68
1,900	1,920	246	229	211	194	176	159	141	124	106	89	71
1,920	1,940	249	232	214	197	179	162	144	127	109	92	74
1,940	1,960	252	235	217	200	182	165	147	130	112	95	77
1,960	1,980	255	238	220	203	185	168	150	133	115	98	80
1,980	2,000	258	241	223	206	188	171	153	136	118	101	83
2,000	2,020	261	244	226	209	191	174	156	139	121	104	86
2,020	2,040	266	247	229	212	194	177	159	142	124	107	89
2,040	2,060	272	250	232	215	197	180	162	145	127	110	92
2,060	2,080	277	253	235	218	200	183	165	148	130	113	95
2,080	2,100	283	256	238	221	203	186	168	151	133	116	98
2,100	2,120	288	259	241	224	206	189	171	154	136	119	101
2,120	2,140	294	262	244	227	209	192	174	157	139	122	104
2,140	2,160	300	267	247	230	212	195	177	160	142	125	107
2,160	2,180	305	272	250	233	215	198	180	163	145	128	110
2,180	2,200	311	278	253	236	218	201	183	166	148	131	113
2,200	2,220	316	284	256	239	221	204	186	169	151	134	116
2,220	2,240	322	289	259	242	224	207	189	172	154	137	119
2,240	2,260	328	295	262	245	227	210	192	175	157	140	122
2,260	2,280	333	300	268	248	230	213	195	178	160	143	125
2,280	2,300	339	306	273	251	233	216	198	181	163	146	128
2,300	2,320	344	312	279	254	236	219	201	184	166	149	131
2,320	2,340	350	317	285	257	239	222	204	187	169	152	134
2,340	2,360	356	323	290	260	242	225	207	190	172	155	137
2,360	2,380	361	328	296	263	245	228	210	193	175	158	140
2,380	2,400	367	334	301	269	248	231	213	196	178	161	143
2,400	2,420	372	340	307	274	251	234	216	199	181	164	146
2,420	2,440	378	345	313	280	254	237	219	202	184	167	149
2,440	2,460	384	351	318	286	257	240	222	205	187	170	152
2,460	2,480	389	356	324	291	260	243	225	208	190	173	155
2,480	2,500	395	362	329	297	264	246	228	211	193	176	158
2,500	2,520	400	368	335	302	270	249	231	214	196	179	161
2,520	2,540	406	373	341	308	275	252	234	217	199	182	164
2,540	2,560	412	379	346	314	281	255	237	220	202	185	167
2,560	2,580	417	384	352	319	286	258	240	223	205	188	170
2,580	2,600	423	390	357	325	292	261	243	226	208	191	173
2,600	2,620	428	396	363	330	298	265	246	229	211	194	176
2,620	2,640	434	401	369	336	303	271	249	232	214	197	179
2,640	2,660	440	407	374	342	309	276	252	235	217	200	182
2,660	2,680	445	412	380	347	314	282	255	238	220	203	185
2,680	2,700	451	418	385	353	320	287	258	241	223	206	188
2,700	2,720	456	424	391	358	326	293	261	244	226	209	191

$2,720 and over   Use Table 3(b) for a **MARRIED person** on page 34. Also see the instructions on page 32.

A-17

SINGLE Persons—MONTHLY Payroll Period
(For Wages Paid in 20XX)

If the wages are—		And the number of withholding allowances claimed is—										
At least	But less than	0	1	2	3	4	5	6	7	8	9	10
		The amount of income tax to be withheld is—										
$0	$220	0	0	0	0	0	0	0	0	0	0	0
220	230	1	0	0	0	0	0	0	0	0	0	0
230	240	2	0	0	0	0	0	0	0	0	0	0
240	250	4	0	0	0	0	0	0	0	0	0	0
250	260	5	0	0	0	0	0	0	0	0	0	0
260	270	7	0	0	0	0	0	0	0	0	0	0
270	280	8	0	0	0	0	0	0	0	0	0	0
280	290	10	0	0	0	0	0	0	0	0	0	0
290	300	11	0	0	0	0	0	0	0	0	0	0
300	320	13	0	0	0	0	0	0	0	0	0	0
320	340	16	0	0	0	0	0	0	0	0	0	0
340	360	19	0	0	0	0	0	0	0	0	0	0
360	380	22	0	0	0	0	0	0	0	0	0	0
380	400	25	0	0	0	0	0	0	0	0	0	0
400	420	28	0	0	0	0	0	0	0	0	0	0
420	440	31	0	0	0	0	0	0	0	0	0	0
440	460	34	0	0	0	0	0	0	0	0	0	0
460	480	37	2	0	0	0	0	0	0	0	0	0
480	500	40	5	0	0	0	0	0	0	0	0	0
500	520	43	8	0	0	0	0	0	0	0	0	0
520	540	46	11	0	0	0	0	0	0	0	0	0
540	560	49	14	0	0	0	0	0	0	0	0	0
560	580	52	17	0	0	0	0	0	0	0	0	0
580	600	55	20	0	0	0	0	0	0	0	0	0
600	640	60	25	0	0	0	0	0	0	0	0	0
640	680	66	31	0	0	0	0	0	0	0	0	0
680	720	72	37	2	0	0	0	0	0	0	0	0
720	760	78	43	8	0	0	0	0	0	0	0	0
760	800	84	49	14	0	0	0	0	0	0	0	0
800	840	90	55	20	0	0	0	0	0	0	0	0
840	880	96	61	26	0	0	0	0	0	0	0	0
880	920	102	67	32	0	0	0	0	0	0	0	0
920	960	108	73	38	3	0	0	0	0	0	0	0
960	1,000	114	79	44	9	0	0	0	0	0	0	0
1,000	1,040	120	85	50	15	0	0	0	0	0	0	0
1,040	1,080	126	91	56	21	0	0	0	0	0	0	0
1,080	1,120	132	97	62	27	0	0	0	0	0	0	0
1,120	1,160	138	103	68	33	0	0	0	0	0	0	0
1,160	1,200	144	109	74	39	4	0	0	0	0	0	0
1,200	1,240	150	115	80	45	10	0	0	0	0	0	0
1,240	1,280	156	121	86	51	16	0	0	0	0	0	0
1,280	1,320	162	127	92	57	22	0	0	0	0	0	0
1,320	1,360	168	133	98	63	28	0	0	0	0	0	0
1,360	1,400	174	139	104	69	34	0	0	0	0	0	0
1,400	1,440	180	145	110	75	40	5	0	0	0	0	0
1,440	1,480	186	151	116	81	46	11	0	0	0	0	0
1,480	1,520	192	157	122	87	52	17	0	0	0	0	0
1,520	1,560	198	163	128	93	58	23	0	0	0	0	0
1,560	1,600	204	169	134	99	64	29	0	0	0	0	0
1,600	1,640	210	175	140	105	70	35	0	0	0	0	0
1,640	1,680	216	181	146	111	76	41	6	0	0	0	0
1,680	1,720	222	187	152	117	82	47	12	0	0	0	0
1,720	1,760	228	193	158	123	88	53	18	0	0	0	0
1,760	1,800	234	199	164	129	94	59	24	0	0	0	0
1,800	1,840	240	205	170	135	100	65	30	0	0	0	0
1,840	1,880	246	211	176	141	106	71	36	1	0	0	0
1,880	1,920	252	217	182	147	112	77	42	7	0	0	0
1,920	1,960	258	223	188	153	118	83	48	13	0	0	0
1,960	2,000	264	229	194	159	124	89	54	19	0	0	0
2,000	2,040	270	235	200	165	130	95	60	25	0	0	0
2,040	2,080	276	241	206	171	136	101	66	31	0	0	0
2,080	2,120	282	247	212	177	142	107	72	37	2	0	0
2,120	2,160	288	253	218	183	148	113	78	43	8	0	0
2,160	2,200	294	259	224	189	154	119	84	49	14	0	0
2,200	2,240	300	265	230	195	160	125	90	55	20	0	0
2,240	2,280	306	271	236	201	166	131	96	61	26	0	0
2,280	2,320	312	277	242	207	172	137	102	67	32	0	0
2,320	2,360	320	283	248	213	178	143	108	73	38	3	0
2,360	2,400	332	289	254	219	184	149	114	79	44	9	0
2,400	2,440	343	295	260	225	190	155	120	85	50	15	0

SINGLE Persons—MONTHLY Payroll Period

(For Wages Paid in 20XX)

If the wages are—		And the number of withholding allowances claimed is—										
At least	But less than	0	1	2	3	4	5	6	7	8	9	10
		The amount of income tax to be withheld is—										
$2,440	$2,480	354	301	266	231	196	161	126	91	56	21	0
2,480	2,520	365	307	272	237	202	167	132	97	62	27	0
2,520	2,560	376	313	278	243	208	173	138	103	68	33	0
2,560	2,600	388	322	284	249	214	179	144	109	74	39	4
2,600	2,640	399	333	290	255	220	185	150	115	80	45	10
2,640	2,680	410	345	296	261	226	191	156	121	86	51	16
2,680	2,720	421	356	302	267	232	197	162	127	92	57	22
2,720	2,760	432	367	308	273	238	203	168	133	98	63	28
2,760	2,800	444	378	314	279	244	209	174	139	104	69	34
2,800	2,840	455	389	324	285	250	215	180	145	110	75	40
2,840	2,880	466	401	335	291	256	221	186	151	116	81	46
2,880	2,920	477	412	347	297	262	227	192	157	122	87	52
2,920	2,960	488	423	358	303	268	233	198	163	128	93	58
2,960	3,000	500	434	369	309	274	239	204	169	134	99	64
3,000	3,040	511	445	380	315	280	245	210	175	140	105	70
3,040	3,080	522	457	391	326	286	251	216	181	146	111	76
3,080	3,120	533	468	403	337	292	257	222	187	152	117	82
3,120	3,160	544	479	414	348	298	263	228	193	158	123	88
3,160	3,200	556	490	425	360	304	269	234	199	164	129	94
3,200	3,240	567	501	436	371	310	275	240	205	170	135	100
3,240	3,280	578	513	447	382	317	281	246	211	176	141	106
3,280	3,320	589	524	459	393	328	287	252	217	182	147	112
3,320	3,360	600	535	470	404	339	293	258	223	188	153	118
3,360	3,400	612	546	481	416	350	299	264	229	194	159	124
3,400	3,440	623	557	492	427	361	305	270	235	200	165	130
3,440	3,480	634	569	503	438	373	311	276	241	206	171	136
3,480	3,520	645	580	515	449	384	319	282	247	212	177	142
3,520	3,560	656	591	526	460	395	330	288	253	218	183	148
3,560	3,600	668	602	537	472	406	341	294	259	224	189	154
3,600	3,640	679	613	548	483	417	352	300	265	230	195	160
3,640	3,680	690	625	559	494	429	363	306	271	236	201	166
3,680	3,720	701	636	571	505	440	375	312	277	242	207	172
3,720	3,760	712	647	582	516	451	386	320	283	248	213	178
3,760	3,800	724	658	593	528	462	397	332	289	254	219	184
3,800	3,840	735	669	604	539	473	408	343	295	260	225	190
3,840	3,880	746	681	615	550	485	419	354	301	266	231	196
3,880	3,920	757	692	627	561	496	431	365	307	272	237	202
3,920	3,960	768	703	638	572	507	442	376	313	278	243	208
3,960	4,000	780	714	649	584	518	453	388	322	284	249	214
4,000	4,040	791	725	660	595	529	464	399	333	290	255	220
4,040	4,080	802	737	671	606	541	475	410	345	296	261	226
4,080	4,120	813	748	683	617	552	487	421	356	302	267	232
4,120	4,160	824	759	694	628	563	498	432	367	308	273	238
4,160	4,200	836	770	705	640	574	509	444	378	314	279	244
4,200	4,240	847	781	716	651	585	520	455	389	324	285	250
4,240	4,280	858	793	727	662	597	531	466	401	335	291	256
4,280	4,320	869	804	739	673	608	543	477	412	347	297	262
4,320	4,360	880	815	750	684	619	554	488	423	358	303	268
4,360	4,400	892	826	761	696	630	565	500	434	369	309	274
4,400	4,440	903	837	772	707	641	576	511	445	380	315	280
4,440	4,480	914	849	783	718	653	587	522	457	391	326	286
4,480	4,520	925	860	795	729	664	599	533	468	403	337	292
4,520	4,560	936	871	806	740	675	610	544	479	414	348	298
4,560	4,600	948	882	817	752	686	621	556	490	425	360	304
4,600	4,640	959	893	828	763	697	632	567	501	436	371	310
4,640	4,680	970	905	839	774	709	643	578	513	447	382	317
4,680	4,720	981	916	851	785	720	655	589	524	459	393	328
4,720	4,760	992	927	862	796	731	666	600	535	470	404	339
4,760	4,800	1,004	938	873	808	742	677	612	546	481	416	350
4,800	4,840	1,015	949	884	819	753	688	623	557	492	427	361
4,840	4,880	1,026	961	895	830	765	699	634	569	503	438	373
4,880	4,920	1,037	972	907	841	776	711	645	580	515	449	384
4,920	4,960	1,048	983	918	852	787	722	656	591	526	460	395
4,960	5,000	1,060	994	929	864	798	733	668	602	537	472	406
5,000	5,040	1,072	1,005	940	875	809	744	679	613	548	483	417

$5,040 and over   Use Table 4(a) for a **SINGLE person** on page 34. Also see the instructions on page 32.

A-19

MARRIED Persons—MONTHLY Payroll Period

(For Wages Paid in 20XX)

If the wages are—		And the number of withholding allowances claimed is—										
At least	But less than	0	1	2	3	4	5	6	7	8	9	10
		The amount of income tax to be withheld is—										
$0	$540	0	0	0	0	0	0	0	0	0	0	0
540	560	2	0	0	0	0	0	0	0	0	0	0
560	580	5	0	0	0	0	0	0	0	0	0	0
580	600	8	0	0	0	0	0	0	0	0	0	0
600	640	12	0	0	0	0	0	0	0	0	0	0
640	680	18	0	0	0	0	0	0	0	0	0	0
680	720	24	0	0	0	0	0	0	0	0	0	0
720	760	30	0	0	0	0	0	0	0	0	0	0
760	800	36	1	0	0	0	0	0	0	0	0	0
800	840	42	7	0	0	0	0	0	0	0	0	0
840	880	48	13	0	0	0	0	0	0	0	0	0
880	920	54	19	0	0	0	0	0	0	0	0	0
920	960	60	25	0	0	0	0	0	0	0	0	0
960	1,000	66	31	0	0	0	0	0	0	0	0	0
1,000	1,040	72	37	2	0	0	0	0	0	0	0	0
1,040	1,080	78	43	8	0	0	0	0	0	0	0	0
1,080	1,120	84	49	14	0	0	0	0	0	0	0	0
1,120	1,160	90	55	20	0	0	0	0	0	0	0	0
1,160	1,200	96	61	26	0	0	0	0	0	0	0	0
1,200	1,240	102	67	32	0	0	0	0	0	0	0	0
1,240	1,280	108	73	38	3	0	0	0	0	0	0	0
1,280	1,320	114	79	44	9	0	0	0	0	0	0	0
1,320	1,360	120	85	50	15	0	0	0	0	0	0	0
1,360	1,400	126	91	56	21	0	0	0	0	0	0	0
1,400	1,440	132	97	62	27	0	0	0	0	0	0	0
1,440	1,480	138	103	68	33	0	0	0	0	0	0	0
1,480	1,520	144	109	74	39	4	0	0	0	0	0	0
1,520	1,560	150	115	80	45	10	0	0	0	0	0	0
1,560	1,600	156	121	86	51	16	0	0	0	0	0	0
1,600	1,640	162	127	92	57	22	0	0	0	0	0	0
1,640	1,680	168	133	98	63	28	0	0	0	0	0	0
1,680	1,720	174	139	104	69	34	0	0	0	0	0	0
1,720	1,760	180	145	110	75	40	5	0	0	0	0	0
1,760	1,800	186	151	116	81	46	11	0	0	0	0	0
1,800	1,840	192	157	122	87	52	17	0	0	0	0	0
1,840	1,880	198	163	128	93	58	23	0	0	0	0	0
1,880	1,920	204	169	134	99	64	29	0	0	0	0	0
1,920	1,960	210	175	140	105	70	35	0	0	0	0	0
1,960	2,000	216	181	146	111	76	41	6	0	0	0	0
2,000	2,040	222	187	152	117	82	47	12	0	0	0	0
2,040	2,080	228	193	158	123	88	53	18	0	0	0	0
2,080	2,120	234	199	164	129	94	59	24	0	0	0	0
2,120	2,160	240	205	170	135	100	65	30	0	0	0	0
2,160	2,200	246	211	176	141	106	71	36	1	0	0	0
2,200	2,240	252	217	182	147	112	77	42	7	0	0	0
2,240	2,280	258	223	188	153	118	83	48	13	0	0	0
2,280	2,320	264	229	194	159	124	89	54	19	0	0	0
2,320	2,360	270	235	200	165	130	95	60	25	0	0	0
2,360	2,400	276	241	206	171	136	101	66	31	0	0	0
2,400	2,440	282	247	212	177	142	107	72	37	2	0	0
2,440	2,480	288	253	218	183	148	113	78	43	8	0	0
2,480	2,520	294	259	224	189	154	119	84	49	14	0	0
2,520	2,560	300	265	230	195	160	125	90	55	20	0	0
2,560	2,600	306	271	236	201	166	131	96	61	26	0	0
2,600	2,640	312	277	242	207	172	137	102	67	32	0	0
2,640	2,680	318	283	248	213	178	143	108	73	38	3	0
2,680	2,720	324	289	254	219	184	149	114	79	44	9	0
2,720	2,760	330	295	260	225	190	155	120	85	50	15	0
2,760	2,800	336	301	266	231	196	161	126	91	56	21	0
2,800	2,840	342	307	272	237	202	167	132	97	62	27	0
2,840	2,880	348	313	278	243	208	173	138	103	68	33	0
2,880	2,920	354	319	284	249	214	179	144	109	74	39	4
2,920	2,960	360	325	290	255	220	185	150	115	80	45	10
2,960	3,000	366	331	296	261	226	191	156	121	86	51	16
3,000	3,040	372	337	302	267	232	197	162	127	92	57	22
3,040	3,080	378	343	308	273	238	203	168	133	98	63	28
3,080	3,120	384	349	314	279	244	209	174	139	104	69	34
3,120	3,160	390	355	320	285	250	215	180	145	110	75	40
3,160	3,200	396	361	326	291	256	221	186	151	116	81	46
3,200	3,240	402	367	332	297	262	227	192	157	122	87	52

A-20

(For Wages Paid in 20XX)

If the wages are—		And the number of withholding allowances claimed is—										
At least	But less than	0	1	2	3	4	5	6	7	8	9	10
		The amount of income tax to be withheld is—										
$3,240	$3,280	408	373	338	303	268	233	198	163	128	93	58
3,280	3,320	414	379	344	309	274	239	204	169	134	99	64
3,320	3,360	420	385	350	315	280	245	210	175	140	105	70
3,360	3,400	426	391	356	321	286	251	216	181	146	111	76
3,400	3,440	432	397	362	327	292	257	222	187	152	117	82
3,440	3,480	438	403	368	333	298	263	228	193	158	123	88
3,480	3,520	444	409	374	339	304	269	234	199	164	129	94
3,520	3,560	450	415	380	345	310	275	240	205	170	135	100
3,560	3,600	456	421	386	351	316	281	246	211	176	141	106
3,600	3,640	462	427	392	357	322	287	252	217	182	147	112
3,640	3,680	468	433	398	363	328	293	258	223	188	153	118
3,680	3,720	474	439	404	369	334	299	264	229	194	159	124
3,720	3,760	480	445	410	375	340	305	270	235	200	165	130
3,760	3,800	486	451	416	381	346	311	276	241	206	171	136
3,800	3,840	492	457	422	387	352	317	282	247	212	177	142
3,840	3,880	498	463	428	393	358	323	288	253	218	183	148
3,880	3,920	504	469	434	399	364	329	294	259	224	189	154
3,920	3,960	510	475	440	405	370	335	300	265	230	195	160
3,960	4,000	516	481	446	411	376	341	306	271	236	201	166
4,000	4,040	522	487	452	417	382	347	312	277	242	207	172
4,040	4,080	532	493	458	423	388	353	318	283	248	213	178
4,080	4,120	543	499	464	429	394	359	324	289	254	219	184
4,120	4,160	554	505	470	435	400	365	330	295	260	225	190
4,160	4,200	565	511	476	441	406	371	336	301	266	231	196
4,200	4,240	577	517	482	447	412	377	342	307	272	237	202
4,240	4,280	588	523	488	453	418	383	348	313	278	243	208
4,280	4,320	599	534	494	459	424	389	354	319	284	249	214
4,320	4,360	610	545	500	465	430	395	360	325	290	255	220
4,360	4,400	621	556	506	471	436	401	366	331	296	261	226
4,400	4,440	633	567	512	477	442	407	372	337	302	267	232
4,440	4,480	644	579	518	483	448	413	378	343	308	273	238
4,480	4,520	655	590	524	489	454	419	384	349	314	279	244
4,520	4,560	666	601	536	495	460	425	390	355	320	285	250
4,560	4,600	677	612	547	501	466	431	396	361	326	291	256
4,600	4,640	689	623	558	507	472	437	402	367	332	297	262
4,640	4,680	700	635	569	513	478	443	408	373	338	303	268
4,680	4,720	711	646	580	519	484	449	414	379	344	309	274
4,720	4,760	722	657	592	526	490	455	420	385	350	315	280
4,760	4,800	733	668	603	537	496	461	426	391	356	321	286
4,800	4,840	745	679	614	549	502	467	432	397	362	327	292
4,840	4,880	756	691	625	560	508	473	438	403	368	333	298
4,880	4,920	767	702	636	571	514	479	444	409	374	339	304
4,920	4,960	778	713	648	582	520	485	450	415	380	345	310
4,960	5,000	789	724	659	593	528	491	456	421	386	351	316
5,000	5,040	801	735	670	605	539	497	462	427	392	357	322
5,040	5,080	812	747	681	616	551	503	468	433	398	363	328
5,080	5,120	823	758	692	627	562	509	474	439	404	369	334
5,120	5,160	834	769	704	638	573	515	480	445	410	375	340
5,160	5,200	845	780	715	649	584	521	486	451	416	381	346
5,200	5,240	857	791	726	661	595	530	492	457	422	387	352
5,240	5,280	868	803	737	672	607	541	498	463	428	393	358
5,280	5,320	879	814	748	683	618	552	504	469	434	399	364
5,320	5,360	890	825	760	694	629	564	510	475	440	405	370
5,360	5,400	901	836	771	705	640	575	516	481	446	411	376
5,400	5,440	913	847	782	717	651	586	522	487	452	417	382
5,440	5,480	924	859	793	728	663	597	532	493	458	423	388
5,480	5,520	935	870	804	739	674	608	543	499	464	429	394
5,520	5,560	946	881	816	750	685	620	554	505	470	435	400
5,560	5,600	957	892	827	761	696	631	565	511	476	441	406
5,600	5,640	969	903	838	773	707	642	577	517	482	447	412
5,640	5,680	980	915	849	784	719	653	588	523	488	453	418
5,680	5,720	991	926	860	795	730	664	599	534	494	459	424
5,720	5,760	1,002	937	872	806	741	676	610	545	500	465	430
5,760	5,800	1,013	948	883	817	752	687	621	556	506	471	436
5,800	5,840	1,025	959	894	829	763	698	633	567	512	477	442

$5,840 and over   Use Table 4(b) for a **MARRIED person** on page 34. Also see the instructions on page 32.

SINGLE Persons—DAILY OR MISCELLANEOUS Payroll Period

(For Wages Paid in 20XX)

At least	But less than	0	1	2	3	4	5	6	7	8	9	10
		\multicolumn{11}{The amount of income tax to be withheld is—}										
$0	$15	0	0	0	0	0	0	0	0	0	0	0
15	18	1	0	0	0	0	0	0	0	0	0	0
18	21	1	0	0	0	0	0	0	0	0	0	0
21	24	2	0	0	0	0	0	0	0	0	0	0
24	27	2	1	0	0	0	0	0	0	0	0	0
27	30	3	1	0	0	0	0	0	0	0	0	0
30	33	3	2	0	0	0	0	0	0	0	0	0
33	36	4	2	0	0	0	0	0	0	0	0	0
36	39	4	2	1	0	0	0	0	0	0	0	0
39	42	5	3	1	0	0	0	0	0	0	0	0
42	45	5	3	2	0	0	0	0	0	0	0	0
45	48	5	4	2	1	0	0	0	0	0	0	0
48	51	6	4	3	1	0	0	0	0	0	0	0
51	54	6	5	3	2	0	0	0	0	0	0	0
54	57	7	5	4	2	0	0	0	0	0	0	0
57	60	7	6	4	2	1	0	0	0	0	0	0
60	63	8	6	4	3	1	0	0	0	0	0	0
63	66	8	7	5	3	2	0	0	0	0	0	0
66	69	9	7	5	4	2	1	0	0	0	0	0
69	72	9	7	6	4	3	1	0	0	0	0	0
72	75	9	8	6	5	3	1	0	0	0	0	0
75	78	10	8	7	5	3	2	0	0	0	0	0
78	81	10	9	7	6	4	2	1	0	0	0	0
81	84	11	9	8	6	4	3	1	0	0	0	0
84	87	11	10	8	6	5	3	2	0	0	0	0
87	90	12	10	9	7	5	4	2	0	0	0	0
90	93	12	11	9	7	6	4	3	1	0	0	0
93	96	13	11	9	8	6	5	3	1	0	0	0
96	99	13	11	10	8	7	5	3	2	0	0	0
99	102	14	12	10	9	7	5	4	2	1	0	0
102	105	14	12	11	9	8	6	4	3	1	0	0
105	108	14	13	11	10	8	6	5	3	2	0	0
108	111	15	13	12	10	8	7	5	4	2	0	0
111	114	16	14	12	11	9	7	6	4	2	1	0
114	117	17	14	13	11	9	8	6	4	3	1	0
117	120	18	15	13	11	10	8	7	5	3	2	0
120	123	19	16	13	12	10	9	7	5	4	2	1
123	126	19	16	14	12	11	9	7	6	4	3	1
126	129	20	17	14	13	11	10	8	6	5	3	1
129	132	21	18	15	13	12	10	8	7	5	4	2
132	135	22	19	16	14	12	10	9	7	6	4	2
135	138	23	20	17	14	12	11	9	8	6	4	3
138	141	24	21	18	15	13	11	10	8	6	5	3
141	144	24	21	18	15	13	12	10	9	7	5	4
144	147	25	22	19	16	14	12	11	9	7	6	4
147	150	26	23	20	17	14	13	11	9	8	6	5
150	153	27	24	21	18	15	13	12	10	8	7	5
153	156	28	25	22	19	16	14	12	10	9	7	5
156	159	29	26	23	20	17	14	12	11	9	8	6
159	162	29	26	23	20	17	14	13	11	10	8	6
162	165	30	27	24	21	18	15	13	12	10	8	7
165	168	31	28	25	22	19	16	14	12	11	9	7
168	171	32	29	26	23	20	17	14	13	11	9	8
171	174	33	30	27	24	21	18	15	13	11	10	8
174	177	34	31	28	25	22	19	16	13	12	10	9
177	180	35	32	28	25	22	19	16	14	12	11	9
180	183	35	32	29	26	23	20	17	14	13	11	10
183	186	36	33	30	27	24	21	18	15	13	12	10
186	189	37	34	31	28	25	22	19	16	14	12	10
189	192	38	35	32	29	26	23	20	17	14	13	11
192	195	39	36	33	30	27	24	21	18	15	13	11
195	198	40	37	34	31	28	24	21	18	15	13	12
198	201	40	37	34	31	28	25	22	19	16	14	12
201	204	41	38	35	32	29	26	23	20	17	14	13
204	207	42	39	36	33	30	27	24	21	18	15	13
207	210	43	40	37	34	31	28	25	22	19	16	14
210	213	44	41	38	35	32	29	26	23	20	17	14
213	216	45	42	39	36	33	30	27	23	20	17	14
216	219	45	42	39	36	33	30	27	24	21	18	15
219	222	46	43	40	37	34	31	28	25	22	19	16

A-22

SINGLE Persons—DAILY OR MISCELLANEOUS Payroll Period
(For Wages Paid in 20XX)

If the wages are—		And the number of withholding allowances claimed is—										
At least	But less than	0	1	2	3	4	5	6	7	8	9	10
		The amount of income tax to be withheld is—										
$222	$225	47	44	41	38	35	32	29	26	23	20	17
225	228	48	45	42	39	36	33	30	27	24	21	18
228	231	49	46	43	40	37	34	31	28	25	22	19
231	234	50	47	44	41	38	35	32	29	26	23	19
234	237	51	47	44	41	38	35	32	29	26	23	20
237	240	52	48	45	42	39	36	33	30	27	24	21
240	243	52	49	46	43	40	37	34	31	28	25	22
243	246	53	50	47	44	41	38	35	32	29	26	23
246	249	54	51	48	45	42	39	36	33	30	27	24
249	252	55	52	49	46	43	40	37	34	31	28	25
252	255	56	53	50	46	43	40	37	34	31	28	25
255	258	57	54	50	47	44	41	38	35	32	29	26
258	261	58	55	51	48	45	42	39	36	33	30	27
261	264	59	56	52	49	46	43	40	37	34	31	28
264	267	60	57	53	50	47	44	41	38	35	32	29
267	270	61	58	54	51	48	45	42	39	36	33	30
270	273	62	58	55	52	49	45	42	39	36	33	30
273	276	63	59	56	53	49	46	43	40	37	34	31
276	279	64	60	57	54	50	47	44	41	38	35	32
279	282	65	61	58	55	51	48	45	42	39	36	33
282	285	66	62	59	56	52	49	46	43	40	37	34
285	288	66	63	60	56	53	50	47	44	41	38	35
288	291	67	64	61	57	54	51	48	44	41	38	35
291	294	68	65	62	58	55	52	48	45	42	39	36
294	297	69	66	63	59	56	53	49	46	43	40	37
297	300	70	67	63	60	57	53	50	47	44	41	38
300	303	71	68	64	61	58	54	51	48	45	42	39
303	306	72	69	65	62	59	55	52	49	46	43	40
306	309	73	70	66	63	60	56	53	50	47	44	40
309	312	74	71	67	64	61	57	54	51	47	44	41
312	315	75	71	68	65	61	58	55	51	48	45	42
315	318	76	72	69	66	62	59	56	52	49	46	43
318	321	77	73	70	67	63	60	57	53	50	47	44
321	324	78	74	71	68	64	61	58	54	51	48	45
324	327	79	75	72	69	65	62	59	55	52	49	46
327	330	79	76	73	69	66	63	59	56	53	49	46
330	333	80	77	74	70	67	64	60	57	54	50	47
333	336	81	78	75	71	68	65	61	58	55	51	48
336	339	82	79	76	72	69	66	62	59	56	52	49
339	341	83	80	76	73	70	66	63	60	56	53	50
341	343	84	80	77	74	70	67	64	60	57	54	50
343	345	84	81	78	74	71	68	64	61	58	54	51
345	347	85	82	78	75	72	68	65	62	58	55	52
347	349	86	82	79	75	72	69	65	62	59	55	52
349	351	86	83	79	76	73	69	66	63	59	56	53
351	353	87	83	80	77	73	70	67	63	60	57	53
353	355	87	84	81	77	74	71	67	64	61	57	54
355	357	88	85	81	78	75	71	68	65	61	58	55
357	359	89	85	82	79	75	72	69	65	62	59	55
359	361	89	86	83	79	76	73	69	66	63	59	56
361	363	90	87	83	80	77	73	70	66	63	60	56
363	365	90	87	84	80	77	74	70	67	64	60	57
365	367	91	88	84	81	78	74	71	68	64	61	58
367	369	92	88	85	82	78	75	72	68	65	62	58
369	371	92	89	86	82	79	76	72	69	66	62	59
371	373	93	90	86	83	80	76	73	70	66	63	60
373	375	94	90	87	84	80	77	74	70	67	64	60
375	377	94	91	88	84	81	78	74	71	67	64	61
377	379	95	91	88	85	81	78	75	71	68	65	61
379	381	95	92	89	85	82	79	75	72	69	65	62
381	383	96	93	89	86	83	79	76	73	69	66	63
383	385	97	93	90	87	83	80	77	73	70	67	63
385	387	97	94	91	87	84	81	77	74	71	67	64
387	389	98	95	91	88	85	81	78	75	71	68	65
389	391	99	95	92	89	85	82	79	75	72	68	65

$391 and over   Use Table 8(a) for a **SINGLE person** on page 35. Also see the instructions on page 32.

A-23

MARRIED Persons—DAILY OR MISCELLANEOUS Payroll Period

(For Wages Paid in 20XX)

If the wages are—		And the number of withholding allowances claimed is—										
At least	But less than	0	1	2	3	4	5	6	7	8	9	10
		The amount of income tax to be withheld is—										
$0	$27	0	0	0	0	0	0	0	0	0	0	0
27	30	1	0	0	0	0	0	0	0	0	0	0
30	33	1	0	0	0	0	0	0	0	0	0	0
33	36	1	0	0	0	0	0	0	0	0	0	0
36	39	2	0	0	0	0	0	0	0	0	0	0
39	42	2	1	0	0	0	0	0	0	0	0	0
42	45	3	1	0	0	0	0	0	0	0	0	0
45	48	3	2	0	0	0	0	0	0	0	0	0
48	51	4	2	0	0	0	0	0	0	0	0	0
51	54	4	3	1	0	0	0	0	0	0	0	0
54	57	5	3	1	0	0	0	0	0	0	0	0
57	60	5	3	2	0	0	0	0	0	0	0	0
60	63	6	4	2	1	0	0	0	0	0	0	0
63	66	6	4	3	1	0	0	0	0	0	0	0
66	69	6	5	3	2	0	0	0	0	0	0	0
69	72	7	5	4	2	0	0	0	0	0	0	0
72	75	7	6	4	2	1	0	0	0	0	0	0
75	78	8	6	5	3	1	0	0	0	0	0	0
78	81	8	7	5	3	2	0	0	0	0	0	0
81	84	9	7	5	4	2	1	0	0	0	0	0
84	87	9	7	6	4	3	1	0	0	0	0	0
87	90	10	8	6	5	3	1	0	0	0	0	0
90	93	10	8	7	5	4	2	0	0	0	0	0
93	96	10	9	7	6	4	2	1	0	0	0	0
96	99	11	9	8	6	4	3	1	0	0	0	0
99	102	11	10	8	7	5	3	2	0	0	0	0
102	105	12	10	9	7	5	4	2	0	0	0	0
105	108	12	11	9	7	6	4	3	1	0	0	0
108	111	13	11	9	8	6	5	3	1	0	0	0
111	114	13	12	10	8	7	5	3	2	0	0	0
114	117	14	12	10	9	7	6	4	2	1	0	0
117	120	14	12	11	9	8	6	4	3	1	0	0
120	123	15	13	11	10	8	6	5	3	2	0	0
123	126	15	13	12	10	8	7	5	4	2	0	0
126	129	15	14	12	11	9	7	6	4	2	1	0
129	132	16	14	13	11	9	8	6	5	3	1	0
132	135	16	15	13	11	10	8	7	5	3	2	0
135	138	17	15	14	12	10	9	7	5	4	2	1
138	141	17	16	14	12	11	9	8	6	4	3	1
141	144	18	16	14	13	11	10	8	6	5	3	2
144	147	18	16	15	13	12	10	8	7	5	4	2
147	150	19	17	15	14	12	10	9	7	6	4	2
150	153	19	17	16	14	13	11	9	8	6	4	3
153	156	19	18	16	15	13	11	10	8	7	5	3
156	159	20	18	17	15	13	12	10	9	7	5	4
159	162	20	19	17	16	14	12	11	9	7	6	4
162	165	21	19	18	16	14	13	11	9	8	6	5
165	168	21	20	18	16	15	13	12	10	8	7	5
168	171	22	20	18	17	15	14	12	10	9	7	6
171	174	22	21	19	17	16	14	12	11	9	8	6
174	177	23	21	19	18	16	15	13	11	10	8	6
177	180	23	21	20	18	17	15	13	12	10	9	7
180	183	24	22	20	19	17	15	14	12	11	9	7
183	186	24	22	21	19	17	16	14	13	11	9	8
186	189	25	23	21	20	18	16	15	13	11	10	8
189	192	25	23	22	20	18	17	15	14	12	10	9
192	195	26	24	22	20	19	17	16	14	12	11	9
195	198	27	24	23	21	19	18	16	14	13	11	10
198	201	28	25	23	21	20	18	17	15	13	12	10
201	204	29	26	23	22	20	19	17	15	14	12	11
204	207	30	27	24	22	21	19	17	16	14	13	11
207	210	30	27	24	23	21	19	18	16	15	13	11
210	213	31	28	25	23	22	20	18	17	15	13	12
213	216	32	29	26	24	22	20	19	17	16	14	12
216	219	33	30	27	24	22	21	19	18	16	14	13
219	222	34	31	28	25	23	21	20	18	16	15	13
222	225	35	32	29	26	23	22	20	18	17	15	14
225	228	35	32	29	26	24	22	21	19	17	16	14
228	231	36	33	30	27	24	23	21	19	18	16	15
231	234	37	34	31	28	25	23	21	20	18	17	15

A-24

MARExRIED Persons—DAILY OR MISCELLANEOUS Payroll Period

(For Wages Paid in 20XX)

If the wages are—		And the number of withholding allowances claimed is—										
At least	But less than	0	1	2	3	4	5	6	7	8	9	10
		The amount of income tax to be withheld is—										
$234	$237	38	35	32	29	26	24	22	20	19	17	15
237	240	39	36	33	30	27	24	22	21	19	18	16
240	243	40	37	34	31	28	25	23	21	20	18	16
243	246	41	38	35	31	28	25	23	22	20	18	17
246	249	41	38	35	32	29	26	24	22	20	19	17
249	252	42	39	36	33	30	27	24	23	21	19	18
252	255	43	40	37	34	31	28	25	23	21	20	18
255	258	44	41	38	35	32	29	26	23	22	20	19
258	261	45	42	39	36	33	30	27	24	22	21	19
261	264	46	43	40	37	34	31	27	24	23	21	20
264	267	46	43	40	37	34	31	28	25	23	22	20
267	270	47	44	41	38	35	32	29	26	24	22	20
270	273	48	45	42	39	36	33	30	27	24	22	21
273	276	49	46	43	40	37	34	31	28	25	23	21
276	279	50	47	44	41	38	35	32	29	26	23	22
279	282	51	48	45	42	39	36	33	30	26	24	22
282	285	51	48	45	42	39	36	33	30	27	24	23
285	288	52	49	46	43	40	37	34	31	28	25	23
288	291	53	50	47	44	41	38	35	32	29	26	24
291	294	54	51	48	45	42	39	36	33	30	27	24
294	297	55	52	49	46	43	40	37	34	31	28	25
297	300	56	53	50	47	44	41	38	35	32	29	26
300	303	56	53	50	47	44	41	38	35	32	29	26
303	306	57	54	51	48	45	42	39	36	33	30	27
306	309	58	55	52	49	46	43	40	37	34	31	28
309	312	59	56	53	50	47	44	41	38	35	32	29
312	315	60	57	54	51	48	45	42	39	36	33	30
315	318	61	58	55	52	49	46	43	40	37	34	31
318	321	62	59	56	52	49	46	43	40	37	34	31
321	324	62	59	56	53	50	47	44	41	38	35	32
324	327	63	60	57	54	51	48	45	42	39	36	33
327	330	64	61	58	55	52	49	46	43	40	37	34
330	333	65	62	59	56	53	50	47	44	41	38	35
333	336	66	63	60	57	54	51	48	45	42	39	36
336	339	67	64	61	58	55	52	48	45	42	39	36
339	341	67	64	61	58	55	52	49	46	43	40	37
341	343	68	65	62	59	56	53	50	47	44	41	38
343	345	68	65	62	59	56	53	50	47	44	41	38
345	347	69	66	63	60	57	54	51	48	45	42	39
347	349	70	67	63	60	57	54	51	48	45	42	39
349	351	70	67	64	61	58	55	52	49	46	43	40
351	353	71	68	65	62	59	56	53	50	47	44	40
353	355	71	68	65	62	59	56	53	50	47	44	41
355	357	72	69	66	63	60	57	54	51	48	45	42
357	359	72	69	66	63	60	57	54	51	48	45	42
359	361	73	70	67	64	61	58	55	52	49	46	43
361	363	73	70	67	64	61	58	55	52	49	46	43
363	365	74	71	68	65	62	59	56	53	50	47	44
365	367	75	72	69	66	62	59	56	53	50	47	44
367	369	75	72	69	66	63	60	57	54	51	48	45
369	371	76	73	70	67	64	61	58	55	52	49	46
371	373	76	73	70	67	64	61	58	55	52	49	46
373	375	77	74	71	68	65	62	59	56	53	50	47
375	377	77	74	71	68	65	62	59	56	53	50	47
377	379	78	75	72	69	66	63	60	57	54	51	48
379	381	78	75	72	69	66	63	60	57	54	51	48
381	383	79	76	73	70	67	64	61	58	55	52	49
383	385	80	77	74	71	68	65	62	58	55	52	49
385	387	80	77	74	71	68	65	62	59	56	53	50
387	389	81	78	75	72	69	66	63	60	57	54	51
389	391	81	78	75	72	69	66	63	60	57	54	51
391	393	82	79	76	73	70	67	64	61	58	55	52
393	395	83	79	76	73	70	67	64	61	58	55	52
395	397	83	80	77	74	71	68	65	62	59	56	53
397	399	84	81	77	74	71	68	65	62	59	56	53

$399 and over   Use Table 8(b) for a **MARRIED person** on page 35. Also see the instructions on **page 32**.

A-25

6.2% Social Security Employee Tax Table

Note: *Wages subject to social security are generally also subject to the Medicare tax.*

Wages at least	But less than	Tax to be withheld	Wages at least	But less than	Tax to be withheld	Wages at least	But less than	Tax to be withheld	Wages at least	But less than	Tax to be withheld
$0.00	$0.09	$0.00	$13.47	$13.63	$.84	$27.02	$27.18	$1.68	$40.57	$40.73	$2.52
.09	.25	.01	13.63	13.80	.85	27.18	27.34	1.69	40.73	40.89	2.53
.25	.41	.02	13.80	13.96	.86	27.34	27.50	1.70	40.89	41.05	2.54
.41	.57	.03	13.96	14.12	.87	27.50	27.67	1.71	41.05	41.21	2.55
.57	.73	.04	14.12	14.28	.88	27.67	27.83	1.72	41.21	41.38	2.56
.73	.89	.05	14.28	14.44	.89	27.83	27.99	1.73	41.38	41.54	2.57
.89	1.05	.06	14.44	14.60	.90	27.99	28.15	1.74	41.54	41.70	2.58
1.05	1.21	.07	14.60	14.76	.91	28.15	28.31	1.75	41.70	41.86	2.59
1.21	1.38	.08	14.76	14.92	.92	28.31	28.47	1.76	41.86	42.02	2.60
1.38	1.54	.09	14.92	15.09	.93	28.47	28.63	1.77	42.02	42.18	2.61
1.54	1.70	.10	15.09	15.25	.94	28.63	28.80	1.78	42.18	42.34	2.62
1.70	1.86	.11	15.25	15.41	.95	28.80	28.96	1.79	42.34	42.50	2.63
1.86	2.02	.12	15.41	15.57	.96	28.96	29.12	1.80	42.50	42.67	2.64
2.02	2.18	.13	15.57	15.73	.97	29.12	29.28	1.81	42.67	42.83	2.65
2.18	2.34	.14	15.73	15.89	.98	29.28	29.44	1.82	42.83	42.99	2.66
2.34	2.50	.15	15.89	16.05	.99	29.44	29.60	1.83	42.99	43.15	2.67
2.50	2.67	.16	16.05	16.21	1.00	29.60	29.76	1.84	43.15	43.31	2.68
2.67	2.83	.17	16.21	16.38	1.01	29.76	29.92	1.85	43.31	43.47	2.69
2.83	2.99	.18	16.38	16.54	1.02	29.92	30.09	1.86	43.47	43.63	2.70
2.99	3.15	.19	16.54	16.70	1.03	30.09	30.25	1.87	43.63	43.80	2.71
3.15	3.31	.20	16.70	16.86	1.04	30.25	30.41	1.88	43.80	43.96	2.72
3.31	3.47	.21	16.86	17.02	1.05	30.41	30.57	1.89	43.96	44.12	2.73
3.47	3.63	.22	17.02	17.18	1.06	30.57	30.73	1.90	44.12	44.28	2.74
3.63	3.80	.23	17.18	17.34	1.07	30.73	30.89	1.91	44.28	44.44	2.75
3.80	3.96	.24	17.34	17.50	1.08	30.89	31.05	1.92	44.44	44.60	2.76
3.96	4.12	.25	17.50	17.67	1.09	31.05	31.21	1.93	44.60	44.76	2.77
4.12	4.28	.26	17.67	17.83	1.10	31.21	31.38	1.94	44.76	44.92	2.78
4.28	4.44	.27	17.83	17.99	1.11	31.38	31.54	1.95	44.92	45.09	2.79
4.44	4.60	.28	17.99	18.15	1.12	31.54	31.70	1.96	45.09	45.25	2.80
4.60	4.76	.29	18.15	18.31	1.13	31.70	31.86	1.97	45.25	45.41	2.81
4.76	4.92	.30	18.31	18.47	1.14	31.86	32.02	1.98	45.41	45.57	2.82
4.92	5.09	.31	18.47	18.63	1.15	32.02	32.18	1.99	45.57	45.73	2.83
5.09	5.25	.32	18.63	18.80	1.16	32.18	32.34	2.00	45.73	45.89	2.84
5.25	5.41	.33	18.80	18.96	1.17	32.34	32.50	2.01	45.89	46.05	2.85
5.41	5.57	.34	18.96	19.12	1.18	32.50	32.67	2.02	46.05	46.21	2.86
5.57	5.73	.35	19.12	19.28	1.19	32.67	32.83	2.03	46.21	46.38	2.87
5.73	5.89	.36	19.28	19.44	1.20	32.83	32.99	2.04	46.38	46.54	2.88
5.89	6.05	.37	19.44	19.60	1.21	32.99	33.15	2.05	46.54	46.70	2.89
6.05	6.21	.38	19.60	19.76	1.22	33.15	33.31	2.06	46.70	46.86	2.90
6.21	6.38	.39	19.76	19.92	1.23	33.31	33.47	2.07	46.86	47.02	2.91
6.38	6.54	.40	19.92	20.09	1.24	33.47	33.63	2.08	47.02	47.18	2.92
6.54	6.70	.41	20.09	20.25	1.25	33.63	33.80	2.09	47.18	47.34	2.93
6.70	6.86	.42	20.25	20.41	1.26	33.80	33.96	2.10	47.34	47.50	2.94
6.86	7.02	.43	20.41	20.57	1.27	33.96	34.12	2.11	47.50	47.67	2.95
7.02	7.18	.44	20.57	20.73	1.28	34.12	34.28	2.12	47.67	47.83	2.96
7.18	7.34	.45	20.73	20.89	1.29	34.28	34.44	2.13	47.83	47.99	2.97
7.34	7.50	.46	20.89	21.05	1.30	34.44	34.60	2.14	47.99	48.15	2.98
7.50	7.67	.47	21.05	21.21	1.31	34.60	34.76	2.15	48.15	48.31	2.99
7.67	7.83	.48	21.21	21.38	1.32	34.76	34.92	2.16	48.31	48.47	3.00
7.83	7.99	.49	21.38	21.54	1.33	34.92	35.09	2.17	48.47	48.63	3.01
7.99	8.15	.50	21.54	21.70	1.34	35.09	35.25	2.18	48.63	48.80	3.02
8.15	8.31	.51	21.70	21.86	1.35	35.25	35.41	2.19	48.80	48.96	3.03
8.31	8.47	.52	21.86	22.02	1.36	35.41	35.57	2.20	48.96	49.12	3.04
8.47	8.63	.53	22.02	22.18	1.37	35.57	35.73	2.21	49.12	49.28	3.05
8.63	8.80	.54	22.18	22.34	1.38	35.73	35.89	2.22	49.28	49.44	3.06
8.80	8.96	.55	22.34	22.50	1.39	35.89	36.05	2.23	49.44	49.60	3.07
8.96	9.12	.56	22.50	22.67	1.40	36.05	36.21	2.24	49.60	49.76	3.08
9.12	9.28	.57	22.67	22.83	1.41	36.21	36.38	2.25	49.76	49.92	3.09
9.28	9.44	.58	22.83	22.99	1.42	36.38	36.54	2.26	49.92	50.09	3.10
9.44	9.60	.59	22.99	23.15	1.43	36.54	36.70	2.27	50.09	50.25	3.11
9.60	9.76	.60	23.15	23.31	1.44	36.70	36.86	2.28	50.25	50.41	3.12
9.76	9.92	.61	23.31	23.47	1.45	36.86	37.02	2.29	50.41	50.57	3.13
9.92	10.09	.62	23.47	23.63	1.46	37.02	37.18	2.30	50.57	50.73	3.14
10.09	10.25	.63	23.63	23.80	1.47	37.18	37.34	2.31	50.73	50.89	3.15
10.25	10.41	.64	23.80	23.96	1.48	37.34	37.50	2.32	50.89	51.05	3.16
10.41	10.57	.65	23.96	24.12	1.49	37.50	37.67	2.33	51.05	51.21	3.17
10.57	10.73	.66	24.12	24.28	1.50	37.67	37.83	2.34	51.21	51.38	3.18
10.73	10.89	.67	24.28	24.44	1.51	37.83	37.99	2.35	51.38	51.54	3.19
10.89	11.05	.68	24.44	24.60	1.52	37.99	38.15	2.36	51.54	51.70	3.20
11.05	11.21	.69	24.60	24.76	1.53	38.15	38.31	2.37	51.70	51.86	3.21
11.21	11.38	.70	24.76	24.92	1.54	38.31	38.47	2.38	51.86	52.02	3.22
11.38	11.54	.71	24.92	25.09	1.55	38.47	38.63	2.39	52.02	52.18	3.23
11.54	11.70	.72	25.09	25.25	1.56	38.63	38.80	2.40	52.18	52.34	3.24
11.70	11.86	.73	25.25	25.41	1.57	38.80	38.96	2.41	52.34	52.50	3.25
11.86	12.02	.74	25.41	25.57	1.58	38.96	39.12	2.42	52.50	52.67	3.26
12.02	12.18	.75	25.57	25.73	1.59	39.12	39.28	2.43	52.67	52.83	3.27
12.18	12.34	.76	25.73	25.89	1.60	39.28	39.44	2.44	52.83	52.99	3.28
12.34	12.50	.77	25.89	26.05	1.61	39.44	39.60	2.45	52.99	53.15	3.29
12.50	12.67	.78	26.05	26.21	1.62	39.60	39.76	2.46	53.15	53.31	3.30
12.67	12.83	.79	26.21	26.38	1.63	39.76	39.92	2.47	53.31	53.47	3.31
12.83	12.99	.80	26.38	26.54	1.64	39.92	40.09	2.48	53.47	53.63	3.32
12.99	13.15	.81	26.54	26.70	1.65	40.09	40.25	2.49	53.63	53.80	3.33
13.15	13.31	.82	26.70	26.86	1.66	40.25	40.41	2.50	53.80	53.96	3.34
13.31	13.47	.83	26.86	27.02	1.67	40.41	40.57	2.51	53.96	54.12	3.35

A-26

6.2% Social Security Employee Tax Table

Note: *Wages subject to social security are generally also subject to the Medicare tax.*

Wages at least	But less than	Tax to be withheld	Wages at least	But less than	Tax to be withheld	Wages at least	But less than	Tax to be withheld	Wages at least	But less than	Tax to be withheld
$54.12	$54.28	$3.36	$66.54	$66.70	$4.13	$78.96	$79.12	$4.90	$91.38	$91.54	$5.67
54.28	54.44	3.37	66.70	66.86	4.14	79.12	79.28	4.91	91.54	91.70	5.68
54.44	54.60	3.38	66.86	67.02	4.15	79.28	79.44	4.92	91.70	91.86	5.69
54.60	54.76	3.39	67.02	67.18	4.16	79.44	79.60	4.93	91.86	92.02	5.70
54.76	54.92	3.40	67.18	67.34	4.17	79.60	79.76	4.94	92.02	92.18	5.71
54.92	55.09	3.41	67.34	67.50	4.18	79.76	79.92	4.95	92.18	92.34	5.72
55.09	55.25	3.42	67.50	67.67	4.19	79.92	80.09	4.96	92.34	92.50	5.73
55.25	55.41	3.43	67.67	67.83	4.20	80.09	80.25	4.97	92.50	92.67	5.74
55.41	55.57	3.44	67.83	67.99	4.21	80.25	80.41	4.98	92.67	92.83	5.75
55.57	55.73	3.45	67.99	68.15	4.22	80.41	80.57	4.99	92.83	92.99	5.76
55.73	55.89	3.46	68.15	68.31	4.23	80.57	80.73	5.00	92.99	93.15	5.77
55.89	56.05	3.47	68.31	68.47	4.24	80.73	80.89	5.01	93.15	93.31	5.78
56.05	56.21	3.48	68.47	68.63	4.25	80.89	81.05	5.02	93.31	93.47	5.79
56.21	56.38	3.49	68.63	68.80	4.26	81.05	81.21	5.03	93.47	93.63	5.80
56.38	56.54	3.50	68.80	68.96	4.27	81.21	81.38	5.04	93.63	93.80	5.81
56.54	56.70	3.51	68.96	69.12	4.28	81.38	81.54	5.05	93.80	93.96	5.82
56.70	56.86	3.52	69.12	69.28	4.29	81.54	81.70	5.06	93.96	94.12	5.83
56.86	57.02	3.53	69.28	69.44	4.30	81.70	81.86	5.07	94.12	94.28	5.84
57.02	57.18	3.54	69.44	69.60	4.31	81.86	82.02	5.08	94.28	94.44	5.85
57.18	57.34	3.55	69.60	69.76	4.32	82.02	82.18	5.09	94.44	94.60	5.86
57.34	57.50	3.56	69.76	69.92	4.33	82.18	82.34	5.10	94.60	94.76	5.87
57.50	57.67	3.57	69.92	70.09	4.34	82.34	82.50	5.11	94.76	94.92	5.88
57.67	57.83	3.58	70.09	70.25	4.35	82.50	82.67	5.12	94.92	95.09	5.89
57.83	57.99	3.59	70.25	70.41	4.36	82.67	82.83	5.13	95.09	95.25	5.90
57.99	58.15	3.60	70.41	70.57	4.37	82.83	82.99	5.14	95.25	95.41	5.91
58.15	58.31	3.61	70.57	70.73	4.38	82.99	83.15	5.15	95.41	95.57	5.92
58.31	58.47	3.62	70.73	70.89	4.39	83.15	83.31	5.16	95.57	95.73	5.93
58.47	58.63	3.63	70.89	71.05	4.40	83.31	83.47	5.17	95.73	95.89	5.94
58.63	58.80	3.64	71.05	71.21	4.41	83.47	83.63	5.18	95.89	96.05	5.95
58.80	58.96	3.65	71.21	71.38	4.42	83.63	83.80	5.19	96.05	96.21	5.96
58.96	59.12	3.66	71.38	71.54	4.43	83.80	83.96	5.20	96.21	96.38	5.97
59.12	59.28	3.67	71.54	71.70	4.44	83.96	84.12	5.21	96.38	96.54	5.98
59.28	59.44	3.68	71.70	71.86	4.45	84.12	84.28	5.22	96.54	96.70	5.99
59.44	59.60	3.69	71.86	72.02	4.46	84.28	84.44	5.23	96.70	96.86	6.00
59.60	59.76	3.70	72.02	72.18	4.47	84.44	84.60	5.24	96.86	97.02	6.01
59.76	59.92	3.71	72.18	72.34	4.48	84.60	84.76	5.25	97.02	97.18	6.02
59.92	60.09	3.72	72.34	72.50	4.49	84.76	84.92	5.26	97.18	97.34	6.03
60.09	60.25	3.73	72.50	72.67	4.50	84.92	85.09	5.27	97.34	97.50	6.04
60.25	60.41	3.74	72.67	72.83	4.51	85.09	85.25	5.28	97.50	97.67	6.05
60.41	60.57	3.75	72.83	72.99	4.52	85.25	85.41	5.29	97.67	97.83	6.06
60.57	60.73	3.76	72.99	73.15	4.53	85.41	85.57	5.30	97.83	97.99	6.07
60.73	60.89	3.77	73.15	73.31	4.54	85.57	85.73	5.31	97.99	98.15	6.08
60.89	61.05	3.78	73.31	73.47	4.55	85.73	85.89	5.32	98.15	98.31	6.09
61.05	61.21	3.79	73.47	73.63	4.56	85.89	86.05	5.33	98.31	98.47	6.10
61.21	61.38	3.80	73.63	73.80	4.57	86.05	86.21	5.34	98.47	98.63	6.11
61.38	61.54	3.81	73.80	73.96	4.58	86.21	86.38	5.35	98.63	98.80	6.12
61.54	61.70	3.82	73.96	74.12	4.59	86.38	86.54	5.36	98.80	98.96	6.13
61.70	61.86	3.83	74.12	74.28	4.60	86.54	86.70	5.37	98.96	99.12	6.14
61.86	62.02	3.84	74.28	74.44	4.61	86.70	86.86	5.38	99.12	99.28	6.15
62.02	62.18	3.85	74.44	74.60	4.62	86.86	87.02	5.39	99.28	99.44	6.16
62.18	62.34	3.86	74.60	74.76	4.63	87.02	87.18	5.40	99.44	99.60	6.17
62.34	62.50	3.87	74.76	74.92	4.64	87.18	87.34	5.41	99.60	99.76	6.18
62.50	62.67	3.88	74.92	75.09	4.65	87.34	87.50	5.42	99.76	99.92	6.19
62.67	62.83	3.89	75.09	75.25	4.66	87.50	87.67	5.43	99.92	100.00	6.20
62.83	62.99	3.90	75.25	75.41	4.67	87.67	87.83	5.44			
62.99	63.15	3.91	75.41	75.57	4.68	87.83	87.99	5.45			
63.15	63.31	3.92	75.57	75.73	4.69	87.99	88.15	5.46			
63.31	63.47	3.93	75.73	75.89	4.70	88.15	88.31	5.47			
63.47	63.63	3.94	75.89	76.05	4.71	88.31	88.47	5.48			
63.63	63.80	3.95	76.05	76.21	4.72	88.47	88.63	5.49			
63.80	63.96	3.96	76.21	76.38	4.73	88.63	88.80	5.50			
63.96	64.12	3.97	76.38	76.54	4.74	88.80	88.96	5.51			
64.12	64.28	3.98	76.54	76.70	4.75	88.96	89.12	5.52			
64.28	64.44	3.99	76.70	76.86	4.76	89.12	89.28	5.53			
64.44	64.60	4.00	76.86	77.02	4.77	89.28	89.44	5.54			
64.60	64.76	4.01	77.02	77.18	4.78	89.44	89.60	5.55			
64.76	64.92	4.02	77.18	77.34	4.79	89.60	89.76	5.56			
64.92	65.09	4.03	77.34	77.50	4.80	89.76	89.92	5.57			
65.09	65.25	4.04	77.50	77.67	4.81	89.92	90.09	5.58			
65.25	65.41	4.05	77.67	77.83	4.82	90.09	90.25	5.59			
65.41	65.57	4.06	77.83	77.99	4.83	90.25	90.41	5.60			
65.57	65.73	4.07	77.99	78.15	4.84	90.41	90.57	5.61			
65.73	65.89	4.08	78.15	78.31	4.85	90.57	90.73	5.62			
65.89	66.05	4.09	78.31	78.47	4.86	90.73	90.89	5.63			
66.05	66.21	4.10	78.47	78.63	4.87	90.89	91.05	5.64			
66.21	66.38	4.11	78.63	78.80	4.88	91.05	91.21	5.65			
66.38	66.54	4.12	78.80	78.96	4.89	91.21	91.38	5.66			

Wages	Taxes
$100	$6.20
200	12.40
300	18.60
400	24.80
500	31.00
600	37.20
700	43.40
800	49.60
900	55.80
1,000	62.00

A-27

1.45% Medicare Employee Tax Table

Wages at least	But less than	Tax to be withheld	Wages at least	But less than	Tax to be withheld	Wages at least	But less than	Tax to be withheld	Wages at least	But less than	Tax to be withheld
$0.00	$0.35	$0.00	$28.63	$29.32	$.42	$57.59	$58.28	$.84	$86.56	$87.25	$1.26
.35	1.04	.01	29.32	30.00	.43	58.28	58.97	.85	87.25	87.94	1.27
1.04	1.73	.02	30.00	30.69	.44	58.97	59.66	.86	87.94	88.63	1.28
1.73	2.42	.03	30.69	31.38	.45	59.66	60.35	.87	88.63	89.32	1.29
2.42	3.11	.04	31.38	32.07	.46	60.35	61.04	.88	89.32	90.00	1.30
3.11	3.80	.05	32.07	32.76	.47	61.04	61.73	.89	90.00	90.69	1.31
3.80	4.49	.06	32.76	33.45	.48	61.73	62.42	.90	90.69	91.38	1.32
4.49	5.18	.07	33.45	34.14	.49	62.42	63.11	.91	91.38	92.07	1.33
5.18	.5.87	.08	34.14	34.83	.50	63.11	63.80	.92	92.07	92.76	1.34
5.87	6.56	.09	34.83	35.52	.51	63.80	64.49	.93	92.76	93.45	1.35
6.56	7.25	.10	35.52	36.21	.52	64.49	65.18	.94	93.45	94.14	1.36
7.25	7.94	.11	36.21	36.90	.53	65.18	65.87	.95	94.14	94.83	1.37
7.94	8.63	.12	36.90	37.59	.54	65.87	66.56	.96	94.83	95.52	1.38
8.63	9.32	.13	37.59	38.28	.55	66.56	67.25	.97	95.52	96.21	1.39
9.32	10.00	.14	38.28	38.97	.56	67.25	67.94	.98	96.21	96.90	1.40
10.00	10.69	.15	38.97	39.66	.57	67.94	68.63	.99	96.90	97.59	1.41
10.69	11.38	.16	39.66	40.35	.58	68.63	69.32	1.00	97.59	98.28	1.42
11.38	12.07	.17	40.35	41.04	.59	69.32	70.00	1.01	98.28	98.97	1.43
12.07	12.76	.18	41.04	41.73	.60	70.00	70.69	1.02	98.97	99.66	1.44
12.76	13.45	.19	41.73	42.42	.61	70.69	71.38	1.03	99.66	100.00	1.45
13.45	14.14	.20	42.42	43.11	.62	71.38	72.07	1.04			
14.14	14.83	.21	43.11	43.80	.63	72.07	72.76	1.05			
14.83	15.52	.22	43.80	44.49	.64	72.76	73.45	1.06			
15.52	16.21	.23	44.49	45.18	.65	73.45	74.14	1.07			
16.21	16.90	.24	45.18	45.87	.66	74.14	74.83	1.08			
16.90	17.59	.25	45.87	46.56	.67	74.83	75.52	1.09			
17.59	18.28	.26	46.56	47.25	.68	75.52	76.21	1.10			
18.28	18.97	.27	47.25	47.94	.69	76.21	76.90	1.11			
18.97	19.66	.28	47.94	48.63	.70	76.90	77.59	1.12			
19.66	20.35	.29	48.63	49.32	.71	77.59	78.28	1.13			
20.35	21.04	.30	49.32	50.00	.72	78.28	78.97	1.14			
21.04	21.73	.31	50.00	50.69	.73	78.97	79.66	1.15			
21.73	22.42	.32	50.69	51.38	.74	79.66	80.35	1.16			
22.42	23.11	.33	51.38	52.07	.75	80.35	81.04	1.17			
23.11	23.80	.34	52.07	52.76	.76	81.04	81.73	1.18			
23.80	24.49	.35	52.76	53.45	.77	81.73	82.42	1.19			
24.49	25.18	.36	53.45	54.14	.78	82.42	83.11	1.20			
25.18	25.87	.37	54.14	54.83	.79	83.11	83.80	1.21			
25.87	26.56	.38	54.83	55.52	.80	83.80	84.49	1.22			
26.56	27.25	.39	55.52	56.21	.81	84.49	85.18	1.23			
27.25	27.94	.40	56.21	56.90	.82	85.18	85.87	1.24			
27.94	28.63	.41	56.90	57.59	.83	85.87	86.56	1.25			

Wages	Taxes
$100	$1.45
200	2.90
300	4.35
400	5.80
500	7.25
600	8.70
700	10.15
800	11.60
900	13.05
1,000	14.50

A-28

INDEX

Accident claims, taxability of, 273

Account(s), 219, 224–225, 225 (illus.)
   bank, for payroll, 139–141
   chart of, 219, 220 (illus.)
   debt and credit sides of, 219
   for employer payroll taxes, 226–228
   imprest, 256
   for income and FICA taxes payable, 226
   revenue and expense, 218
   T form of, 219
   for voluntary deductions, 228–229
   for wages and salaries expense, 225–226

Accountable plans, 76, 273

Accounting, 216–237
   business transactions and, 217, 218–219, 220 (illus.), 221 (illus.)
   definition of, 217
   financial statements and, 222–223, 223 (illus.), 224 (illus.)
   fundamental accounting equation and, 217–218
   journals and ledgers and, 219
   revenue and expense accounts and, 218. See also Payroll accounting

Accounting process (cycle), 221

Accrual
   of payroll tax liabilities, 227–228
   of vacation pay liability, 231, 234
   of wage and salary liabilities, 227–228, 231

ACH, see Automated Clearing House

Acquisition of Abandonment of Secured Property (Form 1099-A), 192 (table)

Age Discrimination in Employment Act of 1967 (ADEA), 14–15, 16

Agricultural employers, tax reporting requirements for, 178, 180 (exhibit)

Agricultural workers, Federal Unemployment Tax Act and, 107–109

Aliens, employment of, 18, 253

Allowances, see Withholding allowances

Americans with Disabilities Act of 1990, 15, 16–17

Annual Employee Earnings Statement, see Form W-2

Annualized wages method, for federal income tax withholding, 73

Annual Summary and Transmittal of U.S. Information Returns (Form 1096), 190, 194 (exhibit)

Applications software, for computerized payroll systems, 251

Assets
   current, 222
   definition of, 217
   fundamental accounting equation and, 217–218
   intangible, 222
   long-term, 222

Assigned state rate, 275
   controlling, 276–278
   reducing, 278–279

Audit, of payroll accounts, 236–237

Audit trail, 177

Automated Clearing House (ACH), 142–145
   processing schedule of, 143–144

Automated time and attendance systems, 255

Automatic funds transfer, 142

Awards, employee retention and, 267

Back-pay claims, 258

Backup withholding, 169

Badge readers, 31

Balance sheet, 218, 222, 223 (illus.)

Bank accounts
   payroll, 139–141;
   reconciliation of, 140–141

Benefit ratio, 278

Benefit-wage ratio, 278

Biweekly payroll periods, 30

Bona fide occupational qualification (BFOQ), 15

I-1